THE COMPLETE POETICAL
WORKS OF
PERCY BYSSHE SHELLEY

Shelley's draft of 'To Mary Wollstonecraft Godwin', lines 25–36; see pp. 328–9
(*Bod. MS. Shelley adds. e. 12, p. 11*)

THE
COMPLETE POETICAL
WORKS OF
PERCY BYSSHE
SHELLEY

EDITED BY

NEVILLE ROGERS

In four volumes

VOLUME II
1814–1817

OXFORD
AT THE CLARENDON PRESS
1975

Oxford University Press, Ely House, London W. 1

GLASGOW NEW YORK TORONTO MELBOURNE WELLINGTON
CAPE TOWN IBADAN NAIROBI DAR ES SALAAM LUSAKA ADDIS ABABA
DELHI BOMBAY CALCUTTA MADRAS KARACHI LAHORE DACCA
KUALA LUMPUR SINGAPORE HONG KONG TOKYO

ISBN 0 19 812707 3

© *Oxford University Press 1975*

*Printed in Great Britain
at the University Press, Oxford
by Vivian Ridler
Printer to the University*

CONTENTS

Shelley's draft of 'To Mary Wollstonecraft Godwin', lines 25–36   *Frontispiece*

INTRODUCTION TO VOLUME II

   I. Manuscripts and editing   xi

  II. Editorial procedure   xxii

 III. Textual sources of this volume

      1. Autograph Manuscripts   xxiii

      2. Transcripts by Mary Shelley   xxv

      3. Printed Sources   xxvi

  IV. Abbreviations and signs used   xxix

SHORTER POEMS, 1814, 1815

  Stanza, written at Bracknell   3

  Stanzas.—April, 1814   3

  To Mary Wollstonecraft Godwin   4

  To ——: 'Yet look on me . . .'   6

  Reality: 'The pale, the cold, and the moony smile . . .'

                         See Introduction, p. xix

  Mutability   7

  A Summer Evening Churchyard   7

  'Oh! there are spirits of the air . . .'   8

  To Wordsworth   10

  Feelings of a Republican on the Fall of Bonaparte   10

  Two Fragments from the Journal of Claire Clairmont   11

TRANSLATIONS, 1814, 1815

  Sonnet, from the Italian of Dante: 'Guido, I would that . . .'   15

  Sonnet, from the Italian of Cavalcanti: 'Returning from its daily quest . . .'   16

  Note by Mary Shelley on the Poems of 1814, 1815   16

THE DAEMON OF THE WORLD, 1815

  Part I   21

  Part II   30

ALASTOR, OR THE SPIRIT OF SOLITUDE, 1815

Preface   43
Alastor   44
Note by Mary Shelley on *Alastor*   64

MISCELLANEOUS SHORTER POEMS AND FRAGMENTS, 1816

The Sunset   69
Hymn to Intellectual Beauty   71
Mont Blanc   75
  Rejected Lines   80
Verses Written on Receiving a Celandine in a Letter from England   80
  Rejected Lines   83
Three Laments:
  1. On Fanny Godwin: 'Her voice did quiver . . .'   83
  2. On William Shelley: 'Thy little footsteps . . .'   84
  3. On Harriet Shelley, November—1816, 1st version:
     'The cold earth slept below . . .'   85
Fragment: 'Dear home . . .'   86
Fragment: Ghost Story   87
Fragment: Stanzas Addressed to Leigh Hunt
  'For me, my friend, if not that tears did tremble . . .'   87
  'Friend, this I hope . . .'   88
  'A gentle story of two lovers young . . .'   88

TRANSLATIONS, 1816

Four Fragments of Greek Pastoral
  1. Moschus, III. 1–7: 'Ye Dorian woods . . .'   91
  2. Moschus, V: 'When winds that move not . . .'   91
  3. Moschus, VI: 'Pan loved his neighbour Echo . . .'   92
  4. Bion, I. 1–49: 'I mourn Adonis dead . . .'   93
Note by Mary Shelley on the Poems of 1816   94

LAON AND CYTHNA, OR THE REVOLUTION OF THE GOLDEN CITY usually known as THE REVOLT OF ISLAM, 1817

Preface   99
Dedication: To Mary [Wollstonecraft] [Shelley]   106
Canto I   111
Canto II   129
Canto III   144

Canto IV   154
Canto V   164
Canto VI   183
Canto VII   199
Canto VIII   211
Canto IX   220
Canto X   231
Canto XI   245
Canto XII   253
Rejected Passages   265
Note by Mary Shelley on *Laon and Cythna*   270

PRINCE ATHANASE, A Fragment, 1817   277
Additional Lines   290
Note by Mary Shelley on 'Prince Athanase'   291

MISCELLANEOUS SHORTER POEMS AND
FRAGMENTS, 1817
Marianne's Dream   295
To Constantia, Singing   300
Fragment: To Constantia   302
Fragment: To One Singing   303
Fragment: To Music (1)   303
Fragment: To Music (2)   304
Fragment: 'Mighty eagle . . .'   304
To the Lord Chancellor   305
Additional Lines   308
To William Shelley, 1817: 'The billows on the beach . . .'   309
Additional Lines   311
Two Laments:
  1. On Harriet Shelley, Nov. 5, 1816, 2nd version:
    'The cold Earth slept below . . .'   312
  2. On [Harriet Shelley], Nov. 5, 1817:
    'That time is dead for ever, child . . .' 313
Death: 'They die—the dead return not . . .'   314
Otho: Stanzas from the Fragment of a Draft:
  I. 'The mistress and the monitress of earth . . .'   315
  II. 'Dark is the realm of grief . . .'   315

III. 'Those whom nor power, nor lying faith . . .' 315
IV. 'Such thoughts, befitting well a parent's bier . . .' 315
V. 'Thou wert not, Cassius . . .' 316
VI. 'I wrong thee not . . .' 316
Fragment: 'O that a chariot of cloud were mine . . .' 316
Fragment: 'A golden-wingèd Angel stood . . .' 317
Fragment: 'To thirst and find no fill . . .' 317
Fragment: 'Wealth and dominion . . .' 318
Fragment: 'My thoughts arise and fade . . .' 318
Fragment: A Hate-Song 319
Fragment: 'My head is wild with weeping . . .', 2nd version 319
Ozymandias 319
    Fragment of an earlier draft 320
Fragment: 'Serene, in his unconquerable might . . .' 320
Fragment: 'Address to the Human Mind' 321
Fragment: 'Soft pillows for the fiends . . .' 322
Fragment: 'Arise, sweet Mary . . .' 322
Fragment: 'Heigh-ho, wisdom and folly . . .' 322
Translation: Epigram of Plato, cited in the *Apologia* of Apuleius
    'Sweet child, thou star of love and beauty bright . . .' 323
Note by Mary Shelley on the Poems of 1817 323
Extraneous fragments found amid the draft for *Laon and Cythna*:
    1. 'Who with the Devil doth rage and revel . . .' 364
    2. 'He ceased—and approbation like the sound . . .' 364
    3. 'Like a sunbeam on a tempest streaming . . .' 365
    4. 'And with thy sweet eyes awful glance . . .' 365
    5. 'My head is wild with weeping . . .', 1st version 366
    6. 'He ceased. Another rose: one pale and ⟨? weak⟩ . . .' 366
    7. 'And I remember wandering through the shadow . . .' 367
    8. 'My   maiden . . .' 367
    9. 'Thou must have seen it was ⟨? ruined⟩ . . .' 367
    10. 'A simoon to the almond blossom . . .' 368
    11. 'I visit thee but thou art sadly changed . . .' 371
    12. 'These things remain . . .' 371
    13. 'The pine is here . . .' 372
    14. 'A music wild and soft that filled the mid'night air . . .' 372
    15. 'Thou was a homeless cloud . . .' 372

16. 'The wild bull in the mountain and the horse . . .'   373
17. 'As the wintry skies . . .'   374
18. 'How long has Poesy, the widowed mother . . .'   374
19. 'We all act out a false part . . .'   374
20. 'Shapes about my steps assembling . . .'   374

NOTES ON THE TEXT AND CONTENT OF   327
THE POEMS

INDEX OF TITLES   415

INDEX OF FIRST LINES   419

INTRODUCTION TO VOLUME II

I. MANUSCRIPTS AND EDITING

FOR the period of Shelley's early poetry, covered by the poems in the first volume of this edition, comparatively few manuscripts have survived. For the present volume and its successors they are available in embarrassing abundance. The attendant editorial problems demand that the General Introduction[1] be supplemented by a further word.

Everybody knows two things about Shelley's manuscripts. The first is that they fetch enormous prices in the saleroom. The second is that they can be exceedingly difficult to decipher. Much confusion has been generated by individuals whose success in deciphering some particular manuscript has made them and others believe that in transcribing Shelley the scribe they have edited Shelley the poet—or rather a portion of him, for the Fundamentalist,[2] as I have called this simple believer, will always have picked a poem or passage of which the text derives from a single extant manuscript. So long as he does this, he need do no more than print a literal transcription and he will be widely accepted as its editor. Even if the manuscript be one of the wildest and most confused of Shelley's drafts, his transcription will be hailed as 'a scholarly modern edition'; for the claim to have given 'the poem as the poet wrote it' is a bait easily swallowed by the many people who are always incautiously eager to demonstrate their up-to-date identification of what is scholarly with what is modern.[3] Unfortunately for the Fundamentalist, though fortunately for Shelley's text, he cannot get very far. Though he may apply his principle of literal transcription to odd poems and passages, he cannot apply it to Shelley's poetry as a whole. As soon as he encounters, as he must before long, a poem or passage of which two holographs exist he is forced to ask himself 'Which do I transcribe?' He is in much the same plight as his predecessor in the field of classical texts—a plight likened by A. E. Housman[4]

---

[1] See Vol. I, pp. xix–xlii.   [2] See Vol. I, pp. xxx–xxxiii.
[3] For an example of 'the poem as the poet wrote it' cf. Frontispiece of this volume.
[4] Preface to *Manilius*, in *Selected Prose*, ed. John Carter, Cambridge University Press, 1961, p. 35.

to that of a donkey who, finding himself between two bundles of hay, confusedly imagines that if one bundle were removed he would cease to be a donkey. Indeed his plight is a worse one for, since the manuscripts of a Latin or Greek author commonly cover the whole of his works, his predecessor could sometimes remove one or more bundles by a display of logistics designed to show some chosen manuscript as 'the best manuscript'. With the text of Shelley such ingenuity would be wholly precluded by the number and nature of both manuscript and printed sources and the way in which these vary from poem to poem.

The confusion disseminated by the printing of uncorrected anomalies from a manuscript may be sufficiently exemplified by the pronouncement of one reviewer that this represents 'a fairly healthy reaction against the nineteenth-century propensity for amending texts by guesswork based on a critic's personal preference'.[1] Underlying this combination of ignorance with preconception is an unquestioning conviction that for a 'modern edition' no more is required than a correction of 'errors'; that errors are synonymous with careless copying; and that the carelessness simply needs to be set right by new and careful copying, usually from the manuscript (which is more impressive) but sometimes, it may be, from a first edition; the relationship between manuscripts and first editions is left unexplored. Knowing references have been made to Hutchinson's edition as 'an embodiment of nineteenth-century error' and to 'Mary Shelley's habit of rewriting her husband's poems'. Of the true history of Shelley's text a summary is given in the General Introduction,[2] and no further notice of this bibliographical mythology would have been necessary were it not that, in the editing of manuscripts, to obscure the quality of preceding editions is to obscure the requirements of a new one. My historical summary is illustrated in the present volume and its successors by the account given poem by poem, and point by point, of how Shelley's text has come down to us. Paradoxically enough, when the distinguished earlier editors did go wrong it was seldom or never for the reasons alleged by Fundamentalist fantasy but, as a rule, because they allowed themselves to do, on occasions, what the Fundamentalist does all the time—subordinate judgement to a reverential faith in a manuscript or first edition. When this happened it was usually because,

[1] *Times Literary Supplement*, 14 July 1966.
[2] See Vol. I, pp. xix–xxxiii.

with the exception of Mary Shelley—and, as a pioneer, she had special problems of her own—the experience on which they based their judgements was restricted by the limited range of manuscripts at their disposal.

The printing as 'editions' of painstakingly transcribed single poems has recently tended to obscure the basic problems, bypassed by transcribers, which are unavoidable when it comes to the editing of Shelley's text as a whole, and which arise from the number and variety of the manuscripts. They divide, in the first place, into manuscripts of poems which Shelley himself printed and those which were printed after his death; the latter then subdivide into those printed by Mary Shelley and those printed by others. For many poems no manuscripts are recorded; manuscripts of others, available to past editors, have now disappeared. For some poems we have holographs only, for some only transcripts; for others we have both, and, if the transcript should chance to be from a holograph now lost, it may on occasions command at least as much authority as the holograph we have. The holograph may be a draft or it may be a fair copy; sometimes, too, the fair copy has obviously been made from a draft now missing. Very frequently a holograph may be impossible to categorize: for example, it may start as a neat fair copy of lines previously composed and degenerate into a tortured draft of new ones. Those whose expectations of 'new, unpublished poems' have run high may be disappointed by this edition. Wholly unpublished poems are few, and their quality is seldom high. From the textual point of view, the real value of unpublished material must be estimated in terms of what might be called its 'contextual significance': its value often lies less in the intrinsic content than in its relationship to other material, printed or unprinted. The smaller fragments which star Shelley's Notebooks form a special category: they will be examined in Volume III, where they begin to increase in number. Sometimes they are no more than unrelated embryos—a number of these will be found among the 'Shorter Poems' of 1816 and 1817. Sometimes, however, they may be pieced together, in jigsaw fashion, with fragments both printed and unprinted: for example, (pp. 87-8) the 'Stanzas Addressed to Leigh Hunt' and (pp. 315-16) the stanzas drafted for 'Otho'. A notable example of a small gleaning with considerable 'contextual significance' is afforded by the draft of 'Mont Blanc'. The difficulties of the poem are well known. Of lines 27-9, for example, Rossetti observes, 'This clause seems to have no syntactical position.' Those less observant than that shrewd editor have sometimes interpreted the confusion as reflecting a confusion in Shelley's mind. But here, as usual, Shelley's mind is perfectly clear and, though full of Platonic subtlety in style and content alike, so is the poem—the source of the confusion is the tortured draft, which so upset the poet who penned it that, in transcribing it, he omitted two lines. A contributory source of confusion is his imperfect skill with the mechanics of punctuation—a weakness he frankly acknowledged and the remedying of which was not least of the responsibilities he bequeathed to his editors. When the missing lines are restored— see p. 76, where they are numbered '27a' and '28a'—and when the thirty-four-and-a-half-line sentence in which they occur is repunctuated with due regard for its complicated system of parentheses, sense emerges out of nonsense.

The variety of Shelley's manuscripts demands a corresponding variety in the textual treatment of the poems which derive from them. To make this plain to the reader it became necessary to furnish every poem in this volume, and in Volumes III and IV, with a separate textual introduction of its own, and this it seemed more convenient to place at the end of the book rather than at the beginning. Where necessity demanded, my annotation has been divided under the two heads of 'Text' and 'Content'. Under 'Text' is given, first of all, an account of the textual sources, manuscript and printed, then an account of the work of my predecessors and of what I have added to it; following this comes a line-by-line commentary on points in my collation which were too numerous or too complex for discussion within the compass of the footnotes accompanying the text. References are inserted in the latter which direct the reader's attention to the relevant pages of the annotation.

A variorum edition in the strict sense, were such a thing practicable, could do little but confuse those who enjoy and study Shelley's poetry. In the planning of the present edition nothing made this plainer than the manuscripts and editions of *Laon and Cythna*. It was in wrestling with their complex nature and relationships that a general principle was finally evolved for sifting the significant from the less significant and the non-significant which could be extended to the edition as a whole. Of this long poem (4,818 lines in Hutchinson) the following textual sources are available:

A. Shelley's first printing, under the title of *Laon and Cythna*.

B. The poem as reprinted by Shelley, with changes demanded by his publisher, under the title of *The Revolt of Islam*.

C. A manuscript Notebook containing portions of a fair copy.

D, E, F. Three Notebooks containing tortured drafts of most of the poem, together with phrases, lines, and passages rejected by Shelley. A good deal of extraneous matter, including snatches of verse, is scattered through the Notebooks and there are memoranda and excerpts from Shelley's reading, often in Greek.

From the abundance and complexity of the material a threefold problem arose: (1) the establishment of the text in accordance with Shelley's deducible intentions; (2) the presentation of passages and poems hitherto unpublished; (3) the arrangement and presentation of the extraneous matter. Counting the drafts as a single category and the extraneous matter as another one, we have five separate categories of material. How do these categories relate to one another? What significance has each for the new text now required? The chief witness, clearly, must be one of Shelley's own printings. But which? I fancy that the Fundamentalist, whose sense of literary values is usually confused with the values of the saleroom, would choose A on the grounds that it is a first edition. A. E. Housman used to enjoy shocking devotees of his own first editions by pointing out that poets' later editions can sometimes be superior by reason of the corrections they introduce. Shelley did this sometimes, when he got the chance and had happened to notice some of his slips. It would, however, be wrong to prefer B on these grounds, since Shelley's letters clearly show how unwillingly most of his changes were made. Mary Shelley printed B, but her motive was probably discretion (see Notes, p. 361). With the exception of H. Buxton Forman, editors have followed her. That Forman chose A may have been due to his tendency, as a collector of books and manuscripts, to allow saleroom values to outweigh the common-sense evaluation of significant evidence. The present text is based on A—not because it is a 'first edition' but because of the abundant evidence that Shelley preferred it: I join Forman, therefore, in restoring to their original form the passages Shelley was forced to change. But it will by no means do to treat A merely as 'the best text', invoking it as a 'copy-text', somewhat as, in an American law-court, a witness might seek to cover himself by invoking the Fifth Amendment. Not all Shelley's changes represent unwilling submission to his publisher: some are verbal improvements, born of second thoughts. C was carefully collated by Locock and Hutchinson and presented me with few problems. How Fundamentalist doctrine would evaluate the relative sanctity of a fair copy and a first edition I do not know: the choice would seem to involve a practitioner, once again, in the dilemma described by Housman. Logically, of course, what matters is the *nature* of the fair copy: obviously an intermediate copying must carry less weight than a manuscript prepared for the printer. But C, like other intermediate copies, is by no means without its value as a witness, since it can here and there correct an anomaly due either to the printer or to a slip made in transcribing the printer's copy. This is where an editor finds himself confronting what Housman called 'one of the most exacting offices of editorial judgement: the balancing of evidence and the choice of variants'. I have cited C only when it differs from A. It is with D, E, and F that the situation really becomes complicated. In relation to the text printed by Shelley the witness of his drafts must, of course, be rated comparatively low. Sometimes, however, they can correct something that went wrong in later transmission, either through the printer or through some slip made by Shelley or Mary in transcribing: see, under 'Text', the notes on lines 3024-5, 3573, 3642-3, 4535-9.

But what of the greater part of the draft material in D, E, and F—a mass of intercatenated cancelling and emendations, built up in tiers on the pages of these Notebooks? A formal collation would involve something like a grandstand of square-bracketed words and phrases, built up in footnotes to the text, dwarfing the text itself and amounting, at best, to no more than a minute history of embryonic and non-significant verbal change. The principle I eventually adopted was to collate from the draft only what varied *significantly* from the printed text—variants, that is to say, which represented, as far as was discernible, those intentions of Shelley's which were his final ones at the moment when it was penned. Where such variants are ambiguous, for example where he left uncancelled alternatives, I have included both.

This principle, evolved to meet the textual problems of *Laon and Cythna*, has been extended to the rest of Shelley's poetry. Where it seemed likely to defeat its own ends by causing the omission of something significant I have taken leave to depart from it. I collate, for example, a cancelled line from the draft of 'The Sunset', because it interestingly foreshadows a line in *Epipsychidion*; so too with a number of other variants which have interest because they illustrate the poetic genesis of a word or a phrase. For students of Shelley-the-poet a limited number of such illustrations should suffice: to multiply them would be to drift towards the dark night of a variorum edition. For the benefit of those students of Shelley-the-scribe for whom comprehensiveness is, apparently, an end in itself, a literal version is being prepared for separate publication. It may be observed in passing that only when used *pari passu* with manuscripts or reproductions of them can such publications be put to any practical use.

Not the least valuable contribution offered to the text of *Laon and Cythna* by D, E, and F is the stanzas which Shelley rejected from the Dedication and the First Canto and which were privately printed, not without misreadings, by Sir John Shelley-Rolls and Roger Ingpen in *Verse and Prose*, 1934. These, in accordance with the practice of Hutchinson, I have placed at the end of the poem, punctuating and otherwise editing them where I could; where the manuscript was too rough to permit this I have had to content myself with literal transcription. In addition to these more substantial additions to the text I found among the drafts a number of lines and phrases, hitherto unprinted, which seemed worthy of preservation but which would hardly gratify the reader's eye if presented with the text itself. I have placed them in my textual footnotes. H. Buxton Forman, that fine editor, was so far able to see beyond the predilections of a proud owner of manuscripts as to declare, on one occasion, that 'had Shelley lived to have the slightest suspicion that we should venerate his every scrap of paper . . . he would have taken ample care to place [his] notebooks out of our reach'. How best to present the unpresentable is a recurrent problem that all his editors have had to face. It arises again from the extraneous matter—memoranda and snatches of verse—which lurk in D, E, and F among the drafts of the big poem. Logically, I suppose, the general arrangement of my volume might demand the inclusion of the verse-snatches in my text, among the shorter poems and fragments of 1817; since, however, they chiefly consist of broken, barely decipherable lines, impossible to present in any form but a literal, and no less broken, form in print, they would hardly look pretty there. Moreover it is possible that, unperceived by me, there may be some occasional thought-connection between these snatches and passages in *Laon and Cythna*. It seemed best to place them at the end of the volume, in the textual section of the annotation, each accompanied by a note showing to what part of the text it is adjacent in Shelley's draft. This makeshift arrangement I have tried to improve by listing them in my Contents and in my indexes of titles and first lines; in case anybody should seek them in the text, a cross-reference has been inserted at the end of 'Miscellaneous and Shorter Poems of 1817'. The thought-connection between the main poem and the memoranda is usually an obvious and highly significant one, especially in the case of the Greek jottings. They too have been placed in my annotation.

No part of Shelley's text may ever be safely edited without reference to what may be learned from other parts. This is especially true of the numerous fragments of unfinished poems scattered throughout his Notebooks. Some of the problems of interrelationship presented by these can be extremely puzzling. For example, in one of the Notebooks containing the draft of *Laon and Cythna* (Bod. MS. Shelley adds. e. 19) we come across a draft of that mysterious fragment 'My head is wild with weeping . . .'. In another Notebook (Bod. MS. Shelley adds. e. 12) is drafted the slightly different version printed by Rossetti, and by subsequent editors, among the poems of 1818. Which text should be printed now? And what is the date of composition? Let us take the second problem first. Where a fragment contains no internal evidence of date it can sometimes be dated from the known dates of material adjacent to it in the Notebook: thus if a fragment is drafted among pages devoted to the drafting of *Epipsychidion*, say, or *Adonais* it is a reasonable guess that it dates from the period within which we know the one or the other to have been composed. Sometimes too the guess can be confirmed, and the period narrowed down, by verbal connections or connections of thought with Shelley's letters of the period, or with his datable reading. Sometimes too a Notebook will itself provide evidence that Shelley used it during a fairly narrow period. Other Notebooks may contain a wide variety of material composed over two or three years, some of it recopied from earlier MSS., so that dating is correspondingly difficult to deduce. The Notebook e. 12 is one of these. But none of the material in e. 12 bears evidence of an earlier date than 1818 and since e. 19 is almost wholly devoted to the drafting of *Laon and Cythna*, composed in 1817, it is a fair assumption that the e. 19 version is the earlier one and was composed likewise in 1817.

The answer to the first problem is less simple. Had one version of the fragment had the appearance of a draft and the other of a fair copy the latter, obviously, would have been the text to print. Both, unfortunately, are drafts, and untidy ones. To one familiar with Shelley's habits it would seem likely enough that the later draft was one of many such which he rewrote from memory. Does the earlier draft represent his true intentions, subsequently mis-remembered? Or does the later one represent his revised, more mature intentions? To this problem, recurrent among Shelley's manuscripts, there can be no certain answer. All an editor can do here is to attempt an expedient which will make the situation plain to his readers. I have placed the e. 19 version in the textual section of my annotation of *Laon and Cythna* (where perhaps some reader, more discerning than myself, may possibly perceive connections of some sort) and, in accordance with my chronological arrangement of poems, which is based on date of *composition*, I have moved the e. 12 version from among the 'Shorter Poems and Fragments, 1818', which are to be printed in Volume III, and placed it in the present volume among 'Miscellaneous Shorter Poems and Fragments, 1817'; cross-references are given in both places.

A cognate problem arose from the poem I have entitled 'Reality' ('The pale, the cold, and the moony smile . . .') composed by Shelley about 1812–13 and printed in his *Alastor* volume of 1816. Since the Esdaile text differs a good deal from the printed one, some, I suppose, might have held it proper had I printed both texts, each in its place. Since, however, such duplication would have been somewhat confusing to readers, I have thought it sufficient to print the poem (see Vol. I, p. 112) among the Esdaile poems where it chronologically belongs, giving it in the 1816 version, which is obviously Shelley's *ultima manus*, and relegating the Esdaile vari-ants to my Commentary. For the benefit of any who might be searching for the poem in the present volume, cross-references have been inserted in the Table of Contents and in the Indexes of Titles and First Lines.

Two other fragments in this volume have been redated: 'Serene, in his unconquerable might . . .', placed by Hutchinson in 1820, may be shown, on Notebook evidence observed by Locock (see

p. 412), to belong, almost certainly, to 1817; while on internal evidence,[1] 'Lines to a Critic' ('Honey from silkworms . . .') must undoubtedly belong to 1819: Mary Shelley acknowledged this misdating in an erratum slip tipped into her 1824 volume but somehow failed to remember it when preparing her edition of 1839. A more important poem, not printed by Hutchinson, and wrongly placed in 1817 by the editors of the Julian edition, is 'A Ballad'— from a misreading of Shelley's fair copy at Harvard wrongly entitled 'Young Parson Richards'.[2] It belongs to 1819, and will be printed under that date in Volume III.

At times Shelley's poems and fragments have a subtle interrelationship of thought and feeling that is half hidden and half revealed by his working habits. In my General Introduction to this edition (Vol. I, p. xxxiv) I have referred, by way of example, to the editorial problem created by the close relationship between the lament for Fanny Godwin, written in 1816, and the lament for William Shelley, written in 1819—a problem aggravated by the equally close relationship of both poems with versions written in 1816 and 1817 of a lament for Harriet Shelley. These relationships being difficult both to understand and to explain, I have sought to make them a little clearer by my arrangement of the text. The two pieces of 1816 and the supplementary piece of 1819, each headed by its date, have been grouped together under the title of 'Three Laments' and placed among the poems of 1816; the two pieces of 1817 are given among the poems of that year under the title of 'Two Laments'. Cross-references in the footnotes and the full explanations in the Notes (pp. 355–6 and 407–8) should, I hope, serve to clarify these complications. Elsewhere too in this edition, where manuscripts revealed some similar relationship between poems, I have endeavoured to curtail, simplify, or supplement exposition by regrouping and adding simple descriptive titles to the groups.

A kindly critic of the first volume of this edition has expressed a fear lest some of my annotation 'be found to contain an overdose of Plato'. This would not surprise me since, although Platonism is commonly allowed to the Elizabethans and others, it is a strain in early nineteenth-century literature strangely unknown to, or

---

[1] See Rogers, 'Four Missing Pages from the Shelley Notebook in the Harvard College Library', *Keats–Shelley Journal*, iii, 1954.

[2] See William J. McTaggart, *England in 1819 : Church, State and Poverty. A Study, Textual and Historical of 'A Ballad', by Shelley, formerly entitled 'Young Parson Richards'*, Keats–Shelley Memorial Association, 1970.

ignored by, 'Romantic specialists', and it runs counter to popular, romanticized, notions of a 'Romantic poet'. I must leave to the critical attention of others these profound misconceptions about Shelley's period. As far as Shelley's poetry is concerned, it is simply saturated in Plato[1] from the time of *Queen Mab* onwards: we have his word for this and Mary's; and the evidence stands out in everything he wrote, whether poetry, prose, or letters. It will hardly do for the people who, for some odd reason, object to it to hint that his Platonism was invented either by the late James A. Notopoulos, who patiently and exhaustively collected the evidence from his printed works, or by myself, who, independently, performed the same function for the manuscript Notebooks. If the overdosage of Platonism has increased in the present volume and, still more, in its successors that will be because Shelley himself has increased the dose—it is, I take it, the business of the literary, as well as the scientific, analyst to show constituent elements in the proportion in which they appear. Shelley's poetry is, essentially—though with an occasional holiday—a poetry of ideas. Shelley did not live to illuminate his ideas, as he had planned to do, in a series of metaphysical essays, and the difficulty experienced by his readers in discovering what those ideas are has tended to give him something of a reputation for obscurity. Behind the apparent obscurity of Shelley's poetry is a coherence and unity derived, as Sir Maurice Bowra used to stress, from the way he took Plato's theory of Knowledge and applied it to Beauty. In the 'Content' sections of my Notes I have had, necessarily, to cover a vast and varied amount of ground, but my principal concern, like Shelley's, has been with his ideas and with the elaborate system of symbolism with which they are expressed. In my analysis I have carefully weighed the 'contextual significance' of points afforded by his manuscripts together with evidence available from elsewhere. It is with evidence that I have been concerned and I have tried to avoid both theorizing myself and discussion of the theories of others.

[1] For a concise reassessment see William J. McTaggart, 'Some New Inquiries into Shelley's Platonism', *Keats–Shelley Memorial Bulletin*, xxi, 1970.

II. EDITORIAL PROCEDURE

THE nature of Shelley's manuscripts makes it very difficult to standardize procedure in the Textual Commentary. Often enough what has happened in the manuscript can be conventionally shown: for example

7 mute *above* [deep] *e. 12*

or

168 filled *edd.*][fed] filled *E. 4*

Very often however, in Shelley's drafts, the work of his revising pen is too complicated to be succinctly and comprehensibly conveyed, and then, to avoid swelling my commentary with long and laborious accounts of non-significant verbal change, I have had recourse to the formula 'changed from'.

The special problems arising from the many small, unfinished fragments scattered through Shelley's Notebooks will be discussed in the Introduction to Volume III, where they begin to increase very considerably in number. Mary Shelley fitted many of them into the Notes she appended to the various sections of the text. This raised chronological problems which editors have largely remedied by transferring them to the text itself. This arrangement I have retained but, since the Notes had lost a little by the removal of quotations designed to illustrate them, I have restored them in an abbreviated form, using Mary's text, as seemed appropriate, and adding footnotes which will enable the reader to see where it differs from mine.

Sometimes, in my Notes, I have need to refer to a poem which is to appear in Volume III or Volume IV in a form involving a change of the line-numbering as hitherto given. For present convenience such references have been given in accordance with the old line-numbering and, so that the reader may know where to find them, accompanied by the indication '[Hutch.]'.

Additions to Hutchinson's text of 1904, together with redatings, rearrangements, and other changes, are noted either in the Commentary at the foot of the text or, when more detail is needed, in the sections headed 'Text' in the Notes at the end of the volume. A full, separate listing would be impracticable.

III. TEXTUAL SOURCES OF THIS VOLUME

1. *Autograph Manuscripts*

Bodleian Library (Bod.)

Notebook: MS. Shelley E. 4

Prince Athanase
  Additional Lines
To Constantia, Singing
Fragment: To Constantia
Fragment: To One Singing
Fragment: 'To thirst and find no fill . . .'
Fragment: 'Wealth and dominion . . .'
Ozymandias
  Fragment of an Earlier Draft
Fragment: 'Serene, in his unconquerable might . . .'
Fragment: 'Address to the Human Mind'
Fragment: 'Soft pillows for the fiends . . .'
Fragment: 'Arise, sweet Mary . . .'
Fragment: 'Heigh-ho, wisdom and folly . . .'

Notebook: MS. Shelley adds. e. 16

Hymn to Intellectual Beauty
Mont Blanc
Verses Written on Receiving a Celandine (a few lines)
  Rejected Lines
Fragment: Ghost Story
To William Shelley ('The billows on the beach . . .')
  Additional Lines
Death ('They die—the dead return not . . .')
Otho: Stanzas from the Fragment of a Draft
Fragment: 'O that a chariot of cloud . . .'
Fragment: 'My thoughts arise . . .'

Notebook: MS. Shelley adds. e. 12

To Mary Wollstonecraft Godwin
The Sunset
Fragment: 'Dear home . . .'
Translation: Moschus, VI
Lament: On Harriet Shelley, 1816 (2nd version)

Lament: On Harriet Shelley, 1817
Fragment: 'My head is wild with weeping . . .' (2nd version)

Notebook: MS. Shelley adds. e. 8

Fragment: 'Mighty eagle . . .'

Notebook: MS. Shelley adds. e. 9

Fragment: To Music (1)
To the Lord Chancellor
Additional Lines

Notebook: MS. Shelley D. 3

Laon and Cythna (part: see p. 361)
Rejected Passages (part: see p. 394)

Notebook: MS. Shelley adds. e. 14

Laon and Cythna (part: see p. 361)
Rejected Passages (part: see p. 394)

Notebook: MS. Shelley adds. e. 19

Laon and Cythna (part: see p. 361)
Rejected Passages (part : see p. 394)
Fragment: 'My head is wild with weeping . . .' (2nd version)

Notebook: MS. Shelley adds. e. 10

Laon and Cythna (part: see pp. 361-2)
Fragment: To Constantia (part only)

Box of loose sheets: MS. Shelley adds. c. 4

Mont Blanc. Rejected Lines
Three Laments: 1. On Fanny Godwin
              2. On William Shelley
              3. On Harriet Shelley, 1816 (1st version)
Fragment: Stanzas Addressed to Leigh Hunt
Laon and Cythna (two sheets)
To William Shelley. Additional Lines

British Museum (BM)

Two Fragments from the Journal of Claire Clairmont
Queen Mab, 1813 edition, with autograph annotation by Shelley
made for converting the poem into 'The Daemon of the
World', here designated 'BM^b'

Translation: Moschus, VI
Translation: Bion, I
Laon and Cythna (one sheet)

Harvard University Library

Silsbee–Harvard Notebook I (SH I)
  To the Lord Chancellor
  Additional Lines

Silsbee–Harvard Notebook II (SH II)
  Hymn to Intellectual Beauty, sheets of 1817 edition, corrected,
    probably, in Shelley's hand
  To Constantia, Singing

Henry Huntington Library

Bixby–Huntington Notebook I (BH I)
  Fragment: To Music (2)

Bixby–Huntington Notebook II (BH II)
  To ——: 'Yet look on me . . .'
  Fragment: 'Mighty eagle . . .'

Carl H. Pforzheimer Library (Pf.)

Stanza, Written at Bracknell
Queen Mab, 1813 edition, with autograph annotation by
  Shelley made for converting the poem into 'The Daemon
  of the World'. (Formerly owned by H. Buxton Forman and
  designated 'Fn.' in Vol. I)
Fragment: 'Mighty eagle . . .', 1–6

2. *Transcripts by Mary Shelley*

Bodleian Library (Bod.)

Notebook: MS. Shelley adds. d. 7
  To ——: 'Yet look on me . . .'
  Three Laments: 1. On Fanny Godwin, 10–end
                2. On William Shelley, 1–9
  Translation: Bion, I
  To Constantia, Singing
  Fragment: To Constantia
  Fragment: To One Singing
  Fragment: To Music (1)
  Fragment: To Music (2)
  Fragment: 'Mighty eagle . . .'

To William Shelley
  Additional Lines
To William Shelley
Lament: On Harriet Shelley, 1816 (2nd version; part only)
Fragment: 'A golden-wingèd Angel stood . . .'
Fragment: 'To thirst and find no fill . . .'
Fragment: 'Wealth and dominion . . .'
Translation: Epigram of Plato, cited in Apuleius

Notebook: MS. Shelley adds. e. 8
Fragment: 'Mighty eagle . . .'

Notebook: MS. Shelley adds. d. 9
To Mary Wollstonecraft Godwin
Verses Written on Receiving a Celandine. Rejected Lines
Three Laments: 1. On Fanny Godwin, 1–7
                       2. On William Shelley, 1–9
Prince Athanase (part only)
Fragment: To Music (1)
Fragment: To Music (2)
To the Lord Chancellor
To William Shelley ('The billows on the beach . . .') (part only)
Lament: On Harriet Shelley, 1817

Harvard University Library
Silsbee–Harvard Notebook II (SH II)
Verses Written on Receiving a Celandine
Marianne's Dream
To the Lord Chancellor
Translation: Epigram of Plato, cited in Apuleius

Leeds University Library, Cowden Clarke Collection
Fragment: To Music (1)
To the Lord Chancellor
To William Shelley

3. *Printed Sources*

Publications by Shelley:

Alastor; or, The Spirit of Solitude, Baldwin, Cradock, and Joy, and Carpenter and Son, 1816, including:
Stanzas. —— April, 1814

Reality ('The pale, the cold, and the moony smile . . .')
[See Introduction, p. xix]
Mutability
A Summer Evening Churchyard
'Oh! There are spirits of the air . . .'
To Wordsworth
Feelings of a Republican on the Fall of Bonaparte
The Daemon of the World, Part I
Translation: From Moschus, V
Translation: Sonnet from the Italian of Dante

In Leigh Hunt's *Examiner*, 19 Jan. 1817
Hymn to Intellectual Beauty, 1st edn.
In *History of a Six Weeks' Tour*, C. and J. Ollier, 1817
Mont Blanc
Laon and Cythna; or, The Revolution of the Golden City: A Vision
of the Nineteenth Century, C. and J. Ollier, Oct., Nov. 1817
(though postdated 1818), revised as
The Revolt of Islam, C. and J. Ollier, 10 Jan. 1818 (a few copies
bear the date 1817)
In Leigh Hunt's *Examiner*, 11 Jan. 1818
Ozymandias
In the *Oxford University and City Herald*, 31 Jan. 1818
To Constantia, Singing
Rosalind and Helen, C. and J. Ollier, 1819; which includes
Hymn to Intellectual Beauty, 2nd edn.
Ozymandias
In Leigh Hunt's *Literary Pocket-Book*, 1819
Marianne's Dream

Posthumous publications of, or containing, poetry by Shelley:[1]

Leigh Hunt, in the *Literary Pocket-Book*, 1823
The Sunset (part)
Mary Shelley, *Posthumous Poems of Percy Bysshe Shelley*, John and
Henry L. Hunt, 1824
Mary Shelley, *The Poetical Works of Percy Bysshe Shelley*, 4 vols.,
Edward Moxon, 1839; 2nd edn., 1 vol., 1840. [The two edns.
are referred to as 1839[1] and 1839[2]]

---

[1] Transcriptions and modified transcriptions are not listed here: where their help
has been used it is acknowledged. Only valid editions, and those significant in the
textual history of a poem, have been collated.

Thomas Medwin, *The Life of Shelley*, 2 vols., T. C. Newby, 1847. Revised edn., ed. H. Buxton Forman, Oxford University Press, 1913

T. J. Hogg, *The Life of Percy Bysshe Shelley*, vols. 1 and 2, Edward Moxon, 1858. Combined edn. with Trelawny's *Recollections* and Peacock's *Memoirs*, with Introduction by Humbert Wolfe, 2 vols., Dent, 1933

Richard Garnett, *Relics of Shelley*, Edward Moxon, 1862

W. M. Rossetti, *The Poetical Works of Percy Bysshe Shelley*, 2 vols., Edward Moxon, 1870; revised edn., 3 vols., 1878

H. Buxton Forman, *The Poetical Works of Percy Bysshe Shelley*, 4 vols., Reeves and Turner, 1876; 2nd edn., 2 vols., 1882; 3rd edn., 5 vols., Bell, 1892

George E. Woodberry, *The Complete Poetical Works of Percy Bysshe Shelley*, Centenary Edition, 4 vols., Kegan Paul, 1893

C. D. Locock, *An Examination of the Shelley Manuscripts in the Bodleian Library*, Clarendon Press, 1903

Thomas Hutchinson, *The Complete Poetical Works of Shelley*, Clarendon Press, 1904. Reissued, among 'Oxford Standard Authors', 1905

C. D. Locock, *The Poems of Percy Bysshe Shelley*, 2 vols., Methuen, 1911

H. Buxton Forman, *The Note Books of Percy Bysshe Shelley*, 3 vols., privately printed for the Boston Bibliophile Society, 1911

R. Ingpen and W. E. Peck, *The Complete Works of Percy Bysshe Shelley*, Julian Edition, 10 vols., Benn, 1926–30 [*Poems*, 1927]

Sir John Shelley-Rolls and R. Ingpen, *Verse and Prose from the Manuscripts of Percy Bysshe Shelley*, privately printed, 1934

Newman Ivey White, *Shelley*, 2 vols., Secker and Warburg, 1947

Kenneth Neill Cameron, *Shelley and his Circle*, Harvard University Press; London, Oxford University Press, 1961– [vols. i and ii, 1961; vols. iii and iv, 1970]

Frederick L. Jones, *The Letters of Percy Bysshe Shelley*, 2 vols., Clarendon Press, 1964

Marion K. Stocking, *The Journals of Claire Clairmont*, Harvard University Press; London, Oxford University Press, 1968

Claude C. Brew, *Shelley and Mary in 1817* [text and poetical evolution of the Dedication to *Laon and Cythna*], Keats–Shelley Memorial Association, 1971

Miscellaneous publications, used or referred to:

Kenneth Neill Cameron, *The Young Shelley*, Gollancz, 1951

Thomas Constable, *Memoir of the Rev. C. A. Chastel de Boinville*, J. Nisbet, 1880

F. S. Ellis, *A Lexical Concordance to the Works of Percy Bysshe Shelley*, 2 vols., Quaritch, 1892

Humphry House, *Coleridge* (The Clark Lectures), Rupert Hart-Davis, 1953

A. E. Housman, *Selected Prose*, ed. John Carter, Cambridge University Press, 1961

John Livingston Lowes, *The Road to Xanadu*, 2nd revised edn.

William J. McTaggart, *England in 1819: Church, State and Poverty. A Study, Textual and Historical, of 'A Ballad' by Shelley, formerly entitled 'Young Parson Richards'*, Keats–Shelley Memorial Association, 1970

J. A. Notopoulos, 'The Dating of Shelley's Prose', in *PMLA*, lviii, 1943

—— *The Platonism of Shelley*, Duke University Press, 1949

—— 'New Texts of Shelley's Plato', in *Keats–Shelley Journal*, xv, Winter 1966

Neville Rogers, *Shelley at Work*, 2nd edn., Clarendon Press, 1967

Hyder E. Rollins, *Letters of John Keats*, 2 vols., Harvard University Press, 1958

Charles H. Taylor, Jr., *The Early Collected Editions of Shelley's Poems*, Yale University Press, 1958

Hugh Tredennick, *The Last Days of Socrates* (trans. of Plato's *Apology, Crito*, and *Phaedo*), Penguin Books, 1954

IV. ABBREVIATIONS AND SIGNS USED

SHELLEY'S manuscripts are too numerous, and too varied, to permit any system of sigla. The Commentary below the text of each poem begins with details of its manuscript and printed sources. From this such abbreviations as 'Form.', 'Ross.', '1904', '1839[1]', etc. should be self-explanatory, but if an explanation of the operation of my Commentary is needed, it will be found in the General Introduction to this edition, given in Volume I, pp. xxxiv–xlii. The following are the signs used:

$\langle \rangle$ in the text denotes letters or words supplied conjecturally or textually doubtful.

[ ] in the Textual Commentary and sometimes in the text denotes words or letters cancelled in the manuscript.

[ ] in titles denotes words or letters implicit in the manuscript and supplied for clarity.

[at the end of a passage denotes that it is uncompleted in the manuscript.

A gap in a line of poetry denotes that it is uncompleted in the manuscript.

Words and lines from the manuscript which are not part of the text are printed in the Commentary, preceded by an indication of the lines between which they occur, e.g. '16–17', '98–9'.

ADDENDUM

The 'Claris manuscript' of 'Prince Athanase' (see pp. 277, 395) was sold at Sotheby's in 1918 to David Gage Joyce of Chicago, who died in 1937, and inherited by his daughter Beatrice Kean, who died in 1972. From 1918 to 1973 its location was unknown. In September 1973, whilst this volume was in the press, it was sold for $36,000 at the Hanzel Galleries, Chicago. All efforts to trace its new location and owner have failed. From the sale catalogue I have corrected, on p. 282, the last two words of Shelley's footnote, changing 'the difference' (previously printed) to 'this diffidence'. The catalogue states that Shelley placed his footnote at the head of the manuscript. No other textual divergences are mentioned.

SHORTER POEMS
1814, 1815

SHORTER POEMS

1814, 1815

Stanza, written at Bracknell

March 1814

THY dewy looks sink in my breast;
  Thy gentle words stir poison there;
Thou hast disturbed the only rest
  That was the portion of despair!
Subdued to Duty's hard control   5
  I could have borne my wayward lot:
The chains that bind this ruined soul
  Had cankered then—but crushed it not.

Stanzas.—April, 1814

AWAY! the moor is dark beneath the moon,
  Rapid clouds have drank the last pale beam of even:
Away! the gathering winds will call the darkness soon,
  And profoundest midnight shroud the serene lights of heaven.
Pause not! The time is past! Every voice cries, 'Away!'   5
  Tempt not with one last tear thy friend's ungentle mood:
Thy lover's eye, so glazed and cold, dares not entreat thy stay:
  Duty and dereliction guide thee back to solitude.

Away, away! to thy sad and silent home;
  Pour bitter tears on its desolated hearth;   10
Watch the dim shades as like ghosts they go and come,
  And complicate strange webs of melancholy mirth.

STANZA, WRITTEN AT BRACKNELL.   AUTOGRAPH, TITLE, DATE: *Pf., letter to Hogg,*
16 Mar. 1814.   PRINTED: *Hogg, 1858/Hutch. 1904.*   TEXT: *1904/Pf.*
  5 control] control, *Pf. and edd.*

STANZAS.—April, 1814.   MSS.: *Untraced.*   DATE: *See n., p. 327.*   PRINTED: *With*
Alastor, *PBS, 1816/MWS, 1839/Hutch. 1904.*   TITLE: *1816.*   TEXT: *1904/1816.*
  2 drank *1904, 1816*] drunk *1839*   6 tear *1904, 1816*] glance *1839*

The leaves of wasted autumn woods shall float around thine head:
  The blooms of dewy spring shall gleam beneath thy feet:
But thy soul or this world must fade in the frost that binds the dead,
  Ere midnight's frown and morning's smile, ere thou and peace
    may meet.   16

The cloud shadows of midnight possess their own repose,
  For the weary winds are silent, or the moon is in the deep:
Some respite to its turbulence unresting ocean knows;
  Whatever moves, or toils, or grieves, hath its appointed sleep. 20
Thou in the grave shalt rest—yet till the phantoms flee
  Which that house and heath and garden made dear to thee ere-
    while,
Thy remembrance, and repentance, and deep musings are not free
From the music of two voices and the light of one sweet smile.

To Mary Wollstonecraft Godwin

? June 1814

I

MINE eyes were dim with tears unshed;
  Yes, I was firm—thus wert not thou;—
My baffled looks did start yet dread
  To meet thy looks—I could not know
How anxiously they sought to shine   5
With soothing pity upon mine,—

II

To sit and curb the soul's mute rage
  Which preys upon itself alone;
To curse that life which is the cage
  Of fettered grief that dares not groan,   10

15 *See n., p. 327*

TO MARY WOLLSTONECRAFT GODWIN.   AUTOGRAPH: *Bod. MS. Shelley adds. e. 12.*
TRANSCRIPT: *MWS, Bod. MS. Shelley adds. d. 9.*   DATE, TITLE: *See n., p. 328.*
PRINTED: *MWS, 1824/MWS, 1839¹/MWS, 1839²/Hutch. 1904.*   TEXT: *1904/1839/*
1824 and erratum slip/d. 9/e. 12. Considerably repunctuated.

    1 dim *above* [big] [fed] *e. 12*   2 wert *1904, 1839, erratum slip*] did *1824, d. 9,*
e. 12   3 start *e. 12*] fear *1904, 1839, 1824, d. 9*   4 thy *1904, 1839, 1824,*
d. 9] your *above* [thy] *e. 12*   6 upon *uncancelled in e. 12, below into in smaller*
letters, also uncancelled   mine,—] mine. *edd.*   mine *e. 12*   7 mute *above*
[deep] *e. 12*   10 grief *below* [agony] *and both below* pain *e. 12*

Hiding from many a careless eye
The scornèd load of agony,—

III

Whilst thou alone then—not regarded,
　　Though hateless—thou alone shouldst be
To spend years thus, nor be rewarded   15
　　As thou, sweet love, requitedst me
When none were nigh . . . Oh, I did wake
From torture for that moment's sake!

IV

Upon my heart thy accents sweet
　　Of peace and pity fell like dew   20
On flowers half dead;—thy lips did meet
　　Mine tremblingly; thy dark eyes threw
Their soft persuasion on my brain,
Charming away its dream of pain.

V

We are not happy, sweet! our state   25
　　Is strange and full of doubt and fear,
More need for ⟨words⟩ that ills abate;—
　　Reserve or censure come not near
Our sacred friendship, lest there be
No solace left for thee and me.   30

VI

Gentle and good and mild thou art,
　　Nor can I live if thou appear

12 agony,—] agony *upon* misery *e. 12*　　agony. *edd.*　　misery *d. 9*　　　13, 16 thou
edd.] you *d. 9, e. 12*　　13 alone then—not regarded,] alone, then not regarded, *edd.;*
unpunctuated in d. 9 and e. 12　　14 Though hateless—] Tho hateless *e. 12*　　The
⟨*lacuna*⟩ *edd., d. 9*　　thou *edd.*] you *d. 9*　　you *below* [thou] *e. 12*　　shouldst] should
edd., d. 9, e. 12　　15 nor] and *edd., d. 9, e. 12*　　16 requitedst] requited *edd.,*
d. 9, e. 12　　17 nigh . . .] nigh—*e. 12*　　near—*edd., d. 9*　　18 sake!] sake. *edd.*
sake *d. 9, e. 12*　　19 thy *edd.*] your *d. 9*　　your *above* [thy] *e. 12*　　20 peace
edd., d. 9] peace *above* [love] *e. 12*　　23 Their *edd. since 1839, e. 12*] Thy
1824, d. 9　　24 Charming away its dream of pain. *edd., d. 9; changed from* Turning
to bliss its wayward *e. 12*　　25 sweet! *edd.*] sweet; *d. 9*　　sweet *above* [love] *e. 12*
27 for *e. 12*] of *edd., d. 9*　　28 Reserve *edd., d. 9*] Reserve *above* Or pride *e. 12*
30 thee *1904, 1839²*] thou *1839¹*　　you *erratum slip*　　thou *1824*　　you *d. 9* [thou]
you *e. 12*　　32 Nor can I *edd. since 1839, and d. 9*] Nor I can *1824*　　Nor can I
above [I cannot] *e. 12*

Aught but thyself, or turn thine heart
Away from me, or stoop to wear
The mask of scorn, although it be   35
To hide the love thou feel'st for me.

To ——

c. 1814

YET look on me!—take not thine eyes away,
  Which feed upon the love within mine own,
Although it be but the reflected ray
  Of thy sweet beauty from my spirit thrown.
Yet speak to me!—thy voice is as the tone   5
Of my heart's echo, and I think I hear
  That thou yet lovest me, whilst thou, alone,
Like one before a mirror, tak'st no care
Of aught but thine own ⟨? face⟩, imaged too truly there.

And yet I wear out life in watching thee,   10
  A toil so sweet at times; and thou indeed
Art kind when I am sick, and pityest me,
And I [

---

35 scorn, although *edd., d. 9; changed from* anger tho *e. 12*   36 thou feel'st
edd. since 1839] thou feel *1824*   you feel *erratum slip and d. 9*   you *above* [thou] *above*
[you] feel *e. 12*

To ——.   AUTOGRAPH: *BH II.*   TRANSCRIPT: *MWS, Bod. MS. Shelley adds. d. 7.*
DATE: *See n., p. 329.*   PRINTED: *MWS, 1839²/Hutch. 1904/Form.,* Note Books of
Shelley, *1911.*   TITLE: *1839².*   TEXT: *1911/1904/1839²/BH II.*
  3 Although it be *1911, BH II*] Which is indeed *1904, 1839²*   4 thy sweet
1911, BH II] thine own *1904, 1839²*   7 me, whilst thou, alone,] me, whilst thou
alone *1911*   me; yet thou alone *1904, 1839²*   me—yet *underscored, above* [whilst thou
alone] *BH II*   8 tak'st no] takest no *1911*   without *1904, 1839²*   takst no *above*
without *BH II*   9 ⟨? face⟩, imaged too truly there.] ⟨? faith⟩ imaged too truly there
1911   features, imaged there; *1904, 1839². No punctuation in BH II*   9–10 *The
stanza-break, from BH II, was introduced in 1911*   10 thee,] thee *1911, BH II*
thee; *1904, 1839²*   10–11 *BH has, alternatively, uncancelled*

        And yet I wear out life in watching thee
        Whether thou lovest me as looks have said

11 times;] times, *1911, 1904, 1839², BH II*   12 pityest *Ross. 1870*] pity *1911,
1904, 1839², BH II*   me,] me *1911, BH II*   me. *1904, 1839²*   13 And I]
1911 and BH II only

Mutability

1814 or 1815

WE are as clouds that veil the midnight moon;
  How restlessly they speed, and gleam, and quiver,
Streaking the darkness radiantly!—yet soon
  Night closes round, and they are lost for ever:

Or like forgotten lyres, whose dissonant strings   5
  Give various response to each varying blast,
To whose frail frame no second motion brings
  One mood or modulation like the last.

We rest.—A dream has power to poison sleep;
  We rise.—One wandering thought pollutes the day;   10
We feel, conceive or reason, laugh or weep;
  Embrace fond woe, or cast our cares away:

It is the same!—For, be it joy or sorrow,
  The path of its departure still is free:
Man's yesterday may ne'er be like his morrow;   15
  Nought may endure but Mutability.

A Summer Evening Churchyard
Lechlade, Gloucestershire

September 1815

THE wind has swept from the wide atmosphere
Each vapour that obscured the sunset's ray;
And pallid Evening twines its beaming hair
In duskier braids around the languid eyes of Day:
Silence and Twilight, unbeloved of men,   5
Creep hand in hand from yon obscurest glen.

MUTABILITY. MSS.: *Untraced.*   DATE: *See n., p. 329.*   PRINTED: *With* Alastor, *PBS, 1816/Hutch. 1904.*   TITLE: *1816.*   TEXT: *1904/1816.*

A SUMMER EVENING CHURCHYARD. MSS.: *Untraced.*   DATE: *Peacock, Memoirs, 1855. See n., p. 330.*   PRINTED: *With* Alastor, *PBS, 1816/MWS, 1839¹/Hutch. 1904.* TITLE: *1816.*   TEXT: *1904/1839¹/1816.*

They breathe their spells towards the departing day,
Encompassing the earth, air, stars, and sea;
Light, sound, and motion own the potent sway,
Responding to the charm with its own mystery.   10
The winds are still, or the dry church-tower grass
Knows not their gentle motions as they pass.

Thou too, aëreal Pile! whose pinnacles
Point from one shrine like pyramids of fire,
Obeyest in silence their sweet solemn spells,   15
Clothing in hues of heaven thy dim and distant spire,
Around whose lessening and invisible height
Gather among the stars the clouds of night.

The dead are sleeping in their sepulchres:
And, mouldering as they sleep, a thrilling sound,   20
Half sense, half thought, among the darkness stirs,
Breathed from their wormy beds all living things around,
And mingling with the still night and mute sky
Its awful hush is felt inaudibly.

Thus solemnized and softened, death is mild   25
And terrorless as this serenest night:
Here could I hope, like some inquiring child
Sporting on graves, that death did hide from human sight
Sweet secrets, or beside its breathless sleep
That loveliest dreams perpetual watch did keep.   30

'Oh! There are Spirits of the Air . . .'

1814 or 1815

δάκρυσι διοίσω πότμον
ἄποτμον

OH! there are spirits of the air,
    And genii of the evening breeze,
And gentle ghosts, with eyes as fair
    As star-beams among twilight trees:—
Such lovely ministers to meet   5
Oft hast thou turned from men thy lonely feet.

OH! THERE ARE SPIRITS OF THE AIR . . .'.   MSS.: *Untraced.*   DATE: *See n., p. 330.*
PRINTED: *With* Alastor, *PBS, 1816/MWS, 1839¹/Hutch. 1904.*   TITLE: *See n.,*
p. 330.   TEXT: *1904/1816.*
  1 of *1904, 1816*] in *1839¹*

With mountain winds, and babbling springs,
   And moonlight seas, that are the voice
Of these inexplicable things,
   Thou didst hold commune, and rejoice   10
When they did answer thee; but they
Cast, like a worthless boon, thy love away.

And thou hast sought in starry eyes
   Beams that were never meant for thine,
Another's wealth:—tame sacrifice   15
   To a fond faith! still dost thou pine?
Still dost thou hope that greeting hands,
Voice, looks, or lips, may answer thy demands?

Ah! wherefore didst thou build thine hope
   On the false earth's inconstancy?   20
Did thine own mind afford no scope
   Of love, or moving thoughts to thee?
That natural scenes or human smiles
Could steal the power to wind thee in their wiles?

Yes, all the faithless smiles are fled   25
   Whose falsehood left thee broken-hearted;
The glory of the moon is dead;
   Night's ghosts and dreams have now departed;
Thine own soul still is true to thee,
But changed to a foul fiend through misery.   30

This fiend, whose ghastly presence ever
   Beside thee like thy shadow hangs,
Dream not to chase;—the mad endeavour
   Would scourge thee to severer pangs.
Be as thou art. Thy settled fate,   35
Dark as it is, all change would aggravate.

8 moonlight *1904, 1816*] mountain *1839*[1]   24 wiles? *1904*] wiles. *1839*[1], *1816*
28 ghosts *1904, 1816*] ghost *1839*[1]

To Wordsworth

1814 or 1815

POET of Nature, thou hast wept to know
That things depart which never may return:
Childhood and youth, friendship and love's first glow,
Have fled like sweet dreams, leaving thee to mourn.
These common woes I feel. One loss is mine   5
Which thou too feel'st, yet I alone deplore.
Thou wert as a lone star, whose light did shine
On some frail bark in winter's midnight roar:
Thou hast like to a rock-built refuge stood
Above the blind and battling multitude: 10
In honoured poverty thy voice did weave
Songs consecrate to truth and liberty,—
Deserting these, thou leavest me to grieve,
Thus having been, that thou should cease to be.

Feelings of a Republican on the Fall of Bonaparte

1814 or 1815

I HATED thee, fallen tyrant! I did groan
To think that a most unambitious slave,
Like thee, should dance and revel on the grave
Of Liberty. Thou mightst have built thy throne
Where it had stood even now: thou didst prefer   5
A frail and bloody pomp which Time has swept
In fragments towards Oblivion. Massacre,—
For this I prayed,—would on thy sleep have crept,
Treason and Slavery, Rapine, Fear, and Lust,
And stifled thee, their minister. I know   10
Too late, since thou and France are in the dust,
That Virtue owns a more eternal foe
Than Force or Fraud: old Custom, legal Crime,
And bloody Faith, the foulest birth of Time.

To WORDSWORTH. MSS.: *Untraced.*   DATE: *See n., p. 330.*   PRINTED: *With* Alastor, *PBS, 1816/MWS, 1839¹/Hutch. 1904.*   TITLE: *1816.*   TEXT: *1904/1816.*

FEELINGS, ETC. MSS.: *Untraced.*   DATE: *See n., p. 331.*   PRINTED: *With* Alastor, *PBS, 1816/MWS 1839¹/Hutch. 1904.*   TITLE: *1816.*   TEXT: *1904/1816.*

   3 thee,] thou, *1904, 1816*   should] shouldst *1904, 1839¹, 1816*   7–8 Massacre, —/... prayed,—*parenthesis marked by Loc. 1911*   14 Faith, *1839¹*] Faith *1904, 1816*

Two Fragments from the Journal of Claire Clairmont

1814 or 1815

1

The thoughts of my past life
Rise like the ghosts of an unquiet dream
Blackening the cheerful morn.

Now the dark boughs of the Aeolian pine
Swing to the sweeping wind, and the light clouds   5
And the blue sky beyond, so deep and still,
Commingle like a sympathy of sight
With the sweet music!

2

How beautiful it sails
Along the silent and serene expanse,
Blending its solemn and aerial tints
With the pale sky! Now an extinguished moon,
The frail dim spectre of some quenched orb,   5
Beamless and broad on the still air upheld,
It hangs in Heaven's deep azure—like a flame
Sphered by the hand of some belated gnome
That chides for its delay the pausing blush
Where the red light of evening's solemn smile   10
Hangs on the skirts of the exhausted storm,
Or where the embattled clouds of orient day
Allow short respite to the waning stars;
Now the Aeolian chords within yon bower
Most like a moth that mocks the wandering ⟨? fire⟩   15
When mill ⟨*illegible through burning*⟩ ray moons
⟨? Troop⟩ ⟨*illegible through burning*⟩ dream.

Two Fragments, etc.   autograph: *BM. Journal of Claire Clairmont.*   date:
See n., p. 331.   printed: *White,* Shelley, *1947/Stocking,* Journal of Claire Clairmont,
1968.   text: *BM; punctuation added and spelling adjusted.*
    *Written by Shelley on two pages of a notebook used by Claire Clairmont. Both pages
are burned at one edge. Between 1 and 2 a page is missing, so that the connection is open
to a slight doubt.*
    7 Commingle] Commingles *BM*

TRANSLATIONS
1814, 1815

TRANSLATIONS

1814, 1815

Sonnet

From the Italian of Dante

[Guido, i' vorrei che tu e Lapo ed io . . .]

Dante Alighieri to Guido Cavalcanti

GUIDO, I would that Lapo, thou, and I,
Led by some strong enchantment, might ascend
A magic ship, whose charmèd sails should fly
With winds at will where'er our thoughts might wend,
So that no change, nor any evil chance   5
Should mar our joyous voyage; but it might be,
That even satiety should still enhance
Between our hearts their strict community:
And that the bounteous wizard then would place
Vanna and Bice and my gentle love   10
Companions of our wandering, and would grace
With passionate talk, wherever we might rove,
Our time, and each were as content and free
As I believe that thou and I should be.

SONNET FROM DANTE.   MSS.: *Unknown.*   DATE: *See n., p. 331.*   PRINTED: *With*
Alastor, *PBS, 1816/MWS, 1824/MWS, 1839/Hutch. 1904.*   TITLE: *1816.*   TEXT:
1904/1816 recollated.
  5 So *1904, 1839, 1824*] And *1816. See n., p. 332.*   10 love] love, *edd.*

Sonnet

From the Italian of Cavalcanti

[Io vengo il giorno a te infinite volte . . .]

Guido Cavalcanti to Dante Alighieri

RETURNING from its daily quest, my Spirit
Changed thoughts and vile in thee doth weep to find:
It grieves me that thy mild and gentle mind
Those ample virtues which it did inherit
Has lost. Once thou didst loathe the multitude   5
Of blind and madding men: I then loved thee—
I loved thy lofty songs and that sweet mood
When thou wert faithful to thyself and me.
I dare not now, through thy degraded state,
Own the delight thy strains inspire—in vain   10
I seek what once thou wert—we cannot meet
As we were wont. Again and yet again
Ponder my words: so the false Spirit shall fly
And leave to thee thy true integrity.

SONNET FROM CAVALCANTI.   AUTOGRAPH: *Leigh Hunt MS.*, *later owned by Townsend Mayer, now untraced.*   DATE: *See n., p. 332.*   PRINTED, TITLE: *Form. 1876/Hutch. 1904.*   TEXT: *1904/1876 and facsimile reproduced in 1876.*
  6 men:] men—*1904, 1876*   9 now,] now *1904, 1876*   state,] state *1904, 1876*

---

[1] *Notably the Esdaile Poems, not then available. See Vol. I, pp. 81–179.*

NOTE BY MARY SHELLEY ON THE POEMS OF 1814, 1815

As far as possible I have arranged Shelley's Poems in the order in which they were written. Of course, mistakes will occur in placing some of the shorter ones; for, as I have said, many of these were thrown aside, and I never saw them till I had the misery of looking over his writings after the hand that traced them was dust; and some were in the hands of others, and I never saw them till now. The subjects of the poems are often to me an unerring guide; but on other occasions I can only guess, by finding them in the pages of the same manuscript book that contains poems with the date of whose composition I am fully conversant.
    The loss of his early papers prevents my being able to give any of the

poetry of his boyhood.[1] Of the few I give, the greater part were published with *Alastor*; some of them were written previously, some at the same period. The poem beginning 'Oh, there are spirits in the air' was addressed in idea to Coleridge, whom he never knew; and at whose character he could only guess imperfectly, through his writings, and accounts he heard of him from some who knew him well. He regarded his change of opinions as rather an act of will than conviction, and believed that in his inner heart he would be haunted by what Shelley considered the better and holier aspirations of his youth. The summer evening that suggested to him the poem written in the churchyard of Lechlade occurred during his voyage up the Thames in 1815. He had been advised by a physician to live as much as possible in the open air; and a fortnight of a bright warm July[1] was spent in tracing the Thames to its source. He never spent a season more tranquilly than the summer of 1815. He had just recovered from a severe pulmonary attack; the weather was warm and pleasant. He lived near Windsor Forest; and his life was spent under its shades or on the water, meditating subjects for verse. Hitherto, he had chiefly aimed at extending his political doctrines, and attempted so to do by appeals in prose essays to the people, exhorting them to claim their rights; but he had now begun to feel that the time for action was not ripe in England, and that the pen was the only instrument wherewith to prepare the way for better things.

In the scanty journals kept during those years I find a record of the books that Shelley read during several years. During the years of 1814 and 1815 the list is extensive. It includes, in Greek, Homer, Hesiod, Theocritus, the histories of Thucydides and Herodotus, and Diogenes Laertius. In Latin, Petronius, Suetonius, some of the works of Cicero, a large proportion of those of Seneca and Livy. In English, Milton's poems, Wordsworth's *Excursion*, Southey's *Madoc* and *Thalaba*, Locke's *On the Human Understanding*, Bacon's *Novum Organum*. In Italian, Ariosto, Tasso, and Alfieri. In French, the *Rêveries d'un Solitaire* of Rousseau. To these may be added several modern books of travels. He read few novels.

---

[1] *Mary's recollection is at fault; the trip took place towards the end of August. See White, Shelley, i. 414, 698.*

THE DAEMON
OF THE WORLD
A FRAGMENT
1815

THE DAEMON OF THE WORLD

A FRAGMENT[1]

1815

PART I

Nec tantum prodere vati,
Quantum scire licet. Venit aetas omnis in unam
Congeriem, miserumque premunt tot saecula pectus.

LUCAN, *Phars.* v. 176.

HOW wonderful is Death,
Death and his brother Sleep!
One pale as yonder wan and hornèd moon,
  With lips of lurid blue,
The other glowing like the vital morn,   5
  When throned on ocean's wave
  It breathes over the world:
Yet both so passing strange and wonderful!

Hath then the iron-sceptred Skeleton,
Whose reign is in the tainted sepulchres,   10

---

[1] The fragment entitled *The Daemon of the World* is a detached part of a poem which the author does not intend for publication. The metre in which it is composed is that of *Samson Agonistes* and the Italian pastoral drama, and may be considered as the natural measure into which poetical compositions, expressed in harmonious language, necessarily fall.

[Shelley, in the Preface to the *Alastor* volume, 1816.]

THE DAEMON OF THE WORLD. MSS.: *Two copies of* Q.Mab *bearing autograph changes:* BM[b], *once owned by T. J. Wise, of I, II only; Pf., once owned by Forman, of I, II, VIII, IX. See nn., pp. 332 ff.; also commentary on* Q.Mab *in Vol. I, where Pf. is designated* 'Fn.' DATE: *A rehandling, in 1815, of* Q.Mab, *I, II, VIII, IX.* PRINTED: *Part I, with* Alastor, *PBS, 1816/Part II, from Fn./Pf., Form. 1876/1-end, Hutch. 1904.* TITLE: *1816.* TEXT: *1904/1876/collated with* BM[b], *Pf., 1813.*
PART I. 1-8 *For* Q.Mab, *I. 1-8,* BM[b]   3 wan and hornèd *1904, 1876, 1816,* BM[b]] waning *1813*   5 glowing like the vital *1904, 1876, 1816*] rosy as the *1813* morn *1904, 1876, 1816,* BM[b]] day *Pf.*   7 breathes over *1904, 1876, 1816,* BM[b], *Pf.*] blushes o'er *1813*   8 strange and wonderful *1904, 1876, 1816*] strange wonderful BM[b] [dark] wonderful *Pf.* passing wonderful *1813*   9-21 *For* Q.Mab, *I. 9-21,* BM[b]   9 iron-sceptred Skeleton *1904, 1876, 1816*] gloomy Shadow *Pf.* gloomy Power *1813*

To the helldogs that crouch beneath his throne
Cast that fair prey? Must that divinest form,
Which love and admiration cannot view
Without a beating heart, whose azure veins
Steal like dark streams along a field of snow,   15
Whose outline is as fair as marble clothed
In light of some sublimest mind, decay?
    Nor putrefaction's breath
Leave aught of this pure spectacle
    But loathsomeness and ruin?—   20
    Spare aught but a dark theme,
On which the lightest heart might moralize?
Or is it but that downy-wingèd slumbers
Have charmed their nurse coy Silence near her lids
    To watch their own repose?   25
    Will they, when morning's beam
    Flows through those wells of light,
Seek far from noise and day some western cave,
Where woods and streams with soft and pausing winds
    A lulling murmur weave?—   30

    Ianthe doth not sleep
    The dreamless sleep of death:
Nor in her moonlight chamber silently
Doth Henry hear her regular pulses throb,
    Or mark her delicate cheek   35
With interchange of hues mock the broad moon,
    Outwatching weary night,
    Without assured reward.
    Her dewy eyes are closed;
On their translucent lids, whose texture fine   40
Scarce hides the dark blue orbs that burn below
    With unapparent fire,

11 helldogs *BM*[b]] hell dogs *1904, 1876, 1816*   crouch *BM*[b]] couch *1904, 1876,*
1816   19 aught . . . spectacle *1904, 1876, 1816, BM*[b]] entrancing s *changed to*
pure spectacle *Pf.* nothing . . . heavenly sight *1813*   21–38 *For* Q.Mab, *I. 21–36,*
BM[b]   21 aught . . . dark *1904, 1876, 1816, BM*[b]] nothing . . . gloomy *1813*
23 that downy-winged slumbers *1904, 1876, 1816*] that downy-winged *under* [pinioned]
slumbers *BM*[b]   that wanton winged slumbers *Pf.* only a sweet slumber *1813*
24 *Thus edd. and BM*[b]] Stealing o'er sensation *1813*   31–38 *Inserted in BM*[b]
39–47 *For* Q.Mab, *I. 37–44, BM*[b]42 [With fire that is concealed] *Pf.*

The baby Sleep is pillowed:
Her golden tresses shade
The bosom's stainless pride,   45
Twining like tendrils of the parasite
Around a marble column.

Hark! whence that rushing sound?
'Tis like a wondrous strain that sweeps
Around a lonely ruin   50
When west winds sigh and evening waves respond
In whispers from the shore:
'Tis wilder than the unmeasured notes
Which from the unseen lyres of dells and groves
The genii of the breezes sweep.   55
Floating on waves of music and of light,
The chariot of the Daemon of the World
Descends in silent power;
Its shape reposed within; slight as some cloud
That catches but the palest tinge of day   60
When evening yields to night,
Bright as that fibrous woof when stars indue
Its transitory robe.
Four shapeless shadows bright and beautiful
Draw that strange car of glory, reins of light   65
Check their unearthly speed; they stop and fold
Their wings of braided air:
The Daemon leaning from the ethereal car
Gazed on the slumbering maid.
Human eye hath ne'er beheld   70
A shape so wild, so bright, so beautiful,
As that which o'er the maiden's charmèd sleep
Waving a starry wand,
Hung like a mist of light.

46 Twining *1904, 1876, 1816, BM^b*] Curling *1813*   48–56 *For* Q.Mab, *I. 45–58,*
BM^b   51 *Thus edd. and BM^b*] 'Tis softer than the west wind's sigh *1813*
52 *Inserted after* Q.Mab, *I. 50, in BM^b*   54 dells and groves *1904, 1876, 1816,*
BM^b] [caves and woods] *above* dells and groves *Pf.*
55–6   Are like such rays as many coloured streams
                 Throw on the roof of some impending crag *Pf.*

56 light, *1904*] light *1876, 1816*   57–68 *For* Q.Mab, *I. 59–74, BM^b*   57 Fairy
Queen! *1904, 1876, 1816, BM^b*   Universal Queen *Pf.*   69–77 *Inserted in BM^b*

Such sounds as breathed around like odorous winds   75
   Of wakening spring arose,
Filling the chamber and the moonlight sky.

'Maiden, the world's supremest spirit
   Beneath the shadow of her wings
Folds all thy memory doth inherit   80
   From ruin of divinest things,
     Feelings that lure thee to betray,
     And light of thoughts that pass away.

'For thou hast earned a mighty boon,
   The truths which wisest poets see   85
Dimly, thy mind may make its own,
   Rewarding its own majesty,
     Entranced in some diviner mood
     Of self-oblivious solitude.

'Custom, and Faith, and Power thou spurnest;   90
   From hate and awe thy heart is free;
Ardent and pure as day thou burnest,
   For dark and cold mortality
     A living light, to cheer it long,
     The watch-fires of the world among.   95

'Therefore from nature's inner shrine,
   Where gods and fiends in worship bend,
Majestic spirit, be it thine
   The flame to seize, the veil to rend,
     Where the vast snake Eternity   100
     In charmèd sleep doth ever lie.

'All that inspires thy voice of love,
   Or speaks in thy unclosing eyes,
Or through thy frame doth burn or move,
   Or think or feel, awake, arise!   105
     Spirit, leave, for mine and me
     Earth's unsubstantial mimicry!'

78-95 For Q.Mab, I. 79-93, BM[b]   96-114 For Q.Mab, I. 114-33, BM[b]
106 leave, Loc. 1911] leave 1904, 1876, 1816

It ceased, and from the mute and moveless frame
    A radiant Spirit arose,
All beautiful in naked purity.   110
Robed in its human hues it did ascend;
Disparting as it went the silver clouds,
It moved towards the car, and took its seat
    Beside the Daemon shape.

Obedient to the sweep of aëry song,   115
    The mighty ministers
Unfurled their prismy wings.
    The magic car moved on;
The night was fair, innumerable stars
    Studded heaven's dark blue vault;   120
    The eastern wave grew pale
    With the first smile of morn.

    The magic car moved on.
    From the swift sweep of wings
The atmosphere in flaming sparkles flew;   125
    And where the burning wheels
Eddied above the mountain's loftiest peak
    Was traced a line of lightning.
Now far above a rock the utmost verge
    Of the wide earth it flew,   130
The rival of the Andes, whose dark brow
    Frowned o'er the silver sea.

Far, far below the chariot's stormy path,
    Calm as a slumbering babe,
    Tremendous ocean lay.   135
Its broad and silent mirror gave to view
    The pale and waning stars,
    The chariot's fiery track,
    And the grey light of morn
    Tingeing those fleecy clouds   140
That cradled in their folds the infant dawn.

108-9 From the mute frame a lovely ghost arose *Pf.*   111 ascend;] ascend *1904,*
1876, 1816   ascend: *BM*[b]   112 clouds, *1904*] clouds *1876, 1816*   115-22 *For*
Q.Mab, *I. 199-211, BM*[b]   123-32 *For* Q.Mab, *I. 212-21, BM*[b]   133-47 *For*
Q.Mab, *I. 222-36, BM*[b]

The chariot seemed to fly
Through the abyss of an immense concave,
Radiant with million constellations, tinged
    With shades of infinite colour,   145
    And semicircled with a belt
    Flashing incessant meteors.

    As they approached their goal,
The wingèd shadows seemed to gather speed.
The sea no longer was distinguished; earth   150
Appeared a vast and shadowy sphere, suspended
    In the black concave of heaven
    With the sun's cloudless orb,
    Whose rays of rapid light
Parted around the chariot's swifter course,   155
And fell like ocean's feathery spray
    Dashed from the boiling surge
    Before a vessel's prow.

    The magic car moved on.
    Earth's distant orb appeared   160
The smallest light that twinkles in the heavens,
    Whilst round the chariot's way
Innumerable systems widely rolled,
    And countless spheres diffused
    An ever-varying glory.   165
It was a sight of wonder! Some were horned,
And like the moon's argentine crescent hung
In the dark dome of heaven; some did shed
A clear mild beam like Hesperus, while the sea
Yet glows with fading sunlight; others dashed   170
Athwart the night with trains of bickering fire,
Like spherèd worlds to death and ruin driven;
Some shone like stars, and as the chariot passed
    Bedimmed all other light.

147–8 [The magic car moved on.] *BM^b*   148–58 *For* Q .Mab, *I. 237–48, BM^b*
159–88 *For* Q .Mab, *I. 249–77, BM^b*   161 twinkles in the heavens *1904, 1876,
1816*] shines among the stars *Pf.*   163 widely rolled *1904, 1876, 1816, BM^b*]
rolled *1813*   167 And *1904*] And, *1876, 1816*   168 heaven; *1904*] heaven,
1876, 1816

Spirit of Nature! here   175
In this interminable wilderness
Of worlds, at whose involved immensity
    Even soaring fancy staggers,
    Here is thy fitting temple.
    Yet not the lightest leaf   180
That quivers to the passing breeze
    Is less instinct with thee,—
    Yet not the meanest worm,
That lurks in graves and fattens on the dead,
    Less shares thy eternal breath.   185
    Spirit of Nature! thou
Imperishable as this glorious scene,
    Here is thy fitting temple.

If solitude hath ever led thy steps
To the shore of the immeasurable sea,   190
    And thou hast lingered there
    Until the sun's broad orb
Seemed resting on the fiery line of ocean,
Thou must have marked the braided webs of gold
    That without motion hang   195
    Over the sinking sphere:
Thou must have marked the billowy mountain clouds,
Edged with intolerable radiancy,
    Towering like rocks of jet
    Above the burning deep: 200
    And yet there is a moment
    When the sun's highest point
Peers like a star o'er ocean's western edge,
When those far clouds of feathery purple gleam
Like fairy lands girt by some heavenly sea: 205
Then has thy rapt imagination soared
Where in the midst of all existing things
The temple of the mightiest Daemon stands.

---

177 involved immensity *1904, 1876, BM^b*] immensity *1813*   180 lightest *1904,*
1876, 1816, BM^b] slightest *Pf.*   184 dead, *1876, 1816*   187 glorious scene *1904,*
1876, 1816, BM^b] scene *1813*   189–208 *For* Q.Mab, *II. 1–21*

Yet not the golden islands
That gleam amid yon flood of purple light,　　　210
Nor the feathery curtains
That canopy the sun's resplendent couch,
Nor the burnished ocean waves
Paving that gorgeous dome,
So fair, so wonderful a sight　　　215
As the eternal temple could afford.
The elements of all that human thought
Can frame of lovely or sublime, did join
To rear the fabric of the fane, nor aught
Of earth may image forth its majesty.　　　220
Yet likest evening's vault that faëry hall,
As heaven low-resting on the wave it spread
Its floors of flashing light,
Its vast and azure dome;
And on the verge of that obscure abyss　　　225
Where crystal battlements o'erhang the gulf
Of the dark world, ten thousand spheres diffuse
Their lustre through its adamantine gates.

The magic car no longer moved;
The Daemon and the Spirit　　　230
Entered the eternal gates.
Those clouds of aëry gold
That slept in glittering billows
Beneath the azure canopy,
With the ethereal footsteps trembled not;　　　235
While slight and odorous mists
Floated to strains of thrilling melody
Through the vast columns and the pearly shrines.

The Daemon and the Spirit
Approached the overhanging battlement.　　　240
Below lay stretched the boundless universe!
There, far as the remotest line
That limits swift imagination's flight,
Unending orbs mingled in mazy motion,

209-38 *For* Q.Mab, *II. 22-54,* BM^b　　　239-52 *For* Q.Mab, *II. 68-82,* BM^b

Immutably fulfilling   245
Eternal Nature's law.
Above, below, around,
The circling systems formed
A wilderness of harmony.
Each with undeviating aim   250
In eloquent silence through the depths of space
Pursued its wondrous way.—

Awhile the Spirit paused in ecstasy.
Yet soon she saw, as the vast spheres swept by,
Strange things within their belted orbs appear.   255
Like animated frenzies, dimly moved
Shadows, and skeletons, and fiendly shapes,
Thronging round human graves, and o'er the dead
Sculpturing records for each memory
In verse, such as malignant gods pronounce,   260
Blasting the hopes of men, when heaven and hell
Confounded burst in ruin o'er the world:
And they did build vast trophies, instruments
Of murder, human bones, barbaric gold,
Skins torn from living men, and towers of skulls   265
With sightless holes gazing on blinder heaven,
Mitres, and crowns, and brazen chariots stained
With blood, and scrolls of mystic wickedness,
The sanguine codes of venerable crime.
The likeness of a thronèd king came by,   270
When these had passed, bearing upon his brow
A threefold crown; his countenance was calm,
His eye severe and cold; but his right hand
Was charged with bloody coin, and he did gnaw
By fits, with secret smiles, a human heart   275
Concealed beneath his robe; and motley shapes,
A multitudinous throng, around him knelt,
With bosoms bare, and bowed heads, and false looks
Of true submission, as the sphere rolled by.
Brooking no eye to witness their foul shame,   280
Which human hearts must feel, while human tongues

253-86 *Thus 1904, 1876, 1816; missing in BM^b, Pf.*   279 by. *1904*] by, *1876, 1816*

Tremble to speak, they did rage horribly,
Breathing in self-contempt fierce blasphemies
Against the Daemon of the World, and high
Hurling their armèd hands where the pure Spirit,   285
Serene and inaccessibly secure,
Stood on an isolated pinnacle,
The flood of ages combating below,
The depth of the unbounded universe
      Above, and all around   290
Necessity's unchanging harmony.

PART II

'O HAPPY Earth! reality of Heaven!
To which those restless powers that ceaselessly
Throng through the human universe aspire;
Thou consummation of all mortal hope!   295
Thou glorious prize of blindly-working will,
Whose rays, diffused throughout all space and time,
Verge to one point and blend for ever there:
Of purest spirits thou pure dwelling-place!
Where care and sorrow, impotence and crime,   300
Languor, disease and ignorance dare not come:
O happy Earth, reality of Heaven!

   'Genius has seen thee in her passionate dreams,
And dim forebodings of thy loveliness,
Haunting the human heart, have there entwined   305
Those rooted hopes, that the proud Power of Evil
Shall not for ever on this fairest world
Shake pestilence and war, or that his slaves
With blasphemy for prayer, and human blood
For sacrifice, before his shrine for ever   310
In adoration bend, or Erebus

287–91 *For* Q.Mab, *II. 253–7, BM^b*   287 Stood *1904, 1876, 1816, BM^b*]
High *1813*   291 Necessity's *1904, 1876, 1816, BM^b*] Nature's *1813*

PART II. 292–305 *Cf.* Q.Mab, *IX. 1–15, Pf.*   296 will, *Loc. 1911*] will! *1904,*
1876   304 loveliness, *1904*] loveliness *1876, 1816*   306–19 *Inserted in Pf.*
306 Power *1904, 1876*]   Power *above* [God] *Pf.*   311 or Erebus *1904, 1876*] or
[Ere] *above* [that its jaws] Erebus *Pf.*

With all its banded fiends shall not uprise
To overwhelm in envy and revenge
The dauntless and the good, who dare to hurl
Defiance at his throne, girt though it be   315
With Death's omnipotence. Thou hast beheld
His empire, o'er the present and the past;
It was a desolate sight—now gaze on mine,
Futurity. Thou hoary giant Time,
Render thou up thy half-devourèd babes,—   320
And from the cradles of eternity,
Where millions lie lulled to their portioned sleep
By the deep-murmuring stream of passing things,
Tear thou that gloomy shroud.—Spirit, behold
Thy glorious destiny!'

      The Spirit saw   325
The vast frame of the renovated world
Smile in the lap of Chaos, and the sense
Of hope through her fine texture did suffuse
Such varying glow, as summer evening casts
On undulating clouds and deepening lakes.   330
Like the vague sighings of a wind at even,
That wakes the wavelets of the slumbering sea
And dies on the creation of its breath,
And sinks and rises, fails and swells by fits,
Was the sweet stream of thought that with wild motion
Flowed o'er the Spirit's human sympathies.   336
The mighty tide of thought had paused awhile,
Which from the Daemon now like Ocean's stream
Again began to pour.—

      'To me is given
The wonders of the human world to keep—   340
Space, matter, time and mind—let the sight
Renew and strengthen all thy failing hope.

312–13 [Conspiring Hell shall gape to swallow all] *Pf.* 320–5 *Cf.* Q .Mab,
VIII. 5–10 325–30 *Inserted in Pf.* 325 saw *1904, 1876*] [felt] saw *Pf.*
328 through *1904, 1876*] through *above* [on] *Pf.* 329 glow *1904, 1876 ; changed
from* glows *Pf.* 331–6 *Cf.* Q .Mab, *VIII. 23–30* 337–42 *Inserted in Pf.*
337 paused awhile *1904, 1876*] paused awhile *below* [calmly flowed] *Pf.* 339 pour
1904, 1876] [flow] pour *Pf.* 341–2 let . . . hope *changed from* [Futurity / Exposes
all the treasures to thy sight] *Pf.*

All things are recreated, and the flame
Of consentaneous love inspires all life:
The fertile bosom of the earth gives suck   345
To myriads, who still grow beneath her care,
Rewarding her with their pure perfectness:
The balmy breathings of the wind inhale
Her virtues, and diffuse them all abroad:
Health floats amid the gentle atmosphere,   350
Glows in the fruits, and mantles on the stream;
No storms deform the beaming brow of heaven,
Nor scatter in the freshness of its pride
The foliage of the undecaying trees;
But fruits are ever ripe, flowers ever fair,   355
And Autumn proudly bears her matron grace,
Kindling a flush on the fair cheek of Spring,
Whose virgin bloom beneath the ruddy fruit
Reflects its tint and blushes into love.

'The habitable earth is full of bliss;   360
Those wastes of frozen billows that were hurled
By everlasting snow-storms round the poles,
Where matter dared not vegetate nor live,
But ceaseless frost round the vast solitude
Bound its broad zone of stillness, are unloosed;   365
And fragrant zephyrs there from spicy isles
Ruffle the placid ocean-deep, that rolls
Its broad, bright surges to the sloping sand,
Whose roar is wakened into echoings sweet
To murmur through the heaven-breathing groves   370
And melodise with man's blest nature there.

'The vast tract of the parched and sandy waste
Now teems with countless rills and shady woods,
Corn-fields and pastures and white cottages;
And where the startled wilderness did hear   375
A savage conqueror stained in kindred blood,
Hymning his victory, or the milder snake

343-59 *Cf.* Q.Mab, *VIII. 107-23, Pf.*   354 undecaying *1904, 1876, changed in Pf. from*] ever verdant *1813*   360-76 *Cf.* Q.Mab, *VIII. 58-78*   363 not ... nor] *1904, 1876, 1816, changed in Pf. from* not ... or *1813*   372-83 *Cf.* Q.Mab, *VIII. 70-87, Pf.*   372 *inserted in Pf.*] parched and sandy waste *1904, 1876* [parched and *above* the sandy waste *above* [wilderness] *Pf.*   377-9½ *Inserted in Pf.*

Crushing the bones of some frail antelope
Within his brazen folds—the dewy lawn,
Offering sweet incense to the sunrise, smiles   380
To see a babe, before his mother's door,
Share with the green and golden basilisk
That comes to lick his feet, his morning's meal.

'Those trackless deeps, where many a weary sail
Has seen, above the illimitable plain,   385
Morning on night and night on morning rise,
Whilst still no land to greet the wanderer spread
Its shadowy mountains on the sun-bright sea,—
Where the loud roarings of the tempest-waves
So long have mingled with the gusty wind   390
In melancholy loneliness, and swept
The desert of those ocean solitudes,
But vocal to the sea-bird's harrowing shriek,
The bellowing monster, and the rushing storm,—
Now to the sweet and many-mingling sounds   395
Of kindliest human impulses respond:
Those lonely realms bright garden-isles begem,
With lightsome clouds and shining seas between,
And fertile valleys, resonant with bliss,
Whilst green woods overcanopy the wave,   400
Which like a toil-worn labourer leaps to shore,
To meet the kisses of the flowerets there.

'Man chief perceives the change, his being notes
The gradual renovation, and defines
Each movement of its progress on his mind.   405
Man, where the gloom of the long polar night
Lowered o'er the snow-clad rocks and frozen soil,
Where scarce the hardiest herb that braves the frost
Basked in the moonlight's ineffectual glow,
Shrank with the plants, and darkened with the night; 410
Nor where the tropics bound the realms of day
With a broad belt of mingling cloud and flame,

379–83 *Cf.* Q .Mab, *VIII. 79–87*   384–402 *Cf.* Q .Mab, *VIII. 88–106*
403–10 *Cf.* Q .Mab, *VIII. 142–9*   410 night; *1904, 1876*] night. *Loc.*
1911 followed by paragraph as in Q .Mab   411–18 *Cf.* Q .Mab, *VIII.*
166–73

Where blue mists through the unmoving atmosphere
Scattered the seeds of pestilence, and fed
Unnatural vegetation, where the land   415
Teemed with all earthquake, tempest and disease,
Was man a nobler being; slavery
Had crushed him to his country's blood-stained dust.

'Even where the milder zone afforded man
A seeming shelter, yet contagion there,   420
Blighting his being with unnumbered ills,
Spread like a quenchless fire; nor Truth availed
Till late to arrest its progress, or create
That peace which first in bloodless victory waved
Her snowy standard o'er this favoured clime: 425
There man was long the train-bearer of slaves,
The mimic of surrounding misery,
The jackal of Ambition's lion-rage,
The bloodhound of Religion's hungry zeal.

'Here now the human being stands adorning   430
This loveliest earth with taintless body and mind;
Blest from his birth with all bland impulses,
Which gently in his noble bosom wake
All kindly passions and all pure desires.
Him, still from hope to hope the bliss pursuing,   435
Which from the exhaustless lore of human weal
Dawns on the virtuous mind, the thoughts that rise
In time-destroying infiniteness gift
With self-enshrined eternity, that mocks
The unprevailing hoariness of age,   440
And man, once fleeting o'er the transient scene
Swift as an unremembered vision, stands
Immortal upon earth: no longer now
He slays the beast that sports around his dwelling
And horribly devours its mangled flesh,   445
Or drinks its vital blood, which like a stream

419-29 Cf. Q.Mab, *VIII. 187-97*   422-3 *See n., p. 334*   423 create
cancelled but unreplaced, Pf.   430-45 Cf. Q. Mab, *VIII. 198-213*   433 noble
bosom *cancelled but unreplaced, Pf.*   438 infiniteness *1904*] infiniteness, *1876*
446-9 *Inserted in Pf.*

Of poison thro' his fevered veins did flow
Feeding a plague that secretly consumed
His feeble frame, and kindling in his mind
Hatred, despair, and fear and vain belief,   450
The germs of misery, death, disease, and crime.
No longer now the wingèd habitants,
That in the woods their sweet lives sing away,
Flee from the form of man; but gather round,
And prune their sunny feathers on the hands   455
Which little children stretch in friendly sport
Towards these dreadless partners of their play.
All things are void of terror: man has lost
His desolating privilege, and stands
An equal amidst equals: happiness   460
And science dawn though late upon the earth;
Peace cheers the mind, health renovates the frame;
Disease and pleasure cease to mingle here,
Reason and passion cease to combat there;
Whilst mind unfettered o'er the earth extends   465
Its all-subduing energies, and wields
The sceptre of a vast dominion there.

'Mild is the slow necessity of death:
The tranquil spirit fails beneath its grasp,
Without a groan, almost without a fear,   470
Resigned in peace to the necessity,
Calm as a voyager to some distant land,
And full of wonder, full of hope as he.
The deadly germs of languor and disease
Waste in the human frame, and Nature gifts   475
With choicest boons her human worshippers.
How vigorous now the athletic form of age!
How clear its open and unwrinkled brow!
Where neither avarice, cunning, pride, nor care,
Has stamped the seal of grey deformity   480
On all the mingling lineaments of time.

448 consumed *1904, 1876*] [did eat] consumed *Pf.*   450-67 *Cf.* Q .Mab, *VIII.*
216-34   466 Its *1904, 1876*] Their *Pf., 1813. See n., p. 334*   468-83 *Cf.*
Q .Mab, *IX. 57-64*   *475-6 Inserted in Pf.*   477-82 *Cf.* Q . Mab, *IX. 65-70*
480 Has *Loc. 1911*] Had *1904, 1876, Pf. See n., p. 334*

How lovely the intrepid front of youth!
How sweet the smiles of taintless infancy.

'Within the massy prison's mouldering courts,
Fearless and free the ruddy children play,   485
Weaving gay chaplets for their innocent brows
With the green ivy and the red wall-flower,
That mock the dungeon's unavailing gloom;
The ponderous chains, and gratings of strong iron
There rust amid the accumulated ruins   490
Now mingling slowly with their native earth:
There the broad beam of day, which feebly once
Lighted the cheek of lean captivity
With a pale and sickly glare, now freely shines
On the pure smiles of infant playfulness: 495
No more the shuddering voice of hoarse despair
Peals through the echoing vaults, but soothing notes
Of ivy-fingered winds and gladsome birds
And merriment are resonant around.

'The fanes of Fear and Falsehood hear no more   500
The voice that once waked multitudes to war
Thundering through all their aisles: but now respond
To the death dirge of the melancholy wind:
It were a sight of awfulness to see
The works of faith and slavery, so vast,   505
So sumptuous, yet withal so perishing!
Even as the corpse that rests beneath their wall.
A thousand mourners deck the pomp of death
To-day, the breathing marble glows above
To decorate its memory, and tongues   510
Are busy of its life: to-morrow, worms
In silence and in darkness seize their prey.
These ruins soon leave not a rack behind:
Their elements, wide-scattered o'er the globe,
To happier shapes are moulded, and become   515

---

483 *Inserted in Pf.*   484–99 Q.Mab, *IX. 114–29*   489 iron] iron, *edd.*
497 Peals *1904, 1876*] Pealed *Pf. See n., p. 334*   499 are *1904, 1876*] were *Pf. See n.,*
p. 334   500–3 *Inserted in Pf.*   500 *Changed in Pf. from* [Temples, once stained
with falshood,] *Pf.*   500–1 *See n., p. 334*   504–32 *Cf.* Q.Mab, *IX. 105–50*
507 their *1904, 1876*] its *Pf. See n., p. 334*   513 rack] wreck *edd. See Vol. I, p. xxxvii*

Ministrant to all blissful impulses:
Thus human things are perfected, and earth,
Even as a child beneath its mother's love,
Is strengthened in all excellence, and grows
Fairer and nobler with each passing year.   520

'Now Time his dusky pennons o'er the scene
Closes in steadfast darkness, and the future
Fades from our charmèd sight. My task is done:
Thy lore is learned. Earth's wonders are thine own,
With all the fear and all the hope they bring.   525
My spells are past: the present now recurs.
Ah me! a pathless wilderness remains
Yet unsubdued by man's reclaiming hand.

'Yet, human Spirit, bravely hold thy course,—
Let virtue teach thee firmly to pursue   530
The gradual paths of an aspiring change:
For birth and life and death, and that strange state
Before the naked powers that thro' the world
Wander like winds have found a human home,
All tend to perfect happiness, and urge   535
The restless wheels of being on their way,
Whose flashing spokes, instinct with infinite life,
Bicker and burn to gain their destined goal:
For birth but wakes the universal mind,
Whose mighty streams might else in silence flow   540
Thro' the vast world, to individual sense
Of outward shows, whose unexperienced shape
New modes of passion to its frame may lend;
Life is its state of action, and the store
Of all events is aggregated there   545
That variegate the eternal universe;
Death is a gate of dreariness and gloom,
That leads to azure isles and beaming skies
And happy regions of eternal hope.
Therefore, O Spirit! fearlessly bear on: 550
Though storms may break the primrose on its stalk,

---

522 future *Loc. 1911, see n., p. 334*] past *1904, 1876*   529 course, —] course, *1904,
1876*   533-4 *Inserted in Pf. Cf.* Q. Mab, *IX.150.*   535-9 *cf.* Q. Mab. *151-5*
540-1 *Inserted in Pf.*   542-61 *Cf.* Q .Mab, *IX. 156-75. See n., p. 334*

Though frosts may blight the freshness of its bloom,
Yet spring's awakening breath will woo the earth,
To feed with kindliest dews its favourite flower,
That blooms in mossy banks and darksome glens,   555
Lighting the green wood with its sunny smile.

'Fear not then, Spirit, death's disrobing hand,
So welcome when the tyrant is awake,
So welcome when the bigot's hell-torch flares;
'Tis but the voyage of a darksome hour,   560
The transient gulf-dream of a startling sleep.
For what thou art shall perish utterly,
But what is thine may never cease to be;
Death is no foe to virtue: earth has seen
Love's brightest roses on the scaffold bloom,   565
Mingling with freedom's fadeless laurels there,
And presaging the truth of visioned bliss.
Are there not hopes within thee, which this scene
Of linked and gradual being has confirmed?
Hopes that not vainly thou, and living fires   570
Of mind as radiant and as pure as thou,
Have shone upon the paths of men.—Return,
Surpassing Spirit, to that world, where thou
Art destined an eternal war to wage
With tyranny and falsehood, and uproot   575
The germs of misery from the human heart.
Thine is the hand whose piety would soothe
The thorny pillow of unhappy crime,
Whose impotence an easy pardon gains,
Watching its wanderings as a friend's disease: 580
Thine is the brow whose mildness would defy
Its fiercest rage, and brave its sternest will,
When fenced by power and master of the world.
Thou art sincere and good; of resolute mind,
Free from heart-withering custom's cold control,   585
Of passion lofty, pure and unsubdued.
Earth's pride and meanness could not vanquish thee,

562-3 *Inserted in Pf.*   564-9 *Cf.* Q. Mab, *IX. 176-89*   570-3 *Inserted in Pf.*
572 men.—Return, *Loc. 1911*] men—return, *1904, 1876, Pf.*   574-611 *Cf.* Q .Mab,
IX. 190-228

And therefore art thou worthy of the boon
Which thou hast now received: virtue shall keep
Thy footsteps in the path that thou hast trod.   590
And many days of beaming hope shall bless
Thy spotless life of sweet and sacred love.
Go, happy one, and give that bosom joy
    Whose sleepless spirit waits to catch
    Light, life and rapture from thy smile.'   595

    The Daemon called its wingèd ministers.
Speechless with bliss the Spirit mounts the car,
That rolled beside the crystal battlement,
Bending her beamy eyes in thankfulness.
    The burning wheels inflame   600
The steep descent of Heaven's untrodden way.
    Fast and far the chariot flew:
    The mighty globes that rolled
Around the gate of the Eternal Fane
Lessened by slow degrees, and soon appeared   605
Such tiny twinklers as the planet orbs
That ministering on the solar power
With borrowed light pursued their narrower way.
    Earth floated then below:
    The chariot paused a moment;   610
    The Spirit then descended:
    And from the earth departing
    The shadows with swift wings
Speeded like thought upon the light of Heaven.

    The Body and the Soul united then,   615
A gentle start convulsed Ianthe's frame:
Her veiny eyelids quietly unclosed;
Moveless awhile the dark blue orbs remained:
She looked around in wonder and beheld
Henry, who kneeled in silence by her couch,   620
Watching her sleep with looks of speechless love,
    And the bright beaming stars
    That through the casement shone.

596 *Inserted in Pf.*   ministers *1904, 1876*] ministers *above* [messengers] *Pf.*   598
crystal *inserted in Pf.*   612–14 *Inserted in Pf.*   615–23 *Cf.* Q., Mab, *IX. 232–40*

ALASTOR

OR

THE SPIRIT OF SOLITUDE

1815

ALASTOR

OR

THE SPIRIT OF SOLITUDE

1815

PREFACE

THE poem entitled *Alastor* may be considered as allegorical of one of the most interesting situations of the human mind. It represents a youth of uncorrupted feelings and adventurous genius led forth by an imagination inflamed and purified through familiarity with all that is excellent and majestic, to the contemplation of the universe. He drinks deep of the fountains of knowledge, and is still insatiate. The magnificence and beauty of the external world sinks profoundly into the frame of his conceptions, and affords to their modifications a variety not to be exhausted. So long as it is possible for his desires to point towards objects thus infinite and unmeasured, he is joyous, and tranquil, and self-possessed. But the period arrives when these objects cease to suffice. His mind is at length suddenly awakened and thirsts for intercourse with an intelligence similar to itself. He images to himself the Being whom he loves. Conversant with speculations of the sublimest and most perfect natures, the vision in which he embodies his own imaginations unites all of wonderful, or wise, or beautiful, which the poet, the philosopher, or the lover could depicture. The intellectual faculties, the imagination, the functions of sense, have their respective requisitions on the sympathy of corresponding powers in other human beings. The Poet is represented as uniting these requisitions, and attaching them to a single image. He seeks in vain for a prototype of his conception. Blasted by his disappointment, he descends to an untimely grave.

The picture is not barren of instruction to actual men. The Poet's self-centred seclusion was avenged by the furies of an irresistible passion pursuing him to speedy ruin. But that Power which strikes the luminaries of the world with sudden darkness and extinction, by awakening them to too exquisite a perception of its influences, dooms to a slow and poisonous

ALASTOR.   MSS.: *Untraced.*   DATE: *Note by MWS. See below, pp. 64–5.*
PRINTED, TITLE: *PBS, 1816/MWS, 1824/MWS, 1839¹/MWS, 1839²/Hutch. 1904.*
TEXT: *1904/1839²/1839¹/1824/1816.*

decay those meaner spirits that dare to abjure its dominion. Their destiny is more abject and inglorious as their delinquency is more contemptible and pernicious. They who, deluded by no generous error, instigated by no sacred thirst of doubtful knowledge, duped by no illustrious superstition, loving nothing on this earth, and cherishing no hopes beyond, yet keep aloof from sympathies with their kind, rejoicing neither in human joy nor mourning with human grief; these, and such as they, have their apportioned curse. They languish, because none feel with them their common nature. They are morally dead. They are neither friends, nor lovers, nor fathers, nor citizens of the world, nor benefactors of their country. Among those who attempt to exist without human sympathy, the pure and tender-hearted perish through the intensity and passion of their search after its communities, when the vacancy of their spirit suddenly makes itself felt. All else, selfish, blind, and torpid, are those unforeseeing multitudes who constitute, together with their own, the lasting misery and loneliness of the world. Those who love not their fellow-beings live unfruitful lives, and prepare for their old age a miserable grave.

> 'The good die first,
> And they whose hearts are dry as summer dust
> Burn to the socket!'

December 14, 1815.

Nondum amabam, et amare amabam, quaerebam quid amarem, amans amare.—*Confess. St. August.*

EARTH, ocean, air, belovèd brotherhood!
If our great Mother has imbued my soul
With aught of natural piety to feel
Your love, and recompense the boon with mine;
If dewy morn, and odorous noon, and even,   5
With sunset and its gorgeous ministers,
And solemn midnight's tingling silentness—
If autumn's hollow sighs in the sere wood,
And winter robing with pure snow and crowns
Of starry ice the grey grass and bare boughs;   10
If spring's voluptuous pantings when she breathes
Her first sweet kisses—have been dear to me;
If no bright bird, insect, or gentle beast
I consciously have injured, but still loved
And cherished these my kindred;—then forgive   15

2 has *1904, 1824, 1816*] have *1839², 1839¹*   7 silentness—] silentness; *edd.*
12 Kisses—] Kisses, *edd.*

This boast, belovèd brethren, and withdraw
No portion of your wonted favour now!

Mother of this unfathomable world,
Favour my solemn song! for I have loved
Thee ever, and thee only; I have watched   20
Thy shadow, and the darkness of thy steps,
And my heart ever gazes on the depth
Of thy deep mysteries. I have made my bed
In charnels and on coffins, where black Death
Keeps record of the trophies won from thee,   25
Hoping to still these obstinate questionings
Of thee and thine, by forcing some lone ghost
Thy messenger, to render up the tale
Of what we are. In lone and silent hours,
When night makes a weird sound of its own stillness,   30
Like an inspired and desperate alchymist
Staking his very life on some dark hope,
Have I mixed awful talk and asking looks
With my most innocent love, until strange tears
Uniting with those breathless kisses, made   35
Such magic as compels the charmèd night
To render up thy charge. And, though ne'er yet
Thou hast unveiled thy inmost sanctuary,
Enough from incommunicable dream,
And twilight phantasms, and deep noon-day thought,   40
Has shone within me, that serenely now
And moveless, as a long-forgotten lyre
Suspended in the solitary dome
Of some mysterious and deserted fane,
I wait thy breath, Great Parent, that my strain   45
May modulate with murmurs of the air,
And motions of the forests and the sea,
And voice of living beings, and woven hymns
Of night and day, and the deep heart of man.

There was a Poet whose untimely tomb   50
No human hands with pious reverence reared,
But the charmed eddies of autumnal winds

18 world,] world! *edd.*   19 song!] song *edd.*   37 charge. And,]
Charge . . . and *edd.*

Built o'er his mouldering bones a pyramid
Of mouldering leaves in the waste wilderness:—
A lovely youth,—no mourning maiden decked   55
With weeping flowers, or votive cypress wreath,
The lone couch of his everlasting sleep:—
Gentle, and brave, and generous,—no lorn bard
Breathed o'er his dark fate one melodious sigh:
He lived, he died, he sung, in solitude.   60
Strangers have wept to hear his passionate notes,
And virgins, as unknown he passed, have pined
And wasted for fond love of his wild eyes.
The fire of those soft orbs has ceased to burn,
And Silence, too enamoured of that voice,   65
Locks its mute music in her rugged cell.

    By solemn vision, and bright silver dream,
His infancy was nurtured. Every sight
And sound from the vast earth and ambient air
Sent to his heart its choicest impulses.   70
The fountains of divine philosophy
Fled not his thirsting lips, and all of great,
Or good, or lovely, which the sacred past
In truth or fable consecrates, he felt
And knew. When early youth had passed, he left   75
His cold fireside and alienated home
To seek strange truths in undiscovered lands.
Many a wide waste and tangled wilderness
Has lured his fearless steps; and he has bought
With his sweet voice and eyes, from savage men,   80
His rest and food. Nature's most secret steps
He like her shadow has pursued, where'er
The red volcano overcanopies
Its fields of snow and pinnacles of ice
With burning smoke; or where bitumen lakes   85
On black bare pointed islets ever beat
With sluggish surge; or where the secret caves
Rugged and dark, winding among the springs

60 sung *1904, 1824, 1816*] sang *1839², 1839¹*   62 pined *1904, 1839², 1839¹,
1816*] sighed *1824*   65 Silence, too *1904, 1839¹, 1824, 1816*] Silence too, *1839²*
69 air] air, *edd.*   79 he has *1904, 1839², 1939¹, 1816*] as he *1824*   85 smoke;]
smoke, *edd.*   87 surge;] surge, *edd.*

Of fire and poison, inaccessible
To avarice or pride, their starry domes 90
Of diamond and of gold expand above
Numberless and immeasurable halls,
Frequent with crystal column, and clear shrines
Of pearl, and thrones radiant with chrysolite.
Nor had that scene of ampler majesty 95
Than gems or gold, the varying roof of heaven
And the green earth, lost in his heart its claims
To love and wonder; he would linger long
In lonesome vales, making the wild his home,
Until the doves and squirrels would partake 100
From his innocuous hand his bloodless food,
Lured by the gentle meaning of his looks,
And the wild antelope, that starts whene'er
The dry leaf rustles in the brake, suspend
Her timid steps to gaze upon a form 105
More graceful than her own.
               His wandering step,
Obedient to high thoughts, has visited
The awful ruins of the days of old:
Athens, and Tyre, and Balbec, and the waste
Where stood Jerusalem, the fallen towers 110
Of Babylon, the eternal pyramids,
Memphis and Thebes, and whatsoe'er of strange
Sculptured on alabaster obelisk,
Or jasper tomb, or mutilated sphynx,
Dark Æthiopia in her desert hills 115
Conceals. Among the ruined temples there,
Stupendous columns, and wild images
Of more than man, where marble daemons watch
The Zodiac's brazen mystery, and dead men
Hang their mute thoughts on the mute walls around, 120
He lingered, poring on memorials
Of the world's youth; through the long burning day
Gazed on those speechless shapes; nor, when the moon
Filled the mysterious halls with floating shades
Suspended he that task, but ever gazed 125

97 earth,] earth *edd.*   98 wonder;] wonder, *edd.*   106 step,] step *edd.*
115 in *1904, 1839², 1816*] on *1839¹, 1824*   122 youth;] youth, *edd.*   123 shapes;]
shapes, *edd.*

And gazed, till meaning on his vacant mind
Flashed like strong inspiration, and he saw
The thrilling secrets of the birth of time.

Meanwhile an Arab maiden brought his food,
Her daily portion, from her father's tent,   130
And spread her matting for his couch, and stole
From duties and repose to tend his steps:—
Enamoured, yet not daring for deep awe
To speak her love:—and watched his nightly sleep,
Sleepless herself, to gaze upon his lips   135
Parted in slumber, whence the regular breath
Of innocent dreams arose:— then, when red morn
Made paler the pale moon, to her cold home
Wildered, and wan, and panting, she returned.

The Poet wandering on, through Arabie   140
And Persia, and the wild Carmanian waste,
And o'er the aërial mountains which pour down
Indus and Oxus from their icy caves,
In joy and exultation held his way;
Till in the vale of Cashmire, far within   145
Its loneliest dell, where odorous plants entwine
Beneath the hollow rocks a natural bower,
Beside a sparkling rivulet he stretched
His languid limbs. A vision on his sleep
There came, a dream of hopes that never yet   150
Had flushed his cheek. He dreamed a veilèd maid
Sate near him, talking in low solemn tones.
Her voice was like the voice of his own soul
Heard in the calm of thought; its music long,
Like woven sounds of streams and breezes, held   155
His inmost sense suspended in its web
Of many-coloured woof and shifting hues.
Knowledge and truth and virtue were her theme,
And lofty hopes of divine liberty,
Thoughts the most dear to him, and poesy,   160
Herself a poet. Soon the solemn mood
Of her pure mind kindled through all her frame

137 arose:— then] arose: then *edd.*   161 Herself *1904, 1839¹, 1824, 1816*] Himself *1839²*

A permeating fire: wild numbers then
She raised, with voice stifled in tremulous sobs
Subdued by its own pathos: her fair hands   165
Were bare alone, sweeping from some strange harp
Strange symphony, and in their branching veins
The eloquent blood told an ineffable tale.
The beating of her heart was heard to fill
The pauses of her music, and her breath   170
Tumultuously accorded with those fits
Of intermitted song. Sudden she rose,
As if her heart impatiently endured
Its bursting burthen. At the sound he turned,
And saw by the warm light of their own life   175
Her glowing limbs beneath the sinuous veil
Of woven wind, her outspread arms now bare,
Her dark locks floating in the breath of night,
Her beamy bending eyes, her parted lips
Outstretched, and pale, and quivering eagerly.   180
His strong heart sunk and sickened with excess
Of love. He reared his shuddering limbs and quelled
His gasping breath, and spread his arms to meet
Her panting bosom—she drew back a while,
Then, yielding to the irresistible joy,   185
With frantic gesture and short breathless cry
Folded his frame in her dissolving arms.
Now blackness veiled his dizzy eyes, and night
Involved and swallowed up the vision; sleep,
Like a dark flood suspended in its course,   190
Rolled back its impulse on his vacant brain.

    Roused by the shock he started from his trance—
The cold white light of morning, the blue moon
Low in the west, the clear and garish hills,
The distinct valley and the vacant woods,   195
Spread round him where he stood. Whither have fled
The hues of heaven that canopied his bower
Of yesternight? the sounds that soothed his sleep,
The mystery and the majesty of Earth,

174 burthen. At] burthen: at *edd.*   181 sunk *1904, 1824, 1816*] sank *1839², 1839¹*
184 bosom—] bosom: ... *edd.*   196 round him where *1904, 1839², 1839¹, 1816*]
round where *1824*

The joy, the exultation? His wan eyes   200
Gaze on the empty scene as vacantly
As ocean's moon looks on the moon in heaven.
The spirit of sweet human love has sent
A vision to the sleep of him who spurned
Her choicest gifts. He eagerly pursues   205
Beyond the realms of dream that fleeting shade;
He overleaps the bounds. Alas! Alas!
Were limbs, and breath, and being intertwined
Thus treacherously? Lost, lost, for ever lost,
In the wide pathless desert of dim sleep,   210
That beautiful shape! Does the dark gate of Death
Conduct to thy mysterious paradise,
O Sleep? Does the bright arch of rainbow clouds,
And pendent mountains seen in the calm lake,
Lead only to a black and watery depth,   215
While Death's blue vault, with loathliest vapours hung,
Where every shade which the foul grave exhales
Hides its dead eye from the detested day,
Conducts, O Sleep, to thy delightful realms?
This doubt with sudden tide flowed on his heart—   220
The insatiate hope which it awakened stung
His brain even like despair.
                            While daylight held
The sky, the Poet kept mute conference
With his still soul. At night the passion came,
Like the fierce fiend of a distempered dream,   225
And shook him from his rest, and led him forth
Into the darkness.—As an eagle grasped
In folds of the green serpent, feels her breast
Burn with the poison, and precipitates
Through night and day, tempest, and calm, and cloud,
Frantic with dizzying anguish, her blind flight   231
O'er the wide aëry wilderness: thus, driven
By the bright shadow of that lovely dream,
Beneath the cold glare of the desolate night,
Through tangled swamps and deep precipitous dells, 235

207 bounds *1904, 1839², 1839¹, 1816*] bound *1824*   219 Conducts *1904*] Conduct *1839², 1839¹, 1824, 1816, and edd. Form., 1876, suggests* heart;   221 awakened] awakened, *edd.*   232 thus,] thus *edd.*

Startling with careless step the moonlight snake,
He fled. Red morning dawned upon his flight,
Shedding the mockery of its vital hues
Upon his cheek of death. He wandered on
Till vast Aornos seen from Petra's steep 240
Hung o'er the low horizon like a cloud;
Through Balk, and where the desolated tombs
Of Parthian kings scatter to every wind
Their wasting dust, wildly he wandered on,
Day after day a weary waste of hours, 245
Bearing within his life the brooding care
That ever fed on its decaying flame.
And now his limbs were lean; his scattered hair
Sered by the autumn of strange suffering
Sung dirges in the wind; his listless hand 250
Hung like dead bone within its withered skin;
Life, and the lustre that consumed it, shone
As in a furnace burning secretly
From his dark eyes alone. The cottagers,
Who ministered with human charity 255
His human wants, beheld with wondering awe
Their fleeting visitant. The mountaineer,
Encountering on some dizzy precipice
That spectral form, deemed that the Spirit of Wind
With lightning eyes, and eager breath, and feet 260
Disturbing not the drifted snow, had paused
In its career; the infant would conceal
His troubled visage in his mother's robe
In terror at the glare of those wild eyes,
To remember their strange light in many a dream 265
Of after-times; but youthful maidens, taught
By nature, would interpret half the woe
That wasted him, would call him with false names
Brother, and friend, would press his pallid hand
At parting, and watch, dim through tears, the path 270
Of his departure from their father's door.

    At length upon the lone Chorasmian shore
He paused, a wide and melancholy waste

259 Wind] wind *edd.*   262 its *1904, 1839², 1816*] his *1839¹, 1824*

Of putrid marshes. A strong impulse urged
His steps to the sea-shore. A swan was there,   275
Beside a sluggish stream among the reeds.
It rose as he approached, and with strong wings
Scaling the upward sky, bent its bright course
High over the immeasurable main.
His eyes pursued its flight.—'Thou hast a home,   280
Beautiful bird! thou voyagest to thine home,
Where thy sweet mate will twine her downy neck
With thine, and welcome thy return with eyes
Bright in the lustre of their own fond joy.
And what am I that I should linger here,   285
With voice far sweeter than thy dying notes,
Spirit more vast than thine, frame more attuned
To beauty, wasting these surpassing powers
In the deaf air, to the blind earth, and heaven
That echoes not my thoughts?' A gloomy smile   290
Of desperate hope wrinkled his quivering lips.
For Sleep, he knew, kept most relentlessly
Its precious charge, and silent Death exposed,
Faithless perhaps as Sleep, a shadowy lure,
With doubtful smile mocking its own strange charms.   295

Startled by his own thoughts he looked around.
There was no fair fiend near him, not a sight
Or sound of awe but in his own deep mind.
A little shallop floating near the shore
Caught the impatient wandering of his gaze.   300
It had been long abandoned, for its sides
Gaped wide with many a rift, and its frail joints
Swayed with the undulations of the tide.
A restless impulse urged him to embark
And meet lone Death on the drear ocean's waste;   305
For well he knew that mighty Shadow loves
The slimy caverns of the populous deep.

The day was fair and sunny; sea and sky
Drank its inspiring radiance, and the wind
Swept strongly from the shore, blackening the waves.   310

274 marshes. A *1904, 1839², 1816*] marshes—a *1839¹, 1824*   281 bird!] bird; *edd.*
292 Sleep,] sleep, *edd.*   293 Death] death *edd.*   294 Sleep,] sleep, *edd.*
308 sunny:] sunny, *edd.*

Following his eager soul, the wanderer
Leaped in the boat, he spread his cloak aloft
On the bare mast, and took his lonely seat,
And felt the boat speed o'er the tranquil sea
Like a torn cloud before the hurricane.   315

   As one that in a silver vision floats
Obedient to the sweep of odorous winds
Upon resplendent clouds, so rapidly
Along the dark and ruffled waters fled
The straining boat.—A whirlwind swept it on,   320
With fierce gusts and precipitating force,
Through the white ridges of the chafèd sea.
The waves arose. Higher and higher still
Their fierce necks writhed beneath the tempest's scourge
Like serpents struggling in a vulture's grasp.   325
Calm and rejoicing in the fearful war
Of wave ruining on wave, and blast on blast
Descending, and black flood on whirlpool driven
With dark obliterating course, he sate:
As if their genii were the ministers   330
Appointed to conduct him to the light
Of those belovèd eyes, the Poet sate
Holding the steady helm. Evening came on;
The beams of sunset hung their rainbow hues
High 'mid the shifting domes of sheeted spray   335
That canopied his path o'er the waste deep;
Twilight, ascending slowly from the east,
Entwined in duskier wreaths her braided locks
O'er the fair front and radiant eyes of day;
Night followed, clad with stars. On every side   340
More horribly the multitudinous streams
Of ocean's mountainous waste to mutual war
Rushed in dark tumult thundering, as to mock
The calm and spangled sky. The little boat
Still fled before the storm; still fled, like foam   345
Down the steep cataract of a wintry river;
Now pausing on the edge of the riven wave;
Now leaving far behind the bursting mass

327 ruining *1904, 1824, 1816*] running *1839²*, *1839¹*   333 on;] on, *edd.*

That fell, convulsing ocean,—safely fled,
As if that frail and wasted human form,   350
Had been an elemental god.
                              At midnight
The moon arose: and lo! the ethereal cliffs
Of Caucasus, whose icy summits shone
Among the stars like sunlight, and around
Whose caverned base the whirlpools and the waves   355
Bursting and eddying irresistibly
Rage and resound for ever.—Who shall save?—
The boat fled on,—the boiling torrent drove,—
The crags closed round with black and jaggèd arms,
The shattered mountain overhung the sea,   360
And faster still, beyond all human speed,
Suspended on the sweep of the smooth wave,
The little boat was driven. A cavern there
Yawned, and amid its slant and winding depths
Ingulfed the rushing sea. The boat fled on   365
With unrelaxing speed.—'Vision and Love!'
The Poet cried aloud, 'I have beheld
The path of thy departure. Sleep and Death
Shall not divide us long!'

                              The boat pursued
The windings of the cavern. Daylight shone   370
At length upon that gloomy river's flow;
Now, where the fiercest war among the waves
Is calm, on the unfathomable stream
The boat moved slowly. Where the mountain, riven,
Exposed those black depths to the azure sky,   375
Ere yet the flood's enormous volume fell
Even to the base of Caucasus, with sound
That shook the everlasting rocks, the mass
Filled with one whirlpool all that ample chasm;
Stair above stair the eddying waters rose,   380
Circling immeasurably fast, and laved
With alternating dash the gnarlèd roots
Of mighty trees, that stretched their giant arms

---

349 ocean:—safely] ocean: safely *1904*   ocean. Safely *1839²*, *1839¹*, *1824*, *1816*
fled,] fled— *1904*, *1839²*, *1839¹*, *1824*, *1816*   368 Death] death *edd.*

In darkness over it. I' the midst was left,
Reflecting, yet distorting every cloud,   385
A pool of treacherous and tremendous calm.
Seized by the sway of the ascending stream,
With dizzy swiftness, round, and round, and round,
Ridge after ridge the straining boat arose;
Till on the verge of the extremest curve,   390
Where, through an opening of the rocky bank,
The waters overflow, and a smooth spot
Of glassy quiet mid those battling tides
Is left, the boat paused shuddering.—Shall it sink
Down the abyss? Shall the reverting stress   395
Of that resistless gulf embosom it?
Now shall it fall?—A wandering stream of wind,
Breathed from the west, has caught the expanded sail,
And, lo! with gentle motion, between banks
Of mossy slope, and on a placid stream,   400
Beneath a woven grove it sails, and, hark!
The ghastly torrent mingles its far roar
With the breeze murmuring in the musical woods.
Where the embowering trees recede, and leave
A little space of green expanse, the cove   405
Is closed by meeting banks, whose yellow flowers
For ever gaze on their own drooping eyes,
Reflected in the crystal calm. The wave
Of the boat's motion marred their pensive task,
Which nought but vagrant bird, or wanton wind,   410
Or falling spear-grass, or their own decay
Had e'er disturbed before. The Poet longed
To deck with their bright hues his withered hair,
But on his heart its solitude returned,
And he forbore. Not the strong impulse hid   415
In those flushed cheeks, bent eyes, and shadowy frame
Had yet performed its ministry: it hung
Upon his life, as lightning in a cloud
Gleams, hovering ere it vanish, ere the floods
Of night close over it.
                    The noonday sun   420
Now shone upon the forest, one vast mass

389 arose;] arose, *edd.*   402 roar] roar, *edd.*

Of mingling shade, whose brown magnificence
A narrow vale embosoms. There, huge caves,
Scooped in the dark base of their aëry rocks,
Mocking its moans respond and roar for ever.   425
The meeting boughs and implicated leaves
Wove twilight o'er the Poet's path, as, led
By love, or dream, or god, or mightier Death,
He sought in Nature's dearest haunt, some bank,
Her cradle, and his sepulchre. More dark   430
And dark the shades accumulate. The oak,
Expanding its immense and knotty arms,
Embraces the light beech. The pyramids
Of the tall cedar overarching, frame
Most solemn domes within; and far below,   435
Like clouds suspended in an emerald sky,
The ash and the acacia floating hang,
Tremulous and pale. Like restless serpents, clothed
In rainbow and in fire, the parasites,
Starred with ten thousand blossoms, flow around   440
The grey trunks; and, as gamesome infants' eyes,
With gentle meanings, and most innocent wiles,
Fold their beams round the hearts of those that love,
These twine their tendrils with the wedded boughs
Uniting their close union; the woven leaves   445
Make net-work of the dark-blue light of day
And the night's noontide clearness, mutable
As shapes in the weird clouds. Soft mossy lawns
Beneath these canopies extend their swells,
Fragrant with perfumed herbs, and eyed with blooms 450
Minute yet beautiful. One darkest glen
Sends from its woods of musk-rose, twined with jasmine,
A soul-dissolving odour, to invite
To some more lovely mystery. Through the dell,
Silence and Twilight here, twin-sisters, keep   455
Their noonday watch, and sail among the shades,
Like vaporous shapes half seen; beyond, a well,

---

424 their *1904*, *Form. 1876*, *1816*] those *1839²*, *1839¹*, *1824*, rocks   *Loc. 1911*] rocks *other edd.*   425 moans] moans, *edd.*   427 as,] as *edd.*   432 immense and *1904*, *1839²*, *1839¹*, *1816*] immeasurable *1824*   435 within;] within, *edd.*
437 hang,] hang *edd.*   446 dark-blue *Loc. 1911*] dark blue *1904*, *1839²*, *1839¹*, *1824*, *1816*   day] day, *edd.*

Dark, gleaming, and of most translucent wave,
Images all the woven boughs above,
And each depending leaf, and every speck   460
Of azure sky, darting between their chasms;
Nor aught else in the liquid mirror laves
Its portraiture, but some inconstant star
Between one foliaged lattice twinkling fair,
Or painted bird, sleeping beneath the moon,   465
Or gorgeous insect floating motionless,
Unconscious of the day, ere yet his wings
Have spread their glories to the gaze of noon.

Hither the Poet came. His eyes beheld
Their own wan light through the reflected lines   470
Of his thin hair, distinct in the dark depth
Of that still fountain; as the human heart,
Gazing in dreams over the gloomy grave,
Sees its own treacherous likeness there. He heard
The motion of the leaves, the grass that sprung   475
Startled, and glanced and trembled even to feel
An unaccustomed presence, and the sound
Of the sweet brook that from the secret springs
Of that dark fountain rose. A Spirit seemed
To stand beside him, clothed in no bright robes   480
Of shadowy silver or enshrining light,
Borrowed from aught the visible world affords
Of grace, or majesty, or mystery;
But undulating woods, and silent well,
And leaping rivulet, and evening gloom   485
Now deepening the dark shades, for speech assuming,
Held commune with him, as if he and it
Were all that was; only—when his regard
Was raised by intense pensiveness—two eyes,
Two starry eyes, hung in the gloom of thought   490
And seemed with their serene and azure smiles
To beckon him.

---

465 Or *1839²*, *1839¹*] Or, *1904*, *1824*, *1816*, *and edd.*   476 Startled, *Loc. 1911*]
Startled *1904*, *1839²*, *1839¹*, *1824*, *1816*   480 him,] him— *edd.*   484 But] But,
edd.   485 leaping *1904*, *Form. 1876*, *1816*] reaping *1824*   rippling *1839²*, *1839¹*
488 was; only—] was,—only . . . *edd.*   489 pensiveness—] pensiveness, . . . *edd.*
490 thought *Loc. 1911*] thought, *1904*, *1839²*, *1839¹*, *1824*, *1816*

Obedient to the light
That shone within his soul, he went, pursuing
The windings of the dell.—The rivulet,
Wanton and wild, through many a green ravine   495
Beneath the forest flowed. Sometimes it fell
Among the moss with hollow harmony
Dark and profound. Now on the polished stones
It danced; like childhood, laughing as it went:
Then, through the plain in tranquil wanderings crept, 500
Reflecting every herb and drooping bud
That overhung its quietness.—'O stream!
Whose source is inaccessibly profound,
Whither do thy mysterious waters tend?
Thou imagest my life. Thy darksome stillness,   505
Thy dazzling waves, thy loud and hollow gulfs,
Thy searchless fountain, and invisible course
Have each their type in me: and the wide sky,
And measureless ocean may declare as soon
What oozy cavern or what wandering cloud   510
Contains thy waters, as the universe
Tell where these living thoughts reside, when stretched
Upon thy flowers my bloodless limbs shall waste
I' the passing wind!'

Beside the grassy shore
Of the small stream he went; he did impress   515
On the green moss his tremulous step, that caught
Strong shuddering from his burning limbs. As one
Roused by some joyous madness from the couch
Of fever, he did move; yet not, like him,
Forgetful of the grave, where, when the flame   520
Of his frail exultation shall be spent,
He must descend. With rapid steps he went
Beneath the shade of trees, beside the flow
Of the wild babbling rivulet; and now
The forest's solemn canopies were changed   525
For the uniform and lightsome evening sky.
Grey rocks did peep from the spare moss, and stemmed

494 rivulet,] rivulet *edd.*   499 childhood, *Loc. 1911*] childhood *1904, 1839², 1839¹,*
1824, 1816   508 sky] sky, *edd.*   519 yet not,] yet, not *edd.*

The struggling brook: tall spires of windlestrae
Threw their thin shadows down the rugged slope,
And nought but gnarlèd stumps of ancient pines   530
Branchless and blasted, clenched with grasping roots
The unwilling soil. A gradual change was here,
Yet ghastly. For, as fast years flow away,
The smooth brow gathers, and the hair grows thin
And white, and where irradiate dewy eyes   535
Had shone, gleam stony orbs: so from his steps
Bright flowers departed, and the beautiful shade
Of the green groves, with all their odorous winds
And musical motions. Calm, he still pursued
The stream, that with a larger volume now   540
Rolled through the labyrinthine dell; and there
Fretted a path through its descending curves
With its wintry speed. On every side now rose
Rocks, which, in unimaginable forms,
Lifted their black and barren pinnacles   545
In the light of evening, and, its precipice
Obscuring the ravine, disclosed above,
Mid toppling stones, black gulfs and yawning caves,
Whose windings gave ten thousand various tongues
To the loud stream. Lo! where the pass expands   550
Its stony jaws, the abrupt mountain breaks,
And seems, with its accumulated crags,
To overhang the world: for wide expand
Beneath the wan stars and descending moon
Islanded seas, blue mountains, mighty streams,   555
Dim tracts and vast, robed in the lustrous gloom
Of leaden-coloured even, and fiery hills
Mingling their flames with twilight, on the verge
Of the remote horizon. The near scene,
In naked and severe simplicity,   560
Made contrast with the universe. A pine,
Rock-rooted, stretched athwart the vacancy
Its swinging boughs, to each inconstant blast

---

530 stumps *suggested, 1904*] roots *1904, 1839², 1839¹, 1824, 1816. See n., pp. 336–7*
trunks *Ross. 1870*   543–50 *Thus 1904, 1839², 1839¹, 1824, 1816, apart from the second
comma in 546, introduced by Dowden, 1890. See n., p. 340*   556 tracts *1904, 1824,
1816*] tracks *1839², 1839¹*

Yielding one only response, at each pause,
In most familiar cadence,—with the howl   565
The thunder and the hiss of homeless streams
Mingling its solemn song, whilst the broad river,
Foaming and hurrying o'er its rugged path,
Fell into that immeasurable void
Scattering its waters to the passing winds.   570

    Yet the grey precipice and solemn pine
And torrent, were not all;—one silent nook
Was there. Even on the edge of that vast mountain,
Upheld by knotty roots and fallen rocks,
It overlooked in its serenity   575
The dark earth, and the bending vault of stars.
It was a tranquil spot, that seemed to smile
Even in the lap of horror. Ivy clasped
The fissured stones with its entwining arms,
And did embower with leaves for ever green,   580
And berries dark, the smooth and even space
Of its inviolated floor; and here
The children of the autumnal whirlwind bore,
In wanton sport, those bright leaves, whose decay,
Red, yellow, or ethereally pale,   585
Rivals the pride of summer. 'Tis the haunt
Of every gentle wind, whose breath can teach
The wilds to love tranquillity. One step,
One human step alone, has ever broken
The stillness of its solitude:—one voice   590
Alone inspired its echoes;—even that voice
Which hither came, floating among the winds,
And led the loveliest among human forms
To make their wild haunts the depository
Of all the grace and beauty that endued   595
Its motions, render up its majesty,
Scatter its music on the unfeeling storm,
And to the damp leaves and blue cavern mould,
Nurses of rainbow flowers and branching moss,
Commit the colours of that varying cheek,   600
That snowy breast, those dark and drooping eyes.

564 pause, *Loc. 1911*] pause *1904, 1839², 1839¹, 1824, 1816*   565 cadence,—]
cadence, *edd.*   582 floor;] floor, *edd.*

The dim and hornèd moon hung low, and poured
A sea of lustre on the horizon's verge
That overflowed its mountains. Yellow mist
Filled the unbounded atmosphere, and drank   605
Wan moonlight even to fulness: not a star
Shone, not a sound was heard; the very winds,
Danger's grim playmates, on that precipice
Slept, clasped in his embrace.—O storm of Death,
Whose sightless speed divides this sullen night!   610
And thou, colossal Skeleton, that, still
Guiding its irresistible career
In thy devastating omnipotence,
Art king of this frail world! From the red field
Of slaughter, from the reeking hospital,   615
The patriot's sacred couch, the snowy bed
Of innocence, the scaffold and the throne,
A mighty voice invokes thee! Ruin calls
His brother Death. A rare and regal prey
He hath prepared, prowling around the world;   620
Glutted with which thou mayst repose, and men
Go to their graves like flowers or creeping worms,
Nor ever more offer at thy dark shrine
The unheeded tribute of a broken heart.

When on the threshold of the green recess   625
The wanderer's footsteps fell, he knew that death
Was on him. Yet a little, ere it fled,
Did he resign his high and holy soul
To images of the majestic past,
That paused within his passive being now,   630
Like winds that bear sweet music, when they breathe
Through some dim latticed chamber. He did place
His pale lean hand upon the rugged trunk
Of the old pine. Upon an ivied stone
Reclined his languid head, his limbs did rest,   635
Diffused and motionless, on the smooth brink
Of that obscurest chasm;—and thus he lay,
Surrendering to their final impulses

609 O] O, *edd.*   Death,] death! *edd.*   610 night!] night; *edd.*   614 world!]
world, *edd.*   618 thee!] thee. *edd.*

The hovering powers of life. Hope and despair,
The torturers, slept; no mortal pain or fear   640
Marred his repose; the influxes of sense,
And his own being unalloyed by pain,
Yet feebler and more feeble, calmly fed
The stream of thought, till he lay breathing there
At peace, and faintly smiling:—his last sight   645
Was the great moon, which o'er the western line
Of the wide world her mighty horn suspended,
With whose dun beams inwoven darkness seemed
To mingle. Now upon the jaggèd hills
It rests, and still as the divided frame   650
Of the vast meteor sunk, the Poet's blood,
That ever beat in mystic sympathy
With nature's ebb and flow, grew feebler still;
And when two lessening points of light alone
Gleamed through the darkness, the alternate gasp   655
Of his faint respiration scarce did stir
The stagnate night:—till the minutest ray
Was quenched, the pulse yet lingered in his heart.
It paused—it fluttered. But when heaven remained
Utterly black, the murky shades involved   660
An image, silent, cold, and motionless,
As their own voiceless earth and vacant air.
Even as a vapour fed with golden beams
That ministered on sunlight, ere the west
Eclipses it, was now that wondrous frame—   665
No sense, no motion, no divinity—
A fragile lute, on whose harmonious strings
The breath of heaven did wander—a bright stream
Once fed with many-voicèd waves—a dream
Of youth, which night and time have quenched for ever,
Still, dark, and dry, and unremembered now.   671

Oh for Medea's wondrous alchemy,
Which wheresoe'er it fell made the earth gleam
With bright flowers, and the wintry boughs exhale
From vernal blooms fresh fragrance! Oh that God,   675
Profuse of poisons, would concede the chalice

641 repose; *Loc. 1911*] repose, *1904, 1839², 1839¹, 1824, 1816*

Which but one living man has drained, who now,
Vessel of deathless wrath, a slave that feels
No proud exemption in the blighting curse
He bears, over the world wanders for ever,   680
Lone as incarnate death! Oh that the dream
Of dark magician in his visioned cave,
Raking the cinders of a crucible
For life and power, even when his feeble hand
Shakes in its last decay, were the true law   685
Of this so lovely world! But thou art fled
Like some frail exhalation which the dawn
Robes in its golden beams,—ah! thou hast fled!
The brave, the gentle, and the beautiful,
The child of grace and genius. Heartless things   690
Are done and said i' the world, and many worms
And beasts and men live on, and mighty Earth
From sea and mountain, city and wilderness,
In vesper low or joyous orison,
Lifts still its solemn voice:—but thou art fled—   695
Thou canst no longer know or love the shapes
Of this phantasmal scene, who have to thee
Been purest ministers, who are, alas!
Now thou art not! Upon those pallid lips
So sweet even in their silence, on those eyes   700
That image sleep in death, upon that form
Yet safe from the worm's outrage, let no tear
Be shed—not even in thought! Nor, when those hues
Are gone, and those divinest lineaments,
Worn by the senseless wind, shall live alone   705
In the frail pauses of this simple strain,
Let not high verse, mourning the memory
Of that which is no more, or painting's woe
Or sculpture, speak in feeble imagery
Their own cold powers! Art and eloquence,   710
And all the shows o' the world are frail and vain
To weep a loss that turns their lights to shade.
It is a woe too 'deep for tears,' when all

---

687 exhalation *Loc. 1911*] exhalation; *1904, 1839², 1839¹, 1824, 1816*   699 not!]
not. *edd.*   703 thought!] thought *edd.*   710 powers!] powers. *edd.*   712 lights
1904, Form. 1876, 1816] light *1839², 1839¹, 1824*

Is reft at once, when some surpassing Spirit,
Whose light adorned the world around it, leaves   715
Those who remain behind, not sobs or groans,
The passionate tumult of a clinging hope,
But pale despair and cold tranquillity,
Nature's vast frame, the web of human things,
Birth and the grave, that are not as they were.   720

716 not ... or *1904, 1816*] nor ... nor *1839², 1839¹, 1824*   717 hope,] hope; *edd.*

NOTE BY MARY SHELLEY ON *ALASTOR*

Alastor is written in a very different tone from *Queen Mab*. In the latter, Shelley poured out all the cherished speculations of his youth—all the irrepressible emotions of sympathy, censure, and hope, to which the present suffering, and what he considers the proper destiny, of his fellow-creatures, gave birth. *Alastor*, on the contrary, contains an individual interest only. A very few years, with their attendant events, had checked the ardour of Shelley's hopes, though he still thought them well grounded, and that to advance their fulfilment was the noblest task man could achieve.

This is neither the time nor place to speak of the misfortunes that chequered his life. It will be sufficient to say that, in all he did, he at the time of doing it believed himself justified to his own conscience; while the various ills of poverty and loss of friends brought home to him the sad realities of life. Physical suffering had also considerable influence in causing him to turn his eyes inward; inclining him rather to brood over the thoughts and emotions of his own soul than to glance abroad, and to make, as in *Queen Mab*, the whole universe the object and subject of his song. In the Spring of 1815 an eminent physician pronounced that he was dying rapidly of a consumption; abscesses were formed on his lungs, and he suffered acute spasms. Suddenly a complete change took place; and, though through life he was a martyr to pain and debility, every symptom of pulmonary disease vanished. His nerves, which nature had formed sensitive to an unexampled degree, were rendered still more susceptible by the state of his health.

As soon as the peace of 1814 had opened the Continent, he went abroad. He visited some of the more magnificent scenes of Switzerland, and returned to England from Lucerne, by the Reuss and the Rhine. The river-navigation enchanted him. In his favourite poem of *Thalaba*, his imagination had been excited by a description of such a voyage. In the summer of 1815, after a tour along the southern coast of Devonshire and a visit to Clifton, he rented a house on Bishopgate Heath, on the borders of Windsor Forest, where he enjoyed several months of comparative health and tranquil happiness. The later summer months were warm and dry. Accompanied by a few friends, he visited the source of the Thames, making a voyage in a wherry from Windsor to Cricklade. His beautiful stanzas in the churchyard of Lechlade were written on that occasion. *Alastor* was composed on his return. He spent his days under the oak-shades of Windsor Great Park; and the magnificent woodland was a fitting study to inspire the various descriptions of forest-scenery we find in the poem.

None of Shelley's poems is more characteristic than this. The solemn spirit that reigns throughout, the worship of the majesty of nature, the broodings of a poet's heart in solitude—the mingling of the exulting joy which the various aspects of the visible universe inspires with the sad and struggling pangs which human passion imparts—give a touching interest to the whole. The death which he had often contemplated during the last months as certain and near he here represented in such colours as had, in his lonely musings, soothed his soul to peace. The versification sustains the solemn spirit which breathes throughout: it is peculiarly melodious. The poem ought rather to be considered didactic than narrative: it was the outpouring of his own emotions, embodied in the purest form he could conceive, painted in the ideal hues which his brilliant imagination inspired, and softened by the recent anticipation of death.

MISCELLANEOUS
SHORTER POEMS AND
FRAGMENTS
1816

MISCELLANEOUS SHORTER POEMS
AND FRAGMENTS
1816

The Sunset

Spring 1816

THERE late was One within whose subtle being,
As light and wind within some delicate cloud
That fades amid the blue noon's burning sky,
Genius and death contended. None may know
The sweetness of the joy which made his breath   5
Fail, like the trances of the summer air,
When, with the lady of his love, who then
First knew the unreserve of mingled being,
He walked along the pathway of a field
Which to the east a hoar wood shadowed o'er,   10
But to the west was open to the sky.
There now the sun had sunk, but lines of gold
Hung on the ashen clouds, and on the points
Of the far level grass and nodding flowers
And the old dandelion's hoary beard,   15
And, mingled with the shades of twilight, lay

THE SUNSET.   AUTOGRAPH: *a. Now lost; b. Bod. MS. Shelley adds. e. 12.*   DATE:
See n., p. 341.   PRINTED: *9–20, 28–42, from a., Hunt, Lit. Pocket-Bk., 1823/1–end,
minus line 37, from a., MWS, 1824, 1839¹, 1839²/1–end, adding line 37, from Hunt and
MWS, Hutch. 1904/1–end, from b., I and P, 1927.*   TITLE: *1904/* 'Grief. A Fragment'
1823/ 'Sunset. From an Unpublished Poem' *1824.*   TEXT: *1904/1839²/1839¹/1824/
1823, e. 12.*

   1 There late was One *1904 and edd.; changed from* [I had a friend] *e. 12*   3 That
fades *1904 and edd.*] That fades *above* [Fading] *e. 12*   4 death *1904, 1839*] youth
1824, e. 12   6 Fail *1904 and edd.*] [Ebb] Fail *e. 12*   the summer air *for* [a
summer breeze] *e. 12*   7 When *1904 and edd.*] As *e. 12*   8–9 [First seemed
to take his soul into her own] *e. 12*   12 There now *1904 and edd.; changed from*
[The sun had] *e. 12*   gold *1904 and edd.; changed from* [light] *e. 12*   13 Hung
1904 and edd.] [Yet] hung *e. 12*   15 old *changed from* [gay] *e. 12*   beard *1904
and edd.*] hair *e. 12*

On the brown massy woods—and in the east
The broad and burning moon lingeringly rose
Between the black trunks of the crowded trees,
While the faint stars were gathering overhead.—   20
'Is it not strange, Isabel,' said the youth,
'I never saw the sun? We will walk here
To-morrow; thou shalt look on it with me.'

That night the youth and lady mingled lay
In love and sleep—but when the morning came   25
The lady found her lover dead and cold.
Let none believe that God in mercy gave
That stroke. The lady died not, nor grew wild,
But year by year lived on—in truth I think
Her gentleness and patience and sad smiles,   30
And that she did not die, but lived to tend
Her agèd father, were a kind of madness,
If madness 'tis to be unlike the world.
For but to see her were to read the tale
Woven by some subtlest bard, to make hard hearts   35
Dissolve away in wisdom-working grief;—
Her eyes were black and lustreless and wan:
Her eyelashes were worn away with tears,
Her lips and cheeks were like things dead—so pale;
Her hands were thin, and through their wandering veins 40
And weak articulations might be seen
Day's ruddy light. The tomb of thy dead self
Which one vexed ghost inhabits, night and day,
Is all, lost child, that now remains of thee!

18 burning *1904 and edd.*] pallid *e. 12*   lingeringly rose *1904 and edd. ; changed from* [burning] [a]rose *in e. 12*   20 While the *1904 and edd.*] [While the] [And] [one] [two] *e. 12*   21 Isabel *1904 and edd.*] Rosalind *above* [Louisa] *e. 12*
22 *Thus edd. and e. 12 ; wrongly suspected by Form. 1876. See n., p. 342.*   24 the youth and lady *1904 and edd. ; changed from* [these happiest beings] *in e. 12*   28 stroke *1904 and edd. ; changed from* [death] *in e. 12*   29 year by year *1904 and edd.*] years and years *e. 12*   29 *Followed in e. 12 by a cancelled version of line 33*   31 lived to *1904 and edd.*] lived to *above* rather *uncancelled e. 12*   32 father *1904 and edd.*] father *above* [mother] *e. 12*   33 the world *1904 and edd.*] mankind *e. 12*   35 Woven *1904 and edd.*] Woven *above* [Told] *e. 12*   bard *1904 and edd.*] bard *below* [Poet] *e. 12*
36 grief *1904 and edd.*] [tears] grief *e. 12*   37 *Thus 1904, 1823 ; omitted 1839, 1824*
38 worn *1904, 1824, e. 12*] torn *1839*   43 Which one *1904 and edd.*] While a *possibly* Where a *e. 12*

'Inheritor of more than earth can give,   45
Passionless calm and silence unreproved,
Whether the dead find, oh, not sleep! but rest,
And are the uncomplaining things they seem,
Or live, a drop in the deep sea of Love;
Oh, that like thine, mine epitaph were—Peace!'   50
This was the only moan she ever made.

Hymn to Intellectual Beauty

June 1816

I

THE awful shadow of some unseen Power
  Floats though unseen among us,—visiting
  This various world with as inconstant wing
As summer winds that creep from flower to flower;
Like moonbeams that behind some piny mountain shower,   5
    It visits with inconstant glance
    Each human heart and countenance;
Like hues and harmonies of evening,
    Like clouds in starlight widely spread,
    Like memory of music fled,   10
    Like aught that for its grace may be
Dear, and yet dearer for its mystery.

45-7 *Thus 1904, 1824, and edd.; cancelled in e. 12*
48-9   [Or as we most be yielded up to Love
                [Or yielded up to]
                ⟨Or ? love ? or ? live ? we know not⟩
                Or love and life [thine epitaph is peace]
                [And fortunate among thy kind art thou]
                I do desire to rest   *e. 12*
49 live, a *see n., p. 342*] live, or *1904, 1824, and edd.*   live *above* [are a] *e. 12*
HYMN TO INTELLECTUAL BEAUTY. MSS.: *a. Autograph, minus 37–48, Bod. MS. Shelley*
adds. e. 16 ; b. sheets of 1817, corrected, probably, in Shelley's hand, and dated in Mary's,
Harvard, inserted in the Notebook SH II.   DATE: *SH II.*   PRINTED: *Hunt, in the*
Examiner 19 Jan. 1817/with Rosalind and Helen, *PBS, 1819/Hutch. 1904.*   TITLE:
1817/1819.   TEXT: *1904/1819/1817/SH II/e. 16. Repunctuated: see nn., pp. 341–2 ff.*
  2 Floats *1904, 1819, 1817, SH II*] Walks *underlined e. 16*   among *1904, 1819*]
amongst *1817, SH II, e. 16*   3 This various world *1904, 1819, 1817, SH II*] All
that has thought *changed from* All [human *changed to* [living] hearts] *e. 16*   7 heart
1904, 1819, 1817, SH II] mind *above* [heart] *e. 16*   9 widely *1904, 1819, 1817
SH II*] wildly *e. 16*

II

Spirit of BEAUTY, that dost consecrate
  With thine own hues all thou dost shine upon
  Of human thought or form,—where art thou gone?   15
Why dost thou pass away and leave our state,
This dim vast vale of tears, vacant and desolate?
    Ask why the sunlight not for ever
    Weaves rainbows o'er yon mountain-river;
Why aught should fail and fade that once is shown;   20
    Why fear and dream and death and birth
    Cast on the daylight of this earth
    Such gloom,—why man has such a scope
For love and hate, despondency and hope?

III

No voice from some sublimer world hath ever   25
    To sage or poet these responses given:
    Therefore the names of Demon, Ghost, and Heaven,
Remain the records of their vain endeavour—
Frail spells, whose uttered charm might not avail to sever,
    From all we hear and all we see,   30
    Doubt, chance, and mutability.
Thy light alone—like mist o'er mountains driven,
    Or music by the night-wind sent
    Through strings of some still instrument,
    Or moonlight on a midnight stream—   35
Gives grace and truth to life's unquiet dream.

13 dost *1904, 1819*] doth *1817, SH II, e. 16*   14 thine own *1904, 1819, 1817,*
SH II] thine *e. 16*   15 thought *1904, 1819, 1817*] mind *above* [heart] *e. 16*
16 and leave *1904, 1819, 1817, SH II*] leave *e. 16*   17 This dim *1904, 1819, 1817,*
SH II] A dim *e. 16*   18 Ask why *1904, 1819, 1817, SH II*] Ask why *above* [Why
do] *e. 16*   18–19 sunlight . . . Weaves *1904, 1819, 1817, SH II*] sunbeams . . .
Weave *e. 16*   20 Why . . . fade *1904, 1819, 1817, SH II*] Why does aught pass
away *e. 16*   21 fear and dream *1904, 1819, 1817, SH II*] care and pain *e. 16*
24 love *1904, 1819, 1817 SH II*] [joy] love *e. 16*   26 sage or poet *1904, 1819,*
1817, SH II] wisest poets *e. 16*   27 names of Demon, Ghost, *1904, 1819, 1817*]
name of God and ghost *SH II*   names of Ghosts and God *e. 16*   30 *Thus 1904,*
1819, 1817, SH II] From what we hear and we see *e. 16*   34 strings of some still
1904, 1819, 1817, SH II] some unconscious *e. 16*   35 *Thus edd. and SH II*] Or
day[light] on a [woo] [stream] *e. 16*   stream—] stream, *edd., SH. II*   stream *e. 16,*
leaving parenthesis unclosed   36 Gives grace *1904, 1819, 1817, SH II*] Gives grace
below [Sheds light] *e. 16*   unquiet *1904, 1819, 1817, SH II*] tumultuous *e. 16*

IV

Love, Hope, and Self-esteem, like clouds depart
  And come, for some uncertain moments lent.
  Man were immortal, and omnipotent,
Didst thou, unknown and awful as thou art,   40
Keep with thy glorious train firm state within his heart.
    Thou messenger of sympathies,
    That wax and wane in lovers' eyes—
Thou that to human thought art nourishment,
  Like darkness to a dying flame!   45
  Depart not as thy shadow came,
  Depart not—lest the grave should be,
Like life and fear, a dark reality.

V

While yet a boy I sought for ghosts, and sped
  Through many a listening chamber, cave and ruin,   50
  And starlight wood, with fearful steps pursuing
Hopes of high talk with the departed dead.
  I called on poisonous names with which our youth is fed;
    I was not heard, I saw them not:—
    When, musing deeply on the lot   55
Of life, at that sweet time when winds are wooing
  All vital things that wake to bring
  News of buds and blossoming,
  Sudden, thy shadow fell on me;
I shrieked, and clasped my hands in ecstasy!   60

VI

I vowed that I would dedicate my powers
  To thee and thine—have I not kept the vow?
  With beating heart and streaming eyes, even now
I call the phantoms of a thousand hours

37–48 *missing in e. 16*   43 lovers' *1904, 1839*] lover's *1819, 1817, SH II*
44 art *1904, 1839, 1817, SH II*] are *1819*   49–72 *Thus 1904, 1819, 1817, SH II;
stanzas IV and V are reversed in e. 16*   49 While *1904, 1819, 1817, SH II*] When
e. 16   50 listening *1904, 1819, 1817, SH II*] lonely *e. 16*   cave *1904, 1819,
1817, SH II*] vault *e. 16*   51 fearful steps *1904, 1819, 1817, SH II*] franticy *sic,
followed by a space, e. 16*   53 poisonous names *1904, 1819, 1817, SH II*] the false
name *e. 16*   54 I was not heard *1904, 1819, 1817, SH II*] He heard me not *e. 16*
55 When,] When *edd., MSS.*   57 that wake to *1904, 1819, 1817, SH II*] to wake
and *e. 16*   58 buds *SH II, e. 16*] birds *1904, 1819, 1817*

Each from his voiceless grave: they have in visioned bowers 65
    Of studious zeal or love's delight
    Outwatched with me the envious night:
They know that never joy illumed my brow
    Unlinked with hope that thou wouldst free
    This world from its dark slavery—   70
    That thou, O awful LOVELINESS,
Wouldst give whate'er these words cannot express.

VII

The day becomes more solemn and serene
When noon is past: there is a harmony
    In autumn, and a lustre in its sky,   75
Which through the summer is not heard or seen,
As if it could not be, as if it had not been!
        Thus let thy power, which like the truth
        Of nature on my passive youth
    Descended, to my onward life supply   80
        Its calm,—to one who worships thee,
        And every form containing thee,
    Whom, SPIRIT fair, thy spells did bind
To fear himself, and love all human kind.

65 they *1904, 1819, 1817, SH II*] that *e. 16*   bowers *1904 1819, 1817, SH II*]
hours *by dittography from 64, e. 16*   66 love's *1904, Form. 1876*] loves *1819,
1817, SH II, e. 16*   67 envious *underlined in e. 16*   68 They know *1904,
1819, 1817, SH II*] To tell *e. 16*   69 wouldst *1904, 1819, 1817, SH II*] shouldst
e. 16   72 whate'er *1904, 1819, 1817, SH II*] whatever *e. 16*   76 or *MSS.,
and edd. except 1839, which reads* nor   78 Thus . . . which *edd. and SH II;
a blank in e. 16*   81 Its *1904, 1819, 1817, SH II*] Thy *e. 16*   who *1904, 1819,
1817, SH II*] that *e. 16*   83 SPIRIT fair, *1904, 1819, 1817, SH II*] awful Power
e. 16   84 *Below, written by MWS*, Switzerland, June 1816 *SH II.*

Mont Blanc

July 23, 1816

I

THE everlasting universe of things
Flows through the mind, and rolls its rapid waves—
Now dark, now glittering, now reflecting gloom,
Now lending splendour where, from secret springs,
The source of human thought its tribute brings   5
Of waters,—with a sound but half its own,
Such as a feeble brook will oft assume
In the wild woods, among the mountains lone,
Where waterfalls around it leap for ever,
Where woods and winds contend, and a vast river   10
Over its rocks ceaselessly bursts and raves.

II

Thus thou, Ravine of Arve—dark, deep Ravine;—
Thou many-coloured, many-voicèd vale,
Over whose pines and crags and caverns sail
Fast cloud-shadows and sunbeams;—awful scene   15
Where Power, in likeness of the Arve, comes down
From the ice-gulfs that gird his secret throne,
Bursting through these dark mountains like the flame
Of lightning through the tempest;—thou dost lie,
Thy giant brood of pines around thee clinging   20
(Children of elder time, in whose devotion
The chainless winds still come, and ever came

MONT BLANC. AUTOGRAPH: *Bod. MS. Shelley adds. e. 16, inked, in part, over a rubbed or erased pencil draft; much emended, and with some sections cancelled by vertical strokes.* PRINTED: *With* History of a Six Weeks' Tour *PBS, 1817/MWS, 1824/MWS, 1839¹, 1839²/Hutch. 1904.*   UNPRINTED: *27a, 28a.*   TITLE, DATE: *1817.*   TEXT: *1904/ 1839/1824/1817/e. 16, considerably repunctuated. See nn., pp. 348–53 ff.*
    Before line 1 The scene at the extremity of the vale of Servoz *e. 16*   1–2 In day the stream of things / Now move *below which, in e. 16, in a different ink, is a snatch belonging to* Rosalind and Helen   4 springs *edd.*] caves *e. 16*   5 source of human thought *edd.; changed from* [fountain of the mind] *e. 16*   6 sound but half its own *edd.*] wild sound half *e. 16*   10 vast *edd.*] loud *above* [vast] *e. 16*
14 Over whose rocks and *above* pines *and* and caverns *above* [the clouds and sunbeams] sail *e. 16*   15 cloud-shadows *1904*] clouds, shadows *1839* cloud, shadows *1824* cloud shadows *1817, e. 16*   18–48 *For text, punctuation, and syntax see n., pp. 349–51.*

To drink their odours, and their mighty swinging
To hear—an old and solemn harmony),
Thine earthly rainbows stretched across the sweep   25
Of the aethereal waterfall, whose veil
Robes some unsculptured image (even the sleep,   27
The sudden pause which does inhabit thee   27a
Which, when the voices of the desert fail   28
And its hues wane, doth blend them all and steep   28a
Their period in its own eternity),
Thy caverns echoing to the Arve's commotion,   30
A loud, lone sound no other sound can tame;—
Thou art pervaded with that ceaseless motion,
Thou art the path of that unresting sound,
Dizzy Ravine! . . . . . . And, when I gaze on thee,
I seem as in a trance sublime and strange   35
To muse on my own separate fantasy,
My own, my human mind, which passively
Now renders and receives fast influencings,
Holding an unremitting interchange
With the clear universe of things around—   40
One legion of wild thoughts, whose wandering wings
Now float above thy darkness, and now rest
Where that or thou art no unbidden guest,
In the still cave of the witch Poesy—
Seeking among the shadows that pass by   45
(Ghosts of all things that are) some shade of thee,
Some phantom, some faint image; till the breast
From which they fled recalls them, thou art there!

24 solemn *edd.*] solemn *above* [awful] *e. 16*   26 aethereal *edd.*] aerial *e. 16*
waterfall's white veil *changed from* waterfall white-laced *e. 16*   27 even the sleep
e. 16] the strange sleep *edd.*   27a, 28a *e. 16 only; omitted in edd., following PBS,*
1817   27a sudden pause *changed from* momentary death *e. 16*   29 Their
period *above* [tumult] *e. 16*] Wraps all *1817 and edd.*   30–6 *precede line 25 in*
e. 16   33 path *edd.*] path *below* [cave] *e. 16*   34 Dizzy *edd.*] Mighty *e. 16*
35 trance sublime *edd.*] vision deep *e. 16*   36 [I seem] to muse on [separate]
above my own fantasy *e. 16*   38 Now renders and receives *edd.; changed from* [To
render and receive] *e. 16*   39 unremitting *edd.*] unremitted *e. 16*   40 clear
edd.] clear *above* [vast] *e. 16*   41 One legion *edd.; changed from* A [strange mass]
e. 16   42 float *edd.*][rest] float *e. 16*   darkness *edd.*] darkness *above* [wonders] *e. 16*
43 [Where thou art surely no unbidden guest] *e. 16*   44 In *edd.*] Near *above* [In]
e. 16   still *edd.*] still *above* [weird] *e. 16*   witch *edd.*] witch *above* [shade] *e. 16*
46 all *edd.*] [the] *changed to* all *e. 16*   47 phantom *edd.*] likeness *cancelled but*
unreplaced e. 16

III

Some say that gleams of a remoter world
Visit the soul in sleep,—that death is slumber,   50
And that its shapes the busy thoughts outnumber
Of those who wake and live. I look on high:—
Has some unknown omnipotence unfurled
The veil of life and death? Or do I lie
In dream, and does the mightier world of sleep   55
Spread far around and inaccessibly
Its circles? For the very spirit fails,
Driven like a homeless cloud from steep to steep
That vanishes among the viewless gales!
Far, far above, piercing the infinite sky,   60
Mont Blanc appears,—still, snowy, and serene;
Its subject mountains their unearthly forms
Pile round it, ice and rock, broad vales between
Of frozen floods, unfathomable deeps,
Blue as the overhanging heaven, that spread   65
And wind among the accumulated steeps—
A desert peopled by the storms alone,
Save when the eagle brings some hunter's bone,
And the wolf tracks her there. How hideously
Its shapes are heaped around—rude, bare, and high,   70
Ghastly, and scarred, and riven!—Is this the scene

52 on high *edd.*] on high *above* [above] *e. 16*   53 unfurled *quite clear in e. 16;*
upfurled *unnecessarily conjectured by James Thomson ('B.V.')*   56 Spread *e. 16,*
and edd. except 1839, which has Speed   57 very spirit fails *edd.; changed from*
[mind is faint / With aspiration] *e. 16*   58 Driven like a *edd.*] Driven like a *above*
[Climbing among] *above* [from] *e. 16*   58–9 [While far above shapes] *e. 16*
59 That *edd.*] Which *e. 16*   61 appears *apparently cancelled in e. 16*   still snowy
and serene *above* [and all its subject towers] *above* [every pyramid] *above* [below and all
around] *e. 16*   63 round *e. 16*] around *edd., rightly suspected by Form. as a misprint
passed by Shelley*   63–4 [how hideously / They overhang the vale] *followed by a
cancelled first draft of 71–6 beginning* is this the scene *e. 16*   64 floods *edd.*] waves
e. 16   65–6 that spread *above* [spread] [wind] / And wind *above* [spread] among
the [compl]accumulated steeps *e. 16*
67–8   [Column and pinnacle and pyramid]
              [And] [Now clothed in beams]
              [Ice] ⟨? Frost here⟩ makes mockery of human ⟨? forms⟩]
              [Column and pinnacle and pyramid] *Cf. line 104.*
              [And walls]   *e. 16*
69 tracks her there *1904, 1839*] tracts her there *1824, 1817*   watches her *e. 16*
69–70 [Insect or beast or bird inhabited] *e. 16. Cf. line 115.*   70 shapes *edd.*]
rocks *e. 16*

Where the old Earthquake-daemon taught her young
Ruin? Were these their toys? or did a sea
Of fire envelop once this silent snow?
None can reply—all seems eternal now.   75
The wilderness has a mysterious tongue
Which teaches awful doubt, or faith so mild,
So solemn, so serene, that man may be,
In such a faith, with nature reconciled,—
Thou hast a voice, great Mountain, to repeal   80
Large codes of fraud and woe not understood
By all, but which the wise, and great, and good
Interpret, or make felt, or deeply feel!

IV

The fields, the lakes, the forests, and the streams,
Ocean, and all the living things that dwell   85
Within the daedal earth; lightning, and rain,
Earthquake, and fiery flood, and hurricane;
The torpor of the year when feeble dreams
Visit the hidden buds, or dreamless sleep
Holds every future leaf and flower; the bound   90
With which from that detested trance they leap;
The works and ways of man, their death and birth,
And that of him and all that his may be;—
All things that move and breathe with toil and sound
Are born and die, revolve, subside, and swell.   95
Power dwells apart in its tranquillity,
Remote, serene, and inaccessible:
And *this*, the naked countenance of earth,
On which I gaze, even these primaeval mountains
Teach the adverting mind. The glaciers creep   100
Like snakes that watch their prey, from their far fountains,
Slow rolling on; there, many a precipice,

72 old *edd.*] old *above* [dark] *e. 16*   79 In such a *e. 16*] But for such *edd.*, *because
Shelley, nonsensically, printed a cancelled phrase in place of his correction*   80 Thou
hast . . . Mountain *edd.*] Ye have . . . Mountains *e. 16*   84 *changed from* [The
powers that rule the world themselves are still] *e. 16*   86 rain *edd.*] rain *above*
[wind] *e. 16*   87 fiery flood *edd.*] fiery flood *above* [floods of watersprout] *e. 16*
91 that *edd.*] that [its] *e. 16*   92 The works and ways of man *edd.; changed from*
[The cities of mankind] *e. 16*   102 Slow *edd. except 1839, which has* Slowly] Slow
over Slowly *apparently, e. 16*

Frost and the Sun in scorn of mortal power
Have piled: dome, pyramid, and pinnacle,
A city of death, distinct with many a tower 105
And wall impregnable of beaming ice.
Yet not a city, but a flood of ruin
Is there, that from the boundaries of the sky
Rolls its perpetual stream; vast pines are strewing
Its destined path, or in the mangled soil 110
Branchless and shattered stand; the rocks, drawn down
From yon remotest waste, have overthrown
The limits of the dead and living world,
Never to be reclaimed. The dwelling-place
Of insects, beasts, and birds becomes its spoil; 115
Their food and their retreat for ever gone,
So much of life and joy is lost. The race
Of man flies far in dread; his work and dwelling
Vanish, like smoke before the tempest's stream,
And their place is not known. Below, vast caves 120
Shine in the rushing torrents' restless gleam,
Which from those secret chasms in tumult welling
Meet in the vale, and one majestic River,
The breath and blood of distant lands, for ever
Rolls its loud waters to the ocean-waves, 125
Breathes its swift vapours to the circling air.

V

Mont Blanc yet gleams on high:—the power is there,
The still and solemn power of many sights,
And many sounds, and much of life and death.
In the calm darkness of the moonless nights, 130
In the lone glare of day, the snows descend
Upon that Mountain; none beholds them there,
Nor when the flakes burn in the sinking sun,
Or the star-beams dart through them. Winds contend

103 mortal *edd.*] human *e. 16*   107 flood *edd.*] flood *above* [stream] *e. 16*
111 stand; the *edd.*] stand, the *above* and *e. 16*   113 The limits *edd.*] *cancelled but*
unreplaced in e. 16   115 birds *e. 16*] birds, *edd.*   119 like *edd.*] as *for* [like]
e. 16   121 rushing *edd.*] gushing *e. 16*   torrents' *1904, following Ross. 1870*]
torrent's *1839, 1824, 1817*   torrents *e. 16*   125 Rolls *edd.*] Bears *e. 16*   129 life
and death *edd.; changed from* [good and ill] *e. 16*   131 glare *edd.*] light *above*
[glare] *e. 16*   snows descend *edd.: changed from* [snow flakes fall] *e. 16*

Silently there, and heap the snow with breath   135
Rapid and strong, but silently. Its home
The voiceless lightning in these solitudes
Keeps innocently, and like vapour broods
Over the snow. The secret Strength of things
Which governs thought, and to the infinite dome   140
Of Heaven is as a law, inhabits thee.
And what were thou, and earth, and stars, and sea,
If to the human mind's imaginings
Silence and solitude were vacancy?

Rejected Lines

THERE is a voice, not understood by all,
Sent from these desert-caves. It is the roar
Of the rent ice-cliff which the sunbeams call,
Plunging into the vale—it is the blast
Descending on the pines—the torrents pour [5

Verses Written on Receiving a Celandine in a Letter from England

July, 1816

I THOUGHT of thee, fair Celandine,
    As of a flower aery blue
        Yet small—thy leaves methought were wet
With the light of morning dew;
In the same glen thy star did shine   5
    As the primrose and the violet,
And the wild briar bent over thee
And the woodland brook danced under thee.

135 with *edd.*] their *e. 16*   139 Over the snow *followed by* the unpolluted dome /
Of Heaven is not more silent. *uncancelled in e. 16*   140 to the infinite *edd.; changed
from* starry rules the *e. 16*   143–4 *Missing in e. 16*

MONT BLANC. Rejected Lines.   AUTOGRAPH: *Bod. MS. Shelley adds. c. 4, a draft in
pencil.*   PRINTED: *Garn. 1862/Hutch. 1904.*   TEXT: *1904/1862/c. 4. See n., p. 355.*

VERSES WRITTEN ON RECEIVING, ETC.   AUTOGRAPH: *Bod. MS. Shelley adds. e. 16, a
pencil draft, illegible because over it is drafted* 'To William Shelley' *(see below, p. 355).*
TRANSCRIPT, TITLE, DATE: *MWS, SH II.*   PRINTED: *W. E. Peck, Boston Herald,
21 Dec. 1925/I and P, 1927.*   TEXT: *1927/1925/SH II.*
    4 dew;] dew. *edd., SH II*

Lovely thou wert in thine own glen
 Ere thou didst dwell in song or story;   10
  Ere the moonlight of a Poet's mind
  Had arrayed thee with the glory
Whose fountains are the hearts of men—
 Many a thing of vital kind
Had fed and sheltered under thee,   15
Had nourished their thoughts near to thee.

Yes, gentle flower in thy recess,
 None might a sweeter aspect wear;
  Thy young bud drooped so gracefully,
  Thou wert so very fair,   20
Among the fairest, ere the stress
 Of exile, death and injury,
Thus withering and deforming thee,
Had made a mournful type of thee,—

A type of that whence I and thou   25
 Are thus familiar, Celandine—
  A deathless Poet whose young prime
  Was as serene as thine!
But he is changed and withered now,
 Fallen on a cold and evil time;   30
His heart is gone—his fame is dim,
And Infamy sits mocking him.

Celandine! Thou art pale and dead,
 Changed from thy fresh and woodland state,—
  Oh! that thy bard were cold, but he   35
  Has lived too long and late.
Would he were in an honoured grave!
 But that, men say, now must not be,
Since he for impious gold could sell
The love of those who loved him well.   40

18 wear;] wear, *edd.*, *SH II* 21 fairest,] fairest *edd.*, *SH II* 24 thee,—] thee.
edd., *SH II* 28 thine!] thine; *edd.*, *SH II* 34 state,—] state. *edd.*, *SH II*
37 grave!] grave. *edd.*, *SH II*

That he, with all hope else of good
    Should be thus transitory,
        I marvel not, but that his lays
    Have spared not their own glory—
That blood, even the foul god of blood   45
    With most inexpiable praise,
Freedom and truth left desolate,
He has been bought to celebrate!

They were his hopes which he doth scorn;
    They were his foes the fight that won;   50
        That sanction and that condemnation
    Are now forever gone.
They need them not! Truth may not mourn
    That, with a liar's inspiration
Her majesty he did disown   55
Ere he could overlive his own.

They need them not, for Liberty
    Justice and philosophic truth
        From his divine and simple song
    Shall draw immortal youth,   60
When he and thou shall cease to be
    Or be some other thing,—so long
As men may breathe or flowers may blossom
O'er the wide earth's maternal bosom.

The stem whence thou wert disunited   65
    Since thy poor self wast banished hither,
        Now by that priest of Nature's care
    Who sent thee forth to wither,
His window with its blooms has lighted
    And I shall see thy brethren there.   70
And each, like thee, will aye betoken
Love sold, hope dead, and honour broken.

---

43 not,] not; *edd.*, *SH II*   44 glory—] glory. *edd.*, *SH II*   46 inexpiable
SH II] inespicable *edd.*   47 and *SH II*] with *edd.*   62 thing,—] thing, *edd.*,
SH II   66 wast] was *edd.*, *SH II*   72 honour *SH II*] honor *edd.*

Rejected Lines from the draft

ERE thou wert thus companionless
Ere exile, death and injury,
Thus withering and deforming thee,
Had made a mournful type of thee [

The Celandine and this lament,   5
The memory of thy grievous wrong
Will fade and   ?
But genius is omnipotent
To hallow great pure [

Three Laments

1. On Fanny Godwin

1816

I

HER voice did quiver as we parted,
Yet knew I not the heart was broken
From which it came—and I departed
Heeding not the words then spoken—
Misery, oh Misery,   5
This world is all too wide for thee!

VERSES WRITTEN ON RECEIVING, ETC. Rejected Lines.   AUTOGRAPH: *Bod. MS. Shelley adds. e. 16.*   TRANSCRIPT: *MWS. Bod. MS. Shelley adds. d. 9. See n., p. 355.* PRINTED: *1–4, Garn. 1862, and later edd., as belonging to* 'To William Shelley, 1817'. *See above, p. 80, and nn., p. 355.*   UNPRINTED: *5–9.*   TEXT: *e. 16. See n., p. 355.*
    8 *The last two words are cancelled in e. 16*

ON FANNY GODWIN.   AUTOGRAPH: *Bod. MS. Shelley adds. c. 4.*   TRANSCRIPTS: *a. 10–end, MWS, Bod. MS. Shelley adds. d. 7 ; b. 1–7, MWS, Bod. MS. Shelley adds. d. 9.*   DATE: *See n., pp. 355–6.*   PRINTED: *1–6, MWS, 1839¹, 1839², Hutch. 1904/1–end, SR and I, who first gave the connection with the next poem, 1934.*   TITLE: 'On F.G.' *1839¹, 1839²/*'On Fanny Godwin' *1904.*   TEXT: *1934/1904/1839²/1839¹/ MSS.*
    Before 1 *Cancelled opening*
                Friend had I known thy secret grief
                Should we have parted so *above* [ever] *c. 4*
Above, left, Shelley scribbled Did some *and above that* [No sympathy]; *above, right, is drafted the second Lament*   2 the *upon* that *c. 4*] that *edd., d. 9*   3 came— *c. 4*] came, *edd., d. 9*   4 spoken— *c. 4*] spoken, *edd.*   spoken *d. 9*   5 Misery, *d. 9*] Miscry— *edd., c. 4*   oh Misery,] oh misery *c. 4*   O Misery, *1904, 1839*   o misery, *d. 9*   O Misery *1934*   6 thee! *c. 4*] thee. *edd. d. 9*   6–7 *A space in c. 4 indicates a stanza-break*

II

Some secret woes had been mine own,
And they had taught me that the good,
The pur⟨e⟩ [

And that for who are lone and weary   10
The road of life is long and dreary;

III

Some hopes were buried in my heart
Whose spectres haunted me with sadness.

2. *On William Shelley*

[attached to no. 1 in 1819]

I

THY little footsteps on the sand
Of a remote and lonely shore . . .
The twinkling of thine infant hands,
Where now the worm will feed no more . . .
Thy look of mingled love and glee   5
When *one* returned to gaze on thee . . .

7 woes *edd., d. 9*] woes *above* griefs *uncancelled c. 4*   8 good,] good— *1934*   good
c. 4   9 pur⟨e⟩ *c. 4*] pain *1934*   9–10 *A break in c. 4, indicative of a lacuna to
be filled later*   10 And that for who are *c. 4, so changed from* And that for those
who are *so transcribed in d. 7 ; 1934 prints* And that for whom   *The grammar is beyond
repair*   11 road *MSS.*] load *1934   Against this line in d. 7 MWS notes* I think
on F.G. written before Italy   11–12 *A space in c. 4 indicates a stanza-break*
12–13 *To the left* [I heeded] *and below* There was a *c. 4*

ON WILLIAM SHELLEY.   AUTOGRAPH: *Bod. MS. Shelley adds. c. 4. See n., p. 355.*
TRANSCRIPTS: *a. 1–9, MWS, Bod. MS. Shelley adds. d. 7 ;   b. 1–9, MWS, Bod. MS.
Shelley adds. d. 9.*   DATE: *See n., pp. 355–6.*   PRINTED, TITLE: *1–6, MWS, 1839,
Hutch. 1904*/*1–10, S R and I, who first gave the connection with the preceding poem, 1934.*
TEXT: *1934*/*1904*/*1839*/*MSS. For punctuation see n., p. 356.*
2 a *edd., d. 7, d. 9*] a *above* [some] *c. 4*   shore . . .] shore; *edd.* ¨ shore— *changed
from* [sea] *c. 4*   shore *d. 7*   shore, *d. 9*   3 The *edd., d. 7, d. 9*] The *over* [Thy]
c. 4   4 Where *edd., d. 7, d. 9, preceded by* [Upon thy] *in c. 4*   now *edd., d. 7,
d. 9, changed from* [even] *in c. 4*   more . . .] more; *edd.*   more. *c. 4*   more *d. 7*
more, *d. 9*   5 look of mingled *d. 7, c. 4*] mingled look of *edd., d. 9*   6 *one*
MSS.] we *edd.*   thee . . .] thee— *1904*   thee. *other edd.*   thee *MSS.*

II

Thy footsteps on the sand are fled,
Thine eyes are dark, thy hands are cold,
And she is dead, and thou art dead . . .
And we [10

3. *On Harriet Shelley*

November—1816

[1st version; cf. below, p. 312]

I

THE cold earth slept below;
Above the cold sky shone;
And all around, with a chilling sound,
From caves of ice and fields of snow,
The breath of night like death did flow   5
Beneath the sinking moon.

II

The wintry hedge was black;
The green grass was not seen;
The birds did rest on the bare thorn's breast,
Whose roots, beside the pathway track,   10
Had bound their folds o'er many a crack
Which the frost had made between.

7 Thy *1934*] These *d. 7, d. 9*   Thy *changed from* These *c. 4*   fled,] fled *1934,
d. 7, d. 9*   fled *plus a possibly accidental dot c. 4*   8 dark,] dark— *d. 9, c. 4*   dark
d. 7   cold,] cold *1934, d. 7, d. 9*   cold *added below uncancelled* still *c. 4*   9 dead
. . .] dead *1934, d. 7*   dead— *d. 9, c. 4*   *Against this line in d. 7 MWS has noted*
before Italy   10 And we *cancelled, together with the rest of the line which is illegible
c. 4*] And the *1934*   *omitted in d. 7, d. 9*

ON HARRIET SHELLEY, November—1816, 1st Version. AUTOGRAPH: *Bod. MS. Shelley
adds. c. 4.*   DATE: *c. 4, where 1815 is clearly a slip for 1816.*   PRINTED: *Hunt*, Lit.
Pocket-Bk., *1823*/*MWS*, *1824*/*MWS*, *1839*/*Hutch.* 1904.   TITLE: 'November—
1815' *c. 4, 1823*/'Lines' *1824, 1839, 1904.*   TEXT: *1904*/*1839*/*1824*/*1823*/*c. 4.*
1 below; *1824, 1823, c. 4*] below, *1904, 1839*   2 Above *edd.*] Above, *c. 4*
3 *Thus 1904, c. 4*; *two lines in 1839, 1824, 1823*   around, *1904, 1824, 1823, c. 4*]
around *1839*   4 ice *1904, 1839, 1824, 1823*] ice, *c. 4*   snow, *1904, 1824, 1823*]
snow *1839, c. 4*   6 moon. *edd.*] moon.— *c. 4*   7 black;] black, *edd.* black— *c. 4*
8 seen;] seen— *c. 4*   seen, *edd.*   9 *Thus 1904, c. 4*; *two lines in 1839, 1824, 1823*
breast, *1904*] breast *1839, 1824, 1823, c. 4*   10 track, *edd.*] track *c. 4*

III

Thine eyes glowed in the glare
Of the moon's dying light;
As a fen-fire's beam on a sluggish stream   15
Gleams dimly, so the moon shone there,
And it yellowed the strings of thy raven hair
That shook in the wind of night.

IV

The moon made thy lips pale, belovèd;
The wind made thy bosom chill;   20
The night did shed on thy dear head
Its frozen dew, and thou didst lie
Where the bitter breath of the naked sky
Might visit thee at will.

Fragment: 'Dear Home . . .'

Probably 1816

DEAR home, thou scene of joys which now are cold
And grief whose gentle memory now reproves.
Dear home, thou scene of earliest hopes and joys,
The least of whom wronged Memory ever makes
Bitterer than all thine unremembered tears,   5
I visit thee [

15 *Thus 1904, c. 4; two lines in 1839, 1824, 1823*   16 Gleams *edd.*] Gleams *above* [Shines] *c. 4*   17 raven *thus c. 4 and edd., except 1823, which has* tangled *Cf. 2nd version, line 20, p. 312, below*   hair *1839, 1824, 1823, c. 4*] hair, *1904* 19 belovèd; *1839, 1824, 1823*] beloved— *1904, c. 4*   20 chill; *1839, 1824, 1823, c. 4*] chill— *1904*   21 *Thus 1904, c. 4; two lines in 1839, 1824, 1823*   24 will. *edd.*] will.— *c. 4*

FRAGMENT: 'Dear home . . .'   AUTOGRAPH: *Bod. MS. Shelley adds. e. 12. See n., p. 357.*   DATE: *See n.*   PRINTED: *3–5, Garn. 1862, Hutch. 1904/1–end, I and P, 1927.*   TEXT: *1927/1904/1862/e. 12.*
1 home] Home *1927, e. 12*   3 home *1904, 1862*] Home *1927, e. 12* 4 Memory *1904, 1862*] memory *1927, e. 12*   5 tears, *1927*] tears. *1904, 1862* tears *possibly* tears— *e. 12*

Fragment: Ghost Story

1816

A SHOVEL of his ashes took
From the hearth's obscurest nook . . .
 With a body bowed and bent
She tottered forth to the paved courtyard,
 Muttering mysteries as she went . . .   5
Helen and Henry knew that Granny
Was as much afraid of ghosts as any
 And so they followed hard . . .
But Helen clung to her brother's arm
And her own shadow made her shake.   10

Henry [

Fragment:
Stanzas Addressed to Leigh Hunt

1816

FOR me, my friend, if not that tears did tremble
 In my faint cyes, and that my hcart bcat fast
With feelings which made rapture pain resemble,
 Yet, from thy verse that falsehood starts aghast,

FRAGMENT: GHOST STORY. AUTOGRAPH: *Bod. MS. Shelley adds. e. 16.* DATE: *See n., p. 357.* PRINTED: *Garn. 1862/Hutch. 1904.* UNPRINTED: *3, 4, 11.* TITLE: *Ross. 1870/*'Helen and Henry' *I and P, 1927.* TEXT: *1904/1862/e. 16.*
 2 the hearth's *edd.; changed from* the [blazing] hearths *e.* 16 nook . . .] nook, *edd.* nook *e.* 16 3, 4 *omitted in edd.* 4 *preceded by* [A shovel of his] [And tottering] *e.* 16 5 went . . .] went. *edd.* went.— *e.* 16 5–6 [Her grandchildren] fell *possibly* felt *e.* 16 7 ghosts *1862, e.* 16] Ghosts *1904* 9–10 [Look round her there and] *e.* 16 10 shadow *e.* 16] spasm *edd.* 11 Henry [*previously unprinted; presumably the start of a new stanza.*

FRAGMENT: STANZAS, ETC. AUTOGRAPH: *Bod. MS. Shelley adds. c. 4.* DATE: *See n., p. 357.* PRINTED: *1–10, Garn. 1862, Hutch. 1904/18–end, MWS, 1839², Hutch. 1904.* UNPRINTED: *11–17.* TITLE: *See n., p. 357. None in c. 4. 1–10, Ross., Form.,* 'To One Leaving Prison'/*Hutch.* 'To a Friend Released from Prison'/*I and P. 1927,* 'To One Freed from Prison'. TEXT: *1904/1862/c. 4.*
 3 made *changed from* make *c. 4*] make *edd.* 4 *changed from* Yet that thou hast made falsehood look aghast *c. 4* verse *c. 4*] voice *edd.*

I thank thee—let the tyrant keep   5
His chains and bars, yea, let him weep
With rage to see thee freshly risen,
Like strength from slumber, from the prison,
In which he vainly hoped the soul to bind
Which on the chains must prey that fetter humankind. [10

Friend, this I hope ⟨if it be⟩ thou hast ⟨cloven⟩
    The dark, if love offend, ⟨whose shade has woven⟩
        The Universe in its eclipse
            With a ray of thy pure feeling
            By the light of love revealing,   15
Then see fair pleasure smile in peace beside
Majestic Liberty throned as his imperial bride. [

A gentle story of two lovers young,
    Who met in innocence and died in sorrow,
And of one selfish heart, whose rancour clung   20
    Like curses on them; are ye slow to borrow
        The lore of truth from such a tale?
        Or in this world's deserted vale,
            Do ye not see a star of gladness
            Pierce the shadows of its sadness,—   25
When ye are told, that love is a light sent
From Heaven, which none shall quench, to cheer the innocent? [

5–6 tyrant . . ./His *changed from* tyrants . . ./Their *c. 4*   6 bars *c. 4*] tears *edd.*
yea *not in c. 4*   let him *changed from* he [shall]   doth *c. 4*   10 the *edd.*,
omitted in c. 4   11–12 *See n., p. 357*; has woven *conjectural only*   14–15 [When
the highest step of Duty's awful ⟨? throne⟩]/[The seat of glory] *c. 4*   16 fair *changed
from* that *c. 4*   21 are ye *edd.*; *changed in c. 4 from* [art thou] *following* [those]
24 Do ye *edd.*] Dost thou *c. 4*   star *edd.*] star *above* morning *below* [beam] *c. 4*
26 ye are told *above* [thou dost hear] *c. 4*   ye are cold *most edd.*   *Locock accepted
Bradley's correct conjecture.*

TRANSLATIONS
1816

TRANSLATIONS
1816

Four Fragments of Greek Pastoral

I

[Moschus, III. 1–7]

Ye Dorian woods and waves, lament aloud,—
Augment your tide, O streams, with fruitless tears,
For the belovèd Bion is no more.
Let every tender herb and plant and flower,
From each dejected bud and drooping bloom,   5
Shed dews of liquid sorrow, and with breath
Of melancholy sweetness on the wind
Diffuse its languid love; let roses blush,
Anemones grow paler for the loss
Their dells have known; and thou, O hyacinth,   10
Utter thy legend now—yet more, dumb flower,
Than 'Ah! alas!'—thine is no common grief—
Bion the ⟨sweetest singer⟩ is no more.

2

[Moschus, V]

When winds that move not its calm surface sweep
The azure sea, I love the land no more;
The smiles of the serene and tranquil deep
Tempt my unquiet mind.—But when the roar

1. From Moschus, III.   autograph: *Hunt MS., once owned by S. Townsend Mayer. Untraced.*   date: *See n., p. 358.*   printed: *From Hunt MS., Form. 1876/Hutch. 1904.*   text: *1904/1876.*   commentary: *1876.*
  1 *Cancelled reading* Weep, Dorian woods, weep *Hunt*   6 *Cancelled reading* And rivulets mourn; *both* tears *and* sorrow *are left standing, Hunt*   Shed dews of liquid *changed from* Pour forth its dews of *Hunt*   13 ⟨sweetest singer⟩ *edd.; a blank in Hunt. See n., p. 358.*
2. From Moschus, V.   mss.: *Unknown.*   date: *See n., p. 360.*   printed: *With Alastor PBS, 1816/Hutch. 1904.*   text: *1904/ 1816.*

Of Ocean's gray abyss resounds, and foam   5
Gathers upon the sea, and vast waves burst,
I turn from the drear aspect to the home
Of Earth and its deep woods, where, interspersed,
When winds blow loud, pines make sweet melody.
Whose house is some lone bark, whose toil the sea,   10
Whose prey the wandering fish, an evil lot
Has chosen.—But I my languid limbs will fling
Beneath the plane, where the brook's murmuring
Moves the calm spirit, but disturbs it not.

3

[Moschus, VI]

PAN loved his neighbour Echo—but that child
Of Earth and Air pined for the Satyr leaping;
The Satyr loved with wasting madness wild
The bright nymph Lyda,—and so three went weeping.
As Pan loved Echo, Echo loved the Satyr,   5
The Satyr, Lyda; and so love consumed them.—
And thus—to each, which was a woful matter—
To bear what they inflicted Justice doomed them;
For, in as much as each might hate the lover,
Each, loving, so was hated.—Ye that love not   10
Be warned—in thought turn this example over,
That when ye love, the like return ye prove not.

3. FROM MOSCHUS, VI.   AUTOGRAPH: *a. BM, Ashley Coll., together with the next poem*; *b. Bod. MS. Shelley adds. e. 12.*   DATE: *See n., p. 360.*   PRINTED: *MWS, 1824/MWS, 1839/Hutch. 1904.*   TEXT: *1904/1824/e. 12/BM.*
  3 *Thus e. 12, changed from* Who loved, with wasting madness wandering wild,— *apparently the final intention in BM*   4 bright *e. 12, edd.*] fair *BM*   three *e. 12, BM, and edd., except those between 1839 and 1876, which read* the three   7 thus— to each *Ross. 1870*] thus to each— *all other edd., e. 12, BM. See n., p. 358.*   9 in as much *Ross. 1870, Form. 1876, and so changed from* in so much *in BM*] inasmuch *1904, 1824, e. 12 See n., p. 358.*   10 *Thus edd., e. 12 ; changed in BM from* [Be not unkind to those who love ye] [Be timely kind to those who love ye] [This lesson in your minds turn over] [The moral of this song in thought turn over]

4

[Bion, I. 1–49]

I MOURN Adonis dead—loveliest Adonis—
Dead, dead Adonis—and the Loves lament.
Sleep no more, Venus, wrapped in purple woof—
Wake violet-stolèd queen, and weave the crown
Of Death,—'tis Misery calls,—for he is dead.   5

    The lovely one lies wounded in the mountains,
His white thigh struck with the white tooth; he scarce
Yet breathes; and Venus hangs in agony there.
The dark blood wanders o'er his snowy limbs,
His eyes beneath their lids are lustreless,   10
The rose has fled from his wan lips, and there
That kiss is dead, which Venus gathers yet.

    A deep, deep wound Adonis [
A deeper Venus bears within her heart.
See, his belovèd dogs are gathering round—   15
The Oread nymphs are weeping—Aphrodite
With hair unbound is wandering through the woods,
'Wildered, ungirt, unsandalled—the thorns pierce
Her hastening feet and drink her sacred blood.
Bitterly screaming out, she is driven on   20
Through the long vales; and her Assyrian boy,
Her love, her husband, calls—the purple blood
From his struck thigh stains his white navel now,
His bosom, and his neck before like snow.

4. FROM BION, I. AUTOGRAPH: *BM, Ashley Coll., with the preceding poem.* TRAN-
SCRIPT: *MWS, Bod. MS. Shelley adds. d. 7.*   DATE: *See n., p. 360*   PRINTED:
from BM, Form. 1876/Hutch. 1904.   TEXT: *1904/d. 7/BM.*
    4 and weave the crown | Of Death *cancelled in favour of* beat your breast *BM. I
follow Form. See n., p. 359*   7 he scarce *changed from* [and she] *BM*   9 Hangs
over him to catch his passing breath *BM*   12 Venus gathers yet *cancelled but
unreplaced in BM*   14 within *1876, BM*] upon *1904*   17 With hair unbound
changed from [Loosening her hair] *BM*   18 ungirt *cancelled but not replaced in BM*
the thorns pierce *changed from* [and the thorns] *BM*   19 Her hastening feet *changed
from* [Pierce her coming] *BM*   23–4 his . . . his / His . . . his *Emended here from
the Greek. BM has four feminine possessives of which some edd. emend the first.*

'Alas for Cytherea!' the Loves mourn—　　　　　25
The lovely, the beloved is gone—and now
Her sacred beauty vanishes away.
For Venus whilst Adonis lived was fair—
Alas! her loveliness is dead with him.
The oaks and mountains cry, 'Ai! ai! Adonis!'　　　30
The streams change their harmonious tune and groan,
The springs their waters change to tears and weep—
The flowers are withered up with grief.

'Ai! ai!　　　　　　　　　　Adonis is dead!'
Echo resounds　　　　　　　　'Adonis dead!'　　　35
Who will weep not thy dreadful woe, O Venus?
Soon as she saw and knew the mortal wound
Of her Adonis—saw the life-blood flow
From his fair thigh, now wasting,—wailing loud
She clasped him, and cried　　　　　'Stay, Adonis!　　　40
Stay, dearest one,
　　　　　　　　　　　and mix my lips with thine—
Wake yet a while, Adonis—oh, but once,
That I may kiss thee now for the last time—
But for as long as one short kiss may live—　　　45
Oh, let thy breath flow from thy dying soul
Even to my mouth and heart, that I may suck
That ['

30 Ai! ai! *edd.*] Ay ay *BM*　　　31 *omitted in edd. & d. 7; required by the Greek.*
The [rivers] [rills] [streams] change [their harmonious tune and groan] *BM*　　32 *changed from* [The rivers change their streams to tears and weep] *BM*　　35 resounds *changed from* replies *BM*　　39 wailing loud *changed from* [she cried out] *BM*　　43 a while *changed from* [a little while] *BM*

NOTE BY MARY SHELLEY ON THE POEMS OF 1816

SHELLEY wrote little during this year. The poem entitled 'The Sunset' was written in the spring of the year, while still residing at Bishopsgate. He spent the summer on the shores of the Lake of Geneva. The 'Hymn to Intellectual Beauty' was conceived during his voyage round the lake with Lord Byron. He occupied himself during this voyage by reading the *Nouvelle Héloïse* for the first time. The reading it on the very spot where the scenes are laid added to the interest; and he was at once surprised and charmed by the passionate eloquence and earnest enthralling interest that pervade this work. There was something in the character of Saint-Preux, in his abnegation of self, and in the worship he paid to Love, that co-incided with Shelley's own disposition; and, though differing in many of the views and shocked by others, yet the effect of the whole was fascinating and delightful.

'Mont Blanc' was inspired by a view of that mountain and its surround-ing peaks and valleys, as he lingered on the Bridge of Arve on his way through the Valley of Chamouni. Shelley makes the following mention of this poem in his publication of the *History of a Six Weeks' Tour, and Letters from Switzerland*: 'The poem entitled "Mont Blanc" is written by the author of the two letters from Chamouni and Vevai. It was composed under the immediate impression of the deep and powerful feelings excited by the objects which it attempts to describe; and, as an undisci-plined overflowing of the soul, rests its claim to approbation on an attempt to imitate the untamable wildness and inaccessible solemnity from which those feelings sprang.'

This was an eventful year, and less time was given to study than usual. In the list of his reading I find, in Greek, Theocritus, the *Prometheus* of Aeschylus, several of Plutarch's *Lives*, and the works of Lucian. In Latin, Lucretius, Pliny's *Letters*, the *Annals* and *Germany* of Tacitus. In French, the *History of the French Revolution* by Lacretelle. He read for the first time, this year, Montaigne's *Essays*, and regarded them ever after as one of the most delightful and instructive books in the world. The list is scanty in English works: Locke's *Essay*, *Political Justice*, and Coleridge's *Lay Sermon* form nearly the whole. It was his frequent habit to read aloud to me in the evening; in this way we read, this year, the New Testament, *Paradise Lost*, Spenser's *Faerie Queene*, and *Don Quixote*.

LAON AND CYTHNA

OR

THE REVOLUTION OF THE GOLDEN CITY

[Usually known as *The Revolt of Islam*]

1817

LAON AND CYTHNA

OR

THE REVOLUTION OF THE GOLDEN CITY

A Vision of the Nineteenth Century
in the Stanza of Spenser

[Usually known as *The Revolt of Islam*]

1817

"Ὅσαις δὲ βροτὸν ἔθνος ἀγλαΐαις ἁπτόμεσθα
περαίνει πρὸς ἔσχατον
πλόον· ναυσὶ δ᾽ οὔτε πεζὸς ἰὼν ἂν εὕροις
ἐς Ὑπερβορέων ἀγῶνα θαυματὰν ὁδόν.
Pindar, *Pyth. X.*

PREFACE

[1] THE Poem which I now present to the world is an attempt from which I scarcely dare to expect success, and in which a writer of established fame might fail without disgrace. It is an experiment on the temper of the public mind, as to how far a thirst for a happier condition of moral and political society survives, among the enlightened and refined, the tempests which have shaken the age in which we live. I have sought to enlist the harmony of metrical language, the ethereal combinations of the fancy, the rapid and subtle transitions of human passion, all those elements which essentially compose a Poem, in the cause of a liberal and comprehensive

LAON AND CYTHNA. AUTOGRAPH: *a. Fair copy: Preface and parts of Dedication and Canto I, Bod. MS. Shelley D. 3; fragment of Canto IX, Bod. MS. Shelley adds. c. 4; b. Drafts: Bod. MSS. Shelley adds. e. 10, e. 14, e. 19, c. 4; c. Miscellaneous fragments, variously owned. For description of MSS. see Intr., pp. xiv–xviii and nn., pp. 361 ff.* DATE: *See nn., p. 361.* PRINTED: *a. As* Laon and Cythna; or, The Revolution of the Golden City: A Vision of the Nineteenth Century, *PBS, Oct., Nov. 1817 (though postdated '1818'); here called 'LC'; b. slightly revised (see nn., pp. 360–1) as* The Revolt of Islam, *PBS, 10 Jan. 1818; some copies dated '1817'/MWS, 1839¹/1839²/Hutch. 1904; here called 'RI' ('1818' in Textual Commentary indicates that 'RI' does not differ from 'LC'); c. Dedication only: Claude C. Brew, in* Shelley and Mary *in 1817, 1971.* TITLE: *See nn., p. 360.* TEXT: *1971/1904/1839²/1839¹/1818/Shelley's erratum slip in 1818 MSS. Punctuation assisted by Ross. 1870, Loc. 1911. See nn., p. 361.*

morality; and in the view of kindling within the bosoms of my readers a virtuous enthusiasm for those doctrines of liberty and justice, that faith and hope in something good, which neither violence nor misrepresentation nor prejudice can ever totally extinguish among mankind.

[2] For this purpose I have chosen a story of human passion in its most universal character, diversified with moving and romantic adventures, and appealing, in contempt of all artificial opinions or institutions, to the common sympathies of every human breast. I have made no attempt to recommend the motives which I would substitute for those at present governing mankind, by methodical and systematic argument. I would only awaken the feelings, so that the reader should see the beauty of true virtue, and be incited to those inquiries which have led to my moral and political creed, and that of some of the sublimest intellects in the world. The Poem therefore (with the exception of the first canto, which is purely introductory) is narrative, not didactic. It is a succession of pictures illustrating the growth and progress of individual mind aspiring after excellence, and devoted to the love of mankind; its influence in refining and making pure the most daring and uncommon impulses of the imagination, the understanding, and the senses; its impatience at 'all the oppressions which are done under the sun'; its tendency to awaken public hope, and to enlighten and improve mankind; the rapid effects of the application of that tendency; the awakening of an immense nation from their slavery and degradation to a true sense of moral dignity and freedom; the bloodless dethronement of their oppressors, and the unveiling of the religious frauds by which they had been deluded into submission; the tranquillity of successful patriotism, and the universal toleration and benevolence of true philanthropy; the treachery and barbarity of hired soldiers; vice not the object of punishment and hatred, but kindness and pity; the faithlessness of tyrants; the confederacy of the Rulers of the World, and the restoration of the expelled Dynasty by foreign arms; the massacre and extermination of the Patriots, and the victory of established power; the consequences of legitimate despotism,—civil war, famine, plague, superstition, and an utter extinction of the domestic affections; the judicial murder of the advocates of Liberty; the temporary triumph of oppression, that secure earnest of its final and inevitable fall; the transient nature of ignorance and error, and the eternity of genius and virtue. Such is the series of delineations of which the Poem consists. And, if the lofty passions with which it has been my scope to distinguish this story shall not excite in the reader a generous impulse, an ardent thirst for excellence, an interest profound and strong such as belongs to no meaner desires, let not the failure be imputed to a natural unfitness for human sympathy in these sublime and animating themes. It is the business of the Poet to communicate to others the pleasure and the enthusiasm arising out

of those images and feelings in the vivid presence of which within his own mind consists at once his inspiration and his reward.

[3] The panic which, like an epidemic transport, seized upon all classes of men during the excesses consequent upon the French Revolution, is gradually giving place to sanity. It has ceased to be believed that whole generations of mankind ought to consign themselves to a hopeless inheritance of ignorance and misery, because a nation of men who had been dupes and slaves for centuries were incapable of conducting themselves with the wisdom and tranquillity of freemen so soon as some of their fetters were partially loosened. That their conduct could not have been marked by any other characters than ferocity and thoughtlessness is the historical fact from which liberty derives all its recommendations, and falsehood the worst features of its deformity. There is a reflux in the tide of human things which bears the shipwrecked hopes of men into a secure haven after the storms are past. Methinks, those who now live have survived an age of despair.

[4] The French Revolution may be considered as one of those manifestations of a general state of feeling among civilised mankind produced by a defect of correspondence between the knowledge existing in society and the improvement or gradual abolition of political institutions. The year 1788 may be assumed as the epoch of one of the most important crises produced by this feeling. The sympathies connected with that event extended to every bosom. The most generous and amiable natures were those which participated the most extensively in these sympathies. But such a degree of unmingled good was expected as it was impossible to realise. If the Revolution had been in every respect prosperous, then misrule and superstition would lose half their claims to our abhorrence, as fetters which the captive can unlock with the slightest motion of his fingers, and which do not eat with poisonous rust into the soul. The revulsion occasioned by the atrocities of the demagogues, and the re-establishment of successive tyrannies in France, was terrible, and felt in the remotest corner of the civilised world. Could they listen to the plea of reason who had groaned under the calamities of a social state according to the provisions of which one man riots in luxury whilst another famishes for want of bread? Can he who the day before was a trampled slave suddenly become liberal-minded, forbearing, and independent? This is the consequence of the habits of a state of society to be produced by resolute perseverance and indefatigable hope, and long-suffering and long-believing courage, and the systematic efforts of generations of men of intellect and virtue. Such is the lesson which experience teaches now. But, on the first reverses of hope in the progress of French liberty, the sanguine eagerness for good overleaped the solution of these questions, and for a time extinguished itself in the unexpectedness of their result. Thus, many of the

most ardent and tender-hearted of the worshippers of public good have
been morally ruined by what a partial glimpse of the events they deplored
appeared to show as the melancholy desolation of all their cherished
hopes. Hence gloom and misanthropy have become the characteristics of
the age in which we live, the solace of a disappointment that unconsciously
finds relief only in the wilful exaggeration of its own despair. This influ-
ence has tainted the literature of the age with the hoplessness of the minds
from which it flows. Metaphysics,[1] and inquiries into moral and political
science, have become little else than vain attempts to revive exploded
superstitions, or sophisms like those[2] of Mr. Malthus, calculated to lull the
oppressors of mankind into a security of everlasting triumph. Our works
of fiction and poetry have been overshadowed by the same infectious
gloom. But mankind appear to me to be emerging from their trance. I am
aware, methinks, of a slow, gradual, silent change. In that belief I have
composed the following Poem.

[5] I do not presume to enter into competition with our greatest contem-
porary Poets. Yet I am unwilling to tread in the footsteps of any who have
preceded me. I have sought to avoid the imitation of any style of language
or versification peculiar to the original minds of which it is the character;
designing that, even if what I have produced be worthless, it should still
be properly my own. Nor have I permitted any system relating to mere
words to divert the attention of the reader, from whatever interest I may
have succeeded in creating, to my own ingenuity in contriving to disgust
him according to the rules of criticism. I have simply clothed my thoughts
in what appeared to me the most obvious and appropriate language. A
person familiar with nature, and with the most celebrated productions of
the human mind, can scarcely err in following the instinct, with respect to
selection of language, produced by that familiarity.

[6] There is an education peculiarly fitted for a Poet, without which
genius and sensibility can hardly fill the circle of their capacities. No
education, indeed, can entitle to this appellation a dull and unobservant
mind, or one, though neither dull nor unobservant, in which the channels
of communication between thought and expression have been obstructed
or closed. How far it is my fortune to belong to either of the latter classes

Preface. Para. 5 to disgust him] to disgust them *edd. and D. 3*

---

[1] I ought to except Sir W. Drummond's *Academical Questions*; a volume of very
acute and powerful metaphysical criticism.

[2] It is remarkable, as a symptom of the revival of public hope, that Mr. Malthus has
assigned, in the later editions of his work, an indefinite dominion to moral restraint over
the principle of population. This concession answers all the inferences from his doctrine
unfavourable to human improvement, and reduces the *Essay on Population* to a com-
mentary illustrative of the unanswerableness of *Political Justice*.

I cannot know. I aspire to be something better. The circumstances of my accidental education have been favourable to this ambition. I have been familiar from boyhood with mountains and lakes and the sea, and the solitude of forests: Danger, which sports upon the brink of precipices, has been my playmate. I have trodden the glaciers of the Alps, and lived under the eye of Mont Blanc. I have been a wanderer among distant fields. I have sailed down mighty rivers, and seen the sun rise and set, and the stars come forth, whilst I have sailed night and day down a rapid stream among mountains. I have seen populous cities, and have watched the passions which rise and spread, and sink and change, amongst assembled multitudes of men. I have seen the theatre of the more visible ravages of tyranny and war; cities and villages reduced to scattered groups of black and roofless houses, and the naked inhabitants sitting famished upon their desolated thresholds. I have conversed with living men of genius. The poetry of ancient Greece and Rome, and modern Italy, and our own country, has been to me, like external nature, a passion and an enjoyment. Such are the sources from which the materials for the imagery of my Poem have been drawn. I have considered Poetry in its most comprehensive sense; and have read the Poets and the Historians and the Metaphysicians[1] whose writings have been accessible to me, and have looked upon the beautiful and majestic scenery of the earth, as common sources of those elements which it is the province of the Poet to embody and combine. Yet the experience and the feelings to which I refer do not in themselves constitute men Poets, but only prepares them to be the auditors of those who are. How far I shall be found to possess that more essential attribute of Poetry, the power of awakening in others sensations like those which animate my own bosom, is that which, to speak sincerely, I know not; and which, with an acquiescent and contented spirit, I expect to be taught by the effect which I shall produce upon those whom I now address.

[7] I have avoided, as I have said before, the imitation of any contemporary style. But there must be a resemblance, which does not depend upon their own will, between all the writers of any particular age. They cannot escape from subjection to a common influence which arises out of an infinite combination of circumstances belonging to the times in which they live; though each is in a degree the author of the very influence by which his being is thus pervaded. Thus, the tragic poets of the age of Pericles; the Italian revivers of ancient learning; those mighty intellects of our own country that succeeded the Reformation, the translators of the Bible, Shakespeare, Spenser, the dramatists of the reign of Elizabeth,

---

[1] In this sense there may be such a thing as perfectibility in works of fiction, notwithstanding the concession often made by the advocates of human improvement, that perfectibility is a term applicable only to science.

and Lord Bacon;[1] the colder spirits of the interval that succeeded;—all
resemble each other, and differ from every other in their several classes.
In this view of things, Ford can no more be called the imitator of Shake-
speare than Shakespeare the imitator of Ford. There were perhaps few
other points of resemblance between these two men than that which the
universal and inevitable influence of their age produced. And this is an
influence which neither the meanest scribbler nor the sublimest genius
of any era can escape; and which I have not attempted to escape.

[8] I have adopted the stanza of Spenser (a measure inexpressibly beauti-
ful), not because I consider it a finer model of poetical harmony than
the blank verse of Shakespeare and Milton, but because in the latter
there is no shelter for mediocrity; you must either succeed or fail. This
perhaps an aspiring spirit should desire. But I was enticed also by the
brilliancy and magnificence of sound which a mind that has been nourished
upon musical thoughts can produce by a just and harmonious arrange-
ment of the pauses of this measure. Yet there will be found some instances
where I have completely failed in this attempt; and one, which I here
request the reader to consider as an erratum, where there is left, most
inadvertently, an alexandrine in the middle of a stanza.

[9] But in this as in every other respect I have written fearlessly. It is the
misfortune of this age that its Writers, too thoughtless of immortality,
are exquisitely sensible to temporary praise or blame. They write with
the fear of Reviews before their eyes. This system of criticism sprang up
in that torpid interval when Poetry was not. Poetry, and the art which
professes to regulate and limit its powers, cannot subsist together. Lon-
ginus could not have been the contemporary of Homer, nor Boileau
of Horace. Yet this species of criticism never presumed to assert an under-
standing of its own: it has always, unlike true science, followed, not
preceded, the opinion of mankind, and would even now bribe with worth-
less adulation some of our greatest Poets to impose gratuitous fetters on
their own imaginations, and become unconscious accomplices in the
daily murder of all genius either not so aspiring or not so fortunate as
their own. I have sought therefore to write, as I believe that Homer,
Shakespeare, and Milton, wrote, with an utter disregard of anonymous
censure. I am certain that calumny and misrepresentation, though it may
move me to compassion, cannot disturb my peace. I shall understand the
expressive silence of those sagacious enemies who dare not trust them-
selves to speak. I shall endeavour to extract, from the midst of insult and
contempt and maledictions, those admonitions which may tend to correct
whatever imperfections such censurers may discover in this my first
serious appeal to the Public. If certain Critics were as clear-sighted as

---

[1] Milton stands alone in the age which he illumined.

they are malignant, how great would be the benefit to be derived from their virulent writings! As it is, I fear I shall be malicious enough to be amused with their paltry tricks and lame invectives. Should the Public judge that my composition is worthless, I shall indeed bow before the tribunal from which Milton received his crown of immortality; and shall seek to gather, if I live, strength from that defeat, which may nerve me to some new enterprise of thought which may *not* be worthless. I cannot conceive that Lucretius, when he meditated that poem whose doctrines are yet the basis of our metaphysical knowledge, and whose eloquence has been the wonder of mankind, wrote in awe of such censure as the hired sophists of the impure and superstitious noblemen of Rome might affix to what he should produce. It was at the period when Greece was led captive, and Asia made tributary to the Republic, fast verging itself to slavery and ruin, that a multitude of Syrian captives, bigoted to the worship of their obscene Ashtaroth, and the unworthy successors of Socrates and Zeno, found there a precarious subsistence by administering, under the name of freedmen, to the vices and vanities of the great. These wretched men were skilled to plead, with a superficial but plausible set of sophisms, in favour of that contempt for virtue which is the portion of slaves, and that faith in portents, the most fatal substitute for benevolence in the imaginations of men, which, arising from the enslaved communities of the East, then first began to overwhelm the western nations in its stream. Were these the kind of men whose disapprobation the wise and lofty-minded Lucretius should have regarded with a salutary awe? The latest and perhaps the meanest of those who follow in his footsteps would disdain to hold life on such conditions.

[10] The Poem now presented to the Public occupied little more than six months in the composition. That period has been devoted to the task with unremitting ardour and enthusiasm. I have exercised a watchful and earnest criticism on my work as it grew under my hands. I would willingly have sent it forth to the world with that perfection which long labour and revision is said to bestow. But I found that, if I should gain something in exactness by this method, I might lose much of the newness and energy of imagery and language as it flowed fresh from my mind. And, although the mere composition occupied no more than six months, the thoughts thus arranged were slowly gathered in as many years.

[11] I trust that the reader will carefully distinguish between those opinions which have a dramatic propriety in reference to the characters which they are designed to elucidate, and such as are properly my own. The erroneous and degrading idea which men have conceived of a Supreme Being, for instance, is spoken against, but not the Supreme Being itself. The belief which some superstitious persons whom I have brought upon the stage entertain of the Deity, as injurious to the character of his

benevolence, is widely different from my own. In recommending also a great and important change in the spirit which animates the social institutions of mankind, I have avoided all flattery to those violent and malignant passions of our nature which are ever on the watch to mingle with and to alloy the most beneficial innovations. There is no quarter given to Revenge, or Envy, or Prejudice. Love is celebrated everywhere as the sole law which should govern the moral world.

[12] In the personal conduct of my Hero and Heroine, there is one circumstance which was intended to startle the reader from the trance of ordinary life. It was my object to break through the crust of those outworn opinions on which established institutions depend. I have appealed therefore to the most universal of all feelings, and have endeavoured to strengthen the moral sense, by forbidding it to waste its energies in seeking to avoid actions which are only crimes of convention. It is because there is so great a multitude of artificial vices that there are so few real virtues. Those feelings alone which are benevolent or malevolent, are essentially good or bad. The circumstance of which I speak was introduced, however, merely to accustom men to that charity and toleration which the exhibition of a practice widely differing from their own has a tendency to promote.[1] Nothing indeed can be more mischievous than many actions, innocent in themselves, which might bring down upon individuals the bigoted contempt and rage of the multitude.

  [1] The sentiments connected with and characteristic of this circumstance have no personal reference to the Writer.—[Shelley's Note.]

  Para. 12 *omitted in RI*

DEDICATION

There is no danger to a man, that knows
What life and death is: there's not any law
Exceeds his knowledge; neither is it lawful
That he should stoop to any other law.—CHAPMAN.

To Mary [Wollstonecraft] [Shelley]

I

So now my summer task is ended, Mary,
    And I return to thee, mine own heart's home;
As to his Queen some victor Knight of Faëry,
    Earning bright spoils for her enchanted dome;
    Nor thou disdain, that ere my fame become   5

A star among the stars of mortal night,
 If it indeed may cleave its natal gloom,
 Its doubtful promise thus I would unite
With thy belovèd name, thou Child of love and light.

II

The toil which stole from thee so many an hour,   10
 Is ended,—and the fruit is at thy feet!
No longer where the woods to frame a bower
 With interlacèd branches mix and meet,
 Or where with sound like many voices sweet,
Waterfalls leap among wild islands green,   15
 Which framed for my lone boat a lone retreat
Of moss-grown trees and weeds, shall I be seen:
But beside thee, where still my heart has ever been.

III

Thoughts of great deeds were mine, dear Friend, when first
 The clouds which wrap this world from youth did pass. 20
I do remember well the hour which burst
 My spirit's sleep: a fresh May-dawn it was,
 When I walked forth upon the glittering grass,
And wept, I knew not why; until there rose
 From the near schoolroom, voices, that, alas!   25
Were but one echo from a world of woes—
The harsh and grating strife of tyrants and of foes.

IV

And then I clasped my hands and looked around;
 But none was near to mock my streaming eyes,
Which poured their warm drops on the sunny ground;   30
 So, without shame, I spake:—'I will be wise,
 And just, and free, and mild, if in me lies

Dedication. 8 I dedicate to thee whate'er is light *e. 14* 8–9 In future hope *e. 14*
9 belovèd *edd.; underlined in e. 14* love *edd.*] Love *e. 14* 10–18 *II. See*
p. 265, 'Rejected Passages', 1–5. 12–13 [High in the Heavens above are wild-
some] *e. 14* 16 a lone retreat *edd.*] a *caret* retreat *e. 14* 19–27 *III.*
See pp. 265–6, 'Rejected Passages', 6–22. 19–36 *III–IV. See pp. 266–7, 'Rejected
Passages', 23–41.* 21 I do remember well *edd.*] And I remember *e. 14*
22 sleep: *edd.*] sleep; . . . *e. 14. See n., p. 363.* May-dawn *edd.*] May morn *e. 14*
27 grating strife *edd.*] mingled din *e. 14* 28 around;] around— *1971, 1904, 1818*
around, *1839* 30 ground;] ground— *edd.* 31 spake *edd.*] spoke *e. 14*
32 just, and free *edd.*] good, and just *e. 14*

Such power, for I grow weary to behold
The selfish and the strong still tyrannize
Without reproach or check.' I then controlled   35
My tears, my heart grew calm, and I was meek and bold.

                              V

And from that hour did I with earnest thought
   Heap knowledge from forbidden mines of lore,
Yet nothing that my tyrants knew or taught
   I cared to learn, but from that secret store   40
   Wrought linkèd armour for my soul, before
It might walk forth to war among mankind;
   Thus power and hope were strengthened more and more
Within me, till there came upon my mind
A sense of loneliness, a thirst with which I pined.   45

                             VI

Alas, that love should be a blight and snare
   To those who seek all sympathies in one!—
Such once I sought in vain; then black despair,
   The shadow of a starless night, was thrown
   Over the world in which I moved alone:—   50
Yet never found I one not false to me,
   Hard hearts, and cold, like weights of icy stone
Which crushed and withered mine—that could not be
Aught but a lifeless clod, until revived by thee.

                            VII

Thou Friend, whose presence on my wintry heart   55
   Fell, like bright Spring upon some herbless plain;
How beautiful and calm and free thou wert
   In thy young wisdom, when the mortal chain
   Of Custom thou didst burst and rend in twain,

44–5 *V. See p. 267,* '*Rejected Passages*', *42–3.*   46–54 *VI. See p. 267,* '*Rejected
Passages*', *44–51.*   46 snare *edd.*] snare, *e. 14*   48 vain; *edd.*] vain. *e. 14*
53 Which . . . that *edd.*] That . . . [Which] *e. 14*   54 clod *1971, 1904*] clog
1839, 1818. See n., p. 364.   54–5 [Thou who like spring upon the herbless
changed to wintry earth Didst suddenly descend] *e. 14*   53 mine—] mine *edd.*
55 Friend *1818*] friend *e. 14*   56 plain *edd.*] plains *e. 14*

And walk as free as light the clouds among, 60
    Which many an envious slave then breathed in vain
From his dim dungeon; and my spirit sprung
To meet thee from the woes which had begirt it long!

VIII

No more alone through the world's wilderness,
    Although I trod the paths of high intent, 65
I journeyed now: no more companionless,
    Where solitude is like despair, I went.—
There is the wisdom of a stern content
When Poverty can blight the just and good,
    When Infamy dares mock the innocent, 70
And cherished friends turn with the multitude
To trample: this was ours, and we unshaken stood!

IX

Now has descended a serener hour,
    And with inconstant fortune, friends return;
Though suffering leaves the knowledge and the power 75
    Which says 'Let scorn be not repaid with scorn.'
And from thy side two gentle babes are born
To fill our home with smiles, and thus are we
    Most fortunate beneath life's beaming morn;
And these delights, and thou, have been to me 80
The parents of the Song I consecrate to thee.

X

Is it, that now my inexperienced fingers
    But strike the prelude of a loftier strain?
Or, must the lyre on which my spirit lingers
    Soon pause in silence, ne'er to sound again, 85
    Though it might shake the Anarch Custom's reign,

---

60 walk] walked *edd. & e. 10*   62 dungeon;] dungeon, *edd.*   63 long!
1904] long *other edd.; unpunctuated in e. 14*   63–4 And so the youthful foe of
tyranny *e. 14*   64 No more alone *edd.*] Thus not in [fear] *e. 14*   65 paths of high
edd.] path of one sublime *e. 14*   67 Where *edd.*] When *e. 14*   68 stern *edd.*]
high *e. 14*   69 can blight *edd.*] doth blast *above* [did blight] *e. 14*   70 dares
edd.] can *e. 14*   72 trample: *edd.*] trample,; *e. 14. Cf. line 22 and n., p. 363.*   ours,
edd.] ours;. *e. 14*   81 Song *edd.; changed from* [Work] *in e. 14*   83 strike *edd.*]
wake *e. 14*   86 [Tho it might charm the slave to burst his chain] *e. 14*

And charm the minds of men to Truth's own sway
   Holier than was Amphion's? I would fain
Reply in hope—but I am worn away,
And Death and Love are yet contending for their prey.   90

XI

And what art thou? I know, but dare not speak:
   Time may interpret to his silent years.
Yet in the paleness of thy thoughtful cheek,
   And in the light thine ample forehead wears,
   And in thy sweetest smiles, and in thy tears,   95
And in thy gentle speech, a prophecy
   Is whispered, to subdue my fondest fears:
And through thine eyes, even in thy soul I see
A lamp of vestal fire burning internally.

XII

They say that thou wert lovely from thy birth,   100
   Of glorious parents, thou aspiring Child.
I wonder not—for One then left this earth
   Whose life was like a setting planet mild,
   Which clothed thee in the radiance undefiled
Of its departing glory; still her fame   105
   Shines on thee, through the tempests dark and wild
Which shake these latter days; and thou canst claim
The shelter, from thy Sire, of an immortal name.

XIII

One voice came forth from many a mighty spirit,
   Which was the echo of three thousand years;   110
And the tumultuous world stood mute to hear it,
   As some lone man who in a desert hears
   The music of his home:—unwonted fears

87 [And by Truths Loves] *e. 14*   89 worn away *edd.*] frail and *minus rhyme-word e. 14*   92 his silent *edd.*] his silent *below* [his listening] *below* [a thousand] *below* [the listening] *e. 14*   93 paleness *edd.; changed from* [silence] *e. 14*   97 whispered *edd.*] spoken *e. 14*   99 vestal *edd.*] [silent] *below* [vestal] *e. 14*   102 earth *edd.*] Earth *e. 14*   103 [Whose fame is as a star serene and mild] *e. 14*   103–4 [brightening as darkness deepened] *e. 14*   109–17 XIII. See *p. 267*, '*Rejected Passages*', 52–9.
109 A voice went forth from that unshaken Spirit *e. 14*   112 in a desert *edd.*] on a sudden *e. 14*

Fell on the pale oppressors of our race,
   And Faith, and Custom, and low-thoughted cares,   115
Like thunder-stricken dragons, for a space
Left the torn human heart, their food and dwelling-place.

XIV

Truth's deathless voice pauses among mankind!
   If there must be no response to my cry—
If men must rise and stamp with fury blind   120
   On his pure name who loves them,—thou and I,
Sweet friend! can look from our tranquillity
Like lamps into the world's tempestuous night,—
   Two tranquil stars, while clouds are passing by
Which wrap them from the foundering seaman's sight,   125
That burn from year to year with unextinguished light.

CANTO I

I

WHEN the last hope of trampled France had failed
   Like a brief dream of unremaining glory,
From visions of despair I rose, and scaled
   The peak of an aëreal promontory,   130
   Whose caverned base with the vexed surge was hoary;
And saw the golden dawn break forth, and waken
   Each cloud, and every wave:—but transitory
The calm: for sudden, the firm earth was shaken,
As if by the last wreck its frame were overtaken.   135

II

So as I stood, one blast of muttering thunder
   Burst in far peals along the waveless deep,
When, gathering fast, around, above, and under,

114-15 [And] [The free leapt forth in joy] *e. 14*   115-16 [Fled from a thousand hearts and found no] *e. 14*   117 Left the deep human heart which is their dwelling place *e. 14*   118-26 *XIV. See p. 267, 'Rejected Passages', 60-7.*

   Canto I. 127 *For the opening of Canto I as first drafted in e. 19 see 'Rejected Passages' 1-72, pp. 268-70, below. Preceding these come a. an excerpt of French prose; b. an embryonic draft of lines 268-70, roughly repeated in c. 4; c. an extraneous prose memorandum followed by a broken fragment of extraneous verse; d. an editorial query by MWS.; e. a four-word memorandum by Shelley. See n., pp. 364-5.*   136 muttering *changed from* [smothered] *e. 19*

Long trains of tremulous mist began to creep,
Until their complicating lines did steep   140
The orient sun in shadow:—not a sound
Was heard; one horrible repose did keep
The forests and the floods, and all around
Darkness more dread than night was poured upon the ground.

III

Hark! 'tis the rushing of a wind that sweeps   145
Earth and the ocean. See! the lightnings yawn
Deluging Heaven with fire, and the lashed deeps
Glitter and boil beneath: it rages on,
One mighty stream, whirlwind and waves upthrown,
Lightning, and hail, and darkness eddying by.   150
There is a pause—the sea-birds, that were gone
Into their caves to shriek, come forth, to spy
What calm has fall'n on earth, what light is in the sky.

IV

For, where the irresistible storm had cloven
That fearful darkness, the blue sky was seen   155
Fretted with many a fair cloud interwoven
Most delicately, and the ocean green,
Beneath that opening spot of blue serene,
Quivered like burning emerald: calm was spread
On all below; but far on high, between   160
Earth and the upper air, the vast clouds fled,
Countless and swift as leaves on autumn's tempest shed.

V

For ever, as the war became more fierce
Between the whirlwinds and the rack on high,
That spot grew more serene; blue light did pierce   165
That woof of those white clouds, which seemed to lie
Far, deep, and motionless; while through the sky

162-3 *For lines drafted to follow here see p. 270,* 'Rejected Passages', *73–81.*
164 rack *changed from* [mists] *e. 19*

The pallid semicircle of the moon
   Passed on, in slow and moving majesty;
Its upper horn arrayed in mists, which soon   170
But slowly fled, like dew beneath the beams of noon.

VI

I could not choose but gaze; a fascination
   Dwelt in that moon, and sky, and clouds, which drew
My fancy thither, and in expectation
   Of what I knew not, I remained:—the hue   175
   Of the white moon, amid that heaven so blue,
Suddenly stained with shadow did appear;
   A speck, a cloud, a shape, approaching grew,
Like a great ship in the sun's sinking sphere
Beheld afar at sea, and swift it came anear.   180

VII

Even like a bark, which from a chasm of mountains,
   Dark, vast, and overhanging, on a river
Which there collects the strength of all its fountains,
   Comes forth, whilst with the speed its frame doth quiver,
   Sails, oars, and stream, tending to one endeavour;   185
So, from that chasm of light a wingèd Form
   On all the winds of heaven approaching ever
Floated, dilating as it came: the storm
Pursued it with fierce blasts, and lightnings swift and warm.

VIII

A course precipitous, of dizzy speed,   190
   Suspending thought and breath; a monstrous sight!
For in the air do I behold indeed
   An Eagle and a Serpent wreathed in fight:—
   And now relaxing its impetuous flight,
Before the aëreal rock on which I stood,   195
   The Eagle, hovering, wheeled to left and right,
And hung with lingering wings over the flood,
And startled with its yells the wide air's solitude.

IX

A shaft of light upon its wings descended,
  And every golden feather gleamed therein—   200
Feather and scale, inextricably blended.
  The Serpent's mailed and many-coloured skin
  Shone through the plumes its coils were twined within
By many a swoln and knotted fold, and high
  And far, the neck, receding lithe and thin,   205
Sustained a crested head, which warily
Shifted and glanced before the Eagle's steadfast eye.

X

Around, around, in ceaseless circles wheeling
  With clang of wings and scream, the Eagle sailed
Incessantly—sometimes on high concealing   210
  Its lessening orbs, sometimes as if it failed,
  Drooped through the air; and still it shrieked and wailed,
And casting back its eager head, with beak
  And talon unremittingly assailed
The wreathèd Serpent, who did ever seek   215
Upon his enemy's heart a mortal wound to wreak.

XI

What life, what power, was kindled and arose
  Within the sphere of that appalling fray!
For, from the encounter of those wondrous foes,
  A vapour like the sea's suspended spray   220
  Hung gathered: in the void air, far away,
Floated the shattered plumes; bright scales did leap,
  Where'er the Eagle's talons made their way,
Like sparks into the darkness;—as they sweep,
Blood stains the snowy foam of the tumultuous deep.   225

XII

Swift chances in that combat—many a check,
  And many a change, a dark and wild turmoil;
Sometimes the Snake around his enemy's neck

201 scale, *1904*] scale *1839, 1818*   203 plumes *1904, 1818*] plume; *1839*
205 neck, *1904*] neck *1839, 1818*   217 What life, what power, *1904, 1839*] What
life what power *1818*

Locked in stiff rings his adamantine coil,
Until the Eagle, faint with pain and toil,   230
Remitted his strong flight, and near the sea
Languidly fluttered, hopeless so to foil
His adversary, who then reared on high
His red and burning crest, radiant with victory.

XIII

Then on the white edge of the bursting surge,   235
Where they had sunk together, would the Snake
Relax his suffocating grasp, and scourge
The wind with his wild writhings; for to break
That chain of torment, the vast bird would shake
The strength of his unconquerable wings   240
As in despair, and with his sinewy neck,
Dissolve in sudden shock those linkèd rings,
Then soar—as swift as smoke from a volcano springs.

XIV

Wile baffled wile, and strength encountered strength,
Thus long, but unprevailing:—the event   245
Of that portentous fight appeared at length:
Until the lamp of day was almost spent
It had endured, when lifeless, stark, and rent,
Hung high that mighty Serpent, and at last
Fell to the sea, while o'er the continent,   250
With clang of wings and scream the Eagle passed,
Heavily borne away on the exhausted blast.

XV

And with it fled the tempest, so that ocean
And earth and sky shone through the atmosphere—
Only, 'twas strange to see the red commotion   255
Of waves like mountains o'er the sinking sphere
Of sunset sweep, and their fierce roar to hear
Amid the calm; down the steep path I wound
To the sea-shore—the evening was most clear

And beautiful, and there the sea I found   260
Calm as a cradled child in dreamless slumber bound.

XVI

There was a Woman, beautiful as morning,
    Sitting beneath the rocks, upon the sand
Of the waste sea—fair as one flower adorning
    An icy wilderness; each delicate hand   265
    Lay crossed upon her bosom, and the band
Of her dark hair had fall'n, and so she sate
    Looking upon the waves; on the bare strand
Upon the sea-mark a small boat did wait,
Fair as herself, like Love by Hope left desolate.   270

XVII

It seemed that this fair Shape had looked upon
    That unimaginable fight, and now
That her sweet eyes were weary of the sun,
    As brightly it illustrated her woe;
    For in the tears which silently to flow   275
Paused not, its lustre hung: she watching aye
    The foam-wreaths which the faint tide wove below
Upon the spangled sands, groaned heavily,
And after every groan looked up over the sea.

XVIII

And when she saw the wounded Serpent make   280
    His path between the waves, her lips grew pale,
Parted, and quivered; the tears ceased to break
    From her immovable eyes; no voice of wail
    Escaped her; but she rose, and on the gale
Loosening her star-bright robe and shadowy hair   285
    Poured forth her voice; the caverns of the vale
That opened to the ocean, caught it there,
And filled with silver sounds the overflowing air.

261-70 *Hereabouts, in the draft (e. 19), are memoranda and four lines of extraneous
verse, too broken for transcription. See n., p. 365.*   265 wilderness;] wilderness— *edd.*

XIX

She spake in language whose strange melody
  Might not belong to earth. I heard, alone,   290
What made its music more melodious be,
    The pity and the love of every tone;
    But to the Snake those accents sweet were known
His native tongue and hers; nor did he beat
    The hoar spray idly then, but winding on   295
Through the green shadows of the waves that meet
Near to the shore, did pause beside her snowy feet.

XX

Then on the sands the Woman sate again,
  And wept and clasped her hands, and all between,
Renewed the unintelligible strain   300
    Of her melodious voice and eloquent mien;
    And she unveiled her bosom, and the green
And glancing shadows of the sea did play
    O'er its marmoreal depth:—one moment seen,
For ere the next, the Serpent did obey   305
Her voice, and, coiled in rest in her embrace it lay.

XXI

Then she arose, and smiled on me with eyes
  Serene yet sorrowing, like that planet fair,
While yet the daylight lingereth in the skies
    Which cleaves with arrowy beams the dark-red air,   310
    And said: 'To grieve is wise, but the despair
Was weak and vain which led thee here from sleep:
    This shalt thou know, and more, if thou dost dare
With me and with this Serpent, o'er the deep,
A voyage divine and strange, companionship to keep.'   315

XXII

Her voice was like the wildest, saddest tone,
  Yet sweet, of some loved voice heard long ago.
I wept. 'Shall this fair woman all alone,
  Over the sea with that fierce Serpent go?

307–15 *Above Stanza XXI in e. 19 the words* Demon Lover. *See n., p. 365.*

His head is on her heart, and who can know   320
How soon he may devour his feeble prey?'—
Such were my thoughts, when the tide gan to flow;
And that strange boat like the moon's shade did sway
Amid reflected stars that in the waters lay:—

XXIII

A boat of rare device, which had no sail   325
    But its own curvèd prow of thin moonstone,
Wrought like a web of texture fine and frail,
    To catch those gentlest winds which are not known
    To breathe, but by the steady speed alone
With which it cleaves the sparkling sea; and now   330
    We are embarked—the mountains hang and frown
Over the starry deep that gleams below,
A vast and dim expanse, as o'er the waves we go.

XXIV

And as we sailed, a strange and awful tale
    That Woman told, like such mysterious dream   335
As makes the slumberer's cheek with wonder pale!
    'Twas midnight, and around, a shoreless stream,
    Wide ocean rolled, when that majestic theme
Shrined in her heart found utterance, and she bent
    Her looks on mine; those eyes a kindling beam   340
Of love divine into my spirit sent,
And ere her lips could move, made the air eloquent.

XXV

'Speak not to me, but hear! Much shalt thou learn,
    Much must remain unthought, and more untold,
In the dark Future's ever-flowing urn: 345
    Know then that from the depth of ages old
    Two Powers o'er mortal things dominion hold

323 boat *1904*] boat, *1839, 1818*   324 lay:— *1904*] lay. *1839, 1818*   331–3 *For
punctuation and meaning see n., p. 365.*   331 embarked— *1904, D. 3*] embarked,
1839, 1818   332 below, *1904*] below *1839, 1818*   343 Speak . . . hear *edd.*] List,
Stranger, list O list! *D. 3*   345 *Followed in e. 19 by a memorandum and two frag-
ments of extraneous verse. See n., pp. 365–6.*   346 then *D. 3*] then, *edd.*   old *D. 3*]
old, *edd.*

Ruling the world with a divided lot,
  Immortal, all-pervading, manifold,
Twin Genii, equal Gods—when life and thought   350
Sprang forth, they burst the womb of inessential Nought.

XXVI

'The earliest dweller of the world, alone,
  Stood on the verge of chaos. Lo! afar
O'er the wide wild abyss two meteors shone,
  Sprung from the depth of its tempestuous jar: 355
  A blood-red Comet and the Morning Star
Mingling their beams in combat. As he stood,
  All thoughts within his mind waged mutual war,
In dreadful sympathy; when to the flood
That fair Star fell, he turned and shed his brother's blood.

XXVII

'Thus evil triumphed, and the Spirit of evil,   361
  One Power of many shapes which none may know,
One Shape of many names; the Fiend did revel
  In victory, reigning o'er a world of woe,
  For the new race of man went to and fro,   365
Famished and homeless, loathed and loathing, wild,
  And hating good—for his immortal foe
He changed from starry shape, beauteous and mild,
To a dire Snake, with man and beast unreconciled.

XXVIII

'The darkness lingering o'er the dawn of things,   370
  Was Evil's breath and life; this made him strong
To soar aloft with overshadowing wings;
  And the great Spirit of Good did creep among
  The nations of mankind, and every tongue
Cursed, and blasphemed him as he passed; for none   375
  Knew good from evil, though their names were hung
In mockery o'er the fane where many a groan,
As King, and Lord, and God, the conquering Fiend did own,—

357 combat. As] combat—as *edd.*, D. 3   359 sympathy; when] sympathy—when
edd., D. 3.   367 foe] foe, *1904, 1839, 1818*   375 Cursed, *1818*] Cursed *1904, 1839*
378 own,— *1904*] own. *1839, 1818*   own D. 3

XXIX

'The Fiend, whose name was Legion; Death, Decay,
 Earthquake and Blight, and Want, and Madness pale,
Wingèd and wan diseases, an array   381
  Numerous as leaves that strew the autumnal gale;
  Poison, a snake in flowers, beneath the veil
Of food and mirth hiding his mortal head;
  And, without whom all these might nought avail, 385
Fear, Hatred, Faith, and Tyranny, who spread
Those subtle nets which snare the living and the dead.

XXX

'His spirit is their power, and they, his slaves
 In air, and light, and thought, and language, dwell;
And keep their state from palaces to graves,   390
  In all resorts of men—invisible
  But when, in ebon mirror, Nightmare fell
To tyrant or impostor bids them rise—
  Black-wingèd demon forms, whom, from the hell,
His reign and dwelling beneath nether skies,   395
He loosens to their dark and blasting ministries.

XXXI

'In the world's youth his empire was as firm
 As its foundations . . . Soon, the Spirit of Good,
Though in the likeness of a loathsome worm,
  Sprang from the billows of the formless flood, 400
  Which shrank and fled; and with that Fiend of blood
Renewed the doubtful war . . . Thrones then first shook,
  And earth's immense and trampled multitude
In hope on their own powers began to look,
And Fear, the demon pale, his sanguine shrine forsook. 405

XXXII

'Then Greece arose, and to its bards and sages,
 In dream, the golden-pinioned Genii came,
 Even where they slept amid the night of ages,

384 mirth *1904, D. 3*] mirth, *1839, 1818* 388 they, *D. 3*] they *edd.* 391 men—]
men, *edd.*   393 rise—] rise, *edd.*, rise *D. 3*   394 forms,] forms— *edd.*,
D. 3   397–402 *I follow Hutch. and Loc. in accepting from D. 3 Shelley's dotted
suspension points, replaced in most edd. by dashes. See n., pp. 366–7.* 398 Soon, *1818*,
D. 3] Soon *1904, 1839* 403 multitude *1904, D. 3*] multitude, *1839, 1818*

Steeping their hearts in the divinest flame
Which thy breath kindled, Power of holiest name!   410
And oft in cycles since, when darkness gave
New weapons to thy foe, their sunlike fame
Upon the combat shone—a light to save,
Like Paradise spread forth beyond the shadowy grave.

XXXIII

'Such is this conflict—when mankind doth strive   415
With its oppressors in a strife of blood,
Or when free thoughts, like lightnings, are alive,
And in each bosom of the multitude
Justice and truth with Custom's hydra brood
Wage silent war; when Priests and Kings dissemble   420
In smiles or frowns their fierce disquietude,
When round pure hearts a host of hopes assemble,
The Snake and Eagle meet—the world's foundations tremble!

XXXIV

'Thou hast beheld that fight—when to thy home
Thou dost return, steep not its hearth in tears;   425
Though thou may'st hear that earth is now become
The tyrant's garbage, which to his compeers,
The vile reward of their dishonoured years,
He will dividing give.—The victor Fiend,
Omnipotent of yore, now quails, and fears   430
His triumph dearly won, which soon will lend
An impulse swift and sure to his approaching end.

XXXV

'List, stranger, list, mine is an human form,
Like that thou wearest—touch me—shrink not now!
My hand thou feel'st is not a ghost's, but warm   435
With human blood.—'Twas many years ago,
Since first my thirsting soul aspired to know
The secrets of this wondrous world, when deep

409 flame *1904*] flame, *1839, 1818*   417 lightnings, *1904, 1839*] lightnings *1818*
419 truth *1904*] truth, *1839, 1818*   brood *1904*] brood, *1839, 1818*   422 hearts
1904] hearts, *1839, 1818*   429 Fiend, *1904*] Fiend *1839, 1818*

My heart was pierced with sympathy for woe
Which could not be mine own—and thought did keep,
In dream, unnatural watch beside an infant's sleep.   441

XXXVI

'Woe could not be mine own, since far from men
I dwelt, a free and happy orphan child,
By the sea-shore, in a deep mountain-glen;
And near the waves, and through the forests wild,   445
I roamed, to storm and darkness reconciled:
For I was calm while tempest shook the sky:
But when the breathless heavens in beauty smiled,
I wept, sweet tears, yet too tumultuously
For peace, and clasped my hands aloft in ecstasy.   450

XXXVII

'These were forebodings of my fate—before
A woman's heart beat in my virgin breast
It had been nurtured in divinest lore:
A dying poet gave me books, and blessed
With wild but holy talk the sweet unrest   455
In which I watched him as he died away—
A youth with hoary hair—a fleeting guest
Of our lone mountains: and this lore did sway
My spirit like a storm, contending there alway.

XXXVIII

'Thus the dark tale which history doth unfold   460
I knew, but not, methinks, as others know,
For they weep not; and Wisdom had unrolled
The clouds which hide the gulf of mortal woe,—
To few can she that warning vision show—
For I loved all things with intense devotion;   465
So that, when Hope's deep source in fullest flow,
Like earthquake, did uplift the stagnant ocean
Of human thoughts, mine shook beneath the wide commotion.

439 sympathy] sympathy, *edd.*   440 keep, *1904*] keep *1839, 1818*   449 wept,
1818 and edd.] wept *D. 3*   452 breast *D. 3*] breast, *edd.*   458 mountains: *1904*]
mountains— *1839, 1818*   460 unfold *1904*] unfold, *1839, 1818*   463 woe,—
1904] woe: *1839, 1818*   464 show— *1904*] show, *1839, 1818*   466 that,] that
edd., D. 3   468 thoughts,] thoughts—*edd., D. 3*   commotion *D. 3*] emotion *edd.*

XXXIX

'When first the living blood through all these veins
  Kindled a thought in sense, great France sprang forth,
And seized, as if to break, the ponderous chains   471
  Which bind in woe the nations of the earth.
  I saw, and started from my cottage-hearth;
And to the clouds and waves in tameless gladness
  Shrieked, till they caught immeasurable mirth,   475
And laughed in light and music: soon, sweet madness
Was poured upon my heart, a soft and thrilling sadness.

XL

'Deep slumber fell on me:—my dreams were fire—
  Soft and delightful thoughts did rest and hover
Like shadows o'er my brain; and strange desire,   480
  The tempest of a passion, raging over
  My tranquil soul, its depths with light did cover,—
Which passed; and calm, and darkness, sweeter far,
  Came—then I loved; but not a human lover!
For when I rose from sleep, the Morning Star   485
Shone through the woodbine-wreaths which round my case-
    ment were.

XLI

''Twas like an eye which seemed to smile on me.
  I watched, till by the sun made pale, it sank
Under the billows of the heaving sea;
  But from its beams deep love my spirit drank,   490
  And to my brain the boundless world now shrank
Into one thought—one image—yes, for ever!
  Even like the dayspring, poured on vapours dank,
The beams of that one Star did shoot and quiver
Through my benighted mind—and were extinguished never.

XLII

'The day passed thus: at night, methought in dream   496
  A shape of speechless beauty did appear:
It stood like light on a careering stream

---

474 gladness *1839, 1818 D.3*] gladness, *1904*   475 mirth,] mirth— *edd.*   mirth
D. 3   478 fire— *1904, D. 3*] fire, *1839, 1818*   482 cover,— *1904*] cover, *1839,*
1818   483 far, *1904*] far *1839, 1818*

Of golden clouds which shook the atmosphere;—
A wingèd youth, his radiant brow did wear   500
The Morning Star: a wild dissolving bliss
Over my frame he breathed, approaching near,
And bent his eyes of kindling tenderness
Near mine, and on my lips impressed a lingering kiss,

XLIII

'And said: "A Spirit loves thee, mortal maiden: 505
How wilt thou prove thy worth?" Then joy and sleep
Together fled, my soul was deeply laden,
And to the shore I went to muse and weep;
But as I moved, over my heart did creep
A joy less soft, but more profound and strong   510
Than my sweet dream; and it forbade to keep
The path of the sea-shore: that Spirit's tongue
Seemed whispering in my heart, and bore my steps along.

XLIV

'How, to that vast and peopled city led,
Which was a field of holy warfare then,   515
I walked among the dying and the dead,
And shared in fearless deeds with evil men,
Calm as an angel in the dragon's den—
How I braved death for liberty and truth,
And spurned at peace, and power, and fame—and when
Those hopes had lost the glory of their youth,   521
How sadly I returned—might move the hearer's ruth:

XLV

'Warm tears throng fast! the tale may not be said—
Know then, that when this grief had been subdued,
I was not left, like others, cold and dead;   525
The Spirit whom I loved in solitude
Sustained his child: the tempest-shaken wood,

499 atmosphere;—] atmosphere; *edd.*   504 kiss, *Form. 1876*] kiss,— *1904*   kiss.
1839, 1818   505 maiden:] maiden, *edd.*   517 men, *1904*] men. *1839, 1818*
520 fame— *1904, D. 3*] fame; *1839, 1818*   526 loved *1839, 1818, D. 3*] loved, *1904*

The waves, the fountains, and the hush of night—
These were his voice, and well I understood
His smile divine, when the calm sea was bright   530
With silent stars, and Heaven was breathless with delight.

XLVI

'In lonely glens, amid the roar of rivers,
    When the dim nights were moonless, have I known
Joys which no tongue can tell; my pale lip quivers
    When thought revisits them:—know thou alone,   535
    That after many wondrous years were flown,
I was awakened by a shriek of woe;
    And over me a mystic robe was thrown,
By viewless hands, and a bright Star did glow
Before my steps—the Snake then met his mortal foe.'   540

XLVII

'Thou fearest not then the Serpent on thy heart?'
    'Fear it!' she said, with brief and passionate cry,
And spake no more: that silence made me start—
    I looked, and we were sailing pleasantly,
    Swift as a cloud between the sea and sky;   545
Beneath the rising moon seen far away,
    Mountains of ice, like sapphire, piled on high,
Hemming the horizon round, in silence lay
On the still waters—these we did approach alway.

XLVIII

And swift and swifter grew the vessel's motion,   550
    So that a dizzy trance fell on my brain—
Wild music woke me: we had passed the ocean
    Which girds the pole, Nature's remotest reign—
    And we glode fast o'er a pellucid plain
Of waters, azure with the noontide day.   555
    Ethereal mountains shone around—a Fane
Stood in the midst, girt by green isles which lay
On the blue sunny deep, resplendent far away.

530 sea was *1904, 1839, 1818*] seas were *D. 3*   545 sky; *1904, D. 3*] sky *1839,*
1818   546 away, *1904, D. 3*] away; *1839, 1818*   547 high, *1904, D. 3*] high
1839, 1818

XLIX

It was a Temple, such as mortal hand
  Has never built, nor ecstasy, nor dream   560
Reared in the cities of enchanted land:
    'Twas likest Heaven, ere yet day's purple stream
    Ebbs o'er the western forest, while the gleam
Of the unrisen moon among the clouds
  Is gathering—when with many a golden beam   565
The thronging constellations rush in crowds,
Paving with fire the sky and the marmoreal floods:—

L

Like what may be conceived of this vast dome,
  When from the depths which thought can seldom pierce
Genius beholds it rise, his native home,   570
    Girt by the deserts of the Universe,
    Yet, nor in painting's light, or mightier verse,
Or sculpture's marble language, can invest
    That shape to mortal sense—such glooms immerse
That incommunicable sight, and rest   575
Upon the labouring brain and overburdened breast.

LI

Winding among the lawny islands fair,
  Whose blosmy forests starred the shadowy deep,
The wingless boat paused where an ivory stair
    Its fretwork in the crystal sea did steep,   580
    Encircling that vast Fane's aërial heap:
We disembarked, and through a portal wide
    We passed—whose roof of moonstone carved, did keep
A glimmering o'er the forms on every side,
Sculptures like life and thought; immovable, deep-eyed. 585

LII

We came to a vast hall, whose glorious roof
  Was diamond, which had drank the lightning's sheen
In darkness, and now poured it through the woof

---

560 dream *1904, D. 3*] dream, *1839, 1818*   567 floods:—*for continuity, Loc. 1911*]
floods, *1904, 1839, 1818*   571 Universe, *1839*] Universe; *1904, D. 3,* Universe *1818*
573 language, *1904, 1839*] language *1818*

Of spell-inwoven clouds hung there to screen
  Its blinding splendour—through such veil was seen   590
That work of subtlest power, divine and rare:
  Orb above orb, with starry shapes between,
And hornèd moons, and meteors strange and fair,
On night-black columns poised—one hollow hemisphere!

LIII

Ten thousand columns in that quivering light   595
  Distinct, between whose shafts wound far away
The long and labyrinthine aisles, more bright
  With their own radiance than the Heaven of Day;
  And on the jasper walls around, there lay
Paintings, the poesy of mightiest thought,   600
  Which did the Spirit's history display;
A tale of passionate change, divinely taught,
Which, in their wingèd dance, unconscious Genii wrought.

LIV

Beneath there sate, on many a sapphire throne,
  The Great, who had departed from mankind,   605
A mighty Senate;—some, whose white hair shone
  Like mountain snow, mild, beautiful, and blind;
  Some, female forms, whose gestures beamed with mind;
And ardent youths, and children bright and fair;
  And some had lyres whose strings were intertwined   610
With pale and clinging flames, which ever there
Waked faint yet thrilling sounds that pierced the crystal air.

LV

One seat was vacant in the midst, a throne,
  Reared on a pyramid like sculptured flame,
Distinct with circling steps which rested on   615
  Their own deep fire—soon as the Woman came
  Into that hall, she shrieked the Spirit's name
And fell, and vanished slowly from the sight.
  Darkness arose from her dissolving frame,
Which gathering, filled that dome of woven light,   620
Blotting its spherèd stars with supernatural night.

596 Distinct,] Distinct— *edd.*   597 aisles,] aisles— *edd.*   604 Beneath there sate,] Beneath, there sate *edd, D. 3*   607 blind; *1904*] blind, *1839, 1818, D. 3*   618 fell, *D. 3*] fell; *edd.*

LVI

Then first two glittering lights were seen to glide
  In circles on the amethystine floor,
Small serpent eyes trailing from side to side,
  Like meteors on a river's grassy shore;   625
  They round each other rolled, dilating more
And more—then rose, commingling into one,
  One clear and mighty planet hanging o'er
A cloud of deepest shadow, which was thrown
Athwart the glowing steps and the crystalline throne.   630

LVII

The cloud which rested on that cone of flame
  Was cloven; beneath the planet sate a Form,
Fairer than tongue can speak or thought may frame,
  The radiance of whose limbs rose-like and warm
  Flowed forth, and did with softest light inform   635
The shadowy dome, the sculptures, and the state
  Of those assembled shapes—with clinging charm
Sinking upon their hearts and mine. He sate
Majestic, yet most mild—calm, yet compassionate.

LVIII

Wonder and joy a passing faintness threw   640
  Over my brow—a hand supported me,
Whose touch was magic strength: an eye of blue
  Looked into mine, like moonlight, soothingly;
  And a voice said:—'Thou must a listener be
This day—two mighty Spirits now return,   645
  Like birds of calm, from the world's raging sea,
They pour fresh light from Hope's immortal urn;
A tale of human power—despair not—list and learn!'

LIX

I looked, and lo! one stood forth eloquently,
  His eyes were dark and deep, and the clear brow   650
Which shadowed them was like the morning sky,
  The cloudless Heaven of Spring, when in their flow
  Through the bright air, the soft winds as they blow

622 first D.3] first, edd.   625 shore;] shore, edd., shore D. 3   638 mine. He
1904] mine—He 1839, 1818

Wake the green world; his gestures did obey
　　The oracular mind that made his features glow;   655
And where his curvèd lips half-open lay,
Passion's divinest stream had made impetuous way.

LX

Beneath the darkness of his outspread hair
　　He stood thus beautiful; but there was One
Who sate beside him like his shadow there,   660
　　And held his hand—far lovelier; she was known
　　To be thus fair, by the few lines alone
Which through her floating locks and gathered cloak,
　　Glances of soul-dissolving glory, shone:—
None else beheld her eyes—in him they woke   665
Memories which found a tongue as thus he silence broke.

CANTO II

I

THE starlight smile of children, the sweet looks
　　Of women, the fair breast from which I fed,
The murmur of the unreposing brooks,
　　And the green light which, shifting overhead,   670
　　Some tangled bower of vines around me shed,
The shells on the sea-sand, and the wild flowers,
　　The lamplight through the rafters cheerly spread
And on the twining flax—in life's young hours
These sights and sounds did nurse my spirit's folded powers.

II

In Argolis, beside the echoing sea,   676
　　Such impulses within my mortal frame
Arose, and they were dear to memory,
　　Like tokens of the dead:—but others came
　　Soon, in another shape: the wondrous fame   680

---

654 world;] world— *edd.*　　655 glow;] glow, *edd.*　　661 lovelier;] lovelier— *edd.*
665 *Followed in e. 19 by two lines of extraneous verse. See n., p. 367.*　　666 tongue
1904] tongue *1839, 1818*

Canto II. 670 which, *1904, 1839*] which *1818*　　673 spread] spread, *edd.*
675 spirit's *1904, 1839*] Spirits' *1818. See n., p. 367.*

Of the past world, the vital words and deeds
  Of minds whom neither time nor change can tame,
Traditions dark and old, whence evil creeds
Start forth, and whose dim shade a stream of poison feeds.

III

I heard, as all have heard, the various story   685
  Of human life, and wept unwilling tears.
Feeble historians of its shame and glory,
    False disputants on all its hopes and fears,
    Victims who worshipped ruin, chroniclers
Of daily scorn, and slaves who loathed their state   690
    Yet, flattering Power, had given its ministers
  A throne of judgement in the grave:—'twas fate,
That among such as these my youth should seek its mate.

IV

The land in which I lived, by a fell bane
  Was withered up. Tyrants dwelt side by side,   695
And stabled in our homes,—until the chain
    Stifled the captive's cry, and to abide
    That blasting curse men had no shame—all vied
In evil, slave and despot; fear with lust
    Strange fellowship through mutual hate had tied,   700
  Like two dark serpents tangled in the dust,
Which on the paths of men their mingling poison thrust.

V

Earth, our bright home, its mountains and its waters,
  And the ethereal shapes which are suspended
Over its green expanse, and those fair daughters,   705
    The Clouds, of Sun and Ocean, who have blended
    The colours of the air since first extended
It cradled the young world,—none wandered forth
    To see or feel: a darkness had descended
  On every heart; the light which shows its worth,   710
Must among gentle thoughts and fearless take its birth.

---

689 ruin,] ruin,— *edd.*   691 Yet, flattering Power, *1904*] Yet flattering power
1839, 1818   699 lust *1904, 1839*] lust, *1818*   708 world,—] world, *edd.*

VI

This vital world, this home of happy spirits,
    Was as a dungeon to my blasted kind;
All that despair from murdered hope inherits
    They sought, and in their helpless misery blind,   715
    A deeper prison and heavier chains did find,
And stronger tyrants:—a dark gulf before,
    The realm of a stern Ruler, yawned; behind,
Terror and Time conflicting drove, and bore
On their tempestuous flood the shrieking wretch from shore.

VII

Out of that Ocean's wrecks had Guilt and Woe   721
    Framed a dark dwelling for their homeless thought,
And, starting at the ghosts which to and fro
    Glide o'er its dim and gloomy strand, had brought
    The worship thence which they each other taught.   725
Well might men loathe their life, well might they turn
    Even to the ills again from which they sought
Such refuge after death!—well might they learn
To gaze on this fair world with hopeless unconcern!

VIII

For they all pined in bondage; body and soul,   730
    Tyrant and slave, victim and torturer, bent
Before one Power, to which supreme control,
    Over their will by their own weakness lent,
    Made all its many names omnipotent;
All symbols of things evil, all divine;   735
    And hymns of blood or mockery, which rent
The air from all its fanes, did intertwine
Imposture's impious toils round each discordant shrine.

IX

I heard, as all have heard, life's various story,
    And in no careless heart transcribed the tale;   740
But, from the sneers of men who had grown hoary

---

713 kind; *1904*] kind, *1839, 1818*   729 *Here, in e. 19, follow two snatches of*
extraneous verse. See n., p. 367.   732 control,] control *edd.*

In shame and scorn, from groans of crowds made pale
By famine, from a mother's desolate wail
O'er her polluted child, from innocent blood
Poured on the earth, and brows anxious and pale   745
With the heart's warfare, did I gather food
To feed my many thoughts: a tameless multitude!

X

I wandered through the wrecks of days departed
Far by the desolated shore, when Even
O'er the still sea and jagged islets darted   750
The light of moonrise; in the northern Heaven,
Among the clouds near the horizon driven,
The mountains lay beneath one planet pale;
Around me, broken tombs and columns riven
Looked vast in twilight, and the sorrowing gale   755
Waked in those ruins gray its everlasting wail!

XI

I knew not who had framed these wonders then,
Nor had I heard the story of their deeds;
But dwellings of a race of mightier men,
And monuments of less ungentle creeds   760
Tell their own tale to him who wisely heeds
The language which they speak; and now, to me,
The moonlight making pale the blooming weeds,
The bright stars shining in the breathless sea,
Interpreted those scrolls of mortal mystery: 765

XII

'Such man has been, and such may yet become!
Ay, wiser, greater, gentler, even than they
Who on the fragments of yon shattered dome
Have stamped the sign of power!' I felt the sway
Of the vast stream of ages bear away   770

---

746 warfare,] warfare; *edd.*   749 Even *1911*] even *other edd.*   753 one *1839*
and most edd.] our *1904 and 1818, but corrected in Shelley's erratum slip*   758 Nor
1904, 1839] Nor, *1818*   762 me,] me *edd.*   765 mystery:] mystery. *edd.*
766–9 *Edd., except 1911 ,omit inverted commas.*

My floating thoughts—my heart beat loud and fast—
   Even as a storm let loose beneath the ray
Of the still moon, my spirit onward past
Beneath truth's steady beams upon its tumult cast.

XIII

'It shall be thus no more! too long, too long,   775
   Sons of the glorious dead, have ye lain bound
In darkness and in ruin!—Hope is strong,
   Justice and Truth their wingèd child have found!
   Awake! arise! until the mighty sound
Of your career shall scatter in its gust   780
   The thrones of the oppressor, and the ground
Hide the last altar's unregarded dust,
Whose Idol has so long betrayed your impious trust!'

XIV

'It must be so—I will arise and waken
   The multitude, and like a sulphurous hill,   785
Which on a sudden from its snows has shaken
   The swoon of ages, it shall burst and fill
   The world with cleansing fire: it must, it will—
It may not be restrained!—and who shall stand
   Amid the rocking earthquake steadfast still,   790
But Laon? on high Freedom's desert land
A tower whose marble walls the leaguèd storms withstand!'

XV

One summer night, in commune with the hope
   Thus deeply fed, amid those ruins gray
I watched, beneath the dark sky's starry cope;   795
   And ever from that hour upon me lay
   The burden of this hope, and night or day,
In vision or in dream, clove to my breast:
   Among mankind, or when gone far away
To the lone shores and mountains, 'twas a guest   800
Which followed where I fled, and watched when I did rest.

---

775 ... 784 ... 792 *Edd., except 1870 and 1911, omit inverted commas.*   777 ruin!—
1904] ruin.— *1839*   ruin. *1818*   778 found!] found— *edd.*   783 trust! *1904*]
trust. *1839, 1818*   786 has *1904, 1818*] had *1839*

XVI

These hopes found words through which my spirit sought
  To weave a bondage of such sympathy,
As might create some response to the thought
  Which ruled me now—and as the vapours lie   805
  Bright in the outspread morning's radiancy,
So were these thoughts invested with the light
  Of language; and all bosoms made reply
On which its lustre streamed, whene'er it might
Through darkness wide and deep those trancèd spirits smite.

XVII

Yes, many an eye with dizzy tears was dim,   811
  And oft I thought to clasp my own heart's brother,
When I could feel the listener's senses swim,
  And hear his breath its own swift gaspings smother
  Even as my words evoked them—and another,   815
And yet another, I did fondly deem,
  Felt that we all were sons of one great mother;
And the cold truth such sad reverse did seem,
As to awake in grief from some delightful dream.

XVIII

Yes, oft beside the ruined labyrinth   820
  Which skirts the hoary caves of the green deep,
Did Laon and his friend, on one gray plinth,
  Round whose worn base the wild waves hiss and leap,
  Resting at eve, a lofty converse keep:
And that this friend was false, may now be said   825
  Calmly—that he like other men could weep
Tears which are lies, and could betray and spread
Snares for that guileless heart which for his own had bled.

XIX

Then, had no great aim recompensed my sorrow,
  I must have sought dark respite from its stress   830
In dreamless rest, in sleep that sees no morrow:
  For to tread life's dismaying wilderness
  Without one smile to cheer, one voice to bless,

822 friend, *1904*] friend *1839, 1818*   831 morrow:] morrow— *edd.*

Amid the snares and scoffs of human kind,
　　Is hard. But I betrayed it not, nor less　　　　　835
With love that scorned return, sought to unbind
The interwoven clouds which make its wisdom blind.

XX

With deathless minds which leave where they have passed
　　A path of light, my soul communion knew;
Till from that glorious intercourse, at last,　　　　840
　　As from a mine of magic store, I drew
　　Words which were weapons;—round my heart there grew
The adamantine armour of their power,
　　And from my fancy wings of golden hue
Sprang forth—yet not alone from wisdom's tower,　　845
A minister of truth, these plumes young Laon bore.

XXI

I had a little sister whose fair eyes
　　Were lodestars of delight, which drew me home
When I might wander forth; nor did I prize
　　Aught human thing beneath Heaven's mighty dome　850
　　Beyond this child: so when sad hours were come,
And baffled hope like ice still clung to me,
　　Since kin were cold, and friends had now become
Heartless and false, I turned from all, to be,
Cythna, the only source of tears and smiles to thee.　　855

XXII

What wert thou then? A child most infantine,
　　Yet wandering far beyond that innocent age
In all but its sweet looks and mien divine:
　　Even then, methought, with the world's tyrant rage
　　A patient warfare thy young heart did wage,　　860
When those soft eyes of scarcely conscious thought
　　Some tale, or thine own fancies, would engage
To overflow with tears, or converse fraught
With passion, o'er their depths its fleeting light had wrought.

835 hard. But] hard—but *edd.*　　　　847 An orphan with my parents lived, whose
eyes *RI*　　　861 thought *1904*] thought, *1839, 1818*　　　862 fancies, *1904, 1839*]
fancies *1818*

XXIII

She moved upon this earth a shape of brightness,   865
   A power, that from its objects scarcely drew
One impulse of her being—in her lightness
   Most like some radiant cloud of morning dew,
   Which wanders through the waste air's parchless blue,
To nourish some far desert: she did seem   870
   Beside me, gathering beauty as she grew
Like the bright shade of some immortal dream
Which walks, when tempest sleeps, the wave of life's dark stream.

XXIV

As mine own shadow was this child to me,
   A second self, far dearer and more fair;   875
Which clothed in undissolving radiancy
   All those steep paths which languor and despair
   Of human things, had made so dark and bare,
But which I trod alone—nor, till bereft
   Of friends, and overcome by lonely care,   880
Knew I what solace for that loss was left,
Though by a bitter wound my trusting heart was cleft.

XXV

Once she was dear, now she was all I had
   To love in human life, this sister sweet,
This child of twelve years old—so she was made   885
   My sole associate, and her willing feet
   Wandered with mine where earth and ocean meet,
Beyond the aëreal mountains whose vast cells
   The unreposing billows ever beat,
Through forests wide and old, and lawny dells   890
Where boughs of incense droop over the emerald wells.

XXVI

And warm and light I felt her clasping hand
   When twined in mine: she followed where I went,
Through the lone paths of our immortal land.

---

874 dearer *edd.*] dearer *above* [purer] *e. 19*   876 radiancy *1904, 1839*] radiancy,
1818   884 life, this sister *LC*] life—this playmate *RI*   890 dells *1904*]
dells, *1839, 1818*

It had no waste but some memorial lent   895
    Which strung me to my toil—some monument
Vital with mind: then, Cythna by my side,
    Until the bright and beaming day were spent,
Would rest, with looks entreating to abide,
Too earnest and too sweet ever to be denied.   900

XXVII

And soon I could not have refused her. Thus
    For ever, day and night, we two were ne'er
Parted, but when brief sleep divided us:
    And when the pauses of the lulling air
    Of noon beside the sea, had made a lair   905
For her soothed senses, in my arms she slept,
    And I kept watch over her slumbers there,
While, as the shifting visions o'er her swept,
Amid her innocent rest by turns she smiled and wept.

XXVIII

And, in the murmur of her dreams was heard   910
    Sometimes the name of Laon:—suddenly
She would arise, and, like the secret bird
    Whom sunset wakens, fill the shore and sky
    With her sweet accents—a wild melody—
Hymns which my soul had woven to Freedom,—strong 915
    The source of passion, whence they rose, to be
Triumphant strains, which, like a spirit's tongue,
To the enchanted waves that child of glory sung,

XXIX

Her white arms lifted through the shadowy stream
    Of her loose hair! Oh, excellently great   920
Seemed to me then my purpose, the vast theme
    Of those impassioned songs, when Cythna sate
    Amid the calm which rapture doth create

895 waste *1904*] waste, *1839, 1818*   901 her. Thus] her—thus *edd.*   910–27 *For*
punctuation see n., p. 368   914 melody—] melody! *1904, 1839, 1818*   915 Free-
dom,—] Freedom, *1904, 1839, 1818*   916 passion, *1904, 1839*] passion *1818*
be *1839*] be; *1904, 1818*   918 sung,] sung— *1904*   sung. *1839, 1818*   920 hair!]
hair— *1904, 1839, 1818*

After its tumult—her heart vibrating,
   Her spirit o'er the ocean's floating state   925
From her deep eyes far wandering, on the wing
Of visions that were mine, beyond its utmost spring!

XXX

For, before Cythna loved it, had my song
   Peopled with thoughts the boundless universe,
A mighty congregation, which were strong   930
   Where'er they trod the darkness, to disperse
   The cloud of that unutterable curse
Which clings upon mankind:—all things became
   Slaves to my holy and heroic verse,
Earth, sea and sky, the planets, life and fame   935
And fate, or whate'er else binds the world's wondrous frame.

XXXI

And this belovèd child thus felt the sway
   Of my conceptions, gathering like a cloud
The very wind on which it rolls away:
   Hers too were all my thoughts, ere yet, endowed   940
   With music and with light, their fountains flowed
In poesy; and her still and earnest face,
   Pallid with feelings which intensely glowed
Within, was turned on mine with speechless grace,
Watching the hopes which there her heart had learned to trace.

XXXII

In me, communion with this purest being   946
   Kindled intenser zeal, and made me wise
In knowledge, which, in hers mine own mind seeing,
   Left in the human world few mysteries.
   How without fear of evil or disguise   950
Was Cythna!—what a spirit strong and mild,
   Which death, or pain or peril could despise,
   Yet melt in tenderness! what genius wild
Yet mighty, was enclosed within one simple child!

924 tumult—] tumult, *1904, 1839, 1818*   927 spring!] spring. *edd.*   931 dark-
ness,] darkness *edd.*   940 yet, *1904,* 1839] yet *1818*   948 which, *1904*] which
1839, 1818   949 mysteries.] mysteries: *edd.*

XXXIII

New lore was this—old age, with its gray hair,　　955
　　And wrinkled legends of unworthy things,
And icy sneers, is nought: it cannot dare
　　To burst the chains which life for ever flings
　　On the entangled soul's aspiring wings;
So is it cold and cruel, and is made　　960
　　The careless slave of that dark Power which brings
Evil, like blight, on man, who, still betrayed,
Laughs o'er the grave in which his living hopes are laid.

XXXIV

Nor are the strong and the severe to keep
　　The empire of the world: thus Cythna taught　　965
Even in the visions of her eloquent sleep,
　　Unconscious of the power through which she wrought
　　The woof of such intelligible thought;
As from the tranquil strength which cradled lay
　　In her smile-peopled rest, my spirit sought　　970
Why the deceiver and the slave has sway
O'er heralds so divine of truth's arising day.

XXXV

Within that fairest form, the female mind
　　Untainted by the poison-clouds which rest
On the dark world, a sacred home did find:　　975
　　But else, from the wide earth's maternal breast,
　　Victorious Evil, which had dispossessed
All native power, had those fair children torn,
　　And made them slaves to soothe his vile unrest,
And minister to lust its joys forlorn,　　980
Till they had learned to breathe the atmosphere of scorn.

XXXVI

This misery was but coldly felt, till she
　　Became my only friend, who had endued
My purpose with a wider sympathy;
　　Thus, Cythna mourned with me the servitude　　985
　　In which the half of humankind were mewed

959 wings;] wings, *edd.*　　962 blight, *1904*] blight *1839, 1818*　　who, *1904, 1839*]
who *1818*　　968 thought;] thought, *edd.*

Victims of lust and hate, the slaves of slaves:
   She mourned that grace and power were thrown as food
To the hyaena lust, who, among graves,
Over his loathèd meal, laughing in agony, raves.   990

XXXVII

And I, still gazing on that glorious child,
   Even as these thoughts flushed o'er her:—'Cythna sweet,
Well with the world art thou unreconciled;
   Never will peace and human nature meet
   Till free and equal man and woman greet   995
Domestic peace; and ere this power can make
   In human hearts its calm and holy seat,
This slavery must be broken'—as I spake,
From Cythna's eyes a light of exultation brake.

XXXVIII

She replied earnestly:—'It shall be mine,   1000
   This task, mine, Laon!—thou hast much to gain;
Nor wilt thou at poor Cythna's pride repine,
   If she should lead a happy female train
   To meet thee over the rejoicing plain,
When myriads at thy call shall throng around   1005
   The Golden City.'—Then the child did strain
My arm upon her tremulous heart, and wound
Her own about my neck, till some reply she found.

XXXIX

I smiled, and spake not.—'Wherefore dost thou smile
   At what I say? Laon, I am not weak,   1010
And though my cheek might become pale the while,
   With thee, if thou desirest, will I seek
   Through their array of banded slaves to wreak
Ruin upon the tyrants. I had thought
   It was more hard to turn my unpractised cheek   1015
To scorn and shame, and this beloved spot
And thee, O dearest friend, to leave and murmur not.

987 slaves: _1839_] slaves, _1904, 1818_   992 her:— _1904, 1839_] her— _1839, 1818_
997 seat, _1904, 1839_] seat; _1818_   1009 not.—'Wherefore _1904, 1839_] not—'where-
fore _1818_

XL

'Whence came I what I am? Thou, Laon, knowest
　　How a young child should thus undaunted be;
Methinks, it is a power which thou bestowest,　　　　1020
　　　Through which I seek, by most resembling thee,
　　　So to become most good and great and free;
Yet far beyond this Ocean's utmost roar
　　　In towers and huts are many like to me,
Who, could they see thine eyes, or feel such lore　　　1025
As I have learnt from them, like me would fear no more.

XLI

'Think'st thou that I shall speak unskilfully,
　　And none will heed me? I remember now,
How once, a slave in tortures doomed to die,
　　　Was saved, because in accents sweet and low　　　1030
　　　He sung a song his Judge loved long ago,
As he was led to death.—All shall relent
　　　Who hear me—tears, as mine have flowed, shall flow,
Hearts beat as mine now beats, with such intent
As renovates the world; a will omnipotent!　　　　1035

XLII

'Yes, I will tread Pride's golden palaces,
　　Through Penury's roofless huts and squalid cells
Will I descend, where'er in abjectness
　　　Woman with some vile slave her tyrant dwells;
　　　There with the music of thine own sweet spells　　　1040
Will disenchant the captives, and will pour
　　　For the despairing, from the crystal wells
Of thy deep spirit, reason's mighty lore,
And power shall then abound, and hope arise once more.

XLIII

'Can man be free if woman be a slave?　　　　1045
　　Chain one who lives, and breathes this boundless air,
To the corruption of a closèd grave!

1022 good *1904*] good, *1839, 1818*　　free; *1839*] free, *1904, 1818*　　1027 Think'st
1904, 1818] Thinkest *1839*　　1031 sung *1904, 1818*] sang *1839*　　1033 tears, *1904*]
tears *1839, 1818*　　1039 dwells;] dwells, *edd.*　　1046 air, *1904*] air *1839, 1818*

Can they whose mates are beasts, condemned to bear
  Scorn, heavier far than toil or anguish, dare
To trample their oppressors? in their home   1050
  Among their babes, thou knowest a curse would wear
The shape of woman—hoary Crime would come
Behind, and Fraud rebuild Religion's tottering dome.

XLIV

'I am a child:—I would not yet depart.
  When I go forth alone, bearing the lamp   1055
Aloft which thou hast kindled in my heart,
    Millions of slaves from many a dungeon damp
    Shall leap in joy, as the benumbing cramp
Of ages leaves their limbs—no ill may harm
  Thy Cythna ever—truth its radiant stamp   1060
Has fixed, as an invulnerable charm
Upon her children's brow, dark Falsehood to disarm.

XLV

'Wait yet awhile for the appointed day—
  Thou wilt depart, and I with tears shall stand
Watching thy dim sail skirt the ocean gray;   1065
  Amid the dwellers of this lonely land
  I shall remain alone—and thy command
Shall then dissolve the world's unquiet trance,
  And, multitudinous as the desert sand
Borne on the storm, its millions shall advance,   1070
Thronging round thee, the light of their deliverance.

XLVI

'Then, like the forests of some pathless mountain,
  Which from remotest glens two warring winds
Involve in fire which not the loosened fountain
    Of broadest floods might quench, shall all the kinds 1075
    Of evil, catch from our uniting minds
The spark which must consume them;—Cythna then
  Will have cast off the impotence that binds
Her childhood now, and through the paths of men
Will pass, as the charmed bird that haunts the serpent's den.

1074 fire *1904*] fire. *1839, 1818*

XLVII

'We part!—O Laon, I must dare, nor tremble   1081
   To meet those looks no more!—Oh, heavy stroke!
Sweet brother of my soul! can I dissemble
   The agony of this thought?'—As thus she spoke
   The gathered sobs her quivering accents broke,   1085
And in my arms she hid her beating breast.
   I remained still for tears—sudden she woke
As one awakes from sleep, and wildly pressed
My bosom, her whole frame impetuously possessed.

XLVIII

'We part to meet again—but yon blue waste,   1090
   Yon desert wide and deep holds no recess,
Within whose happy silence thus embraced
   We might survive all ills in one caress:
   Nor doth the grave—I fear 'tis passionless—
Nor yon cold vacant Heaven:—we meet again   1095
   Within the minds of men, whose lips shall bless
Our memory, and whose hopes its light retain
When these dissevered bones are trodden in the plain.'

XLIX

I could not speak, though she had ceased, for now
   The fountains of her feeling, swift and deep,   1100
Seemed to suspend the tumult of their flow;
   So we arose, and by the starlight steep
   Went homeward—neither did we speak nor weep,
But, pale, were calm with passion—thus subdued
   Like evening shades that o'er the mountains creep,   1105
We moved towards our home; where, in this mood,
Each from the other sought refuge in solitude.

1081 dare,] dare *edd.*   1082 stroke! *1904, 1839*] stroke, *1818*   1092 silence]
silence, *edd.*   1104 But, pale, *1904*] But pale, *1839*   But pale *1818*   calm with
passion— *1904*] calm.—With passion *1839*   calm with passion,— *1818. See n., p. 368.*

CANTO III

I

WHAT thoughts had sway over my sister's slumber
   That night, I know not; but my own did seem
As if they did ten thousand years outnumber   1110
   Of waking life, the visions of a dream
   Which hid in one dim gulf the troubled stream
Of mind; a boundless chaos wild and vast,
   Whose limits yet were never memory's theme:
And I lay struggling as its whirlwinds passed,   1115
Sometimes for rapture sick, sometimes for pain aghast.

II

Two hours, whose mighty circle did embrace
   More time than might make gray the infant world,
Rolled thus, a weary and tumultuous space;
   When the third came, like mist on breezes curled, 1120
   From my dim sleep a shadow was unfurled;
Methought, upon the threshold of a cave
   I sate with Cythna; drooping briony, pearled
With dew from the wild streamlet's shattered wave,
Hung where we sate to taste the joys which Nature gave.

III

We lived a day as we were wont to live,   1126
   But Nature had a robe of glory on,
And the bright air o'er every shape did weave
   Intenser hues, so that the herbless stone,
   The leafless bough among the leaves alone,   1130
Had being clearer than its own could be,
   And Cythna's pure and radiant self was shown,
In this strange vision, so divine to me,
That, if I loved before, now love was agony.

Canto III. 1108 over my sister's *LC*] o'er Cythna's lonely *RI*   1110 did *LC*]
might *RI and edd.*   1111 dream *1904*] dream, *1839, 1818*   1125 Hung] Hung,
edd.   1132 shown, *1904*] shown *1839, 1818*   1134 That, *1904*] That *1839,
1818*

IV

Morn fled, noon came, evening, then night descended,   1135
   And we prolonged calm talk beneath the sphere
Of the calm moon—when suddenly was blended
   With our repose a nameless sense of fear;
   And from the cave behind I seemed to hear
Sounds gathering upwards—accents incomplete,   1140
   And stifled shrieks,—and now, more near and near,
A tumult and a rush of thronging feet
The cavern's secret depths beneath the earth did beat.

V

The scene was changed, and away, away, away!
   Through the air and over the sea we sped,   1145
And Cythna in my sheltering bosom lay,
   And the winds bore me—through the darkness spread
   Around, the gaping earth then vomited
Legions of foul and ghastly shapes, which hung
   Upon my flight; and ever, as we fled,   1150
They plucked at Cythna—soon to me then clung
A sense of actual things those monstrous dreams among.

VI

And I lay struggling in the impotence
   Of sleep, while outward life had burst its bound,
Though, still deluded, strove the tortured sense   1155
   To its dire wanderings to adapt the sound
   Which in the light of morn was poured around
Our dwelling. Breathless, pale, and unaware
   I rose, and all the cottage crowded found
With armèd men, whose glittering swords were bare,   1160
And whose degraded limbs the tyrant's garb did wear.

VII

And, ere with rapid lips and gathered brow
   I could demand the cause, a feeble shriek—
It was a feeble shriek, faint, far and low—

1137 when *1904*] when, *1839, 1818*   1150 ever, *1904*] ever *1839, 1818*
1158 dwelling. Breathless,] dwelling—breathless, *edd.*   1162 And, *1904*] And
1839, 1818   1163 cause,] cause— *edd.*   1164 low—] low, *edd.*

Arrested me—my mien grew calm and meek,   1165
And grasping a small knife, I went to seek
That voice among the crowd—'twas Cythna's cry!
Beneath most calm resolve did agony wreak
Its whirlwind rage:—so I passed quietly
Till I beheld, where bound, that dearest child did lie.   1170

VIII

I started to behold her, for delight
And exultation, and a joyance free,
Solemn, serene and lofty, filled the light
Of the calm smile with which she looked on me:
So that I feared some brainless ecstasy,   1175
Wrought from that bitter woe, had wildered her—
'Farewell! farewell!' she said, as I drew nigh.
'At first my peace was marred by this strange stir,
Now I am calm as truth—its chosen minister.

IX

'Look not so, Laon—say farewell in hope: 1180
These bloody men are but the slaves who bear
Their mistress to her task—it was my scope
The slavery where they drag me now, to share,
And among captives willing chains to wear
Awhile—the rest thou knowest—return, dear friend!   1185
Let our first triumph trample the despair
Which would ensnare us now, for in the end,
In victory or in death our hopes and fears must blend.'

X

These words had fallen on my unheeding ear,
Whilst I had watched the motions of the crew   1190
With seeming-careless glance; not many were
Around her, for their comrades just withdrew
To guard some other victim—so I drew
My knife, and with one impulse, suddenly
All unaware three of their number slew,   1195
And grasped a fourth by the throat, and with loud cry
My countrymen invoked to death or liberty!

1180 hope:] hope; *1839* hope *1904, 1818*

XI

What followed then, I know not—for a stroke
  On my raised arm and naked head, came down,
Filling my eyes with blood—when I awoke,   1200
  I felt that they had bound me in my swoon,
  And up a rock which overhangs the town,
By the steep path were bearing me: below,
  The plain was filled with slaughter,—overthrown
The vineyards and the harvests, and the glow   1205
Of blazing roofs shone far o'er the white ocean's flow.

XII

Upon that rock a mighty column stood,
  Whose capital seemed sculptured in the sky,
Which to the wanderers o'er the solitude
  Of distant seas, from ages long gone by,   1210
  Had made a landmark; o'er its height to fly
Scarcely the cloud, the vulture, or the blast,
  Has power—and when the shades of evening lie
On earth and ocean, its carved summits cast
The sunken daylight far through the aërial waste.   1215

XIII

They bore me to a cavern in the hill
  Beneath that column, and unbound me there:
And one did strip me stark; and one did fill
  A vessel from the putrid pool; one bare
  A lighted torch, and four with friendless care   1220
Guided my steps the cavern-paths along,
  Then up a steep and dark and narrow stair
We wound, until the torch's fiery tongue
Amid the gushing day beamless and pallid hung.

XIV

They raised me to the platform of the pile,   1225
  That column's dizzy height:—the grate of brass
Through which they thrust me, open stood the while,

<hr>

1211 made a *1904, 1818*] many a *1839*
1818 ; cf. line 1220   1223 torch's *1904*] torches' *1839,*

As to its ponderous and suspended mass,
  With chains which eat into the flesh, alas,
With brazen links, my naked limbs they bound: 1230
  The grate, as they departed to repass,
With horrid clangour fell, and the far sound
Of their retiring steps in the dense gloom was drowned.

XV

The noon was calm and bright:—around that column
  The overhanging sky and circling sea   1235
Spread forth in silentness profound and solemn
  The darkness of brief frenzy cast on me,
  So that I knew not my own misery:
The islands and the mountains in the day
  Like clouds reposed afar; and I could see   1240
The town among the woods below that lay,
And the dark rocks which bound the bright and glassy bay.

XVI

It was so calm, that scarce the feathery weed
  Sown by some eagle on the topmost stone
Swayed in the air:—so bright, that noon did breed   1245
  No shadow in the sky beside mine own—
  Mine, and the shadow of my chain alone.
Below, the smoke of roofs involved in flame
  Rested like night, all else was clearly shown
In that broad glare, yet sound to me none came,   1250
But of the living blood that ran within my frame.

XVII

The peace of madness fled, and ah, too soon,
  A ship was lying on the sunny main!
Its sails were flagging in the breathless noon—
  Its shadow lay beyond—that sight again   1255
  Waked, with its presence, in my trancèd brain

1229 alas,] alas! *edd.*   1233 was *1839*] were *1818, which edd. have preserved for*
euphony   1237 cast *edd., except Form., who emends to* past *putting a full stop after*
solemn *above*   1248 Below, *1904*] Below *1839, 1818*   1250 that *1904, 1818*]
the *1839*   1252 soon,] soon! *edd.*   1253 main!] main, *edd.*

The stings of a known sorrow, keen and cold:
　I knew that ship bore Cythna o'er the plain
Of waters, to her blighting slavery sold,
And watched it with such thoughts as must remain untold.

XVIII

I watched, until the shades of evening wrapped　　　1261
　Earth like an exhalation. Then the bark
Moved, for that calm was by the sunset snapped.
　It moved a speck upon the Ocean dark:
　Soon the wan stars came forth, and I could mark　　1265
Its path no more. I sought to close mine eyes,
　But like the balls, their lids were stiff and stark;
I would have risen, but ere that I could rise,
My parchèd skin was split with piercing agonies.

XIX

I gnawed my brazen chain, and sought to sever　　　1270
　Its admantine links, that I might die:
O Liberty! forgive the base endeavour,
　Forgive me if, reserved for victory,
　The Champion of thy faith e'er sought to fly.—
That starry night, with its clear silence, sent　　　1275
　Tameless resolve which laughed at misery
Into my soul—linkèd remembrance lent
To that such power, to me such a severe content.

XX

To breathe, to be, to hope, or to despair
　And die, I questioned not; nor, though the Sun　　　1280
Its shafts of agony kindling through the air
　Moved over me, nor though in evening dun,
　Or when the stars their visible courses run,
Or morning, the wide universe was spread
　In dreary calmness round me, did I shun　　　1285
Its presence, nor seek refuge with the dead
From one faint hope whose flower a dropping poison shed.

　1262 exhalation. Then] exhalation—then *edd.*　　　1266 more. I] more!—I] *edd.*
1273 if, *1904, 1839*] if *1818*

XXI

Two days thus passed; I neither raved nor died;
　　Thirst raged within me, like a scorpion's nest
Built in mine entrails; I had spurned aside　　　　　　1290
　　The water-vessel, while despair possessed
　　My thoughts, and now no drop remained. The uprest
Of the third sun brought hunger—but the crust
　　Which had been left, was to my craving breast
Fuel, not food. I chewed the bitter dust,　　　　　　1295
And bit my bloodless arm, and licked the brazen rust.

XXII

My brain began to fail when the fourth morn
　　Burst o'er the golden isles. A fearful sleep,
Which through the caverns dreary and forlorn
　　Of the riven soul, sent its foul dreams to sweep　　1300
　　With whirlwind swiftness—a fall far and deep,—
A gulf, a void, a sense of senselessness—
　　These things dwelt in me, even as shadows keep
Their watch in some dim charnel's loneliness,—
A shoreless sea, a sky sunless and planetless!　　　　1305

XXIII

The forms which peopled this terrific trance
　　I well remember—like a choir of devils,
Around me they involved a giddy dance;
　　Legions seemed gathering from the misty levels
　　Of Ocean, to supply those ceaseless revels,　　　　1310
Foul, ceaseless shadows:—thought could not divide
　　The actual world from these entangling evils,
Which so bemocked themselves that I descried
All shapes like mine own self hideously multiplied.

XXIV

The sense of day and night, of false and true,　　　　1315
　　Was dead within me. Yet two visions burst
That darkness. One, as since that hour I knew,
　　Was not a phantom of the realms accursed,

1288 passed;] passed—*edd.*　　died;] died—*edd.*　　1292 remained.] remained! *edd.*
1298 isles. A] isles—a *edd.*　　1304 loneliness,—] loneliness, *edd.*　　1313 themselves]
themselves, *edd.*　　1314 self] self, *edd.*　　1317 darkness. One] darkness—one *edd.*

Where then my spirit dwelt—but of the first
I know not yet, was it a dream or no.   1320
    But both, though not distincter, were immersed
In hues which, when through memory's waste they flow,
Make their divided streams more bright and rapid now.

XXV

Methought that grate was lifted, and the seven
    Who brought me thither four stiff corpses bare,   1325
And from the frieze to the four winds of Heaven
    Hung them on high by the entangled hair:
    Swarthy were three—the fourth was very fair:
As they retired, the golden moon upsprung,
    And eagerly, out in the giddy air,   1330
Leaning that I might eat, I stretched and clung
Over the shapeless depth in which those corpses hung.

XXVI

A woman's shape, now lank and cold and blue,
    The dwelling of the many-coloured worm,
Hung there; the white and hollow cheek I drew   1335
    To my dry lips—what radiance did inform
    Those horny eyes? whose was that withered form?
Alas, alas! it seemed that Cythna's ghost
    Laughed in those looks, and that the flesh was warm
Within my teeth!—A whirlwind keen as frost   1340
Then in its sinking gulfs my sickening spirit tossed.

XXVII

Then seemed it that a tameless hurricane
    Arose, and bore me in its dark career
Beyond the sun, beyond the stars that wane
    On the verge of formless space—it languished there, 1345
    And dying, left a silence lone and drear,
More horrible than famine:—in the deep
    The shape of an old man did then appear,
Stately and beautiful; that dreadful sleep
His heavenly smiles dispersed, and I could wake and weep.

1324 grate *1904*] gate *1839, 1818, but see line 1226.*   1325 thither *1904*] thither,
1839, 1818   1334 worm, *1904, 1839*] worm *1818*   1335 there; *1904*] there,
1839 there *1818*   1349 beautiful; *1904, 1839*] beautiful, *1818*

XXVIII

And, when the blinding tears had fallen, I saw   1351
  That column, and those corpses, and the moon,
And felt the poisonous tooth of hunger gnaw
  My vitals I rejoiced, as if the boon
  Of senseless death would be accorded soon;—   1355
When from that stony gloom a voice arose,
  Solemn and sweet as when low winds attune
The midnight pines; the grate did then unclose,
And on that reverend form the moonlight did repose.

XXIX

He struck my chains, and gently spake and smiled: 1360
  As they were loosened by that Hermit old,
Mine eyes were of their madness half beguiled,
  To answer those kind looks—he did enfold
  His giant arms around me, to uphold
My wretched frame, my scorchèd limbs he wound   1365
  In linen moist and balmy, and as cold
As dew to drooping leaves;—the chain, with sound
Like earthquake, through the chasm of that steep stair did
    bound,

XXX

As, lifting me, it fell!—What next I heard,
  Were billows leaping on the harbour-bar,   1370
And the shrill sea-wind, whose breath idly stirred
  My hair;—I looked abroad, and saw a star
  Shining beside a sail, and distant far
That mountain and its column, the known mark
  Of those who in the wide deep wandering are,   1375
So that I feared some Spirit, fell and dark,
In trance had laid me thus within a fiendish bark.

XXXI

For now indeed, over the salt sea-billow
  I sailed, yet dared not look upon the shape
Of him who ruled the helm, although the pillow   1380

1351 And, *1904, 1839*] And *1818*   1351–4 *Asyntactical. Sense might be restored
by a conjecture of* and *for* I *in 1554*   1369 As, *1904, 1839*] As *1818*   1369–
70. *See n., p. 368.*   1377 laid *1870*] lain *other edd. See n., p. 369.*   1379 sailed,]
sailed: *edd.*

For my light head was hollowed in his lap,
  And my bare limbs his mantle did enwrap,
Fearing it was a fiend; at last, he bent
  O'er me his aged face, as if to snap
Those dreadful thoughts the gentle grandsire bent,   1385
And to my inmost soul his soothing looks he sent.

XXXII

A soft and healing potion to my lips
  At intervals he raised—now looked on high,
To mark if yet the starry giant dips
  His zone in the dim sea—now cheeringly,   1390
  Though he said little, did he speak to me.
'It is a friend beside thee—take good cheer,
  Poor victim, thou art now at liberty!'
I joyed as those a human tone to hear,
Who in cells deep and lone have languished many a year,—

XXXIII

A dim and feeble joy, whose glimpses oft   1396
  Were quenched in a relapse of wildering dreams,
Yet still methought we sailed, until aloft
  The stars of night grew pallid, and the beams
  Of morn descended on the ocean-streams;   1400
And still that aged man, so grand and mild,
  Tended me, even as some sick mother seems
To hang in hope over a dying child,
Till in the azure East darkness again was piled.

XXXIV

And then the night-wind steaming from the shore,   1405
  Sent odours dying sweet across the sea,
And the swift waves the little boat which bore,
  Were cut by its keen keel, though slantingly;
  Soon I could hear the leaves sigh, and could see

1395 year,—] year. *edd.*   1400 ocean-streams;] ocean-streams, *edd.*
1405 steaming *edd., except Ross.*, *who has* streaming *but cf.* 2247 *and* Prom. Unb. *I.*
329, II. ii. 53.   1407 waves . . . boat *suggested by Loc. for the* boat . . . waves *of
other edd.*

The myrtle-blossoms starring the dim grove,   1410
   As past the pebbly beach the boat did flee
On sidelong wing, into a silent cove,
Where ebon pines a shade under the starlight wove.

CANTO IV

I

THE old man took the oars, and soon the bark
   Smote on the beach beside a tower of stone;   1415
It was a crumbling heap, whose portal dark
   With blooming ivy-trails was overgrown;
   Upon whose floor the spangling sands were strown,
And rarest sea-shells, which the eternal flood,
   Slave to the mother of the months, had thrown   1420
Within the walls of that gray tower, which stood
A changeling of man's art, nursed amid Nature's brood.

II

When the old man his boat had anchorèd,
   He wound me in his arms with tender care,
And very few, but kindly words he said,   1425
   And bore me through the tower adown a stair,
   Whose smooth descent some ceaseless step to wear
For many a year had fallen.—We came at last
   To a small chamber, which with mosses rare
Was tapestried, where me his soft hands placed   1430
Upon a couch of grass and oak-leaves interlaced.

III

The moon was darting through the lattices
   Its yellow light, warm as the beams of day—
So warm, that to admit the dewy breeze,
   The old man opened them; the moonlight lay   1435
   Upon a lake whose waters wove their play
Even to the threshold of that lonely home:
   Within was seen in the dim wavering ray
The antique sculptured roof, and many a tome
Whose lore had made that sage all that he had become.   1440

Canto IV. 1428 fallen.—We *1904, 1839*] fallen—We *1818*

IV

The rock-built barrier of the sea was past,—
    And I was on the margin of a lake,
A lonely lake, amid the forests vast
    And snowy mountains:—did my spirit wake
    From sleep as many-coloured as the snake   1445
That girds eternity? in life and truth,
    Might not my heart its cravings ever slake?
Was Cythna then a dream, and all my youth,
And all its hopes and fears, and all its joy and ruth?

V

Thus madness came again,—a milder madness,   1450
    Which darkened nought but time's unquiet flow
With supernatural shades of clinging sadness.
    That gentle Hermit, in my helpless woe,
    By my sick couch was busy to and fro,
Like a strong spirit ministrant of good: 1455
    When I was healed, he led me forth to show
The wonders of his sylvan solitude,
And we together sate by that isle-fretted flood.

VI

He knew his soothing words to weave with skill
    From all my madness told; like mine own heart,   1460
Of Cythna would he question me, until
    That thrilling name had ceased to make me start,
    From his familiar lips. It was not art,
Of wisdom and of justice when he spoke—
    When mid soft looks of pity, there would dart   1465
A glance as keen as is the lightning's stroke
When it doth rive the knots of some ancestral oak.

VII

Thus slowly from my brain the darkness rolled,
    My thoughts their due array did re-assume
Through the enchantments of that Hermit old;   1470
    Then I bethought me of the glorious doom
    Of those who sternly struggle to relume

1445 sleep *1904*] sleep, *1839, 1818*   1452 sadness.] sadness, *edd.*   1463 lips. It]
lips—it *edd.*

The lamp of Hope o'er man's bewildered lot,
 And, sitting by the waters, in the gloom
Of eve, to that friend's heart I told my thought—   1475
That heart which had grown old, but had corrupted not.

VIII

That hoary man had spent his livelong age
 In converse with the dead, who leave the stamp
Of ever-burning thoughts on many a page,
  When they are gone into the senseless damp   1480
 Of graves;—his spirit thus became a lamp
Of splendour, like to those on which it fed:
  Through peopled haunts, the City and the Camp,
Deep thirst for knowledge had his footsteps led,
And all the ways of men among mankind he read.   1485

IX

But custom maketh blind and obdurate
 The loftiest hearts:—he had beheld the woe
In which mankind was bound, but deemed that fate
  Which made them abject, would preserve them so;
  And in such faith, some steadfast joy to know,   1490
He sought this cell: but when fame went abroad,
  That one in Argolis did undergo
Torture for liberty, and that the crowd
High truths from gifted lips had heard and understood,

X

And that the multitude was gathering wide,—   1495
 His spirit leaped within his aged frame,
In lonely peace he could no more abide,
  But to the land on which the victor's flame
  Had fed, my native land, the Hermit came.
Each heart was there a shield, and every tongue   1500
  Was as a sword, of truth—young Laon's name
Rallied their secret hopes, though tyrants sung
Hymns of triumphant joy our scattered tribes among.

  1482 fed: *1904*] fed. *1839* fed *1818*   1494 understood,] understood; *edd.*
1495 wide,— *1904*] wide, *1839* wide; *1818*   1499 came.] came: *edd.*
1501 sword, *1904*] sword *1839, 1818*

XI

He came to the lone column on the rock,
　　And with his sweet and mighty eloquence　　1505
The hearts of those who watched it did unlock,
　　And made them melt in tears of penitence.
　　They gave him entrance free to bear me thence.
'Since this,' the old man said, 'seven years are spent,
　　While slowly truth on thy benighted sense　　1510
Has crept; the hope which wildered it has lent
Meanwhile to me the power of a sublime intent.

XII

'Yes, from the records of my youthful state,
　　And from the lore of bards and sages old,
From whatsoe'er my wakened thoughts create　　1515
　　Out of the hopes of thine aspirings bold,
　　Have I collected language to unfold
Truth to my countrymen; from shore to shore
　　Doctrines of human power my words have told;
They have been heard, and men aspire to more　　1520
Than they have ever gained or ever lost of yore.

XIII

'In secret chambers parents read, and weep,
　　My writings to their babes, no longer blind;
And young men gather when their tyrants sleep,
　　And vows of faith each to the other bind;　　1525
　　And marriageable maidens, who have pined
With love, till life seemed melting through their look,
　　A warmer zeal, a nobler hope now find;
And every bosom thus is rapt and shook,
Like autumn's myriad leaves in one swoln mountain-brook.

XIV

'The tyrants of the Golden City tremble　　1531
　　At voices which are heard about the streets,
The ministers of fraud can scarce dissemble
　　The lies of their own heart; but when one meets
　　Another at the shrine, he inly weets,　　1535

1512 Meanwhile] Meanwhile, *edd.*　　　1519 told; *1839*] told, *1904, 1818*

Though he says nothing, that the truth is known;
   Murderers are pale upon the judgement-seats,
And gold grows vile even to the wealthy crone,
And laughter fills the Fane, and curses shake the Throne.

XV

'Kind thoughts, and mighty hopes, and gentle deeds   1540
   Abound; for fearless love, and the pure law
Of mild equality and peace, succeeds
   To faiths which long have held the world in awe,
   Bloody and false, and cold:—as whirlpools draw
All wrecks of Ocean to their chasm, the sway   1545
   Of thy strong genius, Laon, which foresaw
This hope, compels all spirits to obey,
Which round thy secret strength now throng in wide array.

XVI

'For I have been thy passive instrument'—
   (As thus the old man spake, his countenance   1550
Gleamed on me like a spirit's)—'thou hast lent
   To me, to all, the power to advance
   Towards this unforeseen deliverance
From our ancestral chains—ay, thou didst rear
   That lamp of hope on high, which time nor chance   1555
Nor change may not extinguish, and my share
Of good was o'er the world its gathered beams to bear.

XVII

'But I, alas! am both unknown and old,
   And though the woof of wisdom I know well
To dye in hues of language, I am cold   1560
   In seeming, and the hopes which inly dwell,
   My manners note that I did long repel;
But Laon's name to the tumultuous throng
   Were like the star whose beams the waves compel
And tempests, and his soul-subduing tongue   1565
Were as a lance to quell the mailèd crest of wrong.

1541 Abound;] Abound, *edd.*   1555 chance *1904*] chance, *1839, 1818*
1557 good *1839*] good, *1904, 1818*

XVIII

'Perchance blood need not flow, if thou at length
   Wouldst rise; perchance the very slaves would spare
Their brethren and themselves; great is the strength
   Of words—for lately did a maiden fair,   1570
   Who from her childhood has been taught to bear
The tyrant's heaviest yoke, arise, and make
   Her sex the law of truth and freedom hear,
And with these quiet words—'For thine own sake
I prithee spare me;'—did with ruth so take   1575

XIX

'All hearts, that even the torturer who had bound
   Her meek calm frame, ere it was yet impaled,
Loosened her, weeping then; nor could be found
   One human hand to harm her—unassailed
   Therefore she walks through the great City, veiled   1580
In virtue's adamantine eloquence,
   'Gainst scorn, and death and pain thus trebly mailed,
And blending, in the smiles of that defence,
The Serpent and the Dove, Wisdom and Innocence.

XX

'The wild-eyed women throng around her path: 1585
   From their luxurious dungeons, from the dust
Of meaner thralls, from the oppressor's wrath,
   Or the caresses of his sated lust
   They congregate:—in her they put their trust;
The tyrants send their armèd slaves to quell   1590
   Her power;—they, even like a thunder-gust
Caught by some forest, bend beneath the spell
Of that young maiden's speech, and to their chiefs rebel.

XXI

'Thus she doth equal laws and justice teach
   To woman, outraged and polluted long;   1595
Gathering the sweetest fruit in human reach

1567 flow,] flow; *edd.*   1568 rise; *1839*] rise *1904, 1818*   1578 her,
1904] her *1839, 1818*   1583 blending, *1904*] blending *1839, 1818*

For those fair hands now free, while armèd wrong
Trembles before her look, though it be strong;
Thousands thus dwell beside her, virgins bright,
    And matrons with their babes, a stately throng!   1600
Lovers renew the vows which they did plight
In early faith, and hearts long parted now unite,

XXII

'And homeless orphans find a home near her,
    And those poor victims of the proud, no less,
Fair wrecks, on whom the smiling world with stir,   1605
    Thrusts the redemption of its wickedness:—
    In squalid huts, and in its palaces
Sits Lust alone, while o'er the land is borne
    Her voice, whose awful sweetness doth repress
All evil, and her foes relenting turn,   1610
And cast the vote of love in hope's abandoned urn.

XXIII

'So in the populous City, a young maiden
    Has baffled Havoc of the prey which he
Marks as his own, whene'er with chains o'erladen
    Men make them arms to hurl down tyranny,—   1615
    False arbiter between the bound and free;
And o'er the land, in hamlets and in towns
    The multitudes collect tumultuously,
    And throng in arms; but tyranny disowns
Their claim, and gathers strength around its trembling thrones.

XXIV

'Blood soon, although unwillingly, to shed,   1621
    The free cannot forbear—the Queen of Slaves,
The hoodwinked Angel of the blind and dead,
    Custom, with iron mace points to the graves
    Where her own standard desolately waves   1625

1613 Havoc *1904, 1839*] havoc *1818*   1615 tyranny,— *1904*] tyranny, *1839*,
1818   1621 unwillingly, *1904, 1839*] unwillingly *1818*   1625 Where *1904*,
1839] When *1818*

Over the dust of Prophets and of Kings.
　Many yet stand in her array—"she paves
Her path with human hearts," and o'er it flings
The wildering gloom of her immeasurable wings.

XXV

'There is a plain beneath the City's wall,　　　　　1630
　Bounded by misty mountains, wide and vast;
Millions there lift at Freedom's thrilling call
　Ten thousand standards wide; they load the blast
　Which bears one sound of many voices past,
And startles on his throne their sceptred foe:　　　1635
　He sits amid his idle pomp aghast,
And that his power hath passed away, doth know—
Why pause the victor swords to seal his overthrow?

XXVI

'The tyrant's guards resistance yet maintain:
　Fearless, and fierce, and hard as beasts of blood,　1640
They stand a speck amid the peopled plain;
　Carnage and ruin have been made their food
　From infancy; ill has become their good,
And for its hateful sake their will has wove
　The chains which eat their hearts; the multitude　1645
Surrounding them, with words of human love,
Seek from their own decay their stubborn minds to move.

XXVII

'Over the land is felt a sudden pause,
　As night and day those ruthless bands around,
The watch of love is kept:—a trance which awes　　1650
　The thoughts of men with hope—as, when the sound
　Of whirlwind, whose fierce blasts the waves and clouds
　　confound,
Dies suddenly, the mariner in fear
　Feels silence sink upon his heart—thus bound,
The conquerors pause, and oh! may freemen ne'er　　1655
Clasp the relentless knees of Dread the murderer!

1631 vast; *1839*] vast, *1904, 1818*　　　　1633 wide; *1839*] wide, *1904, 1818*
1640 blood, *1904*] blood; *1839, 1818*　　1643 infancy;] infancy—*edd.*　　1645 hearts;]
hearts— *edd.*　　1649 around, *1904*] around *1839, 1818*　　1651 as, *1904*] as
1839, 1818

XXVIII

'If blood be shed, 'tis but a change and choice
  Of bonds,—from slavery to cowardice:
A wretched fall!—Uplift thy charmèd voice!
  Pour on those evil men the love that lies   1660
  Hovering within those spirit-soothing eyes—
Arise, my friend, farewell!'—As thus he spake,
  From the green earth lightly I did arise,
As one out of dim dreams that doth awake,
And looked upon the depth of that reposing lake.   1665

XXIX

I saw my countenance reflected there;—
  And then my youth fell on me like a wind
Descending on still waters—my thin hair
  Was prematurely gray, my face was lined
  With channels, such as suffering leaves behind,   1670
Not age; my brow was pale, but in my cheek
  And lips a flush of gnawing fire did find
Their food and dwelling; though mine eyes might speak
A subtle mind and strong within a frame thus weak,

XXX

And though their lustre now was spent and faded,   1675
  Yet in my hollow looks and withered mien
The likeness of a shape for which was braided
  The brightest woof of genius still was seen—
  One who, methought, had gone from the world's scene,
And left it vacant—'twas her brother's face—   1680
  It might resemble her—it once had been
The mirror of her thoughts, and still the grace
Which her mind's shadow cast, left there a lingering trace.

XXXI

What then was I? She slumbered with the dead.
  Glory and joy and peace, had come and gone.   1685
Doth the cloud perish, when the beams are fled

1658 cowardice:] cowardice *edd.*   1673 Their *edd., except Ross.*, *who* amends
to Its. *See n., p. 386.*   1674 weak,] weak. *edd.*   1675 was *edd.; the*
were *of 1818 is corrected by Shelley in the erratum slip.*   1678 genius] genius, *edd.*
1680 brother's *LC*] lover's *RI. See n., p. 369.*

Which steeped its skirts in gold? or, dark and lone,
  Doth it not through the paths of night unknown,
On outspread wings of its own wind upborne
  Pour rain upon the earth? The stars are shown,   1690
When the cold moon sharpens her silver horn
Under the sea, and make the wide night not forlorn.

XXXII

Strengthened in heart, yet sad, that aged man
  I left, with interchange of looks and tears,
And lingering speech, and to the camp began   1695
  My way. O'er many a mountain-chain which rears
  Its hundred crests aloft, my spirit bears
My frame, o'er many a dale and many a moor;
  And gaily now meseems serene earth wears
The blosmy spring's star-bright investiture,   1700
A vision which aught sad from sadness might allure.

XXXIII

My powers revived within me, and I went
  As one whom winds waft o'er the bending grass,
Through many a vale of that broad continent.
  At night when I reposed, fair dreams did pass   1705
  Before my pillow;—my own Cythna was,
Not like a child of death, among them ever;
  When I arose from rest, a woful mass
  That gentlest sleep seemed from my life to sever,
As if the light of youth were not withdrawn for ever.   1710

XXXIV

Aye as I went, that maiden who had reared
  The torch of Truth afar, of whose high deeds
The Hermit in his pilgrimage had heard,
  Haunted my thoughts.—Ah, Hope its sickness feeds
  With whatso'er it finds, or flowers or weeds!   1715
Could she be Cythna?—Was that corpse a shade
  Such as self-torturing thought from madness breeds?
Why was this hope not torture? Yet it made
A light around my steps which would not ever fade.

1687 or, *1904*] or *1839, 1818*   1698 frame,] frame; *edd.*   moor;] moor,
edd.   1700 blosmy *1904, 1818*] bloomy *1839*   1701 aught *1904, 1839*] ought
1818   1706 was, *1904*] was *1839, 1818*

CANTO V

I

Over the utmost hill at length I sped,   1720
    A snowy steep:—the moon was hanging low
Over the Asian mountains, and outspread
    The plain, the City, and the camp below,
    Skirted the midnight ocean's glimmering flow;
The City's moonlit spires and myriad lamps,   1725
    Like stars in a sublunar sky did glow,
And fires blazed far amid the scattered camps,
Like springs of flame, which burst where'er swift Earthquake
    stamps.

II

All slept but those in watchful arms who stood,
    And those who sate tending the beacon's light;   1730
And the few sounds from that vast multitude
    Made silence more profound.—Oh, what a might
    Of human thought was cradled in that night!
How many hearts impenetrably veiled
    Beat underneath its shade! What secret fight   1735
Evil and good, in woven passions mailed,
Waged through that silent throng—a war that never failed!

III

And now the Power of Good held victory,
    So, through the labyrinth of many a tent,
Among the silent millions who did lie   1740
    In innocent sleep, exultingly I went;
    The moon had left Heaven desert now, but lent
From eastern morn the first faint lustre showed
    An armèd youth—over his spear he bent
His downward face.—'A friend!' I cried aloud,   1745
And quickly common hopes made freemen understood.

Canto V. 1724 flow; *1904*] flow *1839, 1818*   1730 light;] light, *edd.*   1732 pro-
found.—Oh, *1904*] profound—Oh, *1839, 1818*   1734 veiled *1904, 1839*] veiled,
1818   1735 shade! What] shade, what *edd.*   1737 throng—] throng; *edd.*
1738 victory, *1904*] victory *1818*   1745 face.— *1904, 1839*] face— *1818*

IV

I sate beside him while the morning beam
  Crept slowly over Heaven, and talked with him
Of those immortal hopes—a glorious theme,
    Which led us forth, until the stars grew dim!   1750
    And all the while, methought, his voice did swim
As if it drownèd in remembrance were
  Of thoughts which make the moist eyes overbrim:
At last, when daylight 'gan to fill the air,
He looked on me, and cried in wonder—'Thou art here!' 1755

V

Then, suddenly, I knew it was the youth
  In whom its earliest hopes my spirit found;
But envious tongues had stained his spotless truth,
    And thoughtless pride his love in silence bound,
    And shame and sorrow mine in toils had wound,   1760
Whilst he was innocent, and I deluded.
  The truth now came upon me; on the ground
Tears of repenting joy, which fast intruded,
Fell fast, and o'er its peace our mingling spirits brooded.

VI

Thus while with rapid lips and earnest eyes   1765
  We talked, a sound of sweeping conflict spread,
As from the earth did suddenly arise;
    From every tent roused by that clamour dread,
    Our bands outsprung and seized their arms—we sped
Towards the sound: our tribes were gathering far.   1770
  Those sanguine slaves amid ten thousand dead
Stabbed in their sleep, trampled in treacherous war
The gentle hearts whose power their lives had sought to spare.

VII

Like rabid snakes, that sting some gentle child
  Who brings them food, when winter false and fair   1775
Allures them forth with its cold smiles, so wild

1749 hopes—] hopes *edd.*   theme,] theme! *edd.*   1750 dim!] dim: *edd.*
1751 swim *1904*] swim, *1839, 1818*   1761 deluded.] deluded; *edd.*   1762 me;]
me, *edd.*   1765 Thus while] Thus, while *edd. See n., p. 369*   1766 spread, *1839
1818*] spread *1904*   1770 far. *1904*] far, *1839, 1818*   1772 war *1904*] war,
1839, 1818

They rage among the camp;—they overbear
The patriot hosts—confusion, then despair
Descends like night—when 'Laon!' one did cry.—
Like a bright ghost from Heaven that shout did scare
The slaves, and widening through the vaulted sky,   1781
Seemed sent from Earth to Heaven in sign of victory.

VIII

In sudden panic those false murderers fled,
Like insect tribes before the northern gale:
But swifter still, our hosts encompassèd   1785
Their shattered ranks, and in a craggy vale,
Where even their fierce despair might nought avail,
Hemmed them around!—And then revenge and fear
Made the high virtue of the patriots fail:
One pointed on his foe the mortal spear—   1790
I rushed before its point, and cried, 'Forbear, forbear!'

IX

The spear transfixed my arm that was uplifted
In swift expostulation, and the blood
Gushed round its point: I smiled, and—'Oh! thou gifted
With eloquence which shall not be withstood,   1795
Flow thus!'—I cried in joy, 'thou vital flood,
Until my heart be dry, ere thus the cause
For which thou wert aught worthy be subdued!—
Ah, ye are pale,—ye weep,—your passions pause,—
'Tis well! ye feel the truth of love's benignant laws.   1800

X

'Soldiers, our brethren and our friends are slain.
Ye murdered them, I think, as they did sleep!
Alas, what have ye done? the slightest pain
Which ye might suffer, there were eyes to weep,
But ye have quenched them—there were smiles to steep
Your hearts in balm, but they are lost in woe;   1806
And those whom love did set his watch to keep
Around your tents, truth's freedom to bestow,
Ye stabbed as they did sleep—but they forgive ye now.

1779 cry.—] cry: edd.   1787 avail, 1904, 1839] avail 1818   1798 subdued!—]
subdued— edd.   1804 weep, 1904] weep; 1839, 1818   1808 tents, 1904]
tents 1839, 1818

XI

'Oh wherefore should ill ever flow from ill,   1810
    And pain still keener pain for ever breed?
We all are brethren—even the slaves who kill
    For hire, are men; and to avenge misdeed
    On the misdoer, doth but Misery feed
With her own broken heart! O Earth, O Heaven!   1815
    And thou, dread Nature, which to every deed
And all that lives or is, to be hast given,
Even as to thee have these done ill, and are forgiven!

XII

'Join then your hands and hearts, and let the past
    Be as a grave which gives not up its dead   1820
To evil thoughts.'—A film then overcast
    My sense with dimness, for the wound, which bled
    Freshly, swift shadows o'er mine eyes had shed.
When I awoke, I lay mid friends and foes,
    And earnest countenances on me shed   1825
The light of questioning looks, whilst one did close
My wound with balmiest herbs, and soothed me to repose;

XIII

And one whose spear had pierced me, leaned beside,
    With quivering lips and humid eyes;—and all
Seemed like some brothers on a journey wide   1830
    Gone forth, whom now strange meeting did befall
    In a strange land, round one whom they might call
Their friend, their chief, their father, for assay
    Of peril, which had saved them from the thrall
Of death, now suffering. Thus the vast array   1835
Of those fraternal bands were reconciled that day.

XIV

Lifting the thunder of their acclamation,
    Towards the City then the multitude,
And I among them, went in joy—a nation

1817 lives *1904*] lives, *1839, 1818*   is, to be *1904*] is to be *1839, 1818*   hast
Ross. 1870] hath *1904, 1839, 1818*   1828 one whose *edd. ; Form.* suggests he,
whose   beside, *1904*] beside *1839, 1818*

Made free by love;—a mighty brotherhood   1840
Linked by a jealous interchange of good;
A glorious pageant, more magnificent
    Than kingly slaves arrayed in gold and blood,
When they return from carnage, and are sent
In triumph bright beneath the populous battlement.   1845

XV

Afar, the city-walls were thronged on high,
    And myriads on each giddy turret clung,
And to each spire far lessening in the sky
    Bright pennons on the idle winds were hung;
    As we approached, a shout of joyance sprung   1850
At once from all the crowd, as if the vast
    And peopled Earth its boundless skies among
The sudden clamour of delight had cast,
When from before its face some general wreck had passed.

XVI

Our armies through the City's hundred gates   1855
    Were poured, like brooks which to the rocky lair
Of some deep lake, whose silence them awaits,
    Throng from the mountains when the storms are there;
    And, as we passed through the calm sunny air,
A thousand flower-inwoven crowns were shed,   1860
    The token flowers of truth and freedom fair,
And fairest hands bound them on many a head,
Those angels of love's heaven, that over all was spread.

XVII

I trod as one tranced in some rapturous vision:
    Those bloody bands so lately reconciled,   1865
Were, ever as they went, by the contrition
    Of anger turned to love, from ill beguiled,
    And every one on them more gently smiled,
Because they had done evil:—the sweet awe
    Of such mild looks made their own hearts grow mild,
And did with soft attraction ever draw   1871
Their spirits to the love of freedom's equal law.

1848 sky *1904*] sky, *1839, 1818*   1858 there;] there *edd.*   1859 air,] air
edd.   1867 love, *1904*] love *1839, 1818*.

XVIII

And they, and all, in one loud symphony
  My name with Liberty commingling, lifted,
'The friend and the preserver of the free!   1875
  The parent of this joy!' and fair eyes gifted
  With feelings, caught from one who had uplifted
The light of a great spirit, round me shone;
  And all the shapes of this grand scenery shifted
Like restless clouds before the steadfast sun.   1880
Where was that Maid? I asked, but it was known of none.

XIX

Laone was the name her love had chosen,
  For she was nameless, and her birth none knew:
Where was Laone now?—The words were frozen
  Within my lips with fear; but to subdue   1885
  Such dreadful hope, to my great task was due,
And when at length one brought reply, that she
  To-morrow would appear, I then withdrew
To judge what need for that great throng might be,
For now the stars came thick over the twilight sea.   1890

XX

Yet need was none for rest or food to care,
  Even though that multitude was passing great,
Since each one for the other did prepare
  All kindly succour. Therefore to the gate
  Of the Imperial House, now desolate,   1895
I passed, and there was found aghast, alone,
  The fallen Tyrant!—Silently he sate
Upon the footstool of his golden throne,
Which, starred with sunny gems, in its own lustre shone.

XXI

Alone, but for one child, who led before him   1900
  A graceful dance: the only living thing
Of all the crowd, which thither to adore him
  Flocked yesterday, who solace sought to bring
  In his abandonment!—She knew the King

1880 sun.] sun,— *edd.*   1882 *See n., p. 369.*   1894 succour.] succour— *edd.*
1899 Which, *1904, 1839*] Which 1818

Had praised her dance of yore, and now she wove   1905
   Its circles, aye weeping and murmuring
Mid her sad task of unregarded love,
That to no smiles it might his speechless sadness move.

XXII

She fled to him, and wildly clasped his feet
   When human steps were heard:—he moved nor spoke,
Nor changed his hue, nor raised his looks to meet   1911
   The gaze of strangers. Our loud entrance woke
   The echoes of the hall, which circling broke
The calm of its recesses,—like a tomb
   Its sculptured walls vacantly to the stroke   1915
Of footfalls answered, and the twilight's gloom
Lay like a charnel's mist within the radiant dome.

XXIII

The little child stood up when we came nigh;
   Her lips and cheeks seemed very pale and wan,
But on her forehead, and within her eye   1920
   Lay beauty, which makes hearts that feed thereon
   Sick with excess of sweetness; on the throne
She leaned;—the King, with gathered brow, and lips
   Wreathed by long scorn, did inly sneer and frown
With hue like that when some great painter dips   1925
His pencil in the gloom of earthquake and eclipse.

XXIV

She stood beside him like a rainbow braided
   Within some storm, when scarce its shadows vast
From the blue paths of the swift sun have faded;
   A sweet and solemn smile, like Cythna's, cast   1930
   One moment's light, which made my heart beat fast,
O'er that child's parted lips—a gleam of bliss,
   A shade of vanished days. As the tears passed
Which wrapped it, even as with a father's kiss
I pressed those softest eyes in trembling tenderness.   1935

1912 strangers. Our] strangers—our *edd.*   1916 gloom *1904, 1839*] gloom, *1818*
1923 King, *1904, 1839*] King *1818*   1933 days. As] days,—as *edd.*

XXV

The sceptred wretch then from that solitude
  I drew, and, of his change compassionate,
With words of sadness soothed his rugged mood.
    But he, while pride and fear held deep debate,
    With sullen guile of ill-dissembled hate   1940
Glared on me as a toothless snake might glare:
  Pity, not scorn I felt, though desolate
The desolator now, and unaware
The curses which he mocked had caught him by the hair.

XXVI

I led him forth from that which now might seem   1945
  A gorgeous grave: through portals sculptured deep
With imagery beautiful as dream
    We went, and left the shades which tend on sleep
    Over its unregarded gold to keep
Their silent watch.—The child trod faintingly,   1950
  And as she went, the tears which she did weep
Glanced in the starlight; wildered seemèd she,
And when I spake for sobs she could not answer me.

XXVII

At last the tyrant cried, 'She hungers, slave,
  Stab her, or give her bread!'—It was a tone   1955
Such as sick fancies in a new-made grave
    Might hear. I trembled, for the truth was known;
    He with this child had thus been left alone,
And neither had gone forth for food,—but he
  In mingled pride and awe cowered near his throne, 1960
And she a nursling of captivity
Knew nought beyond those walls, nor what such change
      might be.

XXVIII

And he was troubled at a charm withdrawn
  Thus suddenly; that sceptres ruled no more—
That even from gold the dreadful strength was gone 1965

1953 spake] spake, *edd.*   1957 known; *1904*] known, *1839, 1818*   1965 gone
1839] gone, *1904, 1818*

Which once made all things subject to its power.
　Such wonder seized him, as if hour by hour
The past had come again; and the swift fall
　Of one so great and terrible of yore
To desolateness, in the hearts of all   1970
Like wonder stirred, who saw such awful change befall.

XXIX

A mighty crowd, such as the wide land pours
　Once in a thousand years, now gathered round
The fallen tyrant;—like the rush of showers
　Of hail in spring, pattering along the ground,   1975
　Their many footsteps fell, else came no sound
From the wide multitude; that lonely man
　Then knew the burden of his change, and found,
Concealing in the dust his visage wan,
Refuge from the keen looks which through his bosom ran.

XXX

And he was faint withal; I sate beside him   1981
　Upon the earth, and took that child so fair
From his weak arms, that ill might none betide him
　Or her;—when food was brought to them, her share
To his averted lips the child did bear,   1985
But, when she saw he had enough, she ate
　And wept the while;—the lonely man's despair
Hunger then overcame, and of his state
Forgetful, on the dust as in a trance he sate.

XXXI

Slowly the silence of the multitudes   1990
　Passed, as when far is heard in some lone dell
The gathering of a wind among the woods.
　'And he is fallen!' they cry, 'he who did dwell
　Like famine or the plague, or aught more fell
Among our homes, is fallen! the murderer   1995
　Who slaked his thirsting soul as from a well
Of blood and tears with ruin! he is here!
Sunk in a gulf of scorn from which none may him rear!'

1966 power.] power— *edd.*   1969 yore *1839*] yore, *1904, 1818*   1992 woods.]
woods— *edd.*

XXXII

Then was heard—'He who judged let him be brought
   To judgement! blood for blood cries from the soil   2000
On which his crimes have deep pollution wrought!
   Shall Othman only unavenged despoil?
   Shall they who by the stress of grinding toil
Wrest from the unwilling earth his luxuries
   Perish for crime, while his foul blood may boil,   2005
Or creep within his veins at will?—Arise!
And to high justice make her chosen sacrifice.'

XXXIII

'What do ye seek? what fear ye,' then I cried,
   Suddenly starting forth, 'that ye should shed
The blood of Othman?—if your hearts are tried   2010
   In the true love of freedom, cease to dread
   This one poor lonely man. Beneath Heaven spread
In purest light above us all, through earth,
   Maternal earth, who doth her sweet smiles shed
For all, let him go free; until the worth   2015
Of human nature win from these a second birth.

XXXIV

'What call ye *justice*? Is there one who ne'er
   In secret thought has wished another's ill?—
Are ye all pure? Let those stand forth who hear,
   And tremble not. Shall they insult and kill,   2020
   If such they be? their mild eyes can they fill
With the false anger of the hypocrite?
   Alas, such were not pure,—the chastened will
Of virtue sees that justice is the light
Of love, and not revenge, and terror and despite.'   2025

XXXV

The murmur of the people, slowly dying,
   Paused as I spake; then those who near me were,
   Cast gentle looks where the lone man was lying

2008 ye, *1904*] ye? *1839, 1818*   2010 Othman?— *1904*] Othman— *1839, 1818*
2012 man. Beneath] man—beneath *edd.*   2014 earth, *1904*] earth *1839, 1818*
2023 pure,— *1904*] pure— *1839, 1818*   2026 people, *1904, 1839*] people
1818   2027 spake; *1839*] spake, *1904, 1818*

Shrouding his head, which now that infant fair
Clasped on her lap in silence;—through the air   2030
Sobs were then heard, and many kissed my feet
In pity's madness, and to the despair
Of him whom late they cursed, a solace sweet
His very victims brought—soft looks and speeches meet.

XXXVI

Then to a home for his repose assigned,   2035
Accompanied by the still throng he went
In silence, where, to soothe his rankling mind,
Some likeness of his ancient state was lent;
And if his heart could have been innocent
As those who pardoned him, he might have ended   2040
His days in peace; but his straight lips were bent,
Men said, into a smile which guile portended,
A sight with which that child like hope with fear was blended.

XXXVII

'Twas midnight now, the eve of that great day
Whereon the many nations at whose call   2045
The chains of earth, like mist melted away,
Decreed to hold a sacred festival,
A rite to attest the equality of all
Who live. So to their homes, to dream or wake
All went. The sleepless silence did recall   2050
Laone to my thoughts, with hopes that make
The flood recede from which their thirst they seek to slake.

XXXVIII

The dawn flowed forth, and from its purple fountains
I drank those hopes which make the spirit quail,
As to the plain between the misty mountains   2055
And the great City, with a countenance pale
I went:—it was a sight which might avail
To make men weep exulting tears, for whom
Now first from human power the reverend veil
Was torn, to see Earth from her general womb   2060
Pour forth her swarming sons to a fraternal doom;

2037 where, *1904, 1839*] where *1818*   2046 earth,] earth *edd.*   2054 quail,
1904, 1839] quail; *1818*

XXXIX

To see, far glancing in the misty morning,
　　The signs of that innumerable host;
To hear one sound of many made, the warning
　　Of Earth to Heaven from its free children tossed;　　2065
　　While the eternal hills, and the sea lost
In wavering light, and, starring the blue sky
　　The city's myriad spires of gold, almost
With human joy made mute society—
Its witnesses with men who must hereafter be;　　2070

XL

To see, like some vast island from the Ocean,
　　The Altar of the Federation rear
Its pile i' the midst, a work, which the devotion
　　Of millions in one night created there,
　　Sudden, as when the moonrise makes appear　　2075
Strange clouds in the east,—a marble pyramid
　　Distinct with steps, that mighty shape did wear
The light of genius; its still shadow hid
Far ships: to know its height the morning mists forbid,—

XLI

To hear the restless multitudes for ever　　2080
　　Around the base of that great Altar flow,
As on some mountain-islet burst and shiver
　　Atlantic waves; and solemnly and slow,
　　As the wind bore that tumult to and fro,
To feel the dreamlike music, which did swim　　2085
　　Like beams through floating clouds on waves below,
Falling in pauses, from that Altar dim
As silver-sounding tongues breathed an aëreal hymn.

XLII

To hear, to see, to live, was on that morn
　　Lethean joy! so that all those assembled　　2090
Cast off their memories of the past outworn;

2063 host;] host *edd.*　　2065 tossed;] tossed, *edd.*　　2069 society— *1904*]
society *1839* society, *1818*　　2070 be;] be. *edd.*　　2071 see, *1904, 1839*] see *1818*
2073 midst,] midst; *edd.*　　2076 east,—] east; *edd.*　　2077 steps,] steps: *edd.*
2079 forbid,—] forbid! *edd.*　　2083 slow,] slow *edd.*　　2086 below, *1839, 1818,*]
below *1904*

Two only bosoms with their own life trembled,
  And mine was one,—and we had both dissembled;
So with a beating heart I went, and one,
  Who having much, covets yet more, resembled,—   2095
A lost and dear possession, which not won,
He walks in lonely gloom beneath the noonday sun.

XLIII

To the great Pyramid I came: its stair
  With female choirs was thronged, the loveliest
Among the free, grouped with its sculptures rare;   2100
  As I approached, the morning's golden mist,
  Which now the wonder-stricken breezes kissed
With their cold lips, fled, and the summit shone
  Like Athos seen from Samothracia, dressed
In earliest light, by vintagers. And one   2105
Sate there, a female Shape upon an ivory throne:

XLIV

A Form most like the imagined habitant
  Of silver exhalations sprung from dawn,
By winds which feed on sunrise woven, to enchant
  The faiths of men: all mortal eyes were drawn,   2110
  As famished mariners through strange seas gone
Gaze on a burning watch-tower, by the light
  Of those divinest lineaments—alone
With thoughts which none could share, from that fair sight
I turned in sickness, for a veil shrouded her countenance bright.

XLV

And, neither did I hear the acclamations,   2116
  Which from brief silence bursting, filled the air
With her strange name and mine, from all the nations
  Which we, they said, in strength had gathered there
  From the sleep of bondage; nor the vision fair   2120
Of that bright pageantry beheld,—but blind
  And silent as a breathing corpse did fare,
Leaning upon my friend, till like a wind
To fevered cheeks a voice flowed o'er my troubled mind.

2095 resembled,—] resembled; *edd.*   2099 thronged,] thronged: *edd.*   2105 light,
1904] light *1839, 1818*   vintagers. And] vintagers, and *edd.*   2106 throne: *1904*]
throne, *1839, 1818*   2122 silent] silent, *edd.*

XLVI

Like music of some minstrel heavenly-gifted　　　2125
　　To one whom fiends enthral, this voice to me;
Scarce did I wish her veil to be uplifted,
　　I was so calm and joyous.—I could see
　　The platform where we stood, the statues three
Which kept their marble watch on that high shrine,　　2130
　　The multitudes, the mountains, and the sea,—
As when eclipse hath passed, things sudden shine
To men's astonished eyes most clear and crystalline.

XLVII

At first Laone spoke most tremulously:
　　But soon her voice the calmness which it shed　　2135
Gathered, and—'Thou art whom I sought to see,
　　And thou art our first votary here,' she said:
　　'I had a brother once, but he is dead!—
And of all those on the wide earth who breathe,
　　Thou dost resemble him alone—I spread　　2140
This veil between us two, that thou beneath
Shouldst image one who may have been long lost in death.

XLVIII

'For this wilt thou not henceforth pardon me?
　　Yes, but those joys which silence well requite
Forbid reply;—why men have chosen me　　2145
　　To be the Priestess of this holiest rite
　　I scarcely know, but that the floods of light
Which flow over the world, have borne me hither
　　To meet thee, long most dear. And now unite
Thine hand with mine, and may all comfort wither　　2150
From both the hearts whose pulse in joy now beat together,

XLIX

'If our own will as others' law we bind,
　　If the foul worship trampled here we fear;
If as ourselves we cease to love our kind!'—
　　She paused, and pointed upwards—sculptured there　2155
　　Three shapes around her ivory throne appear;

2125 heavenly-gifted] heavenly-gifted, *edd.*　　2131 sea,—] sea; *edd.*　　2135 the
1904, 1818] that *1839*　　2138 brother *LC*] dear friend *RI*　　2149 dear. And] dear;
and *edd.*　　2151 beat *1904, 1818*] beats *1839. See n., p. 369.*

One was a Giant, like a child asleep
 On a loose rock, whose grasp crushed, as it were
In dream, sceptres and crowns; and one did keep
Its watchful eyes in doubt whether to smile or weep; 2160

L

A Woman sitting on the sculptured disk
 Of the broad earth, and feeding from one breast
A human babe and a young basilisk;
 Her looks were sweet as Heaven's when loveliest
 In autumn eves. The third Image was dressed 2165
In white wings swift as clouds in winter skies;
 Beneath his feet, 'mongst ghastliest forms, repressed
Lay Faith, an obscene worm, who sought to rise,
While calmly on the sun he turned his diamond eyes.

LI

Beside that Image then I sate, while she 2170
 Stood, mid the throngs which ever ebbed and flowed,
Like light amid the shadows of the sea
 Cast from one cloudless star, and on the crowd
 That touch which none who feels forgets, bestowed;
And whilst the sun returned the steadfast gaze 2175
 Of the great Image, as o'er Heaven it glode,
That rite had place; it ceased when sunset's blaze
Burned o'er the isles. All stood in joy and deep amaze
 When in the silence of all spirits there
Laone's voice was felt, and through the air 2180
Her thrilling gestures spoke, most eloquently fair:—

1

'Calm art thou as yon sunset!—swift and strong
As new-fledged eagles, beautiful and young,
 That float among the blinding beams of morning;
 And underneath thy feet writhe Faith, and Folly, 2185
Custom, and Hell, and mortal Melancholy!

2176 Image, *1904*] Image *1839, 1818* 2178 isles. All *1904*] isles; all *1839, 1818*
amaze] amaze— *1904* amaze; *1839* amaze. *1818* 2181 fair:— *1904*] fair. *1839*,
1818 2182 sunset!—] sunset! *edd.* 2186 Melancholy!] Melancholy— *edd.*

Hark, the Earth starts to hear the mighty warning
  Of thy voice sublime and holy!
  Its free spirits here assembled,
    See thee, feel thee, know thee now,—   2190
    To thy voice their hearts have trembled
      Like ten thousand clouds which flow
    With one wide wind as it flies!—
Wisdom, thy irresistible children rise
To hail thee, and the elements they chain   2195
And their own will, to swell the glory of thy train!

2

'O Spirit vast and deep as Night and Heaven!
Mother and soul of all to which is given
  The light of life, the loveliness of being,
    Lo! thou dost re-ascend the human heart,   2200
    Thy throne of power, almighty as thou wert
  In dreams of Poets old grown pale by seeing
    The shade of thee:—now, millions start
    To feel thy lightnings through them burning:
      Nature, or God, or Love, or Pleasure,   2205
    Or Sympathy the sad tears turning
      To mutual smiles, a drainless treasure,
  Descends amidst us;—Scorn, and Hate,
Revenge and Selfishness are desolate
A hundred nations swear that there shall be   2210
Pity and Peace and Love, among the good and free!

3

'Eldest of things, divine Equality!
Wisdom and Love are but the slaves of thee,
  The Angels of thy sway, who pour around thee
    Treasures from all the cells of human thought   2215
    And from the Stars, and from the Ocean brought
  And the last living heart whose beatings bound thee.
    The powerful and the wise had sought
    Thy coming; thou, in light descending

2187 Hark,] Hark! *edd.*   2188 holy!] holy; *edd.*   2194 Wisdom,] Wisdom! *edd.*
2196 will, *1904*] will *1839, 1818*   train!] train. *1904, 1839*   train *1818*   2201 wert
1904] wert, *1839, 1818*   2215 thought] thought, *edd.*   2217 thee.] thee: *edd.*
2219 coming; *1839*] coming, *1904, 1818*   thou,] thou *edd.*

O'er the wide land which is thine own,   2220
Like the Spring whose breath is blending
　　All blasts of fragrance into one,
Comest upon the paths of men!—
Earth bares her general bosom to thy ken,
And all her children here in glory meet   2225
To feed upon thy smiles, and clasp thy sacred feet.

4

'My brethren, we are free! the plains and mountains,
The gray sea-shore, the forests and the fountains,
Are haunts of happiest dwellers;—man and woman,
　　Their common bondage burst, may freely borrow   2230
　　From lawless love a solace for their sorrow.
For oft we still must weep, since we are human.
　　A stormy night's serenest morrow,
　　Whose showers are pity's gentle tears,
　　　　Whose clouds are smiles of those that die   2235
　　Like infants without hopes or fears,
　　　　And whose beams are joys that lie
　　In blended hearts, now holds dominion;
The dawn of mind, which upwards on a pinion
Borne, swift as sunrise, far illumines space,   2240
And clasps this barren world in its own bright embrace!

5

'My brethren, we are free! The fruits are glowing
Beneath the stars, and the night winds are flowing
O'er the ripe corn, the birds and beasts are dreaming—
　　Never again may blood of bird or beast   2245
　　Stain with its venomous stream a human feast,
To the pure skies in accusation steaming;
　　Avenging poisons shall have ceased
　　To feed disease and fear and madness;
　　　　The dwellers of the earth and air   2250
　　Shall throng around our steps in gladness
　　　　Seeking their food or refuge there.

2220 own, *1839*] own *1904, 1818*   2227 brethren, *1904, 1839*] brethren *1818*
2231 sorrow.] sorrow; *edd.*   2247 steaming; *1904, 1839*] steaming, *1818*
2249 madness;] madness, *edd.*

Our toil from thought all glorious forms shall cull,
To make this Earth, our home, more beautiful,
And Science, and her sister Poesy,　　　　　　　　2255
Shall clothe in light the fields and cities of the free!

6

'Victory, Victory to the prostrate nations!
Bear witness Night, and ye mute Constellations
Who gaze on us from your crystalline cars!
　Thoughts have gone forth whose powers can sleep no more!
　Victory! Victory! Earth's remotest shore,　　　　2261
Regions which groan beneath the Antarctic stars,
　　The green lands cradled in the roar
　　Of western waves, and wildernesses
　　　Peopled and vast, which skirt the oceans　　2265
　　Where morning dyes her golden tresses,
　　　Shall soon partake our high emotions:
Kings shall turn pale! Almighty Fear
The Fiend-God, when our charmèd name he hear,
Shall fade like shadow from his thousand fanes,　　2270
While Truth with Joy enthroned o'er his lost empire reigns!'

LII

Ere she had ceased, the mists of night entwining
　Their dim woof, floated o'er the infinite throng;
She, like a spirit through the darkness shining,
　In tones whose sweetness silence did prolong,　　2275
　As if to lingering winds they did belong,
Poured forth her inmost soul: a passionate speech
　With wild and thrilling pauses woven among,
Which whoso heard, was mute, for it could teach
To rapture like her own all listening hearts to reach.　　2280

LIII

Her voice was as a mountain-stream which sweeps
　The withered leaves of Autumn to the lake,
And in some deep and narrow bay then sleeps
　In the shadow of the shores; as dead leaves wake
　Under the wave, in flowers and herbs which make　　2285

Those green depths beautiful when skies are blue,
  The multitude so moveless did partake
Such living change, and kindling murmurs flew
  As o'er that speechless calm delight and wonder grew.

LIV

Over the plain the throngs were scattered then   2290
  In groups around the fires, which from the sea
Even to the gorge of the first mountain-glen
  Blazed wide and far; the banquet of the free
  Was spread beneath many a dark cypress-tree,
Beneath whose spires, which swayed in the red flame,   2295
  Reclining, as they ate, of Liberty,
  And Hope, and Justice, and Laone's name,
Earth's children did a woof of happy converse frame.

LV

Their feast was such as Earth, the general mother,
  Pours from her fairest bosom, when she smiles   2300
In the embrace of Autumn;—to each other
  As when some parent fondly reconciles
  Her warring children, she their wrath beguiles
With her own sustenance; they relenting weep—
  Such was this Festival, which from her isles   2305
  And continents, and winds, and oceans deep,
All shapes might throng to share, that fly, or walk, or creep,—

LVI

Might share in peace and innocence, for gore
  Or poison none this festal did pollute,
But piled on high, an overflowing store   2310
  Of pomegranates, and citrons, fairest fruit,
  Melons, and dates, and figs, and many a root
Sweet and sustaining, and bright grapes ere yet
  Accursed fire their mild juice could transmute
Into a mortal bane, and brown corn set   2315
In baskets; with pure streams their thirsting lips they wet.

2295 flame, *1904, e. 10*] light, *1839, 1818. See n., p. 369.*   2304 weep—]
weep: *edd.*   2305 her *Shelley's erratum slip*] their *edd. generally. Cf. Form.*
1876, I. 303, where the correction is noted as made, with I. 195, where it is, in fact, omitted
2307 creep,— *1904*] creep. *1839, 1818*

LVII

Laone had descended from the shrine,
  And every deepest look and holiest mind
Fed on her form, though now those tones divine
  Were silent as she passed; she did unwind   2320
  Her veil, as with the crowds of her own kind
She mixed; some impulse made my heart refrain
  From seeking her that night, so I reclined
Amidst a group, where on the utmost plain
A festal watchfire burned beside the dusky main.   2325

LVIII

And joyous was our feast; pathetic talk,
  And wit, and harmony of choral strains,
While far Orion o'er the waves did walk
  That flow among the isles, held us in chains
  Of sweet captivity, which none disdains   2330
Who feels; but when his zone grew dim in mist
  Which clothes the ocean's bosom, o'er the plains
The multitudes went homeward, to their rest,
Which that delightful day with its own shadow blessed.

CANTO VI

I

BESIDE the dimness of the glimmering sea,   2335
  Weaving swift language from impassioned themes,
With that dear friend I lingered, who to me
  So late had been restored, beneath the gleams
  Of the silver stars; and ever in soft dreams
Of future love and peace sweet converse lapped   2340
  Our willing fancies, till the pallid beams
Of the last watchfire fell, and darkness wrapped
The waves, and each bright chain of floating fire was snapped,

II

And till we came even to the City's wall
  And the great gate; then, none knew whence or why,
Disquiet on the multitudes did fall: 2346

Canto VI. 2343 snapped,] snapped; *1904*   snapped. *1839, 1818*   2345 gate;
1904] gate, *1839, 1818*

And first, one pale and breathless passed us by,
   And stared and spoke not;—then with piercing cry
A troop of wild-eyed women, by the shrieks
   Of their own terror driven,—tumultuously   2350
Hither and thither hurrying with pale cheeks,
Each one from fear unknown a sudden refuge seeks.

III

Then, rallying cries of treason and of danger
   Resounded: and—'They come! to arms! to arms!
The Tyrant is amongst us, and the stranger   2355
   Comes to enslave us in his name! to arms!'
   In vain: for Panic, the pale fiend who charms
Strength to forswear her right, those millions swept
   Like waves before the tempest—these alarms
Came to me, as to know their cause I lept   2360
On the gate's turret, and in rage and grief and scorn I wept!

IV

For to the north I saw the town on fire,
   And its red light made morning pallid now,
Which burst over wide Asia;—louder, higher,
   The yells of victory and the screams of woe   2365
   I heard approach, and saw the throng below
Stream through the gates like foam-wrought waterfalls
   Fed from a thousand storms—the fearful glow
Of bombs flares overhead—at intervals
The red artillery's bolt mangling among them falls.   2370

V

And now the horsemen come—and all was done
   Swifter than I have spoken—I beheld
Their red swords flash in the unrisen sun.
   I rushed among the rout, to have repelled
   That miserable flight—one moment quelled   2375
By voice and looks and eloquent despair,
   As if reproach from their own hearts withheld
Their steps, they stood; but soon came pouring there
New multitudes, and did those rallied bands o'erbear.

2352 seeks.] seeks— *edd.*   2374 rout, *1904*] rout *1839, 1818*   2376 voice
1904] voice, *1839 1818*   looks *1904*] looks, *1839, 1818*

VI

I strove, as, drifted on some cataract   2380
    By irresistible streams, some wretch might strive
Who hears its fatal roar:—the files compact
    Whelmed me, and from the gate availed to drive
    With quickening impulse, as each bolt did rive
Their ranks with bloodier chasm:—into the plain   2385
    Disgorged at length the dead and the alive
In one dread mass, were parted, and the stain
Of blood, from mortal steel fell o'er the fields like rain.

VII

For now the despot's bloodhounds, with their prey
    Unarmed and unaware, were gorging deep   2390
Their gluttony of death; the loose array
    Of horsemen o'er the wide fields murdering sweep,
    And with loud laughter for their tyrant reap
A harvest sown with other hopes, the while,
    Far overhead, ships from Propontis keep   2395
A killing rain of fire:—when the waves smile
As sudden earthquakes light many a volcano-isle,

VIII

Thus sudden, unexpected feast was spread
    For the carrion-fowls of Heaven.—I saw the sight
I moved—I lived—as o'er the heaps of dead,   2400
    Whose stony eyes glared in the morning light
    I trod;—to me there came no thought of flight,
But with loud cries of scorn which whoso heard
    That dreaded death, felt in his veins the might
Of virtuous shame return, the crowd I stirred,   2405
And desperation's hope in many hearts recurred.

IX

A band of brothers gathering round me, made,
    Although unarmed, a steadfast front, and still
Retreating, with stern looks beneath the shade
    Of gathered eyebrows, did the victors fill   2410

2380 as, *1904*] as *1839, 1818*   2389 bloodhounds,] bloodhounds *edd.*   prey
1904] prey, *1839, 1818*   2397 volcano-isle, *1904 (misprinted in 1970 reprint)*] volcano-
isle. *1839, 1818. See n., p. 369.*   2399 sight— *1904, 1839*] sight *1818*

With doubt even in success; deliberate will
Inspired our growing troop; not overthrown
    It gained the shelter of a grassy hill,
And ever still our comrades were hewn down,
And their defenceless limbs beneath our footsteps strown.

X

Immovably we stood—in joy I found,   2416
    Beside me then, firm as a giant pine
Among the mountain-vapours driven around,
    The old man whom I loved—his eyes divine
    With a mild look of courage answered mine;   2420
And my young friend was near, and ardently
    His hand grasped mine a moment—now the line
Of war extended, to our rallying cry
As myriads flocked in love and brotherhood to die.

XI

For ever while the sun was climbing Heaven   2425
    The horseman hewed our unarmed myriads down
Safely, though when by thirst of carnage driven
    Too near, those slaves were swiftly overthrown
    By hundreds leaping on them:—flesh and bone
Soon made our ghastly ramparts; then the shaft   2430
    Of the artillery from the sea was thrown
More fast and fiery, and the conquerors laughed
In pride to hear the wind our screams of torment waft.

XII

For on one side alone the hill gave shelter,
    So vast that phalanx of unconquered men,   2435
And there the living in the blood did welter
    Of the dead and dying, which, in that green glen,
    Like stifled torrents, made a plashy fen
Under the feet. Thus was the butchery waged
    While the sun clomb Heaven's eastern steep—but when
It 'gan to sink, a fiercer combat raged,   2441
For in more doubtful strife the armies were engaged.

2412 troop;] troop, *edd.*   2420 mine;] mine, *edd.*   2426 horseman *1904,*
1818, and, probably, e. 10] horsemen *1839. See n., p. 387.*   2436 the blood *1904,*
1818] their blood *1839*   2437 glen, *1904, 1839*] glen *1818*   2439 feet. Thus]
feet—thus *edd.*   2441 sink,] sink— *edd.*

XIII

Within a cave upon the hill were found
  A bundle of rude pikes, the instrument
Of those who war but on their native ground   2445
  For natural rights: a shout of joyance sent
  Even from our hearts the wide air pierced and rent,
As those few arms the bravest and the best
  Seized, and each sixth, thus armed, did now present
A line which covered and sustained the rest,   2450
A confident phalanx, which the foe on every side invest.

XIV

That onset turned the foes to flight almost;
  But soon they saw their present strength, and knew
That coming night would to our resolute host
  Bring victory; so dismounting, close they drew   2455
  Their glittering files, and then the combat grew
Unequal but most horrible;—and ever
  Our myriads, whom the swift bolt overthrew,
Or the red sword, failed like a mountain-river
Which rushes forth in foam to sink in sands for ever.   2460

XV

Sorrow and shame, to see with their own kind
  Our human brethren mix, like beasts of blood,
To mutual ruin armed by one behind
  Who sits and scoffs!—That friend so mild and good,
  Who like its shadow near my youth had stood,   2465
Was stabbed!—my old preserver's hoary hair
  With the flesh clinging to its roots, was strewed
Under my feet!—I lost all sense or care,
And like the rest I grew desperate and unaware.

XVI

The battle became ghastlier; in the midst   2470
  I paused, and saw how ugly and how fell
O Hate! thou art, even when thy life thou shedd'st

2452 almost; *1904, 1839*] almost *1818*   2462 blood, *1904*] blood *1839, 1818*
2470 ghastlier;] ghastlier— *edd.*   2471 saw] saw, *edd.*

For love. The ground in many a little dell
Was broken, up and down whose steeps befell
Alternate victory and defeat, and there   2475
    The combatants with rage most horrible
Strove, and their eyes started with cracking stare,
And impotent their tongues they lolled into the air,

XVII

Flaccid and foamy, like a mad dog's hanging;
    Want, and Moon-madness, and the Pest's swift bane 2480
When its shafts smite—while yet its bow is twanging—
    Have each their mark and sign—some ghastly stain;
    And this was thine, O War! of hate and pain
Thou loathèd slave. I saw all shapes of death
    And ministered to many, o'er the plain   2485
While carnage in the sunbeam's warmth did seethe,
Till twilight o'er the east wove her serenest wreath.

XVIII

The few who yet survived, resolute and firm
    Around me fought. At the decline of day
Winding above the mountain's snowy term   2490
    New banners shone: they quivered in the ray
    Of the sun's unseen orb. Ere night the array
Of fresh troops hemmed us in. Of those brave bands
    I soon survived alone—and now I lay
Vanquished and faint, the grasp of bloody hands   2495
I felt, and saw on high the glare of falling brands,

XIX

When on my foes a sudden terror came,
    And they fled, scattering—lo! with reinless speed
A black Tartarian horse of giant frame
    Comes trampling over the dead, the living bleed   2500
    Beneath the hoofs of that tremendous steed,
On which, like to an Angel, robed in white,
    Sate one waving a sword;—the hosts recede
And fly, as through their ranks with awful might,
Sweeps in the shadow of eve that Phantom swift and bright;

2480 Pest's swift bane *1839*] pest's swift Bane *1904, 1818. See n., p. 369.*   2492 orb.
Ere] orb—ere *edd.*   2493 in. Of] in—of *edd.*   2496 brands,] brands; *edd.*

XX

And its path made a solitude.—I rose　　　　2506
　　And marked its coming: it relaxed its course
As it approached me, and the wind that flows
　　Through night, bore accents to mine ear whose force
　　Might create smiles in death. The Tartar horse　　　2510
Paused, and I saw the shape its might which swayed,
　　And heard her musical pants, like the sweet source
Of waters in the desert, as she said,
'Mount with me, Laon, now!'—I rapidly obeyed.

XXI

Then: 'Away! away!' she cried, and stretched her sword
　　As 'twere a scourge over the courser's head,　　　2516
And lightly shook the reins.—We spake no word,
　　But like the vapour of the tempest fled
　　Over the plain; her dark hair was dispread
Like the pine's locks upon the lingering blast;　　　2520
　　Over mine eyes its shadowy strings it spread
Fitfully, and the hills and streams fled fast,
As o'er their glimmering forms the steed's broad shadow passed.

XXII

And his hoofs ground the rocks to fire and dust,
　　His strong sides made the torrents rise in spray,　　　2525
And turbulence, as of a whirlwind's gust,
　　Surrounded us;—and still away! away!
　　Through the desert night we sped, while she alway
Gazed on a mountain which we neared, whose crest,
　　Crowned with a marble ruin, in the ray　　　2530
Of the obscure stars gleamed;—its rugged breast
The steed strained up, and then his impulse did arrest

XXIII

A rocky hill which overhung the Ocean:—
　　From that lone ruin, when the steed that panted
　　Paused, might be heard the murmur of the motion　　　2535

2510 death. The] death—the *edd.*　　　2517 reins.—We *1904, 1839*] reins:—We
1818　　　word, *1904, 1839*] word *1818*　　　2526 of *1904, 1818, e. 10*] if *1839*　　　gust,
as suggested by Form.] gust *edd.*　　　2529 crest, *1904*] crest *1839, 1818*　　　2532 arrest]
arrest. *edd., making an anacoluthon of the next line, where* hill *gives the verb a subject*

Of waters, as in spots for ever haunted
By the choicest winds of Heaven, which are enchanted
To music, by the wands of Solitude,
That wizard wild, and the far tents implanted
Upon the plain, be seen by those who stood   2540
Thence marking the dark shore of Ocean's curvèd flood.

XXIV

One moment these were heard and seen—another
Passed; and the two who stood beneath that night
Each only heard, or saw, or felt the other;
As from the lofty steed she did alight,   2545
Cythna, (for, from the eyes whose deepest light
Of love and sadness made my lips feel pale
With influence strange of mournfullest delight,
My own sweet sister looked), with joy did quail,
And felt her strength in tears of human weakness fail.   2550

XXV

And for a space in my embrace she rested,
Her head on my unquiet heart reposing,
While my faint arms her languid frame invested;
At length she looked on me, and half unclosing
Her tremulous lips, said: 'Friend, thy bands were losing
The battle, as I stood before the King   2556
In bonds.—I burst them then, and swiftly choosing
The time, did seize a Tartar's sword, and spring
Upon his horse, and, swift as on the whirlwind's wing,

XXVI

'Have thou and I been borne beyond pursuer,   2560
And we are here.'—Then turning to the steed,
She pressed the white moon on his front with pure
And rose-like lips, and many a fragrant weed
From the green ruin plucked, that he might feed;—
But I to a stone seat that Maiden led,   2565
And kissing her fair eyes, said, 'Thou hast need
Of rest,' and I heaped up the courser's bed
In a green mossy nook, with mountain-flowers dispread.

2537–9 *See n., p. 388.*   2543 night] night, *edd. See n., p. 388.*   2549 sister
LC] Cythna *RI*   2551 And *1904, 1839*] And, *1818*   2559 and, *1904*] and
1839, 1818

XXVII

Within that ruin, where a shattered portal
　　Looks to the eastern stars (abandoned now　　　　2570
By man, to be the home of things immortal,
　　Memories, like awful ghosts which come and go,
　　And must inherit all he builds below
When he is gone), a hall stood, o'er whose roof
　　Fair clinging weeds with ivy pale did grow,　　　　2575
Clasping its gray rents with a verdurous woof,
A hanging dome of leaves, a canopy moon-proof.

XXVIII

The autumnal winds, as if spell-bound, had made
　　A natural couch of leaves in that recess,
Which seasons none disturbed, but in the shade　　　　2580
　　Of flowering parasites did Spring love to dress
　　With their sweet blooms the wintry loneliness
Of those dead leaves, shedding their stars, whene'er
　　The wandering wind her nurslings might caress;
　　Whose intertwining fingers ever there　　　　2585
Made music wild and soft that filled the listening air.

XXIX

We know not where we go, or what sweet dream
　　May pilot us through caverns strange and fair
Of far and pathless passion, while the stream
　　Of life, our bark doth on its whirlpools bear,　　　　2590
　　Spreading swift wings as sails to the dim air;
Nor should we seek to know, so the devotion
　　Of love and gentle thoughts be heard still there
Louder and louder from the utmost Ocean
Of universal life, attuning its commotion.　　　　2595

XXX

To the pure all things are pure! Oblivion wrapped
　　Our spirits, and the fearful overthrow
Of public hope was from our being snapped,

2570–4 *parenthesis marked by Ross. alone.*　　　　2573 below] below, *edd.*
2574 stood,] stood; *edd.*　　　2580 but *1839, 1818*] but, *1904*　　　2581 parasites]
parasites, *edd.*　　　Spring *1904*] spring *1839, 1818*　　　2585 there *1904*] there,
1839, 1818

Though linkèd years had bound it there; for now
A power, a thirst, a knowledge, which below   2600
All thoughts, like light beyond the atmosphere,
    Clothing its clouds with grace, doth ever flow,
Came on us, as we sate in silence there,
Beneath the golden stars of the clear azure air,—

XXXI

In silence which doth follow talk that causes   2605
    The baffled heart to speak with sighs and tears,
When wildering passion swalloweth up the pauses
    Of inexpressive speech. The youthful years
    Which we together passed, their hopes and fears,
The common blood which ran within our frames,   2610
    That likeness of the features which endears
The thoughts expressed by them, our very names,
And all the wingèd hours which speechless memory claims,

XXXII

Had found a voice—and ere that voice did pass,
    The night grew damp and dim, and through a rent   2615
Of the ruin where we sate, from the morass,
    A wandering Meteor by some wild wind sent,
    Hung high in the green dome, to which it lent
A faint and pallid lustre; while the song
    Of blasts, in which its blue hair quivering bent,   2620
Strewed strangest sounds the moving leaves among;
A wondrous light, the sound as of a spirit's tongue.

XXXIII

The Meteor showed the leaves on which we sate,
    And Cythna's glowing arms, and the thick ties
Of her soft hair, which bent with gathered weight   2625
    My neck near hers, her dark and deepening eyes,
    Which, as twin phantoms of one star that lies

2604-8 *For punctuation see n., p. 369.*   2604 air,—] air:— *1904* air. *1839, 1818*
2608 speech. *1870*] speech:— *1904, 1839, 1818*   2610 common blood *LC*
blood itself *RI*   2614 voice—and *1904*] voice:—and *1839, 1818*

O'er a dim well, move, though the star reposes,
    Swam in our mute and liquid ecstasies,
Her marble brow, and eager lips, like roses,   2630
With their own fragrance pale, which Spring but half uncloses.

XXXIV

The Meteor to its far morass returned;
    The beating of our veins one interval
Made still; and then I felt the blood that burned
    Within her frame, mingle with mine, and fall   2635
    Around my heart like fire; and over all
A mist was spread, the sickness of a deep
    And speechless swoon of joy, as might befall
Two disunited spirits when they leap
In union from this earth's obscure and fading sleep.   2640

XXXV

Was it one moment that confounded thus
    All thought, all sense, all feeling, into one
Unutterable power, which shielded us
    Even from our own cold looks, when we had gone
    Into a wide and wild oblivion   2645
Of tumult and of tenderness? or now
    Had ages, such as make the moon and sun,
The seasons, and mankind their changes know,
Left fear and time unfelt by us alone below?

XXXVI

I know not. What are kisses whose fire clasps   2650
    The failing heart in languishment, or limb
Twined within limb? or the quick dying gasps
    Of the life meeting, when the faint eyes swim
    Through tears of a wide mist boundless and dim,
In one caress? What is the strong control   2655
    Which leads the heart that dizzy steep to climb,
Where far over the world those vapours roll,
Which blend two restless frames in one reposing soul?

XXXVII

It is the shadow which doth float unseen,
　　But not unfelt, o'er blind mortality,   2660
Whose divine darkness fled not from that green
　　And lone recess, where lapped in peace did lie
　　Our linkèd frames, till from the changing sky,
That night and still another day had fled;
　　And then I saw and felt. The moon was high,   2665
And clouds, as of a coming storm, were spread
Under its orb,—loud winds were gathering overhead.

XXXVIII

Cythna's sweet lips seemed lurid in the moon,
　　Her fairest limbs with the night wind were chill,
And her dark tresses were all loosely strewn   2670
　　O'er her pale bosom:—all within was still,
　　And the sweet peace of joy did almost fill
The depth of her unfathomable look;—
　　And we sate calmly, though that rocky hill,
The waves contending in its caverns strook,   2675
For they foreknew the storm, and the gray ruin shook.

XXXIX

There we unheeding sate, in the communion
　　Of interchangèd vows, which, with a rite
Of faith most sweet and sacred, stamped our union.—
　　Few were the living hearts which could unite   2680
　　Like ours, or celebrate a bridal-night
With such close sympathies, for to each other
　　Had high and solemn hopes, the gentle might
Of earliest love, and all the thoughts which smother
Cold Evil's power, now linked a sister and a brother.   2685

2661 not *1839*] not, *1904, 1818*   2663 frames, till *1839*] frames till *1904* frames;
till *1818*   2682-5 *In RI:*

　　　With such close sympathies, for they had sprung
　　　　From linkèd youth, and from the gentle might
　　　Of earliest love, delayed and cherished long,
　　Which common hopes and fears made, like a tempest, strong.

XL

And such is Nature's modesty, that those
   Who grow together cannot choose but love,
If faith or custom do not interpose,
   Or common slavery mar what else might move
All gentlest thoughts; as in the sacred grove   2690
Which shades the springs of Ethiopian Nile,
   That living tree, which, if the arrowy dove
Strike with her shadow, shrinks in fear awhile,
But its own kindred leaves clasps while the sunbeams smile,

XLI

And clings to them when darkness may dissever   2695
   The close caresses of all duller plants
Which bloom on the wide earth—thus we for ever
   Were linked, for love had nursed us in the haunts
Where knowledge, from its secret source enchants
Young hearts with the fresh music of its springing,   2700
   Ere yet its gathered flood feeds human wants,—
As the great Nile feeds Egypt; ever flinging
Light on the woven boughs which o'er its waves are swinging.

XLII

The tones of Cythna's voice like echoes were
   Of those far murmuring streams; they rose and fell,
Mixed with mine own in the tempestuous air.   2706
   And so we sate, until our talk befell
Of the late ruin, swift and horrible,
And how those seeds of hope might yet be sown,
   Whose fruit is evil's mortal poison: well   2710
For us, this ruin made a watch-tower lone;
But Cythna's eyes looked faint, and now two days were gone

XLIII

Since she had food:—therefore I did awaken
   The Tartar steed, who, from his ebon mane

2686 modesty *LC*]law divine *RI*   2690–703 *For the construction see n., pp. 369–*
70.   2694 smile,] smile; *edd., missing in e. 10*   2695 them] them, *edd.*
2701 wants,—] wants, *edd.*   2702 Egypt,] Egypt; *edd.*   2706 air.] air,— *edd.*
2710 well] well, *edd., though Loc. notes that this confuses*   2711 lone;] lone, *edd.*
2714 mane *1904*] mane, *1839, 1818*

Soon as the clinging slumbers he had shaken,   2715
　　Bent his thin head to seek the brazen rein,
　　Following me obediently. With pain
Of heart, so deep and dread, that one caress,
　　When lips and heart refuse to part again
Till they have told their fill, could scarce express   2720
The anguish of her mute and fearful tenderness,

XLIV

Cythna beheld me part, as I bestrode
　　That willing steed:—the tempest and the night,
Which gave my path its safety as I rode
　　Down the ravine of rocks, did soon unite   2725
　　The darkness and the tumult of their might
Borne on all winds.—Far through the streaming rain
　　Floating at intervals the garments white
Of Cythna gleamed, and her voice once again
Came to me on the gust, and soon I reached the plain.   2730

XLV

I dreaded not the tempest, nor did he
　　Who bore me, but his eyeballs wide and red
Turned on the lightning's cleft exultingly;
　　And when the earth beneath his tameless tread
　　Shook with the sullen thunder, he would spread   2735
His nostrils to the blast, and joyously
　　Mock the fierce peal with neighings;—thus we sped
O'er the lit plain, and soon I could descry
Where Death and Fire had gorged the spoil of victory.

XLVI

There was a desolate village in a wood   2740
　　Whose bloom-inwoven leaves now scattering fed
The hungry storm; it was a place of blood,
　　A heap of hearthless walls;—the flames were dead
　　Within those dwellings now,—the life had fled
From all those corpses now,—but the wide sky   2745
　　Flooded with lightning was ribbed overhead
By the black rafters, and around did lie
Women, and babes, and men, slaughtered confusedly.

2717 obediently. With] obediently; with *edd.*　　2719 again *1904*] again, *1839*,
1818　　2734 tread] tread, *edd.*

XLVII

Beside the fountain in the market-place
  Dismounting, I beheld those corpses stare   2750
With horny eyes upon each other's face,
    And on the earth and on the vacant air,
    And upon me, close to the waters where
I stooped to slake my thirst;—I shrank to taste,
  For the salt bitterness of blood was there;   2755
But tied the steed beside, and sought in haste
If any yet survived amid that ghastly waste.

XLVIII

No living thing was there beside one woman,
  Whom I found wandering in the streets, and she
Was withered from a likeness of aught human   2760
    Into a fiend, by some strange misery;
    Soon as she heard my steps she leaped on me,
  And glued her burning lips to mine, and laughed
    With a loud, long, and frantic laugh of glee,
And cried, 'Now, Mortal, thou hast deeply quaffed   2765
The Plague's blue kisses—soon millions shall pledge the draught!

XLIX

'My name is Pestilence—this bosom dry
  Once fed two babes—a sister and a brother.
When I came home, one in the blood did lie
    Of three death-wounds—the flames had ate the other!
    Since then I have no longer been a mother,   2771
But I am Pestilence;—hither and thither
    I flit about, that I may slay and smother:—
All lips which I have kissed must surely wither,
But Death's—if thou art he, we'll go to work together!   2775

L

'What seek'st thou here? The moonlight comes in flashes,—
  The dew is rising dankly from the dell—
'Twill moisten her! and thou shalt see the gashes

2765 Now, *1904*, *1839*] Now *1818*   2767 dry *1839*] dry, *1904*, *1818*
2768 brother.] brother— *edd.*

In my sweet boy, now full of worms:—but tell
   First what thou seek'st.'—'I seek for food.'—''Tis well,
Thou shalt have food; Famine, my paramour,   2781
   Waits for us at the feast—cruel and fell
Is Famine, but he drives not from his door
Those whom these lips have kissed, alone. No more, no more!'

LI

As thus she spake, she grasped me with the strength   2785
   Of madness, and by many a ruined hearth
She led, and over many a corpse:—at length
   We came to a lone hut where on the earth
   Which made its floor, she in her ghastly mirth
Gathering from all those homes now desolate,   2790
   Had piled three heaps of loaves, making a dearth
Among the dead—round which she set in state
A ring of cold, stiff babes; silent and stark they sate.

LII

She leaped upon a pile, and lifted high
   Her mad looks to the lightning, and cried: 'Eat!   2795
Share the great feast—to-morrow we must die!'
   And then she spurned the loaves with her pale feet,
   Towards her bloodless guests;—that sight to meet,
Mine eyes and my heart ached, and but that she
   Who loved me, did with absent looks defeat   2800
Despair, I might have raved in sympathy;
But now I took the food that woman offered me;

LIII

And vainly having with her madness striven
   If I might win her to return with me,
Departed. In the eastern beams of Heaven   2805
   The lightning now grew pallid—rapidly,
   As by the shore of the tempestuous sea
The dark steed bore me, and the mountain gray
   Soon echoed to his hoofs, and I could see
Cythna among the rocks, where she alway   2810
Had sate, with anxious eyes fixed on the lingering day.

2788 hut 1904] hut, 1839, 1818

LIV

And joy was ours to meet: she was most pale,
　　Famished, and wet and weary, so I cast
My arms around her, lest her steps should fail
　　As to our home we went,—and, thus embraced,　　　2815
　　Her full heart seemed a deeper joy to taste
Than e'er the prosperous know; the steed behind
　　Trod peacefully along the mountain waste:
We reached our home ere morning could unbind
Night's latest veil, and on our bridal-couch reclined.　　2820

LV

Her chilled heart having cherished in my bosom,
　　And sweetest kisses passed, we two did share
Our peaceful meal:—as an autumnal blossom
　　Which spreads its shrunk leaves in the sunny air
　　After cold showers, like rainbows woven there,—　　2825
Thus in her lips and cheeks the vital spirit
　　Mantled, and in her eyes, an atmosphere
Of health, and hope; and sorrow languished near it,
And fear, and all that dark despondence doth inherit.

CANTO VII

I

So we sate joyous as the morning ray　　　　　2830
　　Which fed upon the wrecks of night and storm
Now lingering on the winds; light airs did play
　　Among the dewy weeds, the sun was warm,
　　And we sate linked in the inwoven charm
Of converse and caresses sweet and deep,—　　　2835
　　Speechless caresses, talk that might disarm
Time, though he wield the darts of death and sleep,
And those thrice mortal barbs in his own poison steep.

II

I told her of my sufferings and my madness,
　　And how, awakened from that dreamy mood　　　2840
By Liberty's uprise, the strength of gladness

2815 went,—and,] went, and *edd.*　　　　2818 waste: *1904*] waste, *1839, 1818*
2822 passed,] past, *edd.*　　　2824 air] air, *edd.*　　　2825 there,—] there, *edd.*
Canto VII. 2835 deep,—] deep, *edd.*

Came to my spirit in my solitude;
And all that now I was; while tears pursued
Each other down her fair and listening cheek
  Fast as the thoughts which fed them, like a flood   2845
From sun-bright dales; and when I ceased to speak,
Her accents soft and sweet the pausing air did wake.

III

She told me a strange tale of strange endurance,
  Like broken memories of many a heart
Woven into one; to which no firm assurance,   2850
  So wild were they, could her own faith impart.
  She said that not a tear did dare to start
From the swoln brain, and that her thoughts were firm
  When from all mortal hope she did depart,
Borne by those slaves across the Ocean's term,   2855
And that she reached the port without one fear infirm.

IV

One was she among many there, the thralls
  Of the cold Tyrant's cruel lust: and they
Laughed mournfully in those polluted halls;
  But she was calm and sad, musing alway   2860
  On loftiest enterprise, till on a day
The Tyrant heard her singing to her lute
  A wild, and sad, and spirit-thrilling lay,
Like winds that die in wastes—one moment mute
The evil thoughts it made, which did his breast pollute.   2865

V

Even when he saw her wondrous loveliness,
  One moment to great Nature's sacred power
He bent, and was no longer passionless;
  But when he bade her to his secret bower
  Be borne, a loveless victim, and she tore   2870
Her locks in agony, and her words of flame
  And mightier looks availed not; then he bore
Again his load of slavery, and became
A king, a heartless beast, a pageant and a name.

2843 was;] was— *1904* was, *1839, 1818*   2848 *In e. 10 the first* strange *is scored through but unreplaced, indicating an intent to revise.*   2849 *In e. 10* broken *is underlined, again indicating an intent to revise.*

VI

She told me what a loathsome agony　　　　2875
　Is that when selfishness mocks love's delight,
Foul as in dream's most fearful imagery
　To dally with the mowing dead—that night
　All torture, fear, or horror made seem light
Which the soul dreams or knows; and when the day　　2880
　Shone on her awful frenzy, from the sight
Where like a Spirit in fleshly chains she lay
Struggling, aghast and pale the Tyrant fled away.

VII

Her madness was a beam of light, a power
　Which dawned through the rent soul; and words it gave,
Gestures, and looks, such as in whirlwinds bore　　2886
　(Which might not be withstood, whence none could save)
　All who approached their sphere,—like some calm wave
Vexed into whirlpools by the chasms beneath;
　And sympathy made each attendant slave　　2890
Fearless and free, and they began to breathe
Deep curses, like the voice of flames far underneath.

VIII

The King felt pale upon his noonday throne:
　At night two slaves he to her chamber sent,—
One was a green and wrinkled eunuch, grown　　2895
　From human shape into an instrument
　Of all things ill—distorted, bowed and bent.
The other was a wretch from infancy
　Made dumb by poison; who nought knew or meant
But to obey: from the fire-isles came he,　　2900
A diver lean and strong, of Oman's coral sea.

IX

They bore her to a bark, and the swift stroke
　Of silent rowers clove the blue moonlight seas,
Until upon their path the morning broke;

2877 dream's *1904*] dreams *1839, 1818*　　　　2880 knows;] knows, *edd.*
2885-6 gave,/ Gestures, and *1904*] gave,/ Gestures and *1839*　gave/ Gestures and *1818.*
See n., p. 370.　　2887 withstood, *LC*] withstood— *RI*　2888 sphere,— *1904*]
sphere, *1839, 1818. See n. (2887-8), p. 370.*　　2894 sent,— *1904*] sent, *1839, 1818*

They anchored then, where, be there calm or breeze, 2905
   The gloomiest of the drear Symplegades
Shakes with the sleepless surge;—the Ethiop there
   Wound his long arms around her, and with knees
Like iron clasped her feet, and plunged with her
Among the closing waves out of the boundless air.   2910

                          X

'Swift as an eagle stooping from the plain
   Of morning light, into some shadowy wood,
He plunged through the green silence of the main,
   Through many a cavern which the eternal flood
   Had scooped, as dark lairs for its monster brood; 2915
And among mighty shapes which fled in wonder,
   And among mightier shadows which pursued
His heels, he wound: until the dark rocks under
He touched a golden chain—a sound arose like thunder.

                          XI

'A stunning clang of massive bolts redoubling   2920
   Beneath the deep—a burst of waters driven
As from the roots of the sea, raging and bubbling:
   And in that roof of crags a space was riven
   Through which there shone the emerald beams of heaven,
Shot through the lines of many waves inwoven,   2925
   Like sunlight through acacia woods at even,
Through which, his way the diver having cloven,
Passed like a spark sent up out of a burning oven.

                          XII

'And then,' she said, 'he laid me in a cave
   Above the waters, by that chasm of sea,   2930
A fountain round and vast, in which the wave
   Imprisoned, boiled and leaped perpetually,
   Down which, one moment resting, he did flee,
Winning the adverse depth; that spacious cell
   Like an hupaithric temple wide and high,   2935
Whose aëry dome is inaccessible,
Was pierced with one round cleft through which the sunbeams
      fell.

2935 hupaithric *1904*] upaithric *1839, 1818, e. 10 See n., p. 389.*

XIII

'Below, the fountain's brink was richly paven
  With the deep's wealth, coral, and pearl, and sand
Like spangling gold, and purple shells engraven   2940
  With mystic legends by no mortal hand.
  Left there, when thronging to the moon's command,
The gathering waves rent the Hesperian gate
  Of mountains; and on such bright floor did stand;
Columns, and shapes like statues, and the state   2945
Of kingless thrones, which Earth did in her heart create.

XIV

'The fiend of madness which had made its prey
  Of my poor heart, was lulled to sleep awhile:
There was an interval of many a day,
  And a sea-eagle brought me food the while,   2950
  Whose nest was built in that untrodden isle,
And who to be the gaoler had been taught
  Of that strange dungeon; as a friend whose smile
Like light and rest at morn and even is sought
That wild bird was to me, till madness misery brought,—

XV

'The misery of a madness slow and creeping,   2956
  Which made the earth seem fire, the sea seem air,
And the white clouds of noon which oft were sleeping,
  In the blue heaven so beautiful and fair,
  Like hosts of ghastly shadows hovering there;   2960
And the sea-eagle looked a fiend, who bore
  Thy mangled limbs for food!—Thus all things were
Transformed into the agony which I wore
Even as a poisoned robe around my bosom's core.

XVI

'Again I knew the day and night fast fleeing,   2695
  The eagle, and the fountain, and the air;
Another frenzy came—there seemed a being
  Within me—a strange load my heart did bear,

2944 mountains;] mountains, *edd.*   2952 who] who, *edd.*   taught *1904*] taught, *1839, 1818*   2954 sought *1904*] sought, *1839, 1813*   2955 brought,—] brought. *edd.*

As if some living thing had made its lair
Even in the fountains of my life:—a long   2970
    And wondrous vision wrought from my despair,
    Then grew, like sweet reality among
Dim visionary woes, an unreposing throng.

XVII

'Methought I was about to be a mother—
    Month after month went by, and still I dreamed   2975
That we should soon be all to one another,
    I and my child; and still new pulses seemed
    To beat beside my heart, and still I deemed
There was a babe within—and, when the rain
    Of winter through the rifted cavern streamed,   2980
Methought, after a lapse of lingering pain,
I saw that lovely shape, which near my heart had lain.

XVIII

'It was a babe, beautiful from its birth,—
    It was like thee, dear love, its eyes were thine,
Its brow, its lips, and so upon the earth   2985
    It laid its fingers, as now rest on mine
    Thine own, belovèd!—'twas a dream divine:
Even to remember how it fled, how swift,
    How utterly, might make the heart repine,—
Though 'twas a dream.'—Then Cythna did uplift   2990
Her looks on mine, as if some doubt she sought to shift,—

XIX

A doubt which would not flee, a tenderness
    Of questioning grief, a source of thronging tears:
Which having passed, as one whom sobs oppress
    She spoke: 'Yes, in the wilderness of years   2995
    Her memory, aye, like a green home appears;
She sucked her fill even at this breast, sweet love,
    For many months. I had no mortal fears;
Methought I felt her lips and breath approve,—
It was a human thing which to my bosom clove.   3000

2979 and, _1904_] and _1839, 1818_   2987 own, belovèd!— _1904_] own, beloved:—
_1839_   own beloved:— _1818_   2991 shift,—] shift, _edd._   2993 tears: _1904_]
tears; _1839, 1818_   2994 Which _1904_] Which, _1839, 1818_   oppress _1904_] op-
prest _1839, 1818_   2996 appears; _1904_] appears. _1839_   appears, _1818_

XX

'I watched the dawn of her first smiles, and soon,
　When zenith-stars were trembling on the wave,
Or when the beams of the invisible moon,
　　Or sun, from many a prism within the cave
　　Their gem-born shadows to the water gave,　　　3005
Her looks would hunt them, and with outspread hand,
　　From the swift lights which might that fountain pave
She would mark one, and laugh when, that command
Slighting, it lingered there, and could not understand.

XXI

'Methought her looks began to talk with me;　　　3010
　And no articulate sounds, but something sweet
Her lips would frame,—so sweet it could not be
　　That it was meaningless; her touch would meet
　　Mine, and our pulses calmly flow and beat
In response while we slept; and on a day　　　3015
　　When I was happiest in that strange retreat,
With heaps of golden shells we two did play,—
Both infants, weaving wings for time's perpetual way.

XXII

'Ere night, methought, her waning eyes were grown
　Weary with joy, and tired with our delight,　　　3020
We, on the earth, like sister twins lay down
　　On one fair mother's bosom:—from that night
　　She fled;—like those illusions clear and bright,
Which dwell in lakes, should the red moon on high
　　Pause ere it wakens tempest;—and her flight,　　　3025
Though 'twas the death of brainless fantasy,
Yet smote my lonesome heart more than all misery.

XXIII

'It seemed that in the dreary night, the diver
　Who brought me thither, came again, and bore
My child away. I saw the waters quiver,　　　3030
　　When he so swiftly sunk, as once before:
　　Then morning came—it shone even as of yore,

3001 soon,] soon *edd.*　　　3007 pave] pave, *edd.*　　　3008 laugh when,] laugh
when *edd.*　　　3012 be] be, *edd.*　　　3024 should *e. 10*] when *edd. See n., p. 370*

But I was changed—the very life was gone
    Out of my heart—I wasted more and more,
Day after day, and sitting there alone,   3035
Vexed the inconstant waves with my perpetual moan.

XXIV

'I was no longer mad, and yet methought
    My breasts were swoln and changed:—in every vein
The blood stood still one moment, while that thought
    Was passing—with a gush of sickening pain   3040
    It ebbed even to its withered springs again,
When my wan eyes in stern resolve I turned
    From that most strange delusion, which would fain
Have waked the dream for which my spirit yearned
With more than human love,—then left it unreturned.   3045

XXV

'So, now my reason was restored to me
    I struggled with that dream, which, like a beast
Most fierce and beauteous, in my memory
    Had made its lair, and on my heart did feast;
    But all that cave and all its shapes, possessed   3050
By thoughts which could not fade, renewed each one
    Some smile, some look, some gesture which had blessed
Me heretofore: I, sitting there alone,
Vexed the inconstant waves with my perpetual moan.

XXVI

'Time passed, I know not whether months or years;   3055
    For day, nor night, nor change of seasons made
Its note, but thoughts and unavailing tears:
    And I became at last even as a shade,
    A smoke, a cloud on which the winds have preyed,
Till it be thin as air; until, one even,   3060
    A Nautilus upon the fountain played,
Spreading his azure sail where breath of Heaven
Descended not, among the waves and whirlpools driven.

3041 again, *Loc. 1911, Ross. 1870*] again: *other edd. See n., p. 370.*   3046 So, . . .
me] So . . . me *1904*   So . . . me, *1839, 1818*   3050 shapes, *1904*] shapes *1839,
1818*   3053-4 *e. 10 supports edd., despite repetition from 3035-6.*

XXVII

'And, when the Eagle came, that lovely thing,
　Oaring with rosy feet its silver boat,　　　　　　　3065
Fled near me as for shelter; on slow wing,
　The Eagle, hovering o'er his prey did float;
　But when he saw that I with fear did note
His purpose, proffering my own food to him,
　The eager plumes subsided on his throat—　　　　3070
He came where that bright child of sea did swim,
And o'er it cast in peace his shadow broad and dim.

XXVIII

'This wakened me, it gave me human strength;
　And hope, I know not whence or wherefore, rose,
But I resumed my ancient powers at length;　　　　3075
　My spirit felt again like one of those—
　Like thine!—whose fate it is to make the woes
Of humankind their prey.—What was this cave?
　Its deep foundation no firm purpose knows
Immutable, resistless, strong to save,　　　　　　3080
Like mind while yet it mocks the all-devouring grave.

XXIX

'And where was Laon? might my heart be dead,
　While that far dearer heart could move and be?
Or whilst over the earth the pall was spread,
　Which I had sworn to rend? I might be free,　　　3085
　Could I but win that friendly bird to me,
To bring me ropes; and long in vain I sought
　By intercourse of mutual imagery
Of objects, if such aid he could be taught;
But fruit, and flowers, and boughs, yet never ropes he brought.

XXX

'We live in our own world, and mine was made　　　3091
　From glorious fantasies of hope departed:
Aye we are darkened with their floating shade,

3064 And, *1904*] And *1839, 1818*　　　　3073 strength; *1904, 1839*] strength *1818*
3076–8 *Punctuation by Loc. 1911 ; other edd. have a comma after* thine *and a dash after*
prey. *Missing in e. 10. See n., p. 370.*　　　　3093 Aye *1904*] Aye, *1839, 1818*

Or cast a lustre on them—time imparted
    Such power to me, I became fearless-hearted,   3095
My eye and voice grew firm, calm was my mind,
    And piercing, like the morn, now it has darted
Its lustre on all hidden things, behind
Yon dim and fading clouds which load the weary wind.

XXXI

'My mind became the book through which I grew   3100
    Wise in all human wisdom, and its cave,
Which like a mine I rifled through and through,
    To me the keeping of its secrets gave—
One mind, the type of all, the moveless wave
Whose calm reflects all moving things that are: 3105
    Necessity, and love, and life, the grave
And sympathy (fountains of hope and fear),
Justice, and truth, and time, and the world's natural sphere.

XXXII

'And on the sand would I make signs to range
    These woofs, as they were woven, of my thought;   3110
Clear, elemental shapes, whose smallest change
    A subtler language within language wrought:
The key of truths which once were dimly taught
In old Crotona;—and sweet melodies
    Of love, in that lorn solitude I caught   3115
From mine own voice in dream, when thy dear eyes
Shone through my sleep, and did that utterance harmonize.

XXXIII

'Thy songs were winds whereon I fled at will,
    As in a wingèd chariot, o'er the plain
Of crystal youth; and thou wert there to fill   3120
    My heart with joy, and there we sate again
On the gray margin of the glimmering main,

3095 me, *1839, 1818*] me— *1904*   3105-7 *For punctuation see n., p. 370.*
3105 are:] are, *1904, 1839, 1818*   3106 grave] grave, *1904, 1839, 1818*
3107 sympathy (fountains . . . fear),] sympathy, fountains . . . fear; *1904, 1839, 1818*
3115 lorn *1904, e. 10*] lone *1839, 1818 Form. notes the correction made by Shelley in his copy of LC*

Happy as then but wiser far, for we
  Smiled on the flowery grave in which were lain
Fear, Faith, and Slavery; and mankind was free,   3125
Equal, and pure, and wise in Wisdom's prophecy.

XXXIV

'For to my will my fancies were as slaves
  To do their sweet and subtile ministries;
And oft from that bright fountain's shadowy waves
  They would make human throngs gather and rise   3130
To combat with my overflowing eyes
And voice made deep with passion—thus I grew
  Familiar with the shock and the surprise
And war of earthly minds, from which I drew
The power which has been mine to frame their thoughts anew.

XXXV

'And thus my prison was the populous earth;   3136
  Where I saw—even as misery dreams of morn
Before the east has given its glory birth—
  Religion's pomp made desolate by the scorn
Of Wisdom's faintest smile, and thrones uptorn,   3140
And dwellings of mild people interspersed
  With undivided fields of ripening corn,
And love made free,—a hope which we have nursed
Even with our blood and tears,—until its glory burst.

XXXVI

'All is not lost! There is some recompense   3145
  For hope whose fountain can be thus profound,—
Even throned Evil's splendid impotence
  Girt by its hell of power, the secret sound
Of hymns to truth and freedom, the dread bound
Of life and death passed fearlessly and well,   3150
  Dungeons wherein the high resolve is found,
Racks which degraded woman's greatness tell,
And what may else be good and irresistible.

3126 pure, *1904, 1839*] pure *1818*   wise] wise, *edd.*   3131 eyes] eyes, *edd.*
3136 earth;] earth— *edd.*   3146 profound—] profound, *edd.*   3147 throned
1839, 1818, e. 10] thronèd *1904, likewise Loc. 1911, Ross. 1870*   impotence] im-
potence, *edd.*   3149 freedom,] freedom— *edd.*

XXXVII

'Such are the thoughts which, like the fires that flare
  In storm-encompassed isles, we cherish yet   3155
In this dark ruin—such were mine even there;
    As in its sleep some odorous violet,
    While yet its leaves with nightly dews are wet,
Breathes in prophetic dreams of day's uprise,
  Or as, ere Scythian frost in fear has met   3160
Spring's messengers descending from the skies,
The buds foreknow their life—this hope must ever rise.

XXXVIII

'So years had passed, when sudden earthquake rent
  The depth of ocean, and the cavern cracked
With sound, as if the world's wide continent   3165
    Had fallen in universal ruin wracked;
    And through the cleft streamed in one cataract
The stifling waters—when I woke, the flood
  Whose banded waves that crystal cave had sacked
Was ebbing round me, and my bright abode   3170
Before me yawned—a chasm desert, and bare, and broad.

XXXIX

'Above me was the sky, beneath the sea:
  I stood upon a point of shattered stone,
And heard loose rocks rushing tumultuously
    With splash and shock into the deep—anon   3175
    All ceased, and there was silence wide and lone.
I felt that I was free! The ocean-spray
  Quivered beneath my feet, the broad Heaven shone
Around, and in my hair the winds did play
Lingering as they pursued their unimpeded way.   3180

XL

'My spirit moved upon the sea like wind
  Which round some thymy cape will lag and hover,
Though it can wake the still cloud, and unbind

3160 Or as,] Or, as *edd.*   3166 wracked; *1839, 1818*] wracked: *1904*
3167 cataract *1904, 1839*] cataract *1818*

The strength of tempest; day was almost over,
　　When through the fading light I could discover　　3185
A ship approaching—its white sails were fed
　　With the north wind—its moving shade did cover
　　The twilight deep;—the mariners in dread
Cast anchor when they saw new rocks around them spread.

XLI

'And when they saw one sitting on a crag,　　3190
　　They sent a boat to me;—the sailors rowed
In awe through many a new and fearful jag
　　Of overhanging rock, through which there flowed
　　The foam of streams that cannot make abode.
They came and questioned me, but when they heard　　3195
　　My voice, they became silent, and they stood
And moved as men in whom new love had stirred
Deep thoughts: so to the ship we passed without a word.

CANTO VIII

I

'I SATE beside the steersman then, and gazing
　　Upon the west, cried, "Spread the sails! Behold!　　3200
The sinking moon is like a watch-tower blazing
　　Over the mountains yet;—the City of Gold
　　Yon cape alone does from the sight withhold;
The stream is fleet—the north breathes steadily
　　Beneath the stars, they tremble with the cold!　　3205
Ye cannot rest upon the dreary sea!—
Haste, haste to the warm home of happier destiny!"

II

'The mariners obeyed—the captain stood
　　Aloof, and, whispering to the pilot, said,
"Alas, alas! I fear we are pursued　　3210
　　By wicked ghosts: a phantom of the dead,
　　The night before we sailed, came to my bed

3188/3191 mariners . . . sailors *1839, 1818, e. 10*] Mariners . . . Sailors *1904. See n.,*
p. 370.
Canto VIII. 3209 and, *1904, 1839*] and *1818*

In dream, like that!" The pilot then replied,
  "It cannot be—she is a human maid—
Her low voice makes you weep—she is some bride,   3215
Or daughter of high birth—she can be nought beside."

III

'We passed the islets, borne by wind and stream,
  And as we sailed, the mariners came near
And thronged around to listen;—in the gleam
    Of the pale moon I stood, as one whom fear   3220
    May not attaint, and my calm voice did rear;
"Ye all are human—yon broad moon gives light
  To millions who the selfsame likeness wear,
Even while I speak—beneath this very night,
Their thoughts flow on like ours, in sadness or delight.   3225

IV

' "What dream ye? Your own hands have built an home,
  Even for yourselves on a beloved shore:
For some, fond eyes are pining till they come—
  How they will greet him when his toils are o'er,
  And laughing babes rush from the well-known door!   3230
Is this your care? ye toil for your own good—
  Ye feel and think—has some immortal power
Such purposes? or, in a human mood,
Dream ye that God thus builds for man in solitude?

V

' "What then is God? Ye mock yourselves, and give   3235
  A human heart to what ye cannot know:
As if the cause of life could think and live!
  'Twere as if man's own works should feel, and show
  The hopes, and fears, and thoughts from which they flow,
And he be like to them! Lo! Plague is free   3240
  To waste, Blight, Poison, Earthquake, Hail, and Snow,
Disease, and Want, and worse Necessity
Of hate and ill, and Pride, and Fear, and Tyranny!

VI

' "What then is God? Some moon-struck sophist stood
　　Watching the shade from his own soul upthrown　　3245
Fill Heaven and darken Earth, and in such mood
　　The Form he saw and worshipped was his own,
　　His likeness in the world's vast mirror shown;
And 'twere an innocent dream, but that a faith
　　Nursed by fear's dew of poison, grows thereon,　　3250
And that men say God has appointed Death
On all who scorn his will, to wreak immortal wrath.

VII

' "Men say they have seen God, and heard from God,
　　Or known from others who have known such things,
And that his will is all our law, a rod　　3255
　　To scourge us into slaves—that Priests and Kings,
　　Custom, domestic sway, ay, all that brings
Man's freeborn soul beneath the oppressor's heel,
　　Are his strong ministers, and that the stings
Of death will make the wise his vengeance feel,　　3260
Though truth and virtue arm their hearts with tenfold steel.

VIII

' "And it is said, that God will punish wrong;
　　Yes, add despair to crime, and pain to pain!
And, his red hell's undying snakes among,
　　Will bind the wretch on whom he fixed a stain,　　3265
　　Which, like a plague, a burden, and a bane,
Clung to him while he lived;—for love and hate,
　　Virtue and vice, they say, are difference vain—
The will of strength is right:— this human state
Tyrants, that they may rule, with lies thus desolate.　　3270

3244 then is God? *LC*] is that Power? *RI*　　3251 God has appointed *LC*] that
Power has chosen *RI*　　3252 his will *LC*] its laws *RI*　　3253 they . . . God. *LC*]
that they themselves have heard and seen *RI*

3255–6　　A Shade, a Form, which Earth and Heaven between
　　　　　Wields an invisible rod—that Priests and Kings, *RI*

3262 that God *LC*] this Power *RI*　　3264 And deepest hell, and deathless snakes
among, *RI*　　And,] And *edd.*　　3265 he fixed *LC*] is fixed *RI*　　3268 say,
LC] say *1904, 1839, RI*　　3269 right:— *Loc. 1911*] right— *edd.*

IX

' "Alas, what strength? Opinion is more frail
    Than yon dim cloud now fading on the moon
Even while we gaze, though it awhile avail
    To hide the orb of truth: and every throne
    Of Earth or Heaven, though shadow, rests thereon,—
One shape of many names:—for this ye plough   3276
    The barren waves of ocean, hence each one
    Is slave or tyrant; all betray and bow,
Command, or kill, or fear, or wreak, or suffer woe.

X

' "Its names are each a sign which maketh holy   3280
    All power—ay, the ghost, the dream, the shade
Of power—lust, falsehood, hate, and pride, and folly;
    The pattern whence all fraud and wrong is made,
    A law to which mankind has been betrayed;
And human love, is as the name well known   3285
    Of a dear mother, whom the murderer laid
    In bloody grave, and into darkness thrown,
Gathered her wildered babes around him as his own.

XI

' "O Love, who to the hearts of wandering men
    Art as the calm to Ocean's weary waves,   3290
Justice, or Truth, or Joy—those only can
    From slavery and religion's labyrinth caves
    Guide us, as one clear star the seaman saves.
To give to all an equal share of good,
    To track the steps of Freedom, though through graves
She pass, to suffer all in patient mood,   3296
To weep for crime, though stained with thy friend's dearest
        blood,—

3274 truth: *Loc. 1911*] truth—*other edd. See n., p. 370.*   3275 shadow, *1904,*
LC] shadow *1839, RI*   thereon,—] thereon, *edd.*   3278 tyrant; *1904, 1839*]
tyrant *LC Form. notes the change made by Shelley in his copy of LC*   3281 the
dream, the shade *1904, 1839, 1818*] the shade, the dream, *e. 10*   3289 hearts . . .
men *1904, 1839, 1818*] hearts . . . man *e. 10 See n., p. 370.*   3290 waves,] waves! *edd.*
3291 Joy—]Joy! *edd.*   3295 Freedom *1904*] freedom *1839, 1818*   3297 blood,—
1904] blood. *1839, 1818*

XII

' "To feel the peace of self-contentment's lot,
　　To own all sympathies, and outrage none,
And in the inmost bowers of sense and thought,　　　3300
　　Until life's sunny day is quite gone down,
　　To sit and smile with Joy, or, not alone,
To kiss salt tears from the worn cheek of Woe;
　　To live, as if to love and live were one,—
This is not faith or law, nor those who bow　　　3305
To thrones on Heaven or Earth, such destiny may know.

XIII

' "But children near their parents tremble now,
　　Because they must obey—one rules another,
For it is said God rules both high and low,
　　And man is made the captive of his brother,　　　3310
　　And Hate is throned on high with Fear her mother,
Above the Highest—and those fountain-cells,
　　Whence love yet flowed when faith had choked all other,
Are darkened—Woman as the bond-slave dwells
Of man a slave; and life is poisoned in its wells.　　　3315

XIV

' "Man seeks for gold in mines, that he may weave
　　A lasting chain for his own slavery;—
In fear and restless care that he may live
　　He toils for others, who must ever be
　　The joyless thralls of like captivity;　　　3320
He murders, for his chiefs delight in ruin;
　　He builds the altar, that its idol's fee
May be his very blood; he is pursuing—
O, blind and willing wretch!—his own obscure undoing.

XV

' "Woman!—she is his slave, she has become　　　3325
　　A thing I weep to speak—the child of scorn,

3309-10 For it is said God . . . / And man LC] And as one Power . . . / So man RI
3311 her 1904, 1839, RI] his LC　　　Form. notes that Shelley did not make the change
in his copy of LC. But see n., p. 370.　　　3314 Woman 1904] Woman, 1839, 1818
bond-slave 1904] bond-slave, 1839, 1818　　　3315 man Loc. 1911] man, 1904, 1839,
1818. See n., p. 370.　　　3324 wretch!— 1904] wretch! 1839, 1818

The outcast of a desolated home;
    Falsehood, and fear, and toil, like waves have worn
    Channels upon her cheek, which smiles adorn,
As calm decks the false ocean:—well ye know   3330
    What Woman is, for none of Woman born,
Can choose but drain the bitter dregs of woe,
Which ever from the oppressed to the oppressors flow.

                          XVI

‘ "This need not be; ye might arise, and will
    That gold should lose its power, and thrones their glory;
That love, which none may bind, be free to fill   3336
    The world, like light; and evil faith, grown hoary
    With crime, be quenched and die.—Yon promontory
Even now eclipses the descending moon!—
    Dungeons and palaces are transitory—   3340
High temples fade like vapour—Man alone
Remains, whose will has power when all beside is gone.

                         XVII

‘ "Let all be free and equal!—From your hearts
    I feel an echo; through my inmost frame
Like sweetest sound, seeking its mate, it darts—   3345
    Whence come ye, friends? Alas, I cannot name
    All that I read of sorrow, toil, and shame,
On your worn faces; as in legends old
    Which make immortal the disastrous fame
Of conquerors and impostors false and bold,   3350
The discord of your hearts I in your looks behold.

                        XVIII

‘ "Whence come ye, friends? from pouring human blood
    Forth on the earth? Or bring ye steel and gold,
That Kings may dupe and slay the multitude?
    Or from the famished poor, pale, weak, and cold,   3355
    Bear ye the earnings of their toil? Unfold!
Speak! Are your hands in slaughter's sanguine hue
    Stained freshly? have your hearts in guile grown old?
    Know yourselves thus! ye shall be pure as dew,
And I will be a friend and sister unto you.   3360

3327 home; *1904*] home. *1839, 1818*   3351 hearts *1839*] hearts, *1904, 1818*

XIX

' "Disguise it not—we have one human heart—
　All mortal thoughts confess a common home:
Blush not for what may to thyself impart
　　Stains of inevitable crime: the doom
　Is this, which has, or may, or must become　　　3365
Thine, and all humankind's. Ye are the spoil
　Which Time thus marks for the devouring tomb,
Thou and thy thoughts and they, and all the toil
Wherewith ye twine the rings of life's perpetual coil.

XX

' "Disguise it not—ye blush for what ye hate,　　　3370
　And Enmity is sister unto Shame;
Look on your mind—it is the book of fate—
　　Ah! it is dark with many a blazoned name
　Of misery—all are mirrors of the same;
But the dark fiend who with his iron pen　　　3375
　Dipped in scorn's fiery poison, makes his fame
Enduring there, would o'er the heads of men
Pass harmless, if they scorned to make their hearts his den.

XXI

' "Yes, it is Hate, that shapeless fiendly thing
　Of many names, all evil, some divine,　　　3380
Whom self-contempt arms with a mortal sting;
　　Which, when the heart its snaky folds entwine
　Is wasted quite; and when it doth repine
To gorge such bitter prey, on all beside
　It turns with ninefold rage, as with its twine　　　3385
When Amphisbaena some fair bird has tied,
Soon o'er the putrid mass he threats on every side.

XXII

' "Reproach not thine own soul, but know thyself,
　Nor hate another's crime, nor loathe thine own.
It is the dark idolatry of self,　　　3390
　　Which, when our thoughts and actions once are gone,
　Demands that man should weep, and bleed, and groan;

3379 Hate, *1839*] Hate— *1904, 1818. For syntax of Stanza XXI see n.*, *pp. 370–1.*
3383 quite;] quite, *edd.*

O vacant expiation! Be at rest.—
   The past is Death's, the future is thine own;
And love and joy can make the foulest breast   3395
A paradise of flowers, where peace might build her nest.

                              XXIII

‘ "Speak thou! whence come ye?"—A youth made reply:
   "Wearily, wearily o'er the boundless deep
We sail;—thou readest well the misery
      Told in these faded eyes, but much doth sleep   3400
      Within, which there the poor heart loves to keep,
Or dare not write on the dishonoured brow;
   Even from our childhood have we learned to steep
The bread of slavery in the tears of woe,
And never dreamed of hope or refuge until now.   3405

                              XXIV

‘ "Yes—I must speak—my secret should have perished
   Even with the heart it wasted, as a brand
Fades in the dying flame whose life it cherished,
      But that no human bosom can withstand
      Thee, wondrous lady, and the mild command   3410
Of thy keen eyes:—yes, we are wretched slaves,
   Who from their wonted loves and native land
Are reft, and bear o'er the dividing waves
The unregarded prey of calm and happy graves.

                               XXV

‘ "We drag afar from pastoral vales the fairest   3415
   Among the daughters of those mountains lone;
We drag them there, where all things best and rarest
      Are stained and trampled:—years have come and gone
      Since, like the ship which bears me, I have known
No thought;—but now the eyes of one dear maid   3420
   On mine with light of mutual love have shone—
She is my life,—I am but as the shade
Of her,—a smoke sent up from ashes, soon to fade.

XXVI

' "For she must perish in the Tyrant's hall—
    Alas, alas!"—He ceased, and by the sail 3425
Sate cowering—but his sobs were heard by all,
    And still before the ocean and the gale
    The ship fled fast till the stars 'gan to fail,
And, round me gathered with mute countenance,
    The seamen gazed, the pilot, worn and pale 3430
With toil, the captain with gray locks, whose glance
Met mine in restless awe—they stood as in a trance.

XXVII

' "Recede not! pause not now! Thou art grown old,
    But Hope will make thee young, for Hope and Youth
Are children of one mother, even Love—behold! 3435
    The eternal stars gaze on us!—is the truth
    Within your soul? care for your own, or ruth
For others' sufferings? do ye thirst to bear
    A heart which not the serpent Custom's tooth
May violate?—Be free! and even here, 3440
Swear to be firm till death!" They cried "We swear! We
    swear!"

XXVIII

'The very darkness shook, as with a blast
    Of subterranean thunder, at the cry;
The hollow shore its thousand echoes cast
    Into the night, as if the sea, and sky, 3445
    And earth, rejoiced with new-born liberty,
For in that name they swore! Bolts were undrawn,
    And on the deck, with unaccustomed eye
The captives gazing stood, and every one 3449
Shrank as the inconstant torch upon her countenance shone.

XXIX

'They were earth's purest children, young and fair,
    With eyes the shrines of unawakened thought,
And brows as bright as spring or morning, ere

3428 fail, *1904*, *1818*] fail. *1839*   3429 And, *1904*] And *1818*, e. 10 All *1839*
3443 thunder, *1904*] thunder *1839*, *1818*

Dark time had there its evil legend wrought
　　In characters of cloud which wither not.—　　3455
The change was like a dream to them; but soon
　　They knew the glory of their altered lot—
　　In the bright wisdom of youth's breathless noon,
Sweet talk, and smiles, and sighs, all bosoms did attune.

XXX

'But one was mute; her cheeks and lips most fair,　　3460
　　Changing their hue like lilies newly blown,
Beneath a bright acacia's shadowy hair,
　　Waved by the wind amid the sunny noon,
　　Showed that her soul was quivering; and full soon
That youth arose, and breathlessly did look　　3465
　　On her and me, as for some speechless boon:
I smiled, and both their hands in mine I took,
And felt a soft delight from what their spirits shook.

CANTO IX

I

'THAT night we anchored in a woody bay,
　　And sleep no more around us dared to hover　　3470
Than, when all doubt and fear has passed away,
　　It shades the couch of some unresting lover,
　　Whose heart is now at rest. Thus night passed over
In mutual joy:—around, a forest grew
　　Of poplars and dark oaks, whose shade did cover　　3475
The waning stars pranked in the waters blue,
And trembled in the wind which from the morning flew.

II

'The joyous mariners, and each free maiden,
　　Now brought from the deep forest many a bough,
With woodland spoil most innocently laden;　　3480
　　Soon wreaths of budding foliage seemed to flow
　　Over the mast and sails, the stern and prow

3457 lot—] lot, *edd*.　　3460 mute;] mute, *edd*.　　3473 rest. Thus] rest:
thus *edd*.

Were canopied with blooming boughs,—the while
On the slant sun's path o'er the waves we go
Rejoicing, like the dwellers of an isle   3485
Doomed to pursue those waves that cannot cease to smile.

III

'The many ships spotting the dark blue deep
With snowy sails, fled fast as ours came nigh,
In fear and wonder; and on every steep
Thousands did gaze; they heard the startling cry,   3490
Like earth's own voice lifted unconquerably
To all her children, the unbounded mirth,
The glorious joy of thy name—Liberty!
They heard!—As o'er the mountains of the earth
From peak to peak leap on the beams of morning's birth:

IV

'So from that cry over the boundless hills   3496
Sudden was caught one universal sound,
Like a volcano's voice, whose thunder fills
Remotest skies,—such glorious madness found
A path through human hearts with stream which drowned
Its struggling fears and cares, dark Custom's brood;   3501
They knew not whence it came, but felt around
A wide contagion poured—they called aloud
On Liberty—that name lived on the sunny flood.

V

'We reached the port.—Alas! from many spirits   3505
The wisdom which had waked that cry, was fled,
Like the brief glory which dark Heaven inherits
From the false dawn, which fades ere it is spread,
Upon the night's devouring darkness shed:
Yet soon bright day will burst—even like a chasm   3510
Of fire, to burn the shrouds outworn and dead
Which wrap the world; a wide enthusiasm,
To cleanse the fevered world as with an earthquake's spasm!

Canto IX. 3490 gaze;] gaze, *edd.*   3496 hills *1904*] hills, *1839*, *1818*
3501 brood; *1904*, *1839*] brood, *1818*   3505 port.—Alas! *1904*] port—alas! *1839*,
1818   3511 dead] dead, *edd.*

VI

'I walked through the great City then, but free
    From shame or fear; those toil-worn mariners   3515
And happy maidens did encompass me;
    And like a subterranean wind that stirs
    Some forest among caves, the hopes and fears
From every human soul a murmur strange
    Made as I passed; and many wept, with tears   3520
Of joy and awe, and wingèd thoughts did range,
And half-extinguished words, which prophesied of change.

VII

'For, with strong speech I tore the veil that hid
    Nature, and Truth, and Liberty, and Love,—
As one who from some mountain's pyramid   3525
    Points to the unrisen sun—the shades approve
    His truth, and flee from every stream and grove.
Thus, gentle thoughts did many a bosom fill,—
    Wisdom, the mail of tried affections wove
For many a heart, and tameless scorn of ill,   3530
Thrice steeped in molten steel the unconquerable will.

VIII

'Some said I was a maniac wild and lost,
    Some that I scarce had risen from the grave,
The Prophet's virgin bride, a heavenly ghost:—
    Some said I was a fiend from my weird cave,   3535
    Who had stolen human shape, and o'er the wave,
The forest, and the mountain came;—some said
    I was the child of God, sent down to save
Women from bonds and death, and on my head
The burden of their sins would frightfully be laid.   3540

IX

'But soon my human words found sympathy
    In human hearts: the purest and the best,
As friend with friend, made common cause with me,
    And they were few, but resolute;—the rest,
    Ere yet success the enterprise had blessed,   3545

3519 soul] soul, *edd.*   3526 sun—the] sun!—the *edd.*   3532 lost,] lost; *edd.*
3533 Some] Some, *edd.*   grave, *1904, 1839*] grave *1818*   3535 said] said, *edd.*
3543 friend, *1904*] friend *1839, 1818*

Leagued with me in their hearts;—their meals, their slumber,
　　Their hourly occupations, were possessed
By hopes which I had armed to overnumber
Those hosts of meaner cares, which life's strong wings en-
　　cumber.

X

'But chiefly women, whom my voice did waken　　　　3550
　　From their cold, careless, willing slavery,
Sought me: one truth their dreary prison had shaken,—
　　They looked around, and lo! they became free!
　　Their many tyrants sitting desolately
In slave-deserted halls, could none restrain;　　　　3555
　　For wrath's red fire had withered in the eye,
Whose lightning once was death,—nor fear, nor gain
Could tempt one captive now to lock another's chain.

XI

'Those who were sent to bind me, wept, and felt
　　Their minds outsoar the bonds which clasped them round,
Even as a waxen shape may waste and melt　　　　3561
　　In the white furnace; and a visioned swound,
　　A pause of hope and awe the City bound,
Which, like the silence of a tempest's birth,
　　When in its awful shadow it has wound　　　　3565
The sun, the wind, the ocean, and the earth,
Hung terrible, ere yet the lightnings have leaped forth.

XII

'Like clouds inwoven in the silent sky,
　　By winds from distant regions meeting there,
In the high name of truth and liberty　　　　3570
　　Around the City millions gathered were
　　By hopes which sprang from many a hidden lair,—
Words which the lore of truth in hues of fame
　　Arrayed, thine own wild songs which in the air
Like homeless odours floated, and the name　　　　3575
Of thee, and many a tongue which thou hadst dipped in flame.

3547 occupations, _1904, 1839_] occupations _1818_　　　3548 overnumber _1904, 1839_]
overnumber, _1818_　　　3552 had _e. 10, as suggested by Form._] has _edd._　　　3564–7 _See
n., p. 371._　　　3570 liberty] liberty, _edd._　　　3571 were] were, _edd._　　　3573 fame
_e. 10_] _1904, Form._ flame _1876_　　　grace _1839, 1818. See n., p. 371._

XIII

'The Tyrant knew his power was gone, but Fear,
  The nurse of Vengeance, bade him wait the event—
That perfidy and custom, gold and prayer,
    And whatsoe'er, when force is impotent,   3580
  To fraud the sceptre of the world has lent,
Might, as he judged, confirm his failing sway.
  Therefore throughout the streets, the Priests he sent
To curse the rebels.—To their God did they
For Earthquake, Plague, and Want kneel in the public way.

XIV

'And grave and hoary men were bribed to tell,   3586
  From seats where law is made the slave of wrong,
How glorious Athens in her splendour fell,
    Because her sons were free,—and that among
    Mankind, the many to the few belong,   3590
By God, and Nature, and Necessity.
  They said, that age was truth, and that the young
Marred with wild hopes the peace of slavery,
With which old times and men had quelled the vain and free.

XV

'And with the falsehood of their poisonous lips   3595
  They breathed on the enduring memory
Of sages and of bards a brief eclipse;
    There was one teacher, and must ever be,   3598
    They said, even God, whom the necessity   3598a
    Of rule and wrong had armed against mankind,   3599
His slave and his avenger there to be;   3600
  That we were weak and sinful, frail and blind,
And that the will of one was peace, and we
Should seek for nought on earth but toil and misery—

3584 God *LC*] gods *RI*   3585 Want] Want, *edd., e. 10*   3591 God, *LC*]
Heaven, *RI*   3598–600 *In RI:*
          . . . . who, necessity
    Had armed with strength and wrong against mankind,
    His slave and his avenger aye to be;
3598a whom] who *LC, e. 10*   3603 misery— *1904*] misery. *1839, 1818*

XVI

' "For thus we might avoid the hell hereafter."
  So spake the hypocrites, who cursed and lied;   3605
Alas, their sway was past, and tears and laughter
  Clung to their hoary hair, withering the pride
  Which in their hollow hearts dared still abide;
And yet obscener slaves with smoother brow,
  And sneers on their strait lips, thin, blue and wide, 3610
Said, that the rule of men was over now,
And hence, the subject world to woman's will must bow;

XVII

'And gold was scattered through the streets, and wine
  Flowed at a hundred feasts within the wall.
In ain! The steady towers in heaven did shine   3615
  As they were wont, nor at the priestly call
  Left Plague her banquet in the Ethiop's hall,
Nor Famine from the rich man's portal came,
  Where at her ease she ever preys on all
Who throng to kneel for food: nor fear nor shame, 3620
Nor faith, nor discord, dimmed hope's newly kindled flame.

XVIII

'For gold was as a god whose faith began
  To fade, so that its worshippers were few,
And Hell and Awe, which in the heart of man
  Is God itself; the Priests its downfall knew,   3625
  As day by day their altars lonelier grew,
Till they were left alone within the fane;
  The shafts of falsehood unpolluting flew,
And the cold sneers of calumny were vain,
The union of the free with discord's brand to stain. 3630

3624–7 *In RI*:

> And Faith itself, which in the heart of man
>   Gives shape, voice, name, to spectral Terror, knew
>   Its downfall, as the altars lonelier grew,
> Till the Priests stood alone within the fane;

XIX

'The rest thou knowest.—Lo! we two are here—
  We have survived a ruin wide and deep—
Strange thoughts are mine.—I cannot grieve or fear;
  Sitting with thee upon this lonely steep
  I smile, though human love should make me weep.   3635
We have survived a joy that knows no sorrow,
  And I do feel a mighty calmness creep
Over my heart, which can no longer borrow
Its hues from chance or change, dark children of to-morrow.

XX

'We know not what will come—yet Laon, dearest,   3640
  Cythna shall be the prophetess of Love,
Her lips shall rob thee of the grace thou wearest,
  To hide thy heart, and clothe the shapes which rove
  Within the homeless Future's wintry grove;
For I now, sitting thus beside thee, seem   3645
  Even with thy breath and blood to live and move,
And violence and wrong are as a dream
Which rolls from steadfast truth, an unreturning stream.

XXI

'The blasts of Autumn drive the wingèd seeds
  Over the earth,—next come the snows, and rain,   3650
And frosts, and storms, which dreary Winter leads
  Out of his Scythian cave, a savage train;
  Behold! Spring sweeps over the world again,
Shedding soft dews from her ethereal wings;
  Flowers on the mountains, fruits over the plain,   3655
And music on the waves and woods she flings,
And love on all that lives, and calm on lifeless things.

XXII

'O Spring, of hope, and love, and youth, and gladness
  Wind-wingèd emblem! brightest, best and fairest!   3659
Whence comest thou, when, with dark Winter's sadness
  The tears that fade in sunny smiles thou sharest?

3633 fear;] fear, *edd.*   3642 Her lips shall rob thee of *edd.*] The Poet who shall
steal, *e. 10. See n., p. 371.*   3643 To hide *edd.*] Around *e. 10*   3648 truth,
1904, 1839] truth *1818*   3661 sharest? *1904, 1839*] sharest; *1818*

Sister of joy, thou art the child who wearest
Thy mother's dying smile, tender and sweet;
Thy mother Autumn, for whose grave thou bearest
Fresh flowers, and beams like flowers, with gentle feet, 3665
Disturbing not the leaves which are her winding-sheet.

XXIII

'Virtue, and Hope, and Love, like light and Heaven,
Surround the world.—We are their chosen slaves.
Has not the whirlwind of our spirit driven
Truth's deathless germs to thought's remotest caves? 3670
Lo, Winter comes!—the grief of many graves,
The frost of death, the tempest of the sword,
The flood of tyranny, whose sanguine waves
Stagnate like ice at Faith, the enchanter's word,
And bind all human hearts in its repose abhorred.   3675

XXIV

'The seeds are sleeping in the soil: meanwhile
The Tyrant peoples dungeons with his prey;
Pale victims on the guarded scaffold smile
Because they cannot speak; and, day by day,
The moon of wasting Science wanes away   3680
Among her stars; and in that darkness vast
The sons of earth to their foul idols pray,
And gray Priests t riumph; and like blight or blast
A shade of selfish care o'er human looks is cast.

XXV

'This is the winter of the world;—and here   3685
We die, even as the winds of Autumn fade,
Expiring in the frore and foggy air.—
Behold! Spring comes, though we must pass, who made
The promise of its birth,—even as the shade
Which from our death, as from a mountain, flings   3690
The future, a broad sunrise; thus arrayed
As with the plumes of overshadowing wings,
From its dark gulf of chains, Earth like an eagle springs.

3674 Faith, *1839, 1818*] Faith *1904*   3677 prey; *1839*] prey, *1904, 1818*
3681 stars;] stars, *edd.*   3683 triumph;] triumph, *edd.*

XXVI

'O dearest love! we shall be dead and cold
    Before this morn may on the world arise;   3695
Wouldst thou the glory of its dawn behold?
    Alas! gaze not on me, but turn thine eyes
    On thine own heart—it is a paradise
Which everlasting Spring has made its own,
    And while drear Winter fills the naked skies,   3700
Sweet streams of sunny thought, and flowers fresh-blown,
Are there, and weave their sounds and odours into one.

XXVII

'In their own hearts the earnest of the hope
    Which made them great, the good will ever find;
And though some envious shades may interlope   3705
    Between the effect and it, One comes behind,
    Who aye the future to the past will bind—
Necessity, whose sightless strength for ever
    Evil with evil, good with good must wind
    In bands of union, which no power may sever: 3710
They must bring forth their kind, and be divided never!

XXVIII

'The good and mighty of departed ages
    And in their graves, the innocent and free,
Heroes, and Poets, and prevailing Sages,
    Who leave the vesture of their majesty   3715
    To adorn and clothe this naked world—and we
Are like to them—such perish, but they leave
    All hope, or love, or truth, or liberty,
Whose forms their mighty spirits could conceive,
To be a rule and law to ages that survive.   3720

XXIX

'So be the turf heaped over our remains
    Even in our happy youth, and that strange lot,
Whate'er it be, when in these mingling veins
    The blood is still, be ours; let sense and thought
    Pass from our being, or be numbered not   3725

3706 One *1904, 1818*] one *1839*   one *converted to* One *e. 10*   3716 world—]
world;— *edd.*   3719 conceive, *1904*] conceive *1839, 1818*

Among the things that are; let those who come
   Behind, for whom our steadfast will has bought
A calm inheritance, a glorious doom,
Insult with careless tread our undivided tomb!

XXX

'Our many thoughts and deeds, our life and love,   3730
   Our happiness, and all that we have been,
Immortally must live, and burn and move,
   When we shall be no more;—the world has seen
   A type of peace; and—as some most serene
And lovely spot to a poor maniac's eye,   3735
   After long years, some sweet and moving scene
Of youthful hope, returning suddenly,
Quells his long madness—thus man shall remember thee.

XXXI

'And Calumny meanwhile shall feed on us,
   As worms devour the dead, and near the throne   3740
And at the altar, most accepted thus
   Shall sneers and curses be;—what we have done
   None shall dare vouch, though it be truly known;
That record shall remain, when they must pass
   Who built their pride on its oblivion;   3745
And fame, in human hope which sculptured was,
Survive the perished scrolls of unenduring brass.

XXXII

'The while we two, beloved, must depart,
   And Sense and Reason, those enchanters fair,
Whose wand of power is hope, would bid the heart   3750
   That gazed beyond the wormy grave despair:
   These eyes, these lips, this blood, seems darkly there
To fade in hideous ruin; no calm sleep
   Peopling with golden dreams the stagnant air,
Seems our obscure and rotting eyes to steep   3755
In joy;—but senseless death—a ruin dark and deep!

3729 tread] tread, *edd.*   tomb!] tomb. *edd.*   3734 and—as *1904*] and as *1839,
1818*   3743 *Followed, in e. 10, by several broken snatches of extraneous verse, and
two prose memoranda. See n., p. 371.*   3752 *One or two edd. give* seem. *But cf.*
'Hymn of Apollo', 34, 'England in 1819', 9; and the Preface to Alastor *fourth sentence*

XXXIII

'These are blind fancies—reason cannot know
  What sense can neither feel, nor thought conceive;
There is delusion in the world—and woe,
  And fear, and pain—we know not whence we live,   3760
  Or why, or how, or what mute Power may give
Their being to each plant, and star, and beast,
  Or even these thoughts.—Come near me! I do weave
A chain I cannot break—I am possessed
With thoughts too swift and strong for one lone human breast.

XXXIV

'Yes, yes—thy kiss is sweet, thy lips are warm!   3766
  O! willingly, belovèd, would these eyes,
Might they no more drink being from thy form,
  Even as to sleep whence we again arise,
  Close their faint orbs in death! I fear nor prize   3770
Aught that can now betide, unshared by thee—
  Yes, Love when Wisdom fails makes Cythna wise:
Darkness and death, if death be true, must be
Dearer than life and hope, if unenjoyed with thee.

XXXV

'Alas, our thoughts flow on with stream, whose waters 3775
  Return not to their fountain—Earth and Heaven,
The Ocean and the Sun, the Clouds their daughters,
  Winter, and Spring, and Morn, and Noon, and Even,
  All that we are or know, is darkly driven
Towards one gulf.—Lo! what a change is come   3780
  Since I first spake—but time shall be forgiven,
Though it change all but thee!'—She ceased. Night's gloom
Meanwhile had fallen on earth from the sky's sunless dome.

XXXVI

Though she had ceased, her countenance uplifted
  To Heaven still spake, with solemn glory bright;   3785
Her dark deep eyes, her lips, whose motions gifted

3763 thoughts.—Come *1904, 1839*] thoughts;—come *1818*   3766 warm!]
warm— *edd.*   3767 willingly, *1904, 1839*] willingly *1818*   3770 death!] death:
edd.   3775 with stream, *Thus edd. and e. 10 : see n., p. 372.*   3782 ceased.
Night's] ceased—night's *edd.*   3785 Heaven] Heaven, *edd.*

The air they breathed with love, her locks undight.
'Fair star of life and love,' I cried, 'my soul's delight,
Why lookest thou on the crystalline skies?
　　O, that my spirit were yon Heaven of night,　　3790
Which gazes on thee with its thousand eyes!'
She turned to me and smiled—that smile was Paradise!

CANTO X

I

W AS there a human spirit in the steed,
　　That thus with his proud voice, ere night was gone,
He broke our linkèd rest? or do indeed　　3795
　　All living things a common nature own,
　　And thought erect an universal throne,
Where many shapes one tribute ever bear?
　　And Earth, their mutual mother, does she groan
To see her sons contend? and makes she bare　　3800
Her breast, that all in peace its drainless stores may share?

II

I have heard friendly sounds from many a tongue
　　Which was not human—the lone nightingale
Has answered me with her most soothing song,
　　Out of her ivy bower, when I sate pale　　3805
　　With grief, and sighed beneath; from many a dale
The antelopes who flocked for food have spoken
　　With happy sounds, and motions, that avail
Like man's own speech; and such was now the token
Of waning night, whose calm by that proud neigh was broken.

III

Each night, that mighty steed bore me abroad,　　3811
　　And I returned with food to our retreat,
And dark intelligence; the blood which flowed
　　Over the fields had stained the courser's feet.
　　Soon the dust drinks that bitter dew,—then meet　　3815

3787 undight. *1904*] undight; *1839, 1818*

Canto X. 3802 tongue *1904, 1839*] tongue, *1818*　　3814 fields *e. 10*] fields, *edd.*
feet.] feet; *edd.*

The vulture, and the wild dog, and the snake,
     The wolf, and the hyæna gray, and eat
The dead in horrid truce: their throngs did make
Behind the steed a chasm like waves in a ship's wake.

IV

For, from the utmost realms of earth, came pouring   3820
     The banded slaves whom every despot sent
At that throned traitor's summons; like the roaring
     Of fire, whose floods the wild deer circumvent
     In the scorched pastures of the south; so bent
The armies of the leaguèd Kings around   3825
     Their files of steel and flame;—the continent
Trembled, as with a zone of ruin bound,
Beneath their feet; the sea shook with their navies' sound.

V

From every nation of the earth they came,
     The multitude of moving heartless things   3830
Whom slaves call men: obediently they came,
     Like sheep whom from the fold the shepherd brings
     To the stall, red with blood; their many kings
Led them, thus erring, from their native land,—
     Tartar and Frank, and millions whom the wings   3835
Of Indian breezes lull, and many a band
The Arctic Anarch sent, and Idumea's sand,

VI

Fertile in prodigies and lies;—so there
     Strange natures made a brotherhood of ill.
The desert savage ceased to grasp in fear   3840
     His Asian shield and bow, when, at the will
     Of Europe's subtler son, the bolt would kill
Some shepherd sitting on a rock secure;
     But smiles of wondering joy his face would fill,
And savage sympathy: those slaves impure,   3845
Each one the other thus from ill to ill did lure.

3819 steed] steed, *edd.*, *e. 10*   3828 feet;] feet, *edd.*   3830 things] things,
edd.   3834 land,—] land; *1904* home; *1839, 1818*   land *below* [home] *e. 10.*
See *n.*, *p. 372.*

VII

For traitorously did that foul Tyrant robe
　His countenance in lies,—even at the hour
When he was snatched from death, then o'er the globe,
　With secret signs from many a mountain-tower,　　3850
　With smoke by day, and fire by night, the power
Of Kings and Priests, those dark conspirators,
　He called:—they knew his cause their own, and swore
Like wolves and serpents to their mutual wars
Strange truce, with many a rite which Earth and Heaven
　abhors.　　　　　　　　　　　　　　　　3855

VIII

Myriads had come—millions were on their way;
　The Tyrant passed, surrounded by the steel
Of hired assassins, through the public way,
　Choked with his country's dead:—his footsteps reel
On the fresh blood—he smiles. 'Ay, now I feel　　3860
I am a King in truth!' he said, and took
　His royal seat, and bade the torturing wheel
Be brought, and fire, and pincers, and the hook,
And scorpions; that his soul on its revenge might look.

IX

'But first, go slay the rebels—why return　　　　3865
　The victor bands?' he said, 'millions yet live,
Of whom the weakest with one word might turn
　The scales of victory yet;—let none survive
　But those within the walls—each fifth shall give
The expiation for his brethren here.—　　　　　3870
　Go forth, and waste and kill!'—'O king, forgive
My speech,' a soldier answered—'but we fear
The spirits of the night, and morn is drawing near;

X

'For we were slaying still without remorse,
　And now that dreadful chief beneath my hand　3875
Defenceless lay, when, on a hell-black horse,

3852 conspirators, *1904*] conspirators *1839, 1818*　　　3854 wolves *1904, 1839*]
wolves, *1818*　　　3860 smiles. *1904, 1839*] smiles *1818*　　　3866 bands?' *1904,*
1839] bands,' *1818*

An Angel bright as day, waving a brand
Which flashed among the stars, passed.'—'Dost thou stand
Parleying with me, thou wretch?' the king replied;
    'Slaves, bind him to the wheel; and of this band,   3880
Whoso will drag that woman to his side
That scared him thus, may burn his dearest foe beside;

XI

'And gold and glory shall be his.—Go forth!'
    They rushed into the plain.—Loud was the roar
Of their career: the horsemen shook the earth;   3885
    The wheeled artillery's speed the pavement tore;
    The infantry, file after file, did pour
Their clouds on the utmost hills. Five days they slew
    Among the wasted fields; the sixth saw gore
Stream through the city; on the seventh, the dew   3890
Of slaughter became stiff, and there was peace anew:

XII

Peace in the desert fields and villages,
    Between the glutted beasts and mangled dead!
Peace in the silent streets! save when the cries
    Of victims to their fiery judgement led,   3895
    Made pale their voiceless lips who seemed to dread
Even in their dearest kindred, lest some tongue
    Be faithless to the fear yet unbetrayed;
Peace in the Tyrant's palace, where the throng
Waste the triumphal hours in festival and song!   3900

XIII

Day after day the burning sun rolled on
    Over the death-polluted land—it came
Out of the east like fire, and fiercely shone
    A lamp of Autumn, ripening with its flame
    The few lone ears of corn;—the sky became   3905

3887 file, did *1904, 1839*] file did *1818*   3898 yet unbetrayed *edd.*] they strove
to hate *e. 10. See n., p. 372.*   3900 *Followed, in e. 10, by a snatch of broken,
extraneous verse and two memoranda. See n., p. 372.*

Stagnate with heat, so that each cloud and blast
  Languished and died,—the thirsting air did claim
All moisture, and a rotting vapour passed
From the unburied dead, invisible and fast.

XIV

First Want, then Plague came on the beasts; their food 3910
  Failed, and they drew the breath of its decay.
Millions on millions, whom the scent of blood
  Had lured, or who, from regions far away,
  Had tracked the hosts in festival array,
From their dark deserts; gaunt and wasting now,   3915
  Stalked like fell shades among their perished prey;
In their green eyes a strange disease did glow,
They sank in hideous spasm, or pains severe and slow.

XV

The fish were poisoned in the streams; the birds
  In the green woods perished; the insect race   3920
Was withered up; the scattered flocks and herds
  Who had survived the wild beasts' hungry chase
  Died moaning, each upon the other's face
In helpless agony gazing; round the City
  All night, the lean hyænas their sad case   3925
Like starving infants wailed; a woeful ditty!
And many a mother wept, pierced with unnatural pity.

XVI

Amid the aëreal minarets on high,
  The Ethiopian vultures fluttering fell
From their long line of brethren in the sky,   3930
  Startling the concourse of mankind.—Too well
  These signs the coming mischief did foretell:—
Strange panic first, a deep and sickening dread
  Within each heart, like ice, did sink and dwell,
A voiceless thought of evil, which did spread   3935
With the quick glance of eyes, like withering lightnings shed.

XVII

Day after day, when the year wanes, the frosts
  Strip its green crown of leaves, till all is bare;
So on those strange and congregated hosts
  Came Famine, a swift shadow, and the air   3940
  Groaned with the burden of a new despair;
Famine, than whom Misrule no deadlier daughter
  Feeds from her thousand breasts, though sleeping there
With lidless eyes, lie Faith, and Plague, and Slaughter,
A ghastly brood conceived of Lethe's sullen water.   3945

XVIII

There was no food, the corn was trampled down,
  The flocks and herds had perished; on the shore
The dead and putrid fish were ever thrown;
  The deeps were foodless, and the winds no more
  Creaked with the weight of birds, but, as before   3950
Those wingèd things sprang forth, were void of shade;
  The vines and orchards, Autumn's golden store,
Were burned;—so that the meanest food was weighed
With gold, and Avarice died before the god it made.

XIX

There was no corn—in the wide market-place   3955
  All loathliest things, even human flesh, was sold;
They weighed it in small scales—and many a face
  Was fixed in eager horror then: his gold
  The miser brought; the tender maid, grown bold
Through hunger, bared her scornèd charms in vain;   3960
  The mother brought her eldest-born, controlled
By instinct blind as love, but turned again
And bade her infant suck, and died in silent pain.

XX

Then fell blue Plague upon the race of man.
  'O, for the sheathèd steel, so late which gave   3965
Oblivion to the dead, when the streets ran
  With brothers' blood! O, that the earthquake's grave
  Would gape, or Ocean lift its stifling wave!'

3945 brood] brood; *edd.*   3950 but, *1904, 1839*] but *1818*   3959 brought;
1904, 1839] brought, *1818*   3967 earthquake's *1904, 1839*] earthquakes *1818*

Vain cries—throughout the streets, thousands pursued
   Each by his fiery torture howl and rave,   3970
Or sit, in frenzy's unimagined mood,
Upon fresh heaps of dead—a ghastly multitude.

XXI

It was not hunger now, but thirst. Each well
   Was choked with rotting corpses, and became
A cauldron of green mist made visible   3975
   At sunrise. Thither still the myriads came,
   Seeking to quench the agony of the flame,
Which raged like poison through their bursting veins;
   Naked they were from torture, without shame,
Spotted with nameless scars and lurid blains,   3980
Childhood, and youth, and age, writhing in savage pains.

XXII

It was not thirst but madness! Many saw
   Their own lean image everywhere, it went
A ghastlier self beside them, till the awe
   Of that dread sight to self-destruction sent   3985
   Those shrieking victims; some, ere life was spent,
Sought, with a horrid sympathy, to shed
   Contagion on the sound; and others rent
Their matted hair, and cried aloud, 'We tread
On fire! Almighty God his hell on earth has spread!'   3990

XXIII

Sometimes the living by the dead were hid.
   Near the great fountain in the public square,
Where corpses made a crumbling pyramid
   Under the sun, was heard one stifled prayer
   For life, in the hot silence of the air;   3995
And strange 'twas, 'mid that hideous heap to see
   Some shrouded in their long and golden hair,
   As if not dead, but slumbering quietly
Like forms which sculptors carve, then love to agony.

3972 dead—] dead; *edd.*   3990 Almighty God *LC*] the avenging Power *RI*
3996 'mid] amid *1904, 1809, 1818. Probably misprinted, as Forman guessed. In e. 10
the stanza is missing.*

XXIV

Famine had spared the palace of the king:—⁣ 4000
   He rioted in festival the while,
He and his guards and priests; but Plague did fling
   One shadow upon all. Famine can smile
   On him who brings it food, and pass, with guile
Of thankful falsehood, like a courtier gray, 4005
   The house-dog of the throne; but many a mile
Comes Plague, a wingèd wolf, who loathes alway
The garbage and the scum that strangers make her prey.

XXV

So, near the throne, amid the gorgeous feast,
   Sheathed in resplendent arms, or loosely dight 4010
To luxury, ere the mockery yet had ceased
   That lingered on his lips, the warrior's might
   Was loosened, and a new and ghastlier night
In dreams of frenzy lapped his eyes; he fell
   Headlong, or with stiff eyeballs sate upright 4015
Among the guests, or raving mad, did tell
Strange truths; a dying seer of dark oppression's hell.

XXVI

The Princes and the Priests were pale with terror;
   That monstrous faith wherewith they ruled mankind
Fell, like a shaft loosed by the bowman's error, 4020
   On their own hearts: they sought and they could find
   No refuge—'twas the blind who led the blind!
So, through the desolate streets to the high fane
   Of their Almighty God, the armies wind
In sad procession: each among the train 4025
To his own Idol lifts his supplications vain.

XXVII

'O God!' they cried, 'we know our secret pride
   Has scorned thee, and thy worship, and thy name;
Secure in human power we have defied

4004 food, *1904, 1839*] food *1818*   4019 mankind *1829*] mankind, *1904, 1818*
4024 The many-tongued and endless armies wind *RI*

Thy fearful might; we bend in fear and shame   4030
Before thy presence; with the dust we claim
Kindred; be merciful, O King of Heaven!
Most justly have we suffered for thy fame
Made dim, but be at length our sins forgiven,
Ere to despair and death thy worshippers be driven.   4035

XXVIII

'O God Almighty! thou alone hast power!
Who can resist thy will? who can restrain
Thy wrath, when on the guilty thou dost shower
The shafts of thy revenge, a blistering rain?
Greatest and best, be merciful again!   4040
Have we not stabbed thine enemies, and made
The Earth an altar, and the Heavens a fane,
Where thou wert worshipped with their blood, and laid
Those hearts in dust which would thy searchless works have
    weighed?

XXIX

'Well didst thou loosen on this impious City   4045
Thine angels of revenge: recall them now;
Thy worshippers, abased, here kneel for pity,
And bind their souls by an immortal vow:
We swear by thee—and to our oath do thou
Give sanction, from thine hell of fiends and flame—   4050
That we will kill with fire and torments slow
The last of those who mocked thy holy name,
And scorned the sacred laws thy prophets did proclaim.'

XXX

Thus they with trembling limbs and pallid lips
Worshipped their own hearts' image, dim and vast,   4055
Scared by the shade wherewith they would eclipse
The light of other minds;—troubled they passed
From the great Temple;—fiercely still and fast

4036 'O God Almighty! *LC*] 'O King of Glory! *RI*   4047 worshippers, *1904*]
worshippers *1839, 1818*   4049 thee—] thee! *edd.*   4050 flame—] flame, *edd.*
4051 slow] slow, *edd.*

The arrows of the plague among them fell,
   And they on one another gazed aghast,   4060
And through the hosts contention wild befell,
As each] of his own God the wondrous works did tell.

XXXI

And Oromaze, and Christ, and Mahomet,
   Moses and Buddh, Zerdusht, and Brahm, and Foh,
A tumult of strange names, which never met   4065
   Before, as watchwords of a single woe,
   Arose; each raging votary 'gan to throw
Aloft his armèd hands, and each did howl
   'Our God alone is God!'—and slaughter now
Would have gone forth, when from beneath a cowl   4070
A voice came forth, which pierced like ice through every soul.

XXXII

He was a Christian Priest from whom it came,
   A zealous man, who led the legioned West,
With words which faith and pride had steeped in flame,
   To quell the rebel Atheists; a dire guest   4075
   Even to his friends was he, for in his breast
Did hate and guile lie watchful, intertwined,
   Twin serpents in one deep and winding nest;
He loathed all faith beside his own, and pined
To wreak his fear of God in vengeance on mankind.   4080

XXXIII

But more he loathed and hated the clear light
   Of wisdom and free thought, and more did fear,
Lest, kindled once, its beams might pierce the night,
   Even where his Idol stood; for, far and near
   Did many a heart in Europe leap to hear   4085
That faith and tyranny were trampled down—
   Many a pale victim, doomed for truth to share
The murderer's cell, or see, with helpless groan,
The priests his children drag for slaves to serve their own.

4062 God *LC*] god *RI*   4063 and Christ *1904*] Joshua *RI*   4072 He was
a Christian *LC*] 'Twas an Iberian *RI*   4073 West, *1904*] west *1839, 1818*
4075 rebel Atheists *LC*] unbelievers *RI*   4080 God *LC*] Heaven *RI*   4086 down—]
down; *edd.*

XXXIV

He dared not kill the infidels with fire   4090
  Or steel, in Europe; the slow agonies
Of legal torture mocked his keen desire:
    So he made truce with those who did despise
    His cradled Idol, and the sacrifice,
Of God to God's own wrath—that Islam's creed   4095
  Might crush for him those deadlier enemies;
For fear of God did in his bosom breed
A jealous hate of man, an unreposing need.

XXXV

'Peace! Peace!' he cried, 'when we are dead, the Day
  Of Judgement comes, and all shall surely know   4100
Whose God is God, each fearfully shall pay
    The errors of his faith in endless woe!
    But there is sent a mortal vengeance now
On earth, because an impious race had spurned
  Him whom we all adore,—a subtle foe,   4105
By whom for ye this dread reward was earned,
And thrones, which rest on faith in God, nigh overturned.

XXXVI

'Think ye, because ye weep, and kneel, and pray,
  That God will lull the pestilence? It rose
Even from beneath his throne, where, many a day,   4110
    His mercy soothed it to a dark repose:
    It walks upon the earth to judge his foes;
And what are thou and I, that he should deign
  To curb his ghastly minister, or close
The gates of death, ere they receive the twain   4115
Who shook with mortal spells his undefended reign?

XXXVII

'Ay, there is famine in the gulf of hell,
  Its giant worms of fire for ever yawn,—
  Their lurid eyes are on us! those who fell

4094-5
      The expiation, and the sacrifice,
      That, though detested, Islam's kindred creed   *RI*

4107 And kingly thrones, which rest on faith, nigh overturned. *RI*   4118 yawn,—
edd. but misprinted in later reprints of 1904

By the swift shafts of pestilence ere dawn,   4120
　Are in their jaws! they hunger for the spawn
Of Satan, their own brethren, who were sent
　To make our souls their spoil. See! see! they fawn
Like dogs, and they will sleep with luxury spent,
When those detested hearts their iron fangs have rent!   4125

XXXVIII

'Our God may then lull Pestilence to sleep:—
　Pile high the pyre of expiation now,
A forest's spoil of boughs; and on the heap
　Pour venomous gums, which sullenly and slow,
　When touched by flame, shall burn, and melt, and flow,
A stream of clinging fire,—and fix on high   4131
　A net of iron, and spread forth below
A couch of snakes, and scorpions, and the fry
Of centipedes and worms, earth's hellish progeny!

XXXIX

'Let Laon and Laone on that pyre,   4135
　Linked tight with burning brass, perish!—then pray
That, with this sacrifice, the withering ire
　Of God may be appeased.' He ceased, and they
　A space stood silent, as far, far away
The echoes of his voice among them died;   4140
　And he knelt down upon the dust, alway
Muttering the curses of his speechless pride,
Whilst shame, and fear, and awe, the armies did divide.

XL

His voice was like a blast that burst the portal
　Of fabled hell; and as he spake, each one   4145
Saw gape beneath the chasms of fire immortal,
　And Heaven above seemed cloven, where, on a throne
　With storms and shadows girt, sate God, alone
Their King and Judge—fear killed in every breast
　All natural pity then, a fear unknown   4150
Before; and with an inward fire possessed,
They raged like homeless beasts whom burning woods invest.

4127 now, *1904*,] now! *1839, 1818*   4128 boughs;] boughs, *edd.*   4138 God
LC] Heaven *RI*   4148 Girt round with storms and shadows, sate alone *RI*
4151 Before;] Before, *edd.*

XLI

'Twas morn.—At noon the public crier went forth,
  Proclaiming through the living and the dead,
'The Monarch saith, that his great Empire's worth   4155
  Is set on Laon and Laone's head:
He who but one yet living here can lead,
  Or who the life from both their hearts can wring,
  Shall be the kingdom's heir, a glorious meed!
But he who both alive can hither bring,   4160
The Princess shall espouse, and reign an equal King.'

XLII

Ere night the pyre was piled, the net of iron
  Was spread above, the fearful couch below;
It overtopped the towers that did environ
  That spacious square; for Fear is never slow   4165
  To build the thrones of Hate, her mate and foe;
So, she scourged forth the maniac multitude
  To rear this pyramid—tottering and slow,
Plague-stricken, foodless, like lean herds pursued
By gadflies, they have piled the heath, and gums, and wood.

XLIII

Night came, a starless and a moonless gloom.   4171
  Until the dawn, those hosts of many a nation
Stood round that pile, as near one lover's tomb
  Two gentle sisters mourn their desolation;
  And in the silence of that expectation,   4175
Was heard on high the reptiles' hiss and crawl—
  It was so deep—save when the devastation
Of the swift pest, with fearful interval,
Marking its path with shrieks, among the crowd would fall.

XLIV

Morn came,—among those sleepless multitudes,   4180
  Madness, and Fear, and Plague, and Famine still
  Heaped corpse on corpse, as in autumnal woods

4153 morn.—At *1904, 1839*] morn—at *1818*   4163 below; *1904, 1839*] below,
1818   4166 foe;] foe, *edd.*   4176 reptiles' *1904, 1839*] reptiles *1818*
4177 deep— *1904*] deep, *1839, 1818*   4178 pest, *1904*] pest *1839, 1818*
8127073   S

The frosts of many a wind with dead leaves fill
   Earth's cold and sullen brooks; in silence, still
The pale survivors stood; ere noon, the fear   4185
   Of Hell became a panic, which did kill
Like hunger or disease, with whispers drear,
As 'Hush! hark! Come they yet? God, God, thine hour is near!'

XLV

And Priests rushed through their ranks, some counterfeiting
   The rage they did inspire, some mad indeed   4190
With their own lies; they said their God was waiting
   To see his enemies writhe, and burn, and bleed,—
   And that, till then, the snakes of Hell had need
Of human souls:—three hundred furnaces
   Soon blazed through the wide City, where, with speed,
Men brought their atheist kindred to appease   4196
God's wrath, and while they burned, knelt round on quivering
    knees.

XLVI

The noontide sun was darkened with that smoke,
   The winds of eve dispersed those ashes gray.
The madness which these rites had lulled, awoke   4200
   Again at sunset.—Who shall dare to say
   The deeds which night and fear brought forth, or weigh
In balance just the good and evil there?
   He might man's deep and searchless heart display,
And cast a light on those dim labyrinths, where   4205
Hope, near imagined chasms, is struggling with despair.

XLVII

'Tis said, a mother dragged three children then,
   To those fierce flames which roast the eyes in the head,
And laughed, and died; and that unholy men,
   Feasting like fiends upon the infidel dead,   4210
   Looked from their meal, and saw an Angel tread

4184 silence, still *1904, 1839, RI*] silence still *LC*   4187 drear, *1904, 1839*]
drear *1818*   4188 God, God, *LC*] Just Heaven! *RI*   4191 God *LC*] god *RI*
4196 atheist *LC*] infidel *RI*   4207 *Stanza XLVII is drafted in the Notebook*
e. 14, which otherwise is devoted to drafts of the Dedication.

The threshold of God's throne, and it was she!
And, on that night, one without doubt or dread
Came to the fire, and said, 'Stop, I am he!
Kill me!'—They burned them both with hellish mockery.

XLVIII

And, one by one, that night, young maidens came, 4216
    Beauteous and calm, like shapes of living stone
Clothed in the light of dreams, and by the flame
    Which shrank as overgorged, they laid them down,
    And sung a low sweet song, of which alone 4220
One word was heard, and that was Liberty;
    And that some kissed their marble feet, with moan
Like love, and died; and then that they did die
With happy smiles, which sunk in white tranquillity.

CANTO XI

I

SHE saw me not—she heard me not—alone 4225
    Upon the mountain's dizzy brink she stood;
She spake not, breathed not, moved not—there was thrown
    Over her look, the shadow of a mood
    Which only clothes the heart in solitude,
A thought of voiceless depth;—she stood alone, 4230
    Above, the Heavens were spread;—below, the flood
Was murmuring in its caves;—the wind had blown
Her hair apart, through which her eyes and forehead shone.

II

A cloud was hanging o'er the western mountains;
    Before its blue and moveless depth were flying 4235
Gray mists poured forth from the unresting fountains
    Of darkness in the north:—the day was dying:—
    Sudden, the sun shone forth, its beams were lying

4212 The threshold of God's throne, *LC*] The visible floor of Heaven, *RI*
4215 Kill me!'—They *1904, 1839*] 'Kill me!' they *1818*   4223 died; *1904*] died,
1839, 1818

Like boiling gold on Ocean, strange to see,
   And on the shattered vapours which, defying   4240
The power of light in vain, tossed restlessly
In the red Heaven, like wrecks in a tempestuous sea.

III

It was a stream of living beams, whose bank
   On either side by the cloud's cleft was made;
And where its chasms that flood of glory drank,   4245
   Its waves gushed forth like fire, and as if swayed
   By some mute tempest, rolled on *her*; the shade
Of her bright image floated on the river
   Of liquid light, which then did end and fade—
Her radiant shape upon its verge did shiver;   4250
Aloft, her flowing hair like strings of flame did quiver.

IV

I stood beside her, but she saw me not—
   She looked upon the sea, and skies, and earth;
Rapture, and love, and admiration wrought
   A passion deeper far than tears, or mirth,   4255
   Or speech, or gesture, or whate'er has birth
From common joy; which with the speechless feeling
   That led her there united, and shot forth
From her far eyes a light of deep revealing,
All but her dearest self from my regard concealing.   4260

V

Her lips were parted, and the measured breath
   Was now heard there;—her dark and intricate eyes
Orb within orb, deeper than sleep or death,
   Absorbed the glories of the burning skies,
   Which, mingling with her heart's deep ecstasies,   4265
Burst from her looks and gestures;—and a light
   Of liquid tenderness, like love, did rise
From her whole frame,—an atmosphere which quite
Arrayed her in its beams, tremulous and soft and bright.

Canto XI. 4240 vapours which, *1839, 1818*] vapours, which *1904*   4259 eyes
1904] eyes, *1839, 1818*   4267 tenderness, *1904, 1839*] tenderness *1818*
4268 frame,— *1839*] frame, *1904, 1818*

VI

She would have clasped me to her glowing frame;   4270
  Those warm and odorous lips might soon have shed
On mine the fragrance and the invisible flame
    Which now the cold winds stole;—she would have laid
    Upon my languid heart her dearest head;
I might have heard her voice, tender and sweet;   4275
    Her eyes mingling with mine, might soon have fed
My soul with their own joy.—One moment yet
I gazed—we parted then, never again to meet!

VII

Never but once to meet on earth again!
  She heard me as I fled—her eager tone   4280
Sunk on my heart, and almost wove a chain
    Around my will to link it with her own,
    So that my stern resolve was almost gone.
'I cannot reach thee! whither dost thou fly?
    My steps are faint—Come back, thou dearest one—   4285
Return, ah me! return!'—The wind passed by
On which those accents died, faint, far, and lingeringly.

VIII

Woe! Woe! that moonless midnight!—Want and Pest
  Were horrible, but one more fell doth rear,
As in a hydra's swarming lair, its crest   4290
    Eminent among those victims—even the Fear
    Of Hell: each girt by the hot atmosphere
Of his blind agony, like a scorpion stung
    By his own rage upon his burning bier
Of circling coals of fire; but still there clung   4295
One hope, like a keen sword on starting threads uphung:

IX

Not death—death was no more refuge or rest;
  Not life—it was despair to be!—not sleep,
For fiends and chasms of fire had dispossessed

4281 Sunk *1904, 1818*] sank *1839*   4286 return!'—The *1904, 1839*] return—the
1818   4288 midnight!— *1904*] midnight.— *1839* midnight— *1818*

All natural dreams: to wake was not to weep,   4300
   But to gaze mad and pallid, at the leap
To which the Future, like a snaky scourge,
   Or like some tyrant's eye, which aye doth keep
Its withering beam upon his slaves, did urge
Their steps; they heard the roar of Hell's sulphureous surge.

X

Each of that multitude, alone, and lost   4306
   To sense of outward things, one hope yet knew;
As on a foam-girt crag some seaman tossed
   Stares at the rising tide, or like the crew
   Whilst now the ship is splitting through and through;
Each, if the tramp of a far steed was heard,   4311
   Started from sick despair, or if there flew
One murmur on the wind, or if some word
Which none can gather yet the distant crowd has stirred.

XI

Why became cheeks, wan with the kiss of death,   4315
   Paler from hope? they had sustained despair.
Why watched those myriads with suspended breath
   Sleepless a second night? they are not here,
   The victims, and hour by hour, a vision drear,
Warm corpses fall upon the clay-cold dead;   4320
   And even in death their lips are wreathed with fear.—
The crowd is mute and moveless—overhead
Silent Arcturus shines—'Ha! hear'st thou not the tread

XII

'Of rushing feet? laughter? the shout, the scream,
   Of triumph not to be contained? See! hark!   4325
They come, they come! give way!' Alas, ye deem
   Falsely—'tis but a crowd of maniacs stark
   Driven, like a troop of spectres, through the dark

4306 multitude, *1904*] multitude *1839, 1818*   4314 yet] yet, *edd.*
4315 cheeks, *1904, 1839*] cheeks *1818*   4318 here, *1904*] here *1839, 1818*
4321 wreathed *1904, 1839²*, *1818*] writhed *1839¹, e. 10. See n., p. 373.*   4326 come!
give *1904, 1839*] come, give *1818*

From the choked well, whence a bright death-fire sprung,
  A lurid earth-star, which dropped many a spark   4330
From its blue train, and spreading widely, clung
To their wild hair, like mist the topmost pines among.

XIII

And many, from the crowd collected there,
  Joined that strange dance in fearful sympathies;
There was the silence of a long despair,   4335
    When the last echo of those terrible cries
    Came from a distant street, like agonies
Stifled afar.—Before the Tyrant's throne
  All night his aged Senate sate, their eyes
In stony expectation fixed; when one   4340
Sudden before them stood, a stranger and alone.

XIV

Dark Priests and haughty Warriors gazed on him
  With baffled wonder, for a hermit's vest
Concealed his face; but, when he spake, his tone,
    Ere yet the matter did their thoughts arrest,—   4345
    Earnest, benignant, calm, as from a breast
Void of all hate or terror—made them start;
  For as with gentle accents he addressed
His speech to them, on each unwilling heart
Unusual awe did fall—a spirit-quelling dart.   4350

XV

'Ye Princes of the Earth, ye sit aghast
  Amid the ruin which yourselves have made—
Yes, Desolation heard your trumpet's blast,
    And sprang from sleep.—Dark Terror has obeyed
    Your bidding! O, that I whom ye have made   4355
Your foe, could set my dearest enemy free
  From pain and fear! But evil casts a shade,
Which cannot pass so soon, and Hate must be
The nurse and parent still of an ill progeny.

4333 many, *1904, 1839*] many *1818*   4341–65 *See n., p. 373.*   4345 arrest,—
1904] arrest, *1839, 1818*   4347 terror—*1904*] terror, *1839, 1818*   4352 made—]
made, *edd.*   4354 sleep.—Dark] sleep!—dark *edd.*   4355 bidding!] bidding—
edd.

XVI

'Ye turn to God for aid in your distress;   4360
   Alas, that ye, the mighty and the wise,
Who, if ye dared, might not aspire to less
   Than ye conceive of power, should fear the lies
   Which thou, and thou, didst frame for mysteries
To blind your slaves:—consider your own thought,   4365
   An empty and a cruel sacrifice
Ye now prepare, for a vain idol wrought
Out of the fears and hate which vain desires have brought.

XVII

'Ye seek for happiness—alas, the day!
   Ye find it not in luxury nor in gold,   4370
Nor in the fame, nor in the envied sway
   For which, O willing slaves to Custom old,
   Severe taskmistress! ye your hearts have sold.
Ye seek for peace, and when ye die, to dream
   No evil dreams: all mortal things are cold   4375
And senseless then; if aught survive, I deem
It must be love and joy, for they immortal seem.

XVIII

'Fear not the future, weep not for the past.
   O, could I win your ears to dare be now
Glorious, and great, and calm! that ye would cast   4380
   Into the dust those symbols of your woe,
   Purple, and gold, and steel! that ye would go
Proclaiming to the nations whence ye came,
   That Want, and Plague, and Fear, from slavery flow;
And that mankind is free, and that the shame   4385
Of royalty and faith is lost in freedom's fame!

XIX

'If thus, 'tis well—if not, I come to say
   That Laon—' while the Stranger spoke, among
The Council sudden tumult and affray

4360 God *LC*] Heaven *RI*   4361 the mighty *1904*, *1839*, *e. 10*] tho mighty
1818. See *n.*, *p. 373*.   4362 ye *1904*, *1839*, *e. 10*] he *1818*   4387 thus, *1904*]
thus *1839*, *1818*

   Arose, for many of those warriors young,   4390
   Had on his eloquent accents fed and hung
Like bees on mountain-flowers; they knew the truth,
   And from their thrones in vindication sprung;
The men of faith and law then without ruth
Drew forth their secret steel, and stabbed each ardent youth.

XX

They stabbed them in the back and sneered—a slave   4396
   Who stood behind the throne, those corpses drew
Each to its bloody, dark, and secret grave;
   And one more daring raised his steel anew
   To pierce the Stranger. 'What hast thou to do   4400
With me, poor wretch?'—Calm, solemn, and severe,
   That voice unstrung his sinews, and he threw
His dagger on the ground, and pale with fear,
Sate silently—his voice then did the Stranger rear.

XXI

'It doth avail not that I weep for ye—   4405
   Ye cannot change, since ye are old and gray,
And ye have chosen your lot—your fame must be
   A book of blood, whence in a milder day
   Men shall learn truth, when ye are wrapped in clay:
Now ye shall triumph. I am Laon's friend,   4410
   And him to your revenge will I betray,
So ye concede one easy boon. Attend!
For now I speak of things which ye can apprehend.

XXII

'There is a People mighty in its youth,
   A land beyond the Oceans of the West,   4415
Where, though with rudest rites, Freedom and Truth
   Are worshipped; from a glorious mother's breast,
   Who, since high Athens fell, among the rest
Sate like the Queen of Nations, but in woe,
   By inbred monsters outraged and oppressed,   4420
Turns to her chainless child for succour now,
It draws the milk of power in wisdom's fullest flow.

4400 Stranger. 'What *1904*] Stranger: 'What *1839, 1818*   4422 It draws *1904,*
1818] And draws *1839*

XXIII

'That land is like an Eagle, whose young gaze
  Feeds on the noontide beam, whose golden plume
Floats moveless on the storm, and in the blaze   4425
  Of sunrise gleams when Earth is wrapped in gloom;
  An epitaph of glory for the tomb
Of murdered Europe may thy fame be made,
  Great People! As the sands shalt thou become;
Thy growth is swift as morn, when night must fade;   4430
The multitudinous Earth shall sleep beneath thy shade.

XXIV

'Yes, in the desert there is built a home
  For Freedom. Genius is made strong to rear
The monuments of man beneath the dome
  Of a new Heaven; myriads assemble there,   4435
  Whom the proud lords of man, in rage or fear,
Drive from their wasted homes: the boon I pray
  Is this—that Cythna shall be convoyed there—
Nay, start not at the name—America!
And then to you this night Laon will I betray.   4440

XXV

'With me do what you will. I am your foe!'
  The light of such a joy as makes the stare
Of hungry snakes like living emeralds glow,
  Shone in a hundred human eyes—'Where, where
  Is Laon? Haste! fly! drag him swiftly here!   4445
We grant thy boon.'—'I put no trust in ye,
  Swear by your dreadful God.'—'We swear, we swear!'
The stranger threw his vest back suddenly,
And smiled in gentle pride, and said, 'Lo! I am he!'

4423 That *1904, 1818*] This *1839*   4428 murdered Europe *edd.*] buried Albion
e. 10   4429 People! *1904, 1839*] People: *1818*   4432 there *1904, Form. 1876,*
justified by e. 10] then *1839, 1818*   4438 convoyed *edd. ; Shelley's emendation of*
conveyed *in his copy of LC*   4447 your dreadful God.' *LC*] the Power ye dread.' *RI*

CANTO XII

I

THE transport of a fierce and monstrous gladness   4450
     Spread through the multitudinous streets, fast flying
Upon the winds of fear; from his dull madness
     The starveling waked, and died in joy; the dying,
     Among the corpses in stark agony lying,
Just heard the happy tidings, and in hope   4455
     Closed their faint eyes; from house to house replying
With loud acclaim, the living shook Heaven's cope,
And filled the startled Earth with echoes. Morn did ope

II

Its pale eyes then; and lo! the long array
     Of guards in golden arms, and Priests beside,   4460
Singing their bloody hymns, whose garbs betray
     The blackness of the faith it seems to hide;
     And see, the Tyrant's gem-wrought chariot glide
Among the gloomy cowls and glittering spears—
     A Shape of light is sitting by his side,   4465
A child most beautiful. I' the midst appears
Laon,—exempt alone from mortal hopes and fears.

III

His head and feet are bare, his hands are bound
     Behind with heavy chains, yet none do wreak
Their scoffs on him, though myriads throng around;   4470
     There are no sneers upon his lip which speak
     That scorn or hate has made him bold; his cheek
Resolve has not turned pale,—his eyes are mild
     And calm, and, like the morn about to break,
Smile on mankind—his heart seems reconciled   4475
To all things and itself, like a reposing child.

Canto XII. 4450–76. *See n., p. 373.*   4452 winds *edd. ; confirmed by e. 10, though*
Ross. reasonably suggested wings   4458 echoes. Morn] echoes: morn *edd.*
4462 it seems *1904, 1839, 1818, e. 10, though Ross. reasonably conjectures* they seem
4474 and, like *1904]* and like *1839, 1818*

IV

Tumult was in the soul of all beside,
  Ill joy, or doubt, or fear; but those who saw
Their tranquil victim pass, felt wonder glide
  Into their brain, and became calm with awe.—   4480
  See, the slow pageant near the pile doth draw.
A thousand torches in the spacious square,
  Borne by the ready slaves of ruthless law,
Await the signal round: the morning fair
Is changed to a dim night by that unnatural glare.   4485

V

And see! beneath a sun-bright canopy,
  Upon a platform level with the pile,
The anxious Tyrant sit, enthroned on high,
  Girt by the chieftains of the host; all smile
  In expectation, but one child: the while   4490
I, Laon, led by mutes, ascend my bier
  Of fire, and look around: each distant isle
Is dark in the bright dawn; towers far and near,
Pierce like reposing flames the tremulous atmosphere.

VI

There was such silence through the host, as when   4495
  An earthquake trampling on some populous town,
Has crushed ten thousand with one tread, and men
  Expect the second; all were mute but one,
  That fairest child, who, bold with love, alone
Stood up before the King, without avail,   4500
  Pleading for Laon's life—her stifled groan
Was heard—she trembled like one aspen pale
Among the gloomy pines of a Norwegian vale.

VII

What were his thoughts linked in the morning sun,
  Among those reptiles, stingless with delay,   4505
Even like a tyrant's wrath?—The signal-gun

4502 one *1904, 1818*] an *1839*

Roared—hark, again! In that dread pause he lay
   As in a quiet dream—the slaves obey—
A thousand torches drop,—and hark, the last
   Bursts on that awful silence; far away,   4510
Millions, with hearts that beat both loud and fast,
Watch for the springing flame expectant and aghast.

VIII

They fly—the torches fall—a cry of fear
   Has startled the triumphant!—they recede!
For ere the cannon's roar has died, they hear   4515
   The tramp of hoofs like earthquake, and a steed
   Dark and gigantic, with the tempest's speed,
Bursts through their ranks: a woman sits thereon,
   Fairer, it seems, than aught that earth can breed,
Calm, radiant, like the phantom of the dawn,   4520
A spirit from the caves of daylight wandering gone.

IX

All thought it was God's Angel come to sweep
   The lingering guilty to their fiery grave;
The Tyrant from his throne in dread did leap,—
   Her innocence his child from fear did save;   4525
   Scared by the faith they feigned, each priestly slave
Knelt for his mercy whom they served with blood,
   And, like the refluence of a mighty wave
Sucked into the loud sea, the multitude
With crushing panic, fled in terror's altered mood.   4530

X

They pause, they blush, they gaze,—a gathering shout
   Bursts like one sound from the ten thousand streams
Of a tempestuous sea:—that sudden rout
   One checked who never in his mildest dreams
   Felt awe from grace or loveliness; the seams   4535

4510 away, *1904*] away *1839, 1818*   4519 Fairer, it seems, than *1904*] Fairer it
seems than *1839, 1818*   4534 checked] checked, *edd., e. 10*   who] who, *edd.*
4535-9 *Considerably repunctuated here. See n., pp. 373–4.*   4535 loveliness; *e. 10*]
loveliness, *edd.*

Of his rent heart so hard and cold a creed
  Had seared with blistering ice.—'But he misdeems
That he is wise whose wounds do only bleed
Inly for self.'—Thus thought that Christian Priest indeed,

XI

And others too, thought he was wise to see,   4540
  In pain, and fear, and hate, something divine,
In love and beauty, no divinity.—
  Now with a bitter smile, whose light did shine
  Like a fiend's hope upon his lips and eyne,
He said, and the persuasion of that sneer   4545
  Rallied his trembling comrades—'Is it mine
To stand alone, when kings and soldiers fear
A woman? God has sent his other victim here.'

XII

'Were it not impious,' said the King, 'to break
  Our holy oath?'—'Impious to keep it, say!'   4550
Shrieked the exulting Priest—'Slaves, to the stake
  Bind her, and on my head the burden lay
  Of her just torments:—at the Judgement Day
Will I stand up before God's golden throne
  And cry, "O Lord, to thee did I betray   4555
An Atheist; but for me she would have known
Another moment's joy! the glory be thine own!" '

XIII

They trembled, but replied not, nor obeyed,
  Pausing in breathless silence. Cythna sprung
From her gigantic steed, who, like a shade   4560
  Chased by the winds, those vacant streets among
  Fled tameless, as the brazen rein she flung
Upon his neck, and kissed his moonèd brow.
  A piteous sight, that one so fair and young,
The clasp of such a fearful death should woo   4565
With smiles of tender joy as beamed from Cythna now.

4537 ice.—'But] ice—but *1904, 1839, 1818*   4538 wise] wise, *1904, 1839, 1818*
4539 self.'—Thus] self—thus *1904, 1839, 1818*   that Christian *LC*] the Iberian *RI*
4541 divine,] divine; *1904, 1839*   divine *1818*   4548 God *LC*] Heaven *RI*   his
LC] its *RI*   4554 God's *LC*] the *RI*   4555 O Heaven, and cry, "To thee
did I betray *RI*   4556 Atheist *LC*] Infidel *RI*   4557 own!" ' *1904*] own."
1839, 1818

XIV

The warm tears burst in spite of faith and fear
　　From many a tremulous eye, but like soft dews
Which feed Spring's earliest buds, hung gathered there,
　　Frozen by doubt,—alas! they could not choose　　　4570
　　But weep; for when her faint limbs did refuse
To climb the pyre, upon the mutes she smiled;
　　And with her eloquent gestures, and the hues
Of her quick lips, even as a weary child
Wins sleep from some fond nurse with its caresses mild,　4575

XV

She won them, though unwilling, her to bind
　　Near me, among the snakes. When there had fled
One soft reproach that was most thrilling kind,
　　She smiled on me, and nothing then we said,
　　But each upon the other's countenance fed　　　4580
Looks of insatiate love; the mighty veil
　　Which doth divide the living and the dead
Was almost rent, the world grew dim and pale,—
All light in Heaven or Earth beside our love did fail.—

XVI

Yet—yet—one brief relapse! Like the last beam　　　4585
　　Of dying flames, the stainless air around
Hung silent and serene—a blood-red gleam
　　Burst upwards, hurling fiercely from the ground
　　The globèd smoke,—I heard the mighty sound
Of its uprise, like a tempestuous ocean;　　　4590
　　And through its chasms I saw, as in a swound,
The tyrant's child fall without life or motion
Before his throne, subdued by some unseen emotion.

4567 fear *1904*] fear, *1839, 1818*　　　4568-9 *anticipated in a fragment jotted in e. 14
on a blank page amid the drafting of the Dedication:*

　　　　　　and hopes like morning dew unshed
　　　　　Trembling on springs unopened buds

4570 choose *1904*] choose, *1839, 1818*　　　4577 there *1904, Form. 1876, justified by*
e. *10*] then *1839, 1818*　　　4585 relapse! Like] relapse, like *edd.*

XVII

And is this death?—The pyre has disappeared,
    The Pestilence, the Tyrant, and the throng;   4595
The flames grow silent—slowly there is heard
    The music of a breath-suspending song,
    Which, like the kiss of love when life is young,
Steeps the faint eyes in darkness sweet and deep;
    With ever-changing notes it floats along,   4600
Till on my passive soul there seemed to creep
A melody, like waves on wrinkled sands that leap.

XVIII

The warm touch of a soft and tremulous hand
    Wakened me then; lo! Cythna sate reclined
Beside me, on the waved and golden sand   4605
    Of a clear pool, upon a bank o'ertwined
    With strange and star-bright flowers, which to the wind
Breathed divine odour; high above, was spread
    The emerald heaven of trees of unknown kind,
Whose moonlike blooms and bright fruit overhead   4610
A shadow which was light upon the waters shed.

XIX

And round about sloped many a lawny mountain
    With incense-bearing forests, and vast caves
Of marble radiance, to that mighty fountain;
    And where the flood its own bright margin laves,   4615
    Their echoes talk with its eternal waves,
Which, from the depths whose jaggèd caverns breed
    Their unreposing strife, it lifts and heaves,—
Till through a chasm of hills they roll, and feed
A river deep, which flies with smooth but arrowy speed.   4620

XX

As we sate gazing in a trance of wonder,
    A boat approached, borne by the musical air
Along the waves which sung and sparkled under

4594 death?—The *1904*] death? The *1839*   death? the *1818*   4611 shadow...
light] shadow, . . . light, *edd.*   4614 radiance, *1904*] radiance *1839, 1818*

Its rapid keel. A wingèd shape sate there,
  A child with silver-shining wings, so fair,   4625
That as her bark did through the waters glide,
  The shadow of the lingering waves did wear
Light, as from starry beams; from side to side
While veering to the wind her plumes the bark did guide.

XXI

The boat was one curved shell of hollow pearl,   4630
  Almost translucent with the light divine
Of her within; the prow and stern did curl
  Hornèd on high, like the young moon supine,
  When o'er dim twilight mountains dark with pine,
It floats upon the sunset's sea of beams,   4635
  Whose golden waves in many a purple line
Fade fast, till borne on sunlight's ebbing streams,
Dilating, on earth's verge the sunken meteor gleams.

XXII

Its keel has struck the sands beside our feet;—
  Then Cythna turned to me, and from her eyes   4640
Which swam with unshed tears, a look more sweet
  Than happy love, a wild and glad surprise,
  Glanced as she spake: 'Ay, this is Paradise
And not a dream, and we are all united!
  Lo, that is mine own child, who in the guise   4645
Of madness came, like day to one benighted
In lonesome woods: my heart is now too well requited!'

XXIII

And then she wept aloud, and in her arms
  Clasped that bright Shape, less marvellously fair
Than her own human hues and living charms;   4650
  Which, as she leaned in passion's silence there,
  Breathed warmth on the cold bosom of the air,
Which seemed to blush and tremble with delight;
  The glossy darkness of her streaming hair
Fell o'er that snowy child, and wrapped from sight   4655
The fond and long embrace which did their hearts unite.

4624 keel. A] keel—a *edd.*   4628 side to side *1911*] side to side, *1904, 1839, 1818*
4643 spake: *1904, 1839*] spake; *1818*

XXIV

Then the bright child, the plumèd Seraph came,
 And fixed its blue and beaming eyes on mine,
And said, 'I was disturbed by tremulous shame
  When once we met, yet knew that I was thine   4660
 From the same hour in which thy lips divine
Kindled a clinging dream within my brain,
  Which ever waked when I might sleep, to twine
Thine image with *her* memory dear—again
We meet; exempted now from mortal fear or pain.   4665

XXV

'When the consuming flames had wrapped ye round,
 The hope which I had cherished went away;
I fell in agony on the senseless ground,
  And hid mine eyes in dust; and far astray
 My mind was gone, when bright, like dawning day,   4670
The Spectre of the Plague before me flew,
  And breathed upon my lips, and seemed to say,
"They wait for thee, belovèd!"—then I knew
The death-mark on my breast, and became calm anew.

XXVI

'It was the calm of love—for I was dying.   4675
 I saw the black and half-extinguished pyre
In its own gray and shrunken ashes lying;
  The pitchy smoke of the departed fire
 Still hung in many a hollow dome and spire
Above the towers, like night; beneath whose shade   4680
 Awed by the ending of their own desire
The armies stood; a vacancy was made
In expectation's depth, and so they stood dismayed.

XXVII

'The frightful silence of that altered mood,
 The tortures of the dying clove alone,   4685
Till one uprose among the multitude,

4669 dust;] dust, *edd.*   4673 thee, beloved!" *1904, 1839*] thee beloved;—" *1818*
4680 towers, *1904, 1839*] towers *1818*

And said—"The flood of time is rolling on,
We stand upon its brink, whilst *they* are gone
To glide in peace down death's mysterious stream.
Have ye done well? They moulder flesh and bone,   4690
Who might have made this life's envenomed dream
A sweeter draught than ye will ever taste, I deem.

XXVIII

' "These perish as the good and great of yore
Have perished, and their murderers will repent,—
Yes, vain and barren tears shall flow before   4695
Yon smoke has faded from the firmament
Even for this cause, that ye who must lament
The death of those that made this world so fair,
Cannot recall them now; but there is lent
To man the wisdom of a high despair,   4700
When such can die, and he live on and linger here.

XXIX

' "Ay, ye may fear not now the Pestilence,
From fabled hell as by a charm withdrawn;
All power and faith must pass, since calmly hence
In torment and in fire have Atheists gone;   4705
And ye must sadly turn away, and moan
In secret, to his home each one returning;
And to long ages shall this hour be known;
And slowly shall its memory, ever burning,
Fill this dark night of things with an eternal morning.   4710

XXX

' "For me the world is grown too void and cold,
Since hope pursues immortal destiny
With steps thus slow—therefore shall ye behold
How Atheists and Republicans can die;
Tell to your children this!" Then suddenly   4715
He sheathed a dagger in his heart and fell;

4694 repent,— *1904*] repent. *1839*   repent, *1818*   4699 there *1904, Form. 1876, almost certainly justified by e. 10*] then *1839, 1818. See n., p. 374.*   4703 withdrawn; *1904, 1839*] withdrawn, *1818*   4705 In pain and fire have unbelievers gone *RI*   4707 returning; *1839*] returning, *1904, 1818*   4714 How those who love, yet fear not, dare to die; *RI*

My brain grew dark in death, and yet to me
There came a murmur from the crowd, to tell
Of deep and mighty change which suddenly befell.

XXXI

'Then suddenly I stood, a wingèd Thought,   4720
   Before the immortal Senate, and the seat
Of that star-shining spirit, whence is wrought
      The strength of its dominion, good and great,
      The better Genius of this world's estate.
His realm around one mighty Fane is spread,   4725
      Elysian islands bright and fortunate,
Calm dwellings of the free and happy dead,
Where I am sent to lead!' These wingèd words she said,

XXXII

And with the silence of her eloquent smile,
   Bade us embark in her divine canoe;   4730
Then at the helm we took our seat, the while
      Above her head those plumes of dazzling hue
      Into the winds' invisible stream she threw,
Sitting beside the prow: like gossamer
On the swift breath of morn, the vessel flew   4735
O'er the bright whirlpools of that fountain fair,
Whose shores receded fast, whilst we seemed lingering there,—

XXXIII

Till down that mighty stream, dark, calm, and fleet,
   Between a chasm of cedarn mountains riven,
Chased by the thronging winds whose viewless feet,   4740
      As swift as twinkling beams, had under heaven
      From woods and waves wild sounds and odours driven,
The boat fled visibly. Three nights and days,
      Borne like a cloud through morn, and noon, and even,
We sailed along the winding watery ways   4745
Of the vast stream, a long and labyrinthine maze,—

4720 stood, a wingèd Thought, *1904*] stood a winged Thought *1839*, *1818*
4728 *Followed, in e. 10, by broken snatches of extraneous verse, interspersed with prose*
memoranda. See n., p. 374.   4734 gossamer *1904*] gossamer, *1839*, *1818*
4737 there,—] there; *edd.*   4738 stream, *1904*] stream *1839*, *1818*.   4740 feet,]
feet *edd.*   4741 had] had, *edd.*   heaven] Heaven, *edd.*   4743 fled *1904*,
1818] flew *1839*   visibly. Three] visibly—three *edd.*   4746–55 *For punctuation*
see n., pp. 374–5.   4746 maze,—] maze. *edd.*

XXXIV

A scene of joy and wonder to behold—
   That river's shapes and shadows changing ever,
When the broad sunrise filled with deepening gold
   Its whirlpools, where all hues did spread and quiver;
   And where melodious falls did burst and shiver   4751
Among rocks clad with flowers, the foam and spray
   Sparkled like stars upon the sunny river,
Or when the moonlight poured a holier day,
One vast and glittering lake around green islands lay.   4755

XXXV

Morn, noon, and even, that boat of pearl outran
   The streams which bore it, like the arrowy cloud
Of tempest, or the speedier thought of man,
   Which flieth forth and cannot make abode;
   Sometimes through forests, deep like night, we glode,
Between the walls of mighty mountains crowned   4761
   With Cyclopean piles, whose turrets proud,
The homes of the departed, dimly frowned
O'er the bright waves which girt their dark foundations round.

XXXVI

Sometimes between the wide and flowering meadows,   4765
   Mile after mile we sailed, and 'twas delight
To see far off the sunbeams chase the shadows
   Over the grass; sometimes beneath the night
   Of wide and vaulted caves, whose roofs were bright
With starry gems, we fled, whilst from their deep   4770
   And dark-green chasms, shades beautiful and white,
Amid sweet sounds across our path would sweep,
Like swift and lovely dreams that walk the waves of sleep.

XXXVII

And ever as we sailed, our minds were full
   Of love and wisdom, which would overflow   4775
   In converse wild, and sweet, and wonderful,

4747 behold— *Loc. 1911*] behold *1904, 1839, 1818*   4749 When *1904*] Where
1839, 1818   sunrise *1904, 1839*] sunrise, *1818*   gold *1904, 1839*] gold, *1818*
4750 quiver; *1904*] quiver, *1839, 1818*   4759 abode; *1904, 1839*] above, *1818*
4776 wonderful, *1904*] wonderful; *1839, 1818*

And in quick smiles whose light would come and go
Like music o'er wide waves, and in the flow
Of sudden tears, and in the mute caress—
    For a deep shade was cleft, and we did know,   4780
That virtue, though obscured on Earth, not less
Survives all mortal change in lasting loveliness.

XXXVIII

Three days and nights we sailed, as thought and feeling
    Number delightful hours—for through the sky
The spherèd lamps of day and night, revealing   4785
    New changes and new glories, rolled on high,
    Sun, Moon, and moonlike lamps, the progeny
Of a diviner Heaven, serene and fair:
    On the fourth day, wild as a windwrought sea
The stream became, and fast and faster bare   4790
The spirit-wingèd boat, steadily speeding there.

XXXIX

Steady and swift, where the waves rolled like mountains
    Within the vast ravine, whose rifts did pour
Tumultuous floods from their ten thousand fountains,
    The thunder of whose earth-uplifting roar   4795
    Made the air sweep in whirlwinds from the shore,
Calm as a shade, the boat of that fair child
    Securely fled, that rapid stress before,
Amid the topmost spray, and sunbows wild,
Wreathed in the silver mist: in joy and pride we smiled.   4800

XL

The torrent of that wide and raging river
    Is passed, and our aëreal speed suspended.
We look behind; a golden mist did quiver
    Where its wild surges with the lake were blended,—
    Our bark hung there, as on a line suspended   4805

4777 go *1904*] go, *1839, 1818*   4804 Where *1904*] When *1839, 1818*   blended,—
1904] blended; *1839, 1818*   4805 on a line *1904*] one line *1839, 1818*

Between two heavens,—that windless waveless lake
  Which four great cataracts from four vales, attended
By mists, aye feed; from rocks and clouds they break,
And of that azure sea a silent refuge make.

XLI

Motionless resting on the lake awhile,   4810
  I saw its marge of snow-bright mountains rear
Their peaks aloft; I saw each radiant isle;
  And in the midst, afar, even like a sphere
  Hung in one hollow sky, did there appear
The Temple of the Spirit. On the sound   4815
  Which issued thence, drawn nearer and more near,
Like the swift moon this glorious earth around,
The charmèd boat approached, and there its haven found.

LAON AND CYTHNA: REJECTED PASSAGES

DEDICATION

[from a draft]

II

No more beside the river's sunny foam,
  Or the lone mossy isles with [bright] weeds wild,
Or in the emerald forests shall I roam
  Or where the woods an emerald hall [
  Weaving a glorious woof of thought, but like a child [5

III (I)

Great aspirations had been mine since first
  The veil which hid this world of human things
Was rent, and dreams divine my heart had nursed,
  Till it grew strong on night-dividing wings
  To visit thought's most unimagined springs.   10

4806 heavens,— *1904*] heavens, *1839, 1818*   lake *1904*] lake; *1839, 1818*
4812 aloft; . . . isle;] aloft, . . . isle, *edd.*   4815 Spirit. On] Spirit; on *edd.*
LAON AND CYTHNA. Rejected Passages. AUTOGRAPH: *Dedication: fair copy, D. 3;
draft, e. 14. Canto I: fair copy, D. 3; draft, e. 19.*   PRINTED: *Dedication: SR and I,
1934; Claude C. Brew, Shelley and Mary in 1817, 1971; Stanza XV only: Loc. 1911*
TEXT: *Dedication: 1971/1934/e. 14 (1–67), D. 3 (68–71). Canto I: 1934/e. 19.*

And I remember well the day and hour,
　One amongst many, of lone wanderings
When Truth first came upon me, and that power
[Which doth the mists]

III (2)

It was a sunny morn of the fresh year   15
　When I walked forth upon the glittering grass,
And deeply my young heart was moved to hear
　The harsh rude voices from the school-room pass:
　So that I wept, all lonely as I was,
And sate awhile in tears grieving to know   20
　That love was not in the raw world, alas!
And each then feared a tyrant or a foe.

III–IV

I feared not those who ruled, nor did I hate
　Mine equals, but was lone, untameable;
Like some wild beast that cannot find its mate: 25
　A solitary　　　　　　　　　gazelle
　Which in the desert wilderness doth dwell
Secure in its own swiftness.

[I feared or hated none, but wept to find]
[That none did love me tho' a gentle child]   30
　Thus solemn feelings on my soul did dwell.
Mine equals shunned a boy so sad and wild;
　And those who ruled me found untameable
The spirit of a meek and gentle child,
For with a bitter scorn of wrong I smiled.   35

When hoary men, or youths of strength mature,
　Struck me with fruitless blows; thus undefiled
[By awe or by submission, inly pure]
[In its own to⟨? rment⟩] my soul did endure
　[And hate grew in me of the law] of crime   40
　In its own　　　　　　　　free and pure [

Dedication. 28–33 *cancelled by criss-cross lines, e. 14.*

V

And thus [my powers] were strengthened more and more
[Un]til for another's love and sympathy I pined.

VI

[And among all its treacherous pitfalls]
  The dedicated foe of tyranny   45
[Like a benighted soul I wandered on
  [And lost] [Not love or will but hope, and power]
  Withered and died away, until revived by thee.

One whom I found was dear but false to me
The other's heart was like a heart of stone   50
  Which crushed and withered mine.

XIII

I speak when I perchance shall soon inherit
  Oblivion, and [my hopes] be quenched in tears.
A voice went forth from that unshaken spirit[1]
  Which was the echo of three thousand years.   55
  And then the world stood mute as one who hears
Strange music in a desert. Truth and Awe
  Cowered in their
  [And earth grew wan] with [supernatural] fears.

XIV

⟨If I must stand alone among mankind   60
  If there must be no response to my voice
If all must rise and stamp in fury blind
  On him who hates no living thing
  And in my blood and infamy rejoice
Till we are dead, yet, Mary, thou and I   65
May see from our dear home's tranquillity
  That we are lights of love in the world's night⟩

---

[1] The author of *An Enquiry concerning Political Justice and its Influence on Morals and Happiness*. [Shelley's footnote.]

44–8 *cancelled by criss-cross lines, e. 14*   **60–7** *on next leaf, cancelled, the comment:*
Many shall feel who dare not speak their feelings.

[from a fair copy]

XV

A colourless and shapeless mist that hovers
Over the birth of dawn—a vale outspread
Beneath the gathering rainbow—gloom that covers   70
The widely-glancing

CANTO I

[from a draft]

Frail clouds arrayed in sunlight lose the glory
  Which they reflect on Earth—they burn and die,
Revive and change like genius, and when hoary
  They streak the sunless air, then suddenly,
  If the white moon shine forth, their shadows lie   5
Like woven pearl beneath its beams; each tone
  Of the many-voicèd forests doth reply
To symphonies diviner than its own,
Then falls and fades like thought when power is past and gone.

The hues of sea and sky and moon and sun,   10
  The music of the desert and the deep,
Are dark or silent—have their changes run
  Thus soon? Or, pale enthusiast, dost thou weep
  Because all things that change and wake and sleep
Tell thine own story? Like the altered glance   15
  Of a dear friend are they? Like thoughts that keep
Their dwelling in a dying countenance,
Or like the thronging shapes of some tempestuous trance?

There is a Power whose passive instrument
  Our nature is—a Spirit that with motion,   20
Invisible and swift, its breath hath sent
  Amongst us, like the wind on the wide Ocean
  Around whose path, though tumult and commotion

68–70 *missing in e. 14, cancelled in D. 3: perhaps wrongly copied from draft of Canto I in e. 19: cf. p. 270, 55–8*   70 rainbow—gloom *D. 3*] rainbow-gleam, *1911*

    Canto I. 1–72 *drafted as the original opening in e. 19*   4 sunless *changed from* twilight *e. 19*   15 thine *e. 19*] their *1934*   story? Like *e. 19*] story like *1934* 16 friend are *e. 19*] friend? are *1934*   they? Like *e. 19*] they like *1934*   19 passive *changed from* subtle *e. 19*   23 though] tho' *e. 19*   the *1934*

Throng fast, deep calm doth follow, and precedeth.
   This Spirit, chained by some remote devotion,   25
Our choice or will demandeth not nor heedeth,
But for its hymns doth touch the human souls it needeth.

All that we know or seek, our loves and hopes,
   Those sweet and subtle thoughts that do entwine
Swift gleamings with the shade that interlopes   30
   Between their visitings, we may repine
   To lose; but they will pass—thou must resign
Joy, hope, love, power and life, when that which gave
   The shadow and the God has need of thine,
Abandoning thee; then no mercy crave,   35
But bow thyself in dust, take shelter in the grave.

The lamps of mind which make this night of earth
   So beautiful, were kindled thus of yore;
All streams of mortal hope hence drew their birth,
   Those lyres of antient song which evermore   40
   Thro' silent years their kindling music pour
Have thus been fed with sweetness,—mighty lyres
   Whose sounds awaken thoughts that sleep no more,
Which that immortal Spirit which respires
In visioned rest has breathed upon their silent wires.   45

It is not then presumption if I watch
   In expectation's mute and breathless mood
Till it descend—may not the fountain catch
   Hues from the green leaves and the daylight wood,
   Even if blank darkness must descend and brood   50
Upon its waves?—Each human phantasy
   Hath such sweet visions in the solitude
Of thought, that this drear world like heaven would be,
Could words invest such dreams with immortality.

25 chained *e. 19*] claimed *1934*   28 our *1934*] power *pencilled above* [our] *e. 19*,
but probably not a correction; cf. line 33.   30 gleamings *e. 19*] gleaming *1934*
38 yore,] yore— *1934*, yore.— *e. 19*   39 hence *e. 19*] whence *1934*, *which Shelley
wrote but he scored out the first letter*   40 Those *e. 19*] The *1934*   41 kind-
ling *e. 19*] mighty *1934*   pour *e. 19*] pour, *1934*   42 sweetness,—] sweetness
1934, e. 19   43 more,] more *1934, e. 19*   44 Which *e. 19*] When *1934*   45 their
e. 19] the *1934*   46 then *e. 19*] thus *1934*   45 their *e. 19*] the *1934*   46 then
e. 19] thus *1934*   48 descend *changed from* return *e. 19*   53 drear-world *above*
human life *uncancelled in e. 19 See n., p. 394*] dream-world *1934*

A colourless and shapeless mist that hovers   55
  Over the birth of morn, a vale outspread
Beneath the gathering rainbow, gloom that covers
  The widely-glancing meteor, ere 'tis sped,—
  Such is the splendour of the mighty dead;
Such, and no more, is living man, yet One   60
  Seeks, ere the doubtful paths of death he tread,
If love and truth be not for ever gone,
To melodize one song to them and them alone.

  With deathless minds, which leave when they have fled
  [Far from the immortal spirits of the past]   65
    A path of light, my soul communion knew,
  Till from that ceaseless intercourse at last
    As from a mine of magic store I drew
  Words which were weapons; round my heart there grew
    The adamantine armour of their power,   70
  And from my fancy wings of golden hue
Sprang forth, whose[

  And as I gazed, 'twas strange methought to feel
    The calmness of the earth grow more profound,
  While all the sky and all its clouds did reel   75
    And quivered and were torn and whirled around
    Like frail foam on the torrent; to resound
  Meanwhile the thunder ceased not, nor the air
    To echo with its deep and sullen sound,
  Nor the red flames to burst; but all did spare   80
That spot of eastern Heaven that was so still and fair.

  55–8c *f. above, p. 268*   58 sped,—] sped— *1934, e. 19*   69 which *e. 19*] [that]
inexplicably 1934   there *ambiguous but probable e. 19*] then *1934*   73–81 *drafted
in e. 19 to follow 162*   73 'twas strange *above* gazed methought *e. 19 ; 1934 reads*
methought 'twas strange

NOTE BY MARY SHELLEY ON
LAON AND CYTHNA
[*THE REVOLT OF ISLAM*]

[1] SHELLEY possessed two remarkable qualities of intellect—a brilliant
imagination, and a logical exactness of reason. His inclinations led him (he
fancied) almost alike to poetry and metaphysical discussions. I say 'he
fancied,' because I believe the former to have been paramount, and that

it would have gained the mastery even had he struggled against it. However, he said that he deliberated at one time whether he should dedicate himself to poetry or metaphysics; and, resolving on the former, he educated himself for it, discarding in a great measure his philosophical pursuits, and engaging himself in the study of the poets of Greece, Italy, and England. To these may be added a constant perusal of portions of the Old Testament—the Psalms, the Book of Job, the Prophet Isaiah, and others, the sublime poetry of which filled him with delight.

[2] As a poet, his intellect and compositions were powerfully influenced by exterior circumstances, and especially by his place of abode. He was very fond of travelling, and ill-health increased this restlessness. The sufferings occasioned by a cold English winter made him pine, especially when our colder spring arrived, for a more genial climate. In 1816 he again visited Switzerland, and rented a house on the banks of the Lake of Geneva; and many a day, in cloud or sunshine, was passed alone in his boat—sailing as the wind listed, or weltering on the calm waters. The majestic aspect of Nature ministered such thoughts as he afterwards enwove in verse. His lines on the Bridge of the Arve, and his 'Hymn to Intellectual Beauty' were written at this time. Perhaps during this summer his genius was checked by association with another poet whose nature was utterly dissimilar to his own, yet who, in the poem he wrote at that time, gave tokens that he shared for a period the more abstract and etherealized inspiration of Shelley. The saddest events awaited his return to England; but such was his fear to wound the feelings of others that he never expressed the anguish he felt, and seldom gave vent to the indignation roused by the persecutions he underwent; while the course of deep unexpressed passion, and the sense of injury, engendered the desire to embody themselves in forms defecated of all the weakness and evil which cling to real life.

[3] He chose therefore for his hero a youth nourished in dreams of liberty, some of whose actions are in direct opposition to the opinions of the world; but who is animated throughout by an ardent love of virtue, and a resolution to confer the boons of political and intellectual freedom on his fellow-creatures. He created for this youth a woman such as he delighted to imagine—full of enthusiasm for the same objects; and they both, with will unvanquished, and the deepest sense of the justice of their cause, met adversity and death. There exists in this poem a memorial of a friend of his youth. The character of the old man who liberates Laon from his tower-prison, and tends on him in sickness, is founded on that of Doctor Lind, who, when Shelley was at Eton, had often stood by to befriend and support him, and whose name he never mentioned without love and veneration.

[4] During the year 1817 we were established at Marlow in Buckingham-shire. Shelley's choice of abode was fixed chiefly by this town being at no great distance from London, and its neighbourhood to the Thames. The poem was written in his boat, as it floated under the beech-groves of Bisham, or during wanderings in the neighbouring country, which is distinguished for peculiar beauty. The chalk hills break into cliffs that overhang the Thames, or form valleys clothed with beech; the wilder portion of the country is rendered beautiful by exuberant vegetation; and the cultivated part is peculiarly fertile. With all this wealth of Nature which, either in the form of gentlemen's parks or soil dedicated to agri-culture, flourishes around, Marlow was inhabited (I hope it is altered now) by a very poor population. The women are lacemakers, and lose their health by sedentary labour, for which they were very ill paid. The Poor-laws ground to the dust not only the paupers, but those who had risen just above that state, and were obliged to pay poor-rates. The changes produced by peace following a long war, and a bad harvest, brought with them the most heart-rending evils to the poor. Shelley afforded what alleviation he could. In the winter, while bringing out his poem, he had a severe attack of ophthalmia, caught while visiting the poor cottages. I mention these things—for this minute and active sympathy with his fellow-creatures gives a thousandfold interest to his speculations, and stamps with reality his pleadings for the human race.

[5] The poem, bold in its opinions and uncompromising in their ex-pression, met with many censurers, not only among those who allow of no virtue but such as supports the cause they espouse, but even among those whose opinions were similar to his own. I extract a portion of a letter written in answer to one of these friends. It best details the impulses of Shelley's mind, and his motives: it was written with entire unreserve; and is therefore a precious monument of his own opinion of his powers, of the purity of his designs, and the ardour with which he clung, in adversity and through the valley of the shadow of death, to views from which he believed the permanent happiness of mankind must eventually spring.

'*Marlow, Dec.* 11, 1817.

[6] 'I have read and considered all that you say about my general powers, and the particular instance of the poem in which I have attempted to develop them. Nothing can be more satisfactory to me than the interest which your admonitions express. But I think you are mistaken in some points with regard to the peculiar nature of my powers, whatever be their amount. I listened with deference and self-suspicion to your censures of *The Revolt of Islam*; but the productions of mine which you commend hold a very low place in my own esteem; and this reassures me, in some

degree at least. The poem was produced by a series of thoughts which filled my mind with unbounded and sustained enthusiasm. I felt the precariousness of my life, and I engaged in this task, resolved to leave some record of myself. Much of what the volume contains was written with the same feeling—as real, though not so prophetic—as the communications of a dying man. I never presumed indeed to consider it anything approaching to faultless; but, when I consider contemporary productions of the same apparent pretensions, I own I was filled with confidence. I felt that it was in many respects a genuine picture of my own mind. I felt that the sentiments were true, not assumed. And in this have I long believed that my power consists; in sympathy, and that part of the imagination which relates to sentiment and contemplation. I am formed, if for anything not in common with the herd of mankind, to apprehend minute and remote distinctions of feeling, whether relative to external nature or the living beings which surround us, and to communicate the conceptions which result from considering either the moral or the material universe as a whole. Of course, I believe these faculties, which perhaps comprehend all that is sublime in man, to exist very imperfectly in my own mind. But, when you advert to my Chancery-paper, a cold, forced, unimpassioned, insignificant piece of cramped and cautious argument, and to the little scrap about *Mandeville*, which expressed my feelings indeed, but cost scarcely two minutes' thought to express, as specimens of my powers more favourable than that which grew as it were from "the agony and bloody sweat" of intellectual travail; surely I must feel that, in some manner, either I am mistaken in believing that I have any talent at all, or you in the selection of the specimens of it.

[7] Yet, after all, I cannot but be conscious, in much of what I write, of an absence of that tranquillity which is the attribute and accompaniment of power. This feeling alone would make your most kind and wise admonitions, on the subject of the economy of intellectual force, valuable to me. And, if I live, or if I see any trust in coming years, doubt not but that I shall do something, whatever it may be, which a serious and earnest estimate of my powers will suggest to me, and which will be in every respect accommodated to their utmost limits.' [Shelley to Godwin.]

PRINCE ATHANASE

A FRAGMENT

1817

PRINCE ATHANASE

A FRAGMENT

1817

THERE was a youth, who, as with toil and travel,
Had grown quite weak and gray before his time;
Nor any could the restless griefs unravel

Which burned within him, withering up his prime
And goading him, like fiends, from land to land.   5
Not his the load of any secret crime,

For nought of ill his heart could understand,
But pity and wild sorrow for the same;
Not his the thirst for glory or command,

Baffled with blast of hope-consuming shame;   10
Nor evil joys which fire the vulgar breast,
And quench in speedy smoke its feeble flame,

Had left within his soul their dark unrest;
Nor what religion fables of the grave
Feared he,—Philosophy's accepted guest.   15

For none than he a purer heart could have,
Or that loved good more for itself alone;
Of nought in heaven or earth was he the slave.

PRINCE ATHANASE. AUTOGRAPH: *a. Bod. MS. Shelley E. 4; b. MS. given by MWS to J. C. Claris in 1824; see n., pp. 395–6. At present unlocated: see Addendum, p. xxx.* TRANSCRIPT: *125–229, 240–70, 279–97, MWS, Bod. MS. Shelley adds. d. 9.* PRINTED: *1–229, 240–69, 279–97, MWS, 1824, 1839[1], and 312–17, MWS, 1839[2]/230–9, 270–8, 288–end, Loc. 1903 all previously published lines, Hutch. 1904.* UNPRINTED: *229a, 229b, 229c, 229d, 271–8b, as here given.* TITLE: *MSS. and 1824.* DATE: *See n., p. 395.* TEXT: *1904/1839/1824/d. 9/E. 4. See nn., pp. 395 ff.*
  1 as with *edd.*] as with *above* [from] long *E. 4* 3 Nor any *edd.*] [Not his] Nor any *above* eer *E. 4* 10 blast *edd.*] blast [stroke] *E. 4* 11 Nor evil *edd.*] [Nor the] evil *E. 4* 12 feeble *edd.*] little *E. 4*

What sorrow, strange, and shadowy, and unknown,
Sent him, a hopeless wanderer, through mankind?—   20
If with a human sadness he did groan,

He had a gentle yet aspiring mind,
Just, innocent, with varied learning fed;
And such a glorious consolation find

In others' joy, when all their own is dead: 25
He loved, and laboured for his kind in grief,
And yet, unlike all others, it is said

That from such toil he never found relief.
Although a child of fortune and of power,
Of an ancestral name the orphan chief,   30

His soul had wedded Wisdom, and her dower
Is love and justice, clothed in which he sate
Apart from men, as in a lonely tower,

Pitying the tumult of their dark estate.—
Yet even in youth did he not e'er abuse   35
The strength of wealth or thought, to consecrate

Those false opinions which the harsh rich use
To blind the world they famish for their pride;
Nor did he hold from any man his dues,

But, like a steward in honest dealings tried,   40
With those who toiled and wept, the poor and wise,
His riches and his cares he did divide.

Fearless he was, and scorning all disguise,
What he dared do or think, though men might start,
He spoke with mild yet unaverted eyes;   45

19 strange *1904, 1839*] deep *1824*   strange *above* [deep] *E. 4, where* shadowy *does
not occur and* What secret sorrow to himself unknown *is changed to* What sorrow strange
and secret and unknown   20 hopeless *edd.*] friendless *E. 4*   22 mind,] mind;
edd.   25 dead *edd.*] fled *E. 4*   26 his kind *edd.*] mankind *E. 4*   28 such toil
edd.] that toil *E. 4*   29 Although a *edd.*] He was the *E. 4*   30 Of an ancestral name
edd.] And though of a high race *E. 4*   orphan *edd.*] orphan *above* [respected] *E. 4*
33 Apart from men *edd.*] Above his kind *E. 4*   36 thought *edd.*] [genius] thought
E. 4   37 harsh *edd.*] hard *E. 4*   38 To blind the world *edd.*] To [bind the]
blind the world *above* [men] *E. 4*   41 With those who toiled and wept *edd.;*
changed from [To those whom it belonged] *E. 4*   43 all *edd.*] aught *E. 4*   44 What
edd.] All *E. 4*   or think *edd.*] or thought *E. 4*   45 yet *edd.*] but *E. 4*

Liberal he was of soul, and frank of heart,
And to his many friends—all loved him well—
Whate'er he knew or felt he would impart,

If words he found those inmost thoughts to tell;
If not, he smiled or wept; and his weak foes   50
He neither spurned nor hated—though with fell

And mortal hate their thousand voices rose,
They passed like aimless arrows from his ear.
Nor did his heart or mind its portal close

To those, or them, or any, whom life's sphere   55
May comprehend within its wide array.
What sadness made that vernal spirit sere?—

He knew not. Though his life, day after day,
Was failing like an unreplenished stream;
Though in his eyes a cloud and burthen lay,   60

Through which his soul, like Vesper's serene beam
Piercing the chasms of ever-rising clouds,
Shone, softly burning; though his lips did seem

Like reeds which quiver in impetuous floods;
And through his sleep, and o'er each waking hour,   65
Thoughts after thoughts, unresting multitudes,

Were driven within him by some secret power,
Which bade them blaze, and live, and roll afar,
Like lights and sounds from haunted tower to tower

46-7 [And neither spurned nor hated his weak foes] *E. 4*   48 Whate'er *edd.*]
Whate'er [All that] *E. 4*   49 he *edd.*] he *above* [were] *E. 4*   those *edd.*] [his]
those *above* [such] *E. 4*   53 passed *edd.*] past *above* [glanced] [And fell] *E. 4*
ear.] ear— *edd.*   54 portal *edd.*] portal *below* [bounties] *E. 4*   55-6 To them or
those, or aught which the world's sphere / Contains within its wide and [manifold] *above*
[human] [bound] [array] *E. 4*   57 that *underlined in E. 4; see n., p. 397.*   59 fail-
ing *edd.*] wasting [withering] *E. 4*   stream;] stream, *edd.*   60 cloud and burthen
edd.; uncancelled alternative load and darkness *E. 4*   61 his soul *edd.*] his soul
above [their light] *E. 4*   62 chasms *edd.*] rifts *E. 4*   rising *edd.*] rising *above*
[flowing] *E. 4*   Piercing *and* rifts *are 'underlined in a different ink, perhaps with a view
to alteration', Loc. 1903.*   63 softly *edd.; changed from* [ever] *preceded by* [like] *E. 4*
64 Quivering like bent reeds beneath quivering floods *changed to* Which quiver in the
dark and homeless floods *E. 4*   65 And through *edd.*] And [He knew not oer]
through *E. 4*   67 Were driven within him by *edd.*] Were driven within him by
above [Obeyed within his mind] *E. 4*   68 blaze *edd.*] [burn] blaze *E. 4*   and roll
afar *for* [as they arose] *E. 4*   69 lights and sounds *Loc. 1911*] lights and sounds,
1904, 1839, 1824   lights and sounds *above* [voices heard] *E. 4*

O'er castled mountains borne, when tempest's war   70
Is levied by the night-contending winds,
And the pale dalesmen watch with eager ear;—

Though such were in his spirit, as the fiends
Which wake and feed an everliving woe,—
What was this grief, which ne'er in other minds   75

A mirror found? He knew not—none could know.
But on whoe'er might question him he turned
The light of his frank eyes, as if to show

He knew not of the grief within that burned,
But asked forbearance with a mournful look;   80
Or spoke in words from which none ever learned

The cause of his disquietude; or shook
With spasms of silent passion; or turned pale:
So that his friends soon rarely undertook

To stir his secret pain without avail;—   85
For all who knew and loved him then perceived
That there was drawn an adamantine veil

Between his heart and mind,—both unrelieved
Wrought in his brain and bosom separate strife.
Some said that he was mad, others believed   90

That memories of an antenatal life
Made this, where now he dwelt, a penal hell;
And others said that such mysterious grief

---

70 *changed from* In castled mountains; When the tempests roar *E. 4*   74 wake
and feed an *1904*] wake and feed on *1839*   wake *above* [nursed] and feed an *above* [his]
E. 4   76 found? He] found,—he *edd.*   know.] know; *edd. Cf. line 58.*   77 might
edd.] did *E. 4*   79 grief *edd.*] griefs *E. 4*   80 But asked forbearance *edd.;*
changed from [But pleaded silence] *itself changed from* [And sadly silent] *But first written
was* [By the sad silence of that eloquent look] *E. 4*   83 silent *edd.*] secret *E. 4*
86 For *edd.*] For [And] *E. 4*   then *edd.*] then [soon] *E. 4*   87 *Thus edd.;*
changed from [That oer his heart was drawn an iron veil]; *above this* [That he spoke all
he knew] *E. 4*   88 both unrelieved *edd.; changed from* [for they believed] *E. 4*
89 Wrought in his *edd.*] Wrought in his *above* [Worked in] His [His words] [Of its
strange burthen] *E. 4*   90 others *edd.*] and some *E. 4*

From God's displeasure, like a darkness, fell
On souls like his, which owned no higher law   95
Than love; love calm, steadfast, invincible

By mortal fear or supernatural awe.
And others: ' 'Tis the shadow of a dream
Which the veiled eye of Memory never saw,

'But through the soul's abyss, like some dark stream   100
Through shattered mines and caverns underground,
Rolls, shaking its foundations; and no beam

'Of joy may rise but it is quenched and drowned
In the dim whirlpools of this dream obscure;
Soon its exhausted waters will have found   105

'A lair of rest beneath thy spirit pure,
O Athanase!—in one so good and great,
Evil or tumult cannot long endure.'

So spake they: idly of another's state
Babbling vain words and fond philosophy;   110
This was their consolation; such debate

Men held with one another; nor did he,
Like one who labours with a human woe,
Decline this talk: as if its theme might be

94 God's displeasure *edd.; changed from* God's own [anger] [wrath] frown *above* [the dark Devil] Fiend *E. 4*   like a darkness *edd.; changed from* aye like a [shadow] *E. 4*
95 *changed from* [By those whose thoughts were free and souls secure] *varied by* which [disdain a law] *and* [scorned to own a law] *E. 4*   96 *changed from* But love secure steadfast invincible *which was first* [That tis its own ⟨tear in MS.⟩] serene fearless invincible *E. 4*   98 "Tis the shadow of a *edd.; changed from* [said twas a forgotten] *E. 4*
99 veiled *edd.*] dim *E. 4*   100 dark *edd.*] deep *above* [dark] *E. 4*   100–1 Thro [In] [the deep caverns of the shattered earth] *above* [caverns of unfathomable gloom] / [Whose waves have never drea] *E. 4*   101 shattered *edd.*] shattered *above* [the dim] *E. 4*   102 Rolls *edd.*] Rolled *E. 4*   103 *changed in E. 4 from* [Of the mind's eye of ⟨? dreamy⟩ thought would they]   may *edd.*] might *E. 4*   rise *Loc. 1911*] rise, *1904, 1839, 1824*   105 Soon its exhausted *edd.*] Soon its exhausted *above* [And soon poured forth its] *E. 4*   105–6 [And thou they said oh Athanase art found] / So [For good and great that from [on] thy spirit pour] [A ray of arrowy ⟨tear in MS.⟩ ht ⟨= ? light⟩ will leap] *E. 4*   106 *changed from* Repose beneath thy spirit calm *above* [bright] and pure *the first word above* then rest *changed from* [A lair] of rest *E. 4*   109 idly *edd.*] idly [vainly] *E. 4*   111 This *edd.*] This [Such] *E. 4* consolation *edd.*] consolation [words] *E. 4*   such debate *edd.*] such debate *above* [which did youth] *E. 4*   112 Men *edd.*] Men [They] *E. 4*   114 this *edd.*] this [such] *E. 4*

Another, not himself, he to and fro   115
Questioned and canvassed it with subtlest wit;
And none but those who loved him best could know

That which he knew not, how it galled and bit
His weary mind, this converse vain and cold;
For like an eyeless nightmare grief did sit   120

Upon his being,— a snake which fold by fold
Pressed out the life of life, a clinging fiend
Which clenched him if he stirred with deadlier hold;—
And so his grief remained—let it remain—untold[1].

Prince Athanase had one belovèd friend,   125
An old, old man, with hair of silver white,
And lips where heavenly smiles would hang and blend

With his wise words; and eyes whose arrowy light
Shone like the reflex of a thousand minds.
He was the last whom superstition's blight   130

Had spared in Greece—the blight that cramps and blinds,—
And in his olive bower at Œnoe
Had sate from earliest youth. Like one who finds

A fertile island in the barren sea,
One mariner who has survived his mates   135
Many a drear month in a great ship—so he

With soul-sustaining songs, and sweet debates
Of ancient lore, there fed his lonely being:—
'The mind becomes that which it contemplates,'—

---

[1] The author was pursuing a fuller development of the ideal character of Athanase, when it struck him that in an attempt at extreme refinement and analysis, his conceptions might be betrayed into the assuming a morbid character. The reader will judge whether he is a loser or gainer by this diffidence. [*Shelley's footnote.*]

116 wit *edd.*] [speech] wit *E. 4*   118 That *edd.*] [How] That *E. 4*   119 mind *edd.; changed from* [brain], *to avoid jingle, E. 4*   120 *changed from* Like an invisible nightmare [did it sit] *E. 4*   121 being,—] being; *edd.*   heart *E. 4*   122 life of life *edd.*] life of joy *E. 4*   124 let it remain *edd.* and must remain *E. 4*   126 white *edd.*] [bright] white *E. 4*   129 minds *edd.*] minds *after vacillation with* [souls] *E. 4*   129–30 *In E. 4 the name* Uberto *is written, and cancelled, three times and the name* Andreas *once*   130 *changed in E. 4 from* [And with warm love did Athanase requite]   130–61 *Cancelled in E. 4. Uncancelled in d. 9, and printed 1824, 1839. See n., p. 397.*   136 drear *edd.*] drear *above* [long] *E. 4*   137 songs *edd.*] songs *above* [books] *E. 4*   138 there fed *edd.*] there fed *above* [nourished] *E. 4*

And thus Zonoras, by forever seeing   140
Their bright creations, grew like wisest men;
And when he heard the crash of nations fleeing

A bloodier power than ruled thy ruins then,
O sacred Hellas! many weary years
He wandered, till the path of Laian's glen   145

Was grass-grown—and the unremembered tears
Were dry in Laian for their honoured chief,
Who fell in Byzant, pierced by Moslem spears.

And as the lady looked with faithful grief
From her high lattice o'er the rugged path,   150
Where she once saw that horseman toil, with brief

And blighting hope, who with the news of death
Struck body and soul as with a mortal blight,
She saw between the chestnuts, far beneath,

An old man toiling up, a weary wight;   155
And soon within her hospitable hall
She saw his white hair glittering in the light

Of the wood fire, and round his shoulders fall;
And his wan visage and his withered mien,
Yet calm and gentle and majestical.   160

And Athanase, her child, who must have been
Then three years old, sate opposite and gazed
In patient silence.

141 Their bright creations *edd.; changed from* [their shadows grew to be] [the form of truth and love] *E. 4. See n., p. 396.*   142 And when he heard *edd.; changed from* [Sudden was heard] *E. 4*   145 *changed from* [One was seen toiling up the mountain glen] *E. 4*   146 *changed from* Was [overgrown with grass,] and the   tears *E. 4*   152 blighting *edd.] apparently cancelled in E. 4, but see n., p. 397.*   who with the news of *edd.; changed from* [which cling to her like] *E. 4*   153 mortal blight *edd.; changed from* [swift disease] *E. 4*   154 saw *edd.]* saw [heard] *E. 4*   between *1904*, *d. 9, E. 4, though the* beneath *cancelled in E. 4 is printed in 1839, 1824*   155 An old man *seemingly cancelled E. 4*   157 hair *E. 4]* hairs *edd., d. 9*   159 And his wan visage *edd.; changed from* [And shadow his wan looks] *E. 4*   withered mien *edd.]* [hollow fa] withered mien *E. 4*   160 and gentle and *edd.]* and   and *d. 9, E. 4*   162 opposite *edd., d. 9]* opposite [to him] *E. 4*

Such was Zonoras; and as daylight finds
One amaranth glittering on the path of frost,   165
When autumn nights have nipped all weaker kinds,

Thus through his age, dark, cold, and tempest-tossed,
Shone truth upon Zonoras; and he filled
From fountains pure, nigh overgrown and lost,

The spirit of Prince Athanase, a child,   170
With soul-sustaining songs of ancient lore
And philosophic wisdom, clear and mild.

And sweet and subtle talk they evermore,
The pupil and the master, shared; until,
Sharing that undiminishable store,   175

The youth, as shadows on a grassy hill
Outrun the winds that chase them, soon outran
His teacher, and did teach with native skill

Strange truths and new to that experienced man;
Still they were friends, as few have ever been   180
Who mark the extremes of life's discordant span.

So in the caverns of the forest green,
Or on the rocks of echoing ocean hoar,
Zonoras and Prince Athanase were seen

By summer woodmen; and when winter's roar   185
Sounded o'er earth and sea its blast of war,
The Balearic fisher, driven from shore,

164 and as daylight finds *edd., d. 9*] [Faith the blight which blinds] daylight *however*, *subsequently being changed to* morning *E. 4*   165 One *1904, 1839, E. 4*] An *1824, d. 9*   glittering *edd., d. 9*] glittering *above* [blooming] *E. 4*   167 Thus through *1904, 1839, E. 4*] Thus had *1824, d. 9*   168 filled *edd.*] [fed] filled *E. 4* 169 pure *edd., d. 9*] clear *above* pure *both apparently cancelled E. 4. See n., p. 396.* 172 *changed from* And moral wisdom firm and pure and mild *E. 4*   173 subtle talk *edd.*] subtle talk *over* [and] sweet [debate] *E. 4*   they evermore, *1904, 1824, d. 9, E. 4*] now evermore *1839*   174-5 [He taught until the pupil] *E. 4* 175 Sharing *edd.*] Sharing [Dividing] *E. 4*   that *1904, edd., except 1824*] that *upon* the *E. 4*   the *d. 9, a miscopying reproduced in 1824, corrected in 1839*   176 as *edd.*] as *above* [like] *E. 4*   shadows *changed to* shadow *E. 4*   177 Outrun *edd.*] Out-runs *changed to* Outrun *E. 4*   them, *edd.*] [them] it *E. 4*   181 extremes *edd.*] extremes *above* [bounds] *E. 4*   182 So *1904, 1839*] And *1824* And [They] *d. 9* So *above* They [And] *E. 4*   183 Or on *1904, changed in E. 4 from* [or by] which was printed in *1839, 1824*   185-90 *In the margin in E. 4 is a memorandum and two lines of verse. See n., p. 399.*

Hanging upon the peakèd wave afar,
Then saw their lamp from Laian's turret gleam,
Piercing the stormy darkness, like a star   190

Which pours beyond the sea one steadfast beam,
Whilst all the constellations of the sky
Seemed reeling through the storm. They did but seem . . .

For, lo! the wintry clouds are all gone by,
And bright Arcturus through yon pines is glowing,   195
And far o'er southern waves, immovably

Belted Orion hangs—warm light is flowing
From the young moon into the sunset's chasm.
'O, summer eve! with power divine, bestowing

'On thine own bird the sweet enthusiasm   200
Which overflows in notes of liquid gladness,
Filling the sky like light! How many a spasm

'Of fevered brains, oppressed with grief and madness,
Were lulled by thee, delightful nightingale!
And these soft waves, murmuring a gentle sadness,   205

'And the far sighings of yon piny dale
Made vocal by some wind we feel not here!—
I bear alone what nothing may avail

'To lighten—a strange load!'—No human ear
Heard this lament; but o'er the visage wan   210
Of Athanase, a ruffling atmosphere

188 Hanging . . . afar *below* Suspended on the bursting *both uncancelled E. 4*
190 Piercing the stormy *edd.; changed from* [Through the tempestuous] *E. 4*
191 Which pours beyond *edd.; changed from* [Shining above] *E. 4, the whole line being
a substitute for* [Immoveable among the mighty stars] *E. 4*   193 reeling through the
storm. They] reeling through the storm . . . They *1904, see n., p. 398;* reeling through
the storm; they *1839* wrecked   they *1824, d. 9* wrecked *above* reeling
through *apparently cancelled* the storm *E. 4*   seem . . .] seem— *1904, 1839, 1824, E. 4*
seem *d. 9*   198 chasm.] chasm,— *edd.*   199 eve *1904, 1839* [night] eve *E. 4*]
night *1824, d. 9*   201 *changed in E. 4 from* Which [overflows in song of joy] fills
[the sky like light and love and joy] gladness   204 nightingale! *1839, 1824*]
nightingale,— *1904, d. 9, E. 4*   206 yon piny *1904, 1839, 1824, E. 4*] one piny *1824, d. 9*
208 *cancelled in E. 4*   209–10 [Heard the lament of Athanase but he] [as] *E. 4*
210–11 but . . . atmosphere *edd.; changed from* but oer the visage pale / Of Athanase
there past an atmosphere *E. 4*

Of dark emotion, a swift shadow, ran,
Like wind upon some forest-bosomed lake,
Glassy and dark.—And that divine old man

Beheld his mystic friend's whole being shake,   215
Even where its inmost depths were gloomiest;
And with a calm and measured voice he spake,

And, with a soft and equal pressure, pressed
That cold lean hand:—'Dost thou remember yet
When the curved moon then lingering in the west   220

'Paused, in yon waves her mighty horns to wet,
As at this hour half resting on the sea?
'Tis just one year—sure thou dost not forget—

'Then Plato's words of light in thee and me
Lingered like moonlight in the moonless east,   225
For we had just then read—thy memory

'Is faithful now—the story of the feast;
And Agathon and Diotima seemed
From death and dark forgetfulness released

To talk with us of all they knew or dreamed   229a
Of love and all its sacred symbols dim' [229b

What was his grief? His heart is deeply laden: 229c
He loved [229d

212 dark *edd.*] dark *above* [swift] *E. 4*   emotion, a swift *edd., d. 9*] emotion, with
[a] swift *E. 4*   213 *changed from* Like [sudden] wind [oer wood embosomed waters
pools] *E. 4*   215 *Thus 1904, 1839, 1824, d. 9, being Shelley's revision of* [Said nothing
though he saw that being shake] *save that* whole *is not in E. 4*   216 gloomiest;]
gloomiest— *edd.*   219–20 [Plato in the] *changed to* [Plato's Symposion *sic*] *changed
to* [How on a rainy evening] *E. 4*   220 curved *edd.*] curved *below* [horned] *below*
[yellow] *E. 4*   222 *See n., p. 398.*   223–4 [We had just finished reading Plato's
book] *E. 4*   224 Then *edd.; omitted E. 4*   229 From . . . forgetfulness *1904,
1839*] from death and dark *1824, d. 9, E. 4. See n., p. 398.*   229a–229d *Unprinted
previously, from E. 4. See n., p. 398.*   229a *The apparent cancellation of the line
may merely indicate an intended revision. As a rhyme-memorandum* redeemed *is pencilled
above. E. 4*   229a–229b [And telling all ⟨?them⟩ that ⟨?⟩] *E. 4*   229b Of
love [divine] [and all its sacred symbols dim] *E. 4*   229c What was his grief? [he
loved not many] *then, possibly another 'apparent' cancellation:* His [soul] heart is deeply
laden *E. 4*

And when the old man saw that on the green   230
Leaves of his opening manhood blight had lighted
He said: 'My friend, one grief alone can wean

A gentle mind from all that once delighted:—
Thou lovest, and thy secret heart is laden
With feelings which should not be unrequited.'   235

And Athanase . . . then smiled, as one o'erladen
With iron chains might smile to talk of bands
Twined round her lover's neck by some blithe maiden,

And said: 'Then I will tell thee all I know.'

'Twas at the season when the Earth upsprings   240
From slumber, as a spherèd angel's child,
Shadowing its eyes with green and golden wings,

Stands up before its mother bright and mild,
Of whose soft voice the air expectant seems—
So stood before the sun, which shone and smiled   245

To see it rise thus joyous from its dreams,
The fresh and radiant Earth. The hoary grove
Waxed green—and flowers burst forth like starry beams;—

The grass in the warm sun did start and move,
And sea-buds burst under the waves serene:—   250
How many a one, though none be near to love,

Loves then the shade of his own soul, half seen
In any mirror—or the spring's plumed minions,
The wingèd leaves amid the copses green;—

230–9 *omitted in edd. before 1904 and in d. 9; printed by Loc. 1903*   231 man-
hood blight had lighted] a blight had *above* [manhood] blight de *E. 4*   manhood
omitted in 1904. See n., p. 399.   232 my friend one grief alone can wean *follows* you
know not whence *in E. 4. See n., p. 399.*   233 mind *1904*] mind *above* [heart] *E. 4*
234 secret *1904*] secret *above* [lonely] *E. 4*   239 'Then . . . know.' *apparently
cancelled in E. 4; hence omitted in 1904. See n., p. 399. There follows after 239,
inconsecutively, the passage printed on p. 290 as 'Additional Lines'*   244 expectant
has a question mark above it in E. 4   246 thus *edd., d. 9*] thus *above* [so] *E. 4*
247 hoary grove *edd., d. 9; changed from* [hoar woods wild] [forests] [hoar] [bare] *E. 4*
249–50 [When night steams up] [and] [each ⟨? living⟩ nerve did] / [And thoughts in
every heart did   and move] *E. 4*   250 under *1904, 1824, d. 9*] beneath *1839*
under *for* [beneath] *E. 4*   253 plumed minions *E. 4*] young minions *edd.* minions
unmetrically d. 9   254 *Except for* wingèd *replacing* [tender] *the line is apparently
cancelled in E. 4*

How many a spirit then puts on the pinions   255
Of fancy, and outrides the lagging blast,
And his own steps—and over wide dominions

Sweeps in his dream-drawn chariot, far and fast,
Exulting, while the wide world shrinks below,
When winter and despondency are past.   260

'Twas at this season that Prince Athanase
Passed the white Alps. Those eagle-baffling mountains
Slept in their shrouds of snow; beside the ways

The waterfalls were voiceless, for their fountains
Were changed to mines of sunless crystal now,   265
Or by the curdling winds—like brazen wings

Which clanged along the mountain's marble brow—
Warped into adamantine fretwork, hung
And filled with frozen light the chasms below.

Vexed by the blast, the great pines groaned and swung 270
⟨Under their load of snow; the soil was hard
And from the steeps a sound like iron flung

On high the dark and purple noon did gird.   273
The ⟨? rayless⟩ 273a
.   .   .   .   .   .   273b

Such as the eagle sees, when he dives down   274
From the grey deserts of wide air, beheld   275
Prince Athanase; and o'er his mien was thrown

256 outrides *changed in E. 4 from* [outstrips] *the reading of edd. and d. 9*
259 Exulting, while *changed in E. 4 from* [More fleet than storms] *the reading of edd.
and d. 9*   261 at . . . Athanase *edd., apparently cancelled under* Prince *in E. 4*
262 white *edd.*] white *above* [aerial] *E. 4*   Alps. Those] Alps—those *edd.*   eagle-
baffling mountains *edd.*] wintry mountains *d. 9* eagle-baffling crags *above* wintry
mountains *uncancelled E. 4 See n., p. 396.*   263 snow;] snow;— *edd.* ⟨? ice⟩ *E. 4*
266 curdling *edd.*] curdling *above* [warping] *E. 4*   269 chasms *1904, E. 4*]
chasm *1839, 1824, d. 9*   270–8 *omitted in edd. before 1904, where Hutch. printed
it from Loc. 1903, except for 271–3, the soil . . . gird, and 278–278b, and many . . . below
which are printed here from E. 4*   271 snow . . . hard *apparently cancelled in E. 4,*
snowflakes *too being rejected, likewise* earth   272 *cancelled, apparently, in E. 4*
steeps *conj. here for* steps *E. 4*   272–3 [The ⟨? rayless⟩ points of] *E. 4*   273 *can-
celled, apparently, in E. 4*   274–278b [Until he came] Such as the eagle sees when
he [dives down] *above* [descends] / From the grey desarts of wide air *above* [the] sky
[a] [plain] [beheld] / /[Spotted with] [saw] [Prince] Athanase and oer his mien was

The shadow of that scene, field after field,
Purple and dim and wide, and many a town   278
Circled with antique towers and walls which yield   278a

Their image in the lucid streams below.⟩   278b

Thou art the wine whose drunkenness is all   279
We can desire, O Love! and happy souls,   280
Ere from thy vine the leaves of autumn fall,

Catch thee, and feed from their o'erflowing bowls
Thousands who thirst for thine ambrosial dew;—
Thou art the radiance which where ocean rolls

Investeth it; and when the heavens are blue   285
Thou fillest them; and when the earth is fair
The shadows of thy moving wings imbue

Its deserts and its mountains, till they wear
Beauty like some light robe;—thou ever soarest
Among the towers of men, and as soft air   290

In spring, which moves the unawakened forest,
Clothing with leaves its branches bare and bleak,
Thou floatest among men; and aye implorest

That which from thee they should implore:—the weak
Alone kneel to thee, offering up the hearts   295
The strong have broken—yet where shall any seek

thrown / The [image] shadow of that scene *above* [landscape]; field after field *above* [far away] / Purple and dim and wide [and many a town] / Circled *above* [Distinct with antique towers and walls which yield] / [Their image in the lucid streams below] *E. 4*

280 We can desire, O [Love], *apparently cancelled* and [mighty] *above* [the wandering souls] happy *above* joyous souls *E. 4*   282 *changed from* [Sup thee until their amethystine bowls] *E. 4*   283 Thousands ... dew *above* [Are overflowing with the purple dew] *E. 4*   thine *1904, E. 4*] thy *1839, 1824, d. 9*   285 Investeth *1904, Ross. 1870, E. 4*] Investest *1839, 1824, d. 9*   and when the heavens are blue *edd.; changed from* [with colours ever new] *E. 4*   287 shadows *Ross. 1870*] shadow *edd. and MSS. But see n., p. 397.*   288 deserts *edd.*] deserts *above* forests *E. 4*   289 Thee like a garment *above* [Loveliness] and Beauty [like] some light robe; *above* garment [fairy-woven] *above* [whose woof is wind] thou ever soarest *E. 4   For* light *1839, 1824, d. 9 read* bright   290 Among the towers of men *edd.; changed from* [Thou floatest among men] *E. 4*

A garment whom thou clothest not? the darts
Of the keen winter storm, barbèd with frost,
Which, from the everlasting snow that parts

The Alps from Heaven, pierce some traveller lost   300
In the wide waved interminable snow
Ungarmented, [

Yes, often when the eyes are cold and dry,
And the lips calm, the Spirit weeps within
Tears bitterer than the blood of agony   305

Trembling in drops on the discoloured skin
Of those who love their kind and therefore perish
In ghastly torture—a sweet medicine

Of peace and sleep are tears, and quietly
Them soothe from whose uplifted eyes they fall   310
But [

Her hair was brown, her spherèd eyes were brown,
And in their dark and liquid moisture swam,
Like the dim orb of the eclipsèd moon;

Yet when the spirit flashed beneath, there came   315
The light from them, as when tears of delight
Double the western planet's serene flame.

ADDITIONAL LINES

[For 125–9, 168–81]

Prince Athanase had one belovèd friend,
An old, old man, with hair of silver white,
And lips where heavenly smiles would hang and blend

298–end *omitted in edd. before 1904, when printed by Hutch. from Loc. 1903*
300 The Alps from Heaven *changed from* [The earth from high Heaven] *above* [The
Laplander from] *E. 4*   305 the blood *1904*] the *above* [Christs] blood *E. 4*
307 their kind *1904*] their [man]kind *E. 4*   perish *1904*] perish *following* [die] [perish]
E. 4. See n., p. 397.   312 spherèd *1904*] spherèd *above* [starry] *E. 4*   316 when
tears of delight *1904; changed from* [of a double star] *E. 4*

PRINCE ATHANASE. Additional Lines. AUTOGRAPH: *These lines, drafted by Shelley in
E. 4, inconsecutively, after line 239, are a repetition and an expansion of lines 125–9 and
168–81.*   PRINTED: *Loc.*, An Examination, *1903: reprinted by Hutch., among his
Notes, 1904.*

With his wise words; and eyes whose arrowy light
Was the reflex of many minds; he filled 5
From fountains pure, nigh overgrown and [lost],

The spirit of Prince Athanase, a child;
And soul-sustaining songs of ancient lore
And philosophic wisdom, clear and mild.

And sweet and subtle talk they evermore 10
The pupil and the master [share], until
Sharing that undiminishable store,

The youth, as clouds thwart a grassy hill
Outrun the winds that chase them, soon outran
His teacher, and did teach with native skill 15

Strange truths and new to that experienced man;
So they were friends, as few have ever been
Who mark the extremes of life's discordant span.

6 [lost] *As Loc. notes, the word, cancelled by Shelley, does not fit the rhyme scheme, and represents a mechanical copying from the earlier version.* 11 [share] *cancelled because of* Sharing *in 12; Shelley left a space for a replacing word.*

NOTE BY MARY SHELLEY ON 'PRINCE ATHANASE'

THE idea Shelley had formed of Prince Athanase was a good deal modelled on *Alastor*. In the first sketch of the poem, he named it *Pandemos and Urania*. Athanase seeks through the world the One whom he may love. He meets, in the ship in which he is embarked, a lady who appears to him to embody his ideal of love and beauty. But she proves to be Pandemos, or the earthly and unworthy Venus; who, after disappointing his cherished dreams and hopes, deserts him. Athanase, crushed by sorrow, pines and dies. 'On his deathbed, the lady who can really reply to his soul comes and kisses his lips' (*The Deathbed of Athanase*). The poet describes her [in the words of the two concluding tercets, p. 290]. This slender note is all we have to aid our imagination in shaping out the form of the poem, such as its author imagined.

MISCELLANEOUS
SHORTER POEMS AND
FRAGMENTS
1817

MISCELLANEOUS SHORTER POEMS
AND FRAGMENTS
1817

Marianne's Dream

May, 1817

I

A PALE Dream came to a Lady fair,
  And said, 'A boon, a boon, I pray!
I know the secrets of the air,
  And things are lost in the glare of day,
Which I can make the sleeping see,   5
If they will put their trust in me.

II

'And thou shalt know of things unknown,
  If thou wilt let me rest between
The veiny lids, whose fringe is thrown
  Over thine eyes so dark and sheen.'   10
And half in hope, and half in fright,
The Lady closed her eyes so bright.

III

At first all deadly shapes were driven
  Tumultuously across her sleep,
And o'er the vast cope of bending heaven   15
  All ghastly-visaged clouds did sweep;
And the Lady ever looked to spy
If the golden sun shone forth on high.

MARIANNE'S DREAM. AUTOGRAPH: *Untraced.*   TRANSCRIPT: *MWS, in SH II.*
PRINTED: *Hunt*, Lit. Pocket-Bk., *1819/MWS, 1824/MWS, 1839/Hutch. 1904.*   TITLE:
SH II/1819. See *n., p. 402.*   DATE: "*Marlow, May, 1817*" *SH II.*   TEXT: *1904/
1839/1824/1819/SH II.*
  2 'A boon *SH II*] A boon *edd.*   10 sheen.'] sheen: *edd.*   sheen *SH II*
18 golden *1904, 1819, SH II*] gold *1839, 1824*

IV

And as towards the east she turned,
  She saw aloft in the morning air,   20
Which now with hues of sunrise burned,
  A great black Anchor rising there;
And wherever the Lady turned her eyes,
It hung before her in the skies.

V

The sky was blue as the summer sea,   25
  The depths were cloudless overhead,
The air was calm as it could be,
  There was no sight or sound of dread,
But that black Anchor floating still
Over the piny eastern hill.   30

VI

The Lady grew sick with a weight of fear
  To see that Anchor ever hanging,
And veiled her eyes; she then did hear
  The sound as of a dim low clanging,
And looked abroad if she might know   35
Was it aught else, or but the flow
Of the blood in her own veins, to and fro.

VII

There was a mist in the sunless air,
  Which shook as it were with an earthquake's shock,
But the very weeds that blossomed there   40
  Were moveless, and each mighty rock
Stood on its basis steadfastly;
The Anchor was seen no more on high.

VIII

But piled around, with summits hid
  In lines of cloud at intervals,   45
Stood many a mountain pyramid,
  Among whose everlasting walls
Two mighty cities shone, and ever
Through the red mist their domes did quiver.

28 or *1904, 1824, 1819, SH II*] nor *1839*   46 pyramid,] pyramid *edd.*

IX

On two dread mountains, from whose crest,   50
   Might seem, the eagle, for her brood,
Would ne'er have hung her dizzy nest,
   Those tower-encircled cities stood.
A vision strange such towers to see,
Sculptured and wrought so gorgeously,   55
Where human art could never be!

X

And columns framed of marble white,
   And giant fanes, dome over dome
Piled, and triumphant gates, all bright
   With workmanship, which could not come   60
From touch of mortal instrument,
Shot o'er the vales, a lustre lent
From its own shapes magnificent.

XI

But still the Lady heard that clang
   Filling the wide air far away;   65
And still the mist whose light did hang
   Among the mountains shook alway,
So that the Lady's heart beat fast,
As, half in joy and half aghast,
On those high domes her look she cast.   70

XII

Sudden, from out that city sprung
   A light that made the earth grow red;
Two flames that each with quivering tongue
   Licked its high domes, and overhead
Among those mighty towers and fanes   75
Dropped fire, as a volcano rains
Its sulphurous ruin on the plains.

56 be!] be. *edd.*   be *SH II*   62 a *Ross. 1870, SH II*] or *other edd. See n.,*
p. 403.   63 *See n., p. 403.*   69 As,] As *edd., SH. II*   joy] joy, *edd., SH. II*

XIII

And hark! a rush as if the deep
  Had burst its bonds; she looked behind
And saw over the eastern steep   80
  A raging flood descend, and wind
Through that wide vale; she felt no fear,
But said within herself, ''Tis clear
These towers are Nature's own, and she
To save them has sent forth the sea.'   85

XIV

And now those raging billows came
  Where that fair Lady sate, and she
Was borne towards the showering flame
  By the wild waves heaped tumultuously,
And, on a little plank, the flow   90
Of the whirlpool bore her to and fro.

XV

The waves were fiercely vomited
  From every tower and every dome,
And dreary light did widely shed
  O'er that vast flood's suspended foam,   95
Beneath the smoke which hung its night
On the stained cope of heaven's light.

XVI

The plank whereon that Lady sate
  Was driven through the chasms, about and about,
Between the peaks so desolate   100
  Of the drowning mountains, in and out,
As the thistle-beard on a whirlwind sails,
While the flood was filling those hollow vales.

80 eastern *SH II*] western *edd., but cf. line 19*   83 "Tis] 'Tis *edd.*   'tis *SH II*
85 sea.'] sea. *edd.*   sea *SH II*   92 waves *1839, 1824, 1819, SH II*] flames *1904,*
following Rossetti's conjecture, 1870   101 mountains *1904, 1819, SH II*] mountain
1839, 1824   102 sails,] sails— *edd.*   sails *SH II*

XVII

At last her plank an eddy crossed,
   And bore her to the city's wall,   105
Which now the flood had reached almost;
   It might the stoutest heart appal
To hear the fire roar and hiss
Through the rifts of those mighty palaces.

XVIII

The eddy whirled her round and round   110
   Before a gorgeous gate, which stood
Piercing the clouds of smoke which bound
   Its aëry arch with light like blood;
She looked on that gate of marble clear,
With wonder that extinguished fear.   115

XIX

For it was filled with sculptures rarest,
   Of forms most beautiful and strange,
Like nothing human, but the fairest
   Of wingèd shapes, whose legions range
Throughout the sleep of those that are,   120
Like this same Lady, good and fair.

XX

And as she looked, still lovelier grew
   Those marble forms;—the sculptor sure
Was a strong spirit, and the hue
   Of his own mind did there endure   125
After the touch, whose power had braided
Such grace, was in some sad change faded.

XXI

She looked, the flames were dim, the flood
   Grew tranquil as a woodland river
Winding through hills in solitude;   130
   Those marble shapes then seemed to quiver,

106 *See n., p. 403.*   109 rifts . . . mighty *uncancelled, above* domes . . . rifted *uncancelled SH II*] domes . . . mighty *edd.*   120 that *1904, 1824, 1839*] that *above* who *SH II* who *1839*

And their fair limbs to float in motion,
Like weeds unfolding in the ocean,

XXII

And their lips moved; one seemed to speak,
　　When suddenly the mountains cracked,　　　　135
And through the chasm the flood did break
　　With an earth-uplifting cataract;
The statues gave a joyous scream,
And on its wings the pale thin Dream
Lifted the Lady from the stream.　　　　　　140

XXIII

The dizzy flight of that phantom pale
　　Waked the fair Lady from her sleep,
And she arose, while from the veil
　　Of her dark eyes the Dream did creep,
And she walked about as one who knew　　　　145
That sleep has sights as clear and true
As any waking eyes can view.

To Constantia, Singing

1817, probably May

I

THY voice slow rising like a Spirit, lingers
O'ershadowing me with soft and lulling wings;
The blood and life within thy snowy fingers
Teach witchcraft to the instrumental strings.

133 ocean,] ocean. *edd.*　ocean *SH II*　　**136** flood *1904, 1824, 1819, SH II*] floor *1839*

To CONSTANTIA, SINGING.　AUTOGRAPH: *a. Confused draft, Bod. MS. Shelley E. 4; b. fair copy lacking line 44, SH II.*　TRANSCRIPT: *a. From E. 4,　MWS, Bod. MS. Shelley adds. d. 7; b. Claire Clairmont, untraced, see n., p. 403.*　PRINTED: Oxford University and City Herald, *signed 'Pleyel' (see n.), PBS, 31 Jan. 1818, reprinted in* Times Literary Supplement, *Judith Chernaik, 3 Feb. 1969/from E. 4, MWS, 1824, 1839, Loc. 1903, Hutch. 1904/from SH II, with line 44 from E. 4, W. E. Peck,* Boston Herald, *21 Dec. 1925.*　TITLE: *1839; see n., p. 403.* 'To Constantia' *SH II, 1818.*　DATE: *See n., p. 403.*　TEXT: *1818/SH II, considerably repunctuated, with line 44 from E. 4. See n., pp. 403-4.*
　　2 me *1818*] it *1925, SH II.*

—My brain is wild—my breath comes quick—   5
   The blood is listening in my frame,
And thronging shadows, fast and thick,
   Fall on my overflowing eyes;
My heart is quivering like a flame;
   As morning dew, that in the sunbeam dies,   10
   I am dissolved in these consuming exstasies.

II

I have no life, Constantia, but in thee,
   Whilst, like the world-surrounding air, thy song
Flows on, and fills all things with melody,—
   Now is thy voice a tempest swift and strong,   15
On which, as one in trance upborne,
   Secure o'er woods and waves I sweep
Rejoicing, like a cloud of morn;
   Now 'tis the breath of summer's night,
Which, where the starry waters sleep   20
   Round western isles with incense-blossoms bright,
   Lingering, suspends my soul in its voluptuous flight.

III

A deep and breathless awe, like the swift change
   Of dreams unseen, but felt in youthful slumbers,
Wild, sweet, yet incommunicably strange,   25
   Thou breathest now in fast ascending numbers,—
The cope of Heaven seems rent and cloven
   By the enchantment of thy strain,
And o'er my shoulders wings are woven
   To follow its sublime career   30
Beyond the mighty moons that wane
   Upon the verge of Nature's utmost sphere,
   Till the world's shadowy walls are past and disappear.—

IV

Cease, cease—for such wild lessons madmen learn!
   Long thus to sink, thus to be lost and die   35

8 eyes;] eyes, *1818* eyes *SH II*   12 thee,] thee; *1818* thee *SH II*   17 woods
1818] rocks *1925, SH II*   24 slumbers,] slumbers: *1818*   slumbers *SH II*
30 career *SH II*] career, *1818*   34 learn!] learn: *1818*   learn *SH II*

Perhaps is death indeed—Constantia turn!
Yes! in thine eyes a power like light doth lie,
Even though the sounds, its voice that were,
    Between thy lips are laid to sleep—
Within thy breath, and on thy hair   40
Like odour, it is lingering yet,—
    And from thy touch like fire doth leap;
Even while I write, my burning cheeks are wet,—
Alas, that the torn heart can bleed, but not forget!

Fragment: To Constantia

1817

I

THE rose that drinks the fountain dew
    In the fragrant air of noon,
Grows pale and blue with altered hue
    In the gaze of the nightly moon;
For the planet of frost, so cold and bright,   5
Makes it wan with her borrowed light.

II

Such is my heart—roses are fair,
    And that at best a withered blossom;
But thy false care did idly wear
    Its withered leaves in a faithless bosom;   10
And fed with love, like air and dew,
    Its growth [

38 were,] were *1818*, SH II   44 *Thus E. 4*] Such things the heart can feel and learn, but not forget! *1818 ; line omitted in SH II*

To CONSTANTIA. AUTOGRAPH: *a. 1–end, Bod. MS. Shelley E. 4; b. 1–5, Bod. MS. Shelley adds. e. 10.*   TRANSCRIPT: *MWS, Bod. MS. Shelley adds. d. 7.*   PRINTED: *From E. 4, MWS, 1839/Loc. 1903/Hutch. 1904.*   TITLE, DATE: *1839.*   TEXT: *1904/1839/E. 4/e. 10.*
    1 The rose *edd.*] red *above three dots above caret, above and between* The rose *E. 4. See n., p. 404.* Roses *e. 10*   that drinks *edd., E. 4*] which drink *e. 10*   2 In the fragrant air *above* [Beneath the gaze] *E. 4*] Beneath the gaze *e. 10*   In the pleasant air *edd.*   3 Grows *edd.*] Grows *for* [Is] *E. 4*   Are *e. 10*   altered *edd.*] altered *above* [changed] *E. 4*   changed *e. 10*   true] true— *edd.*   4 gaze *edd.*] gaze *for* [eye] *E. 4*   eye *e. 10*   4–5 For the frost has been their *uncancelled e. 10*   6 Makes it wan *for* [Shines on it] *E. 4*   7 roses are *changed from* though the roses be *E. 4*   9 But *edd.*] But *above* [Which] *E. 4*   10 *changed from* [in the warmth of a dear but pitiless bosom] *E. 4*

Fragment: To One Singing

1817

MY spirit like a charmèd bark doth swim
  Upon the liquid waves of thy sweet singing,
Far, far away into the regions dim
   Of rapture—as a boat, with swift sails winging
Its way adown some many-winding river,   5
Speeds through dark forests o'er the waters swinging [

Two Fragments: To Music

1817

I

To Mary

SILVER key of the fountain of tears,
  Where the spirit drinks till the brain is wild;
Softest grave of a thousand fears,
   Where their mother, Care, like a drowsy child,
    Is laid asleep in flowers,—   5
O, be they ever loosened, as now,
Till from my bosom and from my brow
The clinging reason [

TO ONE SINGING. AUTOGRAPH: *Bod. MS. Shelley E. 4.* TRANSCRIPT: *MWS, Bod. MS. Shelley adds. d. 7.* PRINTED: *MWS, 1839*/*Loc. 1903*/*Hutch. 1904.* TITLE, DATE: *1839.* TEXT: *1904*/*1839*/*E. 4.*
  1 bark *edd.*] [boat] bark *E. 4*   swim *edd.; changed from* [float] *E. 4*   2 liquid *edd.*] liquid *above* [lulling] *E. 4*   3 Far,] Far *edd.*   [I feel] Far *E. 4*   into *edd.*] into *above* amid *E. 4*   4 Of rapture—as *edd.*] Of rapture as *above* [Even as a rapid] *E. 4*

TO MUSIC (1). AUTOGRAPH: *Bod. MS. Shelley adds. e. 9.* TRANSCRIPTS: *a. MWS, Bod. MS. Shelley adds. d. 7; b. MWS, Bod. MS. Shelley adds. d. 9; c. MWS, Leeds University, Cowden Clarke Coll.* PRINTED: *1–5, MWS, 1839, Hutch. 1904.* UNPRINTED: *6–end.* DATE: *1839.* TITLE: *e. 9, 1839. Sub-title* 'To Mary' *e. 9 (previously unprinted).* TEXT: *1–5, edd. and MSS.; 6–end, e. 9.*
  1 Silver *Form. 1876, later edd., and MSS.*] The silver *1839*   5 flowers,—] flowers. *edd.* flowers *MSS.*

2

Oh, Music, thou art not the 'food of Love';
Unless Love feeds upon its own sweet self
Till it becomes all Music murmurs of.

Fragment: 'Mighty Eagle . . .'

[Probably addressed to the Spirit of Plato]

Probably early May 1817

MIGHTY eagle! thou that soarest
O'er the misty mountain forest,
   And amidst the blaze of morning
Like a cloud of glory hiest,
And when night descends defiest   5
   The embattled tempests' warning,—
Leave thy   habitation
On the verge of desolation [

To Music (2). AUTOGRAPH: *BH I.* TRANSCRIPTS: *a. MWS, Bod. MS. Shelley* adds. d. 7; b. MWS, Bod. MS. Shelley adds. d. 9. PRINTED: *MWS, 1839/Hutch. 1904/Form. 1876 and* Note Books of Shelley *1911.* TITLE, DATE: *1839.* TEXT: *1911/1904/1876/1839/d. 7/d. 9/BH I.*
   1 Oh, *1911, BH I*] No, *other edd., d. 7, d. 9* 'food of Love';] 'food of Love', *1911, 1904, 1876, BH I* God of Love, *1839, d. 7, d. 9* 2 self] self, *1904, 1876, 1839, d. 7, d. 9, BH I*

'MIGHTY EAGLE . . .'. AUTOGRAPH: *a. 1–6, Pf., on a letter from Godwin, 29 Apr. 1817, once owned by Forman; b. Bod. MS. Shelley adds. e. 8; c. BH II.* TRANSCRIPT: *MWS, Bod. MS. Shelley adds. d. 7.* DATE: *See n., p. 381.* PRINTED: *1–6, from Pf., Form. 1882, Hutch. 1904/1–8, from BH II, Form.,* Note Books of Shelley, *1911.* TEXT: *1911, BH II, collated with 1904, Pf., and e. 8.*
   3 amidst *1911, BH II, e. 8*] amid *1904, 1882* blaze *1911, e. 8*] [cl] blaze *BH II* light *1904, 1882* light *above* [clouds] *Pf.* 5–6 defiest . . . / warning *edd. and MSS except e. 8*] the warning / Of the embattled storm defiest *e. 8* 6 warning,—] warning! *1904, 1882* warning *MSS.* 7 Leave] Leaves *1911, BH II*
7–8   Mighty eagle thou whose dwelling
                       Haunts the precipices
                       And the   *e. 8*

To the Lord Chancellor

Probably April 1817

I

THY country's curse is on thee, darkest crest
Of that foul, knotted, many-headed worm
Which rends our Mother's bosom—Priestly Pest!
Masked Resurrection of a buried Form!

II

Thy country's curse is on thee! Justice sold,   5
Truth trampled, Nature's landmarks overthrown,
And heaps of fraud-accumulated gold,
Plead, loud as thunder, at Destruction's throne.

III

And, whilst that sure slow Angel which aye stands
Watching the beck of Mutability   10
Delays to execute her high commands,
And, though a nation weeps, spares thine and thee,

IV

Oh, let a father's curse be on thy soul,
And let a daughter's hope be on thy tomb;
Be both, on thy gray head, a leaden cowl   15
To weigh thee down to thine approaching doom!

TO THE LORD CHANCELLOR.   AUTOGRAPH: *a. Draft, Bod. MS. Shelley adds. e. 9; b. fair copy, SH I.*   TRANSCRIPTS: *a. MWS, Bod. MS. Shelley adds. d. 9; b. and c. MWS, both once owned by Carl Frederickson of Brooklyn ('Fred.'), now untraced; one had Shelley's corrections; d. MWS in SH II; e. MWS, once owned by Leigh Hunt, now untraced; f. MWS, Leeds University, Cowden Clarke Coll.*   DATE: *See n., p. 405.*   PRINTED: *17–36, 53–6, without title, MWS, 1839¹/1–end, with title, MWS, 1839², Hutch. 1904.*   TITLE: *SH I, 1839². Abbreviated or disguised in ªother MSS.*   TEXT: *1904/1839²/ 1839¹/ SH I/transcripts/e. 9. Considerably repunctuated. See n. on pp. 405–6.*

9 sure slow *edd., SH I, SH II*] slow sure *d. 9, Leeds, e. 9*   Angel which aye *edd., SH I, d. 9, Leeds*] Angel where he *e. 9*   Fate which ever *SH II, Fred.*   11 Delays to execute *edd., SH II, d. 9, Leeds; changed in SH I from* Should now delay to do *as drafted in e. 9*   12 though *edd., SH II, Leeds; changed in SH I from* whilst *drafted in e. 9 and followed in d. 9*   13 Oh, *edd.*] O *d. 9, SH II, Leeds* O *above* [Then] *SH I* Then *e. 9*   father's *edd. and MSS.; changed from in SH I* parent's   14 daughter's *edd., SH II, d. 9, Leeds; changed in SH I from* parents *which had replaced the* father's *drafted in e. 9*

V

I curse thee by a parent's outraged love,
    By hopes long cherished and too lately lost,
By gentle feelings thou couldst never prove,
    By griefs which thy stern nature never crossed;   20

VI

By those infantine smiles of happy light,
    Which were a fire within a stranger's hearth,
Quenched even when kindled, in untimely night
    Hiding the promise of a lovely birth;   •

VII

By those unpractised accents of young speech,   25
    Which he who is a father thought to frame
To gentlest lore, such as the wisest teach—
    Thou strike the lyre of mind!—oh, grief and shame!

VIII

By all the happy see in children's growth,
    That undeveloped flower of budding years,   30
Sweetness and sadness interwoven both,
    Source of the sweetest hopes and saddest fears;

IX

By all the days, under a hireling's care,
    Of dull constraint and bitter heaviness,—
O wretched ye if ever any were,—   35
    Sadder than orphans, yet not fatherless!—

X

By the false cant which on their innocent lips
    Must hang like poison on an opening bloom;
By the dark creeds which cover with eclipse
    Their pathway from the cradle to the tomb;   40

21–4 *Cancelled in SH II, though MWS noted 'Insert this'*   24 promise of a *MSS.
and edd. except 1839¹, which has* promises of   27 lore, *edd. and MSS. except Fred.,
which has* love   32 and saddest *edd., SH I, d. 9, Leeds, e. 9*] the saddest *SH II,
Fred.*   33 a *MSS. and edd. except 1904, which has* an   36 yet not fatherless!—]
Yet not fatherless! *edd. and MSS. except SH II and Fred., which have* why not fatherless?
37 innocent *edd. and MSS.; changed in SH I from* [opening]

XI

By thy most impious Hell, and all its terror;
  By all the grief, the madness, and the guilt
Of thine impostures, which must be their error—
  That sand on which thy crumbling power is built;

XII

By thy complicity with lust and hate,   45
  Thy thirst for tears, thy hunger after gold,
The ready frauds which ever on thee wait,
  ₒ The servile arts in which thou hast grown old;

XIII

By thy most killing sneer, and by thy smile,
  By all the snares and nets of thy black den,   50
And—for thou canst outweep the crocodile—
  By thy false tears, those millstones braining men;

XIV

By all the hate which checks a father's love;
  By all the scorn which kills a father's care;
By those most impious hands which dared remove   55
  Nature's high bounds; by thee; and by despair—

XV

Yes, the despair which bids a father groan,
  And cry, 'My children are no longer mine;
The blood within those veins may be mine own,
  But, Tyrant, their polluted souls are thine!'—   60

41–4 *Cancelled in SH II and Fred. and marked 'dele' by MWS. For an alternative version, cancelled, from e. 9, see below, 'Additional Lines', 1–4.*   41/3 terror . . . error *edd. and MSS. except d. 9, which has* terrors . . . errors   43 must *edd. and MSS.; changed in SH I from* [will]   44 crumbling *edd. and MSS.; changed in SH I from* [tottering]   50 snares and nets *SH I, SH II*] arts and snares *1904* acts and snares *1839², d. 9, Leeds* And by the jackals of thy deadly den *e. 9*   53 checks *edd. and MSS. except e. 9, which has* meets   54 kills *edd., SH II, d. 9, Leeds; changed in SH I from the* meets *of e. 9*   55 which *1904 and MSS.*] that *1839²*   58 And . . . mine;] And . . . mine— *edd., SH II, d. 9, Leeds; changed in SH I from* [Thus I no longer called my children mine]   I dare no longer call my children mine. *e. 9*   59 those *edd., d. 9, Leeds*] their *SH II, Fred., SH I possibly, e. 9 possibly*   60 souls are *edd., SH II*] soul is *SH I, d. 9, Leeds, e. 9*

XVI

I curse thee—though I hate thee not.—O slave!
If thou couldst quench the earth-consuming Hell
Of which thou art a daemon, on thy grave
This curse should be a blessing. Fare thee well!

ADDITIONAL LINES

[From the draft]

By all the terrors of thy fabled Hell,
The madness and the sorrow and the guilt,
By all the woes which he can never tell
Who learns not on what here thy power is built [

By the dark creed of thee and of thy crew,   5
With which thou dost infect the infant mind,
A tender floweret on poison dew
Its leaves asleep, a fragrance on the wind, [

[From Shelley's fair copy]

By that sweet voice which who could understand
It frame to sounds of love and lore divine [10

By those pure accents, which at my command
Should have been framed to love and lore divine,
Now like a lute, fretted by some rude hand,
Uttering harsh discords, they must echo thine.

61 O slave! *edd., SH II, d. 9, Leeds; changed in SH I from the* Thou slave *of e. 9,
itself a change from* be given   62 earth-consuming *edd., SH II, d. 9, Leeds; changed
in SH I from* [fierce and sullen] *and* [ever-blazing]   *lacking in e. 9*   63 Of . . .
daemon *edd. and MSS. except SH I, where it is changed from* [Wither thee as thou
crawlest to]

To the Lord Chancellor. Additional Lines.   autograph: *1–8, Bod. MS. Shelley
adds. e. 9, cancelled; 9–14, SH I, cancelled.*   printed: *9–14, I and P, 1927.*   un-
printed: *1–8.*   text: *e. 9, SH I, slightly repunctuated.*
    *1–4 follow line 40 in e. 9   5–8 follow line 64 in e. 9   9–14 follow line 24
in SH I*

To William Shelley

Marlow, 1817

I

THE billows on the beach are leaping around it,
　The bark is weak and frail,
The sea looks black, and the clouds that bound it
　Darkly strew the gale.
Come with me, delightful child,　　　　　　　　　　5
Come with me! Though the wave is wild,
And the winds are loose, we must not stay,
Or the slaves of law may rend thee away.

II

They have taken thy brother and sister dear,
　They have made them unfit for thee;　　　　　　　10
They have withered the smile and dried the tear
　Which should have been sacred to me.
To a blighting faith and a cause of crime
They have bound them slaves in youthly time;
And they will curse my name and thee　　　　　　　15
Because we fearless are and free.

III

Come thou, belovèd as thou art;
　Another sleepeth still
Near thy sweet mother's anxious heart,
　Which thou with joy wilt fill.　　　　　　　　　　20
With fairest smiles of wonder thrown
On that which is indeed our own,
And which in distant lands will be
The dearest playmate unto thee.

TO WILLIAM SHELLEY. AUTOGRAPH: *Pencil draft, written over draft of* Verses Written
on Receiving a Celandine, etc., *Bod. MS. Shelley adds. e. 16.* TRANSCRIPTS: *a. MWS,
Bod. MS. Shelley adds. d. 7 ; b. 1–16 only, MWS, Bod. MS. Shelley adds. d. 9 ; c. MWS,
Leeds University, Cowden Clarke Coll.* PRINTED: *1–8, 33–52, MWS, 1839¹/1–end,
MWS, 1839², Hutch. 1904.* TITLE: *Leeds, 1839.* DATE: *Leeds.* TEXT: *1904/
1839²/1839¹/transcripts/e. 16.*
　1 on the beach *MSS. and edd. except 1839¹, where it is omitted* 5 delightful
MSS.] thou delightful *edd.* 8 law *1839², MSS. except Leeds]* the law *1904, 1839²,
Leeds* 14 time;] time *1839², e. 16* time *over* prime *d. 9* prime *1904, d. 7, Leeds,
probably an intrusion from the Celandine poem* 20 wilt *1839², d. 7, e. 16]* shalt *1904,
Leeds*

IV

Fear not the tyrants will rule for ever,   25
   Or the priests of the evil faith;
They stand on the brink of that raging river,
   Whose waves they have tainted with death.
It is fed from the depth of a thousand dells,
Around them it foams and rages and swells;   30
And their swords and their sceptres I floating see,
Like wrecks on the surge of eternity.

V

Rest, rest, shriek not, thou gentle child!
   The rocking of the boat thou fearest,
And the cold spray and the clamour wild?—   35
   There, sit between us two, thou dearest—
Me and thy mother—well we know
The storm at which thou tremblest so,
With all its dark and hungry graves,
Less cruel than the savage slaves   40
Who hunt thee o'er these sheltering waves.

VI

This hour will in thy memory
   Be a dream of days forgotten long;
We soon shall dwell by the azure sea
Of serene and golden Italy,   45
Or Greece, the Mother of the free;
   And I will teach thine infant tongue
To call upon those heroes old
In their own language, and will mould
Thy growing spirit in the flame   50
Of Grecian lore, that by such name
A patriot's birthright thou mayst claim!

25-32 *Incorporated, with slight variation, in* Rosalind and Helen, *894-901. Omitted in* Leeds.   33 shriek *1839², 1839¹, MSS. except Leeds*] and shriek *1904, Leeds*
36 dearest— *1904, possibly Leeds*] dearest; *1839², 1839¹, which destroys grammar, as does* dearest, *d. 7*   dearest *in the unhelpful draft, e. 16*   41 thee *1839²*] thee *above*
[us] *e. 16*   us *1904, 1839¹, d. 7, Leeds*   42 will *1904, 1839², d. 7, Leeds*] will sometime *1839¹, and in some phrases in e. 16, uncancelled but abortive*   43 forgotten long *1904, Leeds, e. 16*] forgotten *1839², 1839¹, d. 7*   48 those *1904, 1839¹, d. 7 Leeds*] their *1839²*

ADDITIONAL LINES

Mild thoughts of man's ungentle race
  Shall our contented exile reap;
For who that in some happy place
His own free thoughts can freely chase
By woods and waves, can clothe his face   5
  In cynic smiles? Child, we shall weep!—
'Twill be the balm of soothing tears,
Like memories of delightful years
  ⟨When mourning for the toil   war
  Who toil beneath the world's ill star   10
  We feel how meek and calm we are⟩ [

.   .   .   .   .   .

The world is now our dwelling-place;
Where'er the earth onc fading trace
Of what was great and free does keep,
That is our home [15

As an alternative, to follow line 2, the following lines appear

The cynic starts from Pride's embrace
And smile's in Misery's withered face
But thou, sweet child, shalt weep
The woes we share not—many a tear
            that strange war   20
Whose waves we then shall hear ⟨? afar⟩

To WILLIAM SHELLEY. Additional Lines. AUTOGRAPH: *Bod. MSS. Shelley adds.
e. 16, c. 4.* TRANSCRIPT: *(3–11 only) Bod. MS. Shelley adds. d. 7.* PRINTED:
1–6, 12–15, Garn. 1862/Hutch. 1904. See *n.*, *p. 407.* UNPRINTED: *7–11, 16–21.*
TEXT: *1904/1862/d. 7/c. 16/c. 4.*

Two Laments

1. *On Harriet Shelley*

Nov. 5, 1816

[2nd version, written in 1817]

THE cold Earth slept below;
  Above the cold sky shone;
    And all around,
    With a chilling sound,
From caves of ice and fields of snow, 5
The wind of night like death did flow
  Under the sinking moon.

The wintry hedge was black;
  The brown grass was not seen;
    The birds did rest 10
    In the dark thorn's breast,
Whose roots beside the pathway track
Bound the hard soil; and many a crack
  The black frost made between.

Thine eyes glowed in the glare 15
  Of the departing light;
    As a starry beam
    On a deep dark stream
Shines dimly, so the moon shone there,
And it shone thro' the strings of thy tangled hair, 20
  Which shook in the blast of night.

ON HARRIET SHELLEY, Nov. 5, 1816, 2nd Version. AUTOGRAPH: *Combining the next poem, Bod. MS. Shelley adds. e. 12. See Intr., p. xx, p. 84 above, and n., pp. 407–8.* TRAN-SCRIPT: *I, II, III, MWS, Bod. MS. Shelley adds. d. 7.* DATE: *With heading, e. 12, where, however, it is erroneously given as '1815'; cf., pp. 356–7, the similar misdating of the first version, of which it is an 1817 rehandling.* PRINTED: *S-R and I, 1934, where it was first connected with the next poem.* TITLE: *'To' followed by a heavy erasure e. 12; none in d. 7; 'To [   ]' 1934.* TEXT: *1934/e. 12.*

  1 *preceded by* [Come to me] *e. 12*   below;] below, *1934*   below *e. 12*   6 wind *edd.*] wind *above* [breath] *e. 12*   8 black;] black, *1934*   black *e. 12*   9 brown *edd.*] brown *above* [green] *e. 12*   seen;] seen, *1934*   seen *e. 12*   12 roots . . . track *e. 12*] roots, . . . track, *1934*   13 soil;] soil *1934*   clod *above* soil *both uncancelled e. 12*   19 there,] there. *1934*   there *e. 12*   21 blast *above* [wind] *e. 12*

The moon made thy lips pale, belovèd;
  The wind made thy bosom chill;
    The air did shed
    On thy dear head   25
Its frozen dew, and thou didst lie
Where the bitter breath of the naked sky
  Might visit thee at will.

2. On [Harriet Shelley]

Nov. 5, 1817

THAT time is dead for ever, child,
  Drowned, frozen, dead for ever!
    We look on the past,
    And stare aghast
At the spectres wailing, pale and wild,   5
Of hopes which thou and I beguiled
  To death on life's dark river.

The stream we gazed on then rolled by;
  Its waves are unreturning;
    But we yet stand   10
    In a lone land,
Like tombs to mark the memory
Of hopes and fears, which fade and flee
  In the light of life's brief morning.

22 belovèd;] beloved— *1934*   belovèd *e. 12*   23 chill;] chill— *1934*   chill *e. 12*

ON [HARRIET SHELLEY], Nov. 5, 1817. AUTOGRAPH: *Bod. MS. Shelley adds. e. 12.*
TRANSCRIPT: *Bod. MS. Shelley adds. d. 9.*   PRINTED: *MWS, 1924/MWS, 1839/
Hutch. 1904/S–R and I, 1934.*   TITLE: *None in e. 12/*'Lines' *1824, 1839, 1904.*
DATE: *From autograph, above line 1.*   TEXT: *1934/1904/1839/1824/d. 9/e. 12.*
   1 That time *edd.*] That time *above* [those hours] *e. 12*   child, *edd. except 1904*]
child! *1904*   child *e. 12*   5 pale *1904, 1839, 1824, e. 12*] pale, *1934*   wild
1934, e. 12] ghast *1904, 1839, 1824, d. 9*   6 thou and I *1904, 1839, 1824*] I and
thou *1934, e. 12*   8 then *1904, 1839, 1824*] then, *1934, d. 9, e. 12*   rolled by; *edd.,
e. 12*] is past *d. 9*   14 In the light of *edd., d. 9 ; in e. 12 apparently changed to* From
blest *which is misread in 1934 as* Mary blest *but see n., p. 408.*   brief *1934, d. 9, e. 12*]
dim *1904, 1839, 1824*

Death

1817

I

THEY die—the dead return not. Misery
Sits near an open grave and calls them over,
A Youth with hoary hair and haggard eye.
They are the names of kindred, friend and lover,
Which he so feebly calls—they all are gone,   5
Fond wretch, all dead! those vacant names alone,
This most familiar scene, thy pain—
These tombs—alone remain.

II

Misery, my sweetest friend—oh, weep no more!
Thou wilt not be consoled? I wonder not!   10
For I have seen thee from thy dwelling's door
Watch the calm sunset with them, and thy lot
Was even so bright and calm, but transitory;
And now thy hopes are gone, thy hair is hoary;
This most familiar scene, my pain,   15
These tombs—alone remain.

DEATH. AUTOGRAPH: *Bod. MS. Shelley adds. e. 16; two drafts, see n., p. 408.*
PRINTED: *MWS, 1824/MWS, 1839/Hutch. 1904.*   TITLE, DATE: *1824.*   TEXT:
1904/1839/1824/e. 16, second draft, collated with first.
  1 not.] not— *edd., e. 16*   3 haggard *1904, 1839, 1824*] haggard *above* [sunken] *e. 16*
eye.] eye— *edd., e. 16*   4 the names *1904, 1824, e. 16*] names *1839*

4–9   Muttering like madness—yes they all are gone
     .   Fond wretch, thou mayst count their names alone
            Their graves reminding thee of parent, lover
            And friend, thy heart's companions—thou dost groan
            I wonder not for when the shadows come
            And evening falls upon thy lonely home   *e. 16, first draft*

5 calls *1904, 1839, e. 16*] called *1824*   7 thy *e. 16*] my *1904, 1839, 1824*
10 consoled?] consoled— *edd. & MSS.*   12 thy lot *upon* [yon spot] *e. 16*] this spot
edd.   12–13 [Of lawn among the pines may be forgot / When looks and words]
which is changed to Was calm—I weep with thee—that lawny spot / Among the pines
e. 16   13 so] so *above as e. 16*   as *1904, 1839, 1824*   transitory;] transitory, *edd.*
transitory . . *e. 16*   14–15 [Thou sittest in the cold and w] *above* On   winter
cold *above* [Thou lookest on this life with] *e. 16*   15–16 *lacking in second draft;*
supplied from first   15 pain,] pain— *edd., e. 16*

Otho: Stanzas from the Fragment of a Draft
1817

I

THE mistress and the monitress of earth
  Had fallen; her throne was vacant, and upon
Its painted footstool, in unnatural mirth,
    Robed royally, a sceptred skeleton
      Smiled at the praise; the sound whose mystery   5
Was empire, virtue, greatness, now was gone,
      Numbered among what things our memory
      Once having noted cannot cease to be.

II

'Dark is the realm of grief, but human things
  Those may not know who cannot weep for them.   10
Sadness is joy, sweet mother, for she brings
    Such gentle looks as render vain and stem
      Power's hard and heartless triumph. We retrieve
The good that is gone by, while we condemn
      Ourselves in frail humanity and grieve   15
      That much is past, which it did once achieve.

III

'Those whom nor power, nor lying faith, nor toil,
  Nor custom, queen of many slaves, makes blind,
Have ever grieved that man should be the spoil
    Of his own weakness, and with earnest mind   20
      Fed hopes of its redemption; these recur
Chastened by doubtful victory now, and find
      Foundations in this foulest age, that stir
      Me whom they cheer to be their minister.'

IV

Such thoughts, befitting well a parent's bier,   25
  Are mine of Rome when, although desolate,
Its genius yet delayed to disappear
    Even while each palace, fane and trophied gate

OTHO: STANZAS, ETC.   AUTOGRAPH: *Bod. MS. Shelley adds. e. 16.*   PRINTED: *V*, *VI*, *MWS*, *1839*[1], *Hutch. 1904/II. 1–2, III, Garn. 1862, Hutch. 1904.*   UNPRINTED: *I, II. 3–8, IV.*   TITLE, DATE: *See Mary Shelley's Note on Poems of 1817, p. 324.* TEXT: *1904/1862/1839/e. 16. See n., pp. 408–9.*

Showed, like its tomb, what still inhabited
Fallen greatness—even the record of its state   30
Seem[s] like some visage wandering from the dead
To say

V

'Thou wert not, Cassius, and thou couldst not be,
"Last of the Romans"—though thy memory claim
From Brutus his own glory, and on thee   35
Rest the full splendour of his sacred fame—
Nor he who dared make the foul tyrant quail
Amid his cowering senate with thy name:
Though thou and he were great it will avail
To thine own fame that Otho's should not fail.   40

VI

'I wrong thee not—thou wouldst, if thou couldst feel,
Abjure such envious fame. Great Otho died
Like thee—he sanctified his country's steel,
At once the tyrant and tyrannicide,
In his own blood. A deed it was to bring   45
Tears from all men—though full of gentle pride,
Such pride as from impetuous love may spring,
That will not be refused its offering.'

Fragment: 'O that a Chariot of Cloud were Mine . . .'

Probably 1817

O THAT a chariot of cloud were mine—
Of cloud which the tempest weaves in air,
When the moon over the ocean's line
Is spreading the locks of her bright gray hair!
O that a chariot of cloud were mine!   5
I would sail on the waves of the billowy wind
To the mountain peak and the rocky lake,
And the [

'O THAT A CHARIOT OF CLOUD . . .'. AUTOGRAPH: *Bod. MS. Shelley adds. e. 16.*
DATE: *See n., p. 410.*   PRINTED: *Garn. 1862/Hutch. 1904.*   TEXT: *1904/1862/e. 16.*
   1 mine—] mine! *edd.*   mine *e. 16*   2 tempest] wild tempest *edd.* wild tempest
above [winds] *e. 16*   weaves *edd.*] weave *e. 16. See n., p. 410.*   4 hair!] hair. *edd.*
hair *e. 16*

Fragment: 'A golden-wingèd Angel stood . . .'

Probably 1817

A GOLDEN-WINGÈD Angel stood
  Before the Eternal Judgement-seat:
His looks were weird, and Devils' blood
  Stained his dainty hands and feet.
God the Father and God the Son   5
Knew what strife was now begun.
They knew that Satan had broken his chain,
And with millions of daemons in his train,
Was ranging over the world again.

Before the Angel had told his tale,   10
  A sweet and a creeping sound
  Like the rushing of wings was heard around;
And suddenly the lamps grew pale—
The lamps, before the Archangels seven,
That burn continually in Heaven.   15

Fragment: 'To thirst and find no fill . . .'

1817

To thirst and find no fill—to ⟨wail⟩ and wander
With short unsteady steps—to pause and ponder—
To feel the blood run through the veins and tingle
Where busy thought and blind sensation mingle;

'A GOLDEN-WINGÈD ANGEL STOOD . . .'. AUTOGRAPH: *Transcribed by Garn. Now untraced.* TRANSCRIPT: *MWS, Bod. MS. Shelley adds. d. 7.* PRINTED: *Ross. 1870/Hutch. 1904.* DATE: *See n., p. 410.* TEXT: *1904/1870/d. 7.*
  3 weird] wierd *d. 7*   wild *edd.*   5 G-d the F-th-r and G-d the S- *d. 7*] The Father and the Son *edd.*   6 what *d. 7*] that *edd.*

'To THIRST AND FIND NO FILL . . .'. AUTOGRAPH: *Bod. MS. Shelley E. 4.*   TRAN-SCRIPT: *Bod. MS. Shelley adds. d. 7.* PRINTED: *MWS, 1839/Loc. 1903/Hutch. 1904.*
DATE: *1839.* TITLE: *See n., p. 410.* TEXT: *1904/1903/1839¹/E. 4/d. 7. See n., p. 410.*
  1 ⟨wail⟩ *cancelled and doubtfully decipherable in E. 4*   2 short *edd.*] short *above* [uneven] *E. 4*   unsteady *E. 4 and edd., except Form. 1876, which has* uneasy

To nurse the image of unfelt caresses   5
Till ⟨? dazed⟩ imagination just possesses
The half-created shadow, then all the night
Sick [

Fragment: 'Wealth and dominion . . .'

1817

WEALTH and dominion fade into the mass
  Of the great sea of human right and wrong,
When once from our possession they must pass;
  But love, though misdirected, is among
The things which are immortal, and surpass   5
  All that frail stuff which will be—or which was.

Fragment: 'My thoughts arise and fade . . .'

1817

MY thoughts arise and fade in solitude,
  The verse that would invest them melts away
  Like moonlight in the beam of spreading day:
How beautiful they were, how firm they stood,
  Freckling the starry sky like woven pearl!   5

6 ⟨? dazed⟩ imagination] dize *apparently*, *correcting* dizzy imagination *above* [life is half created shadow] *E. 4*   7 The half created shadow—[then to tremble] *below* none turning *uncancelled*, *above* and clasping air *uncancelled* E. 4   8 [To find the form that] [dim] [then to grow] *above* [then to borrow] *above* [all the night] *E. 4*

'WEALTH AND DOMINION . . .'.   AUTOGRAPH: *Bod. MS. Shelley E. 4.*   TRANSCRIPT: *Bod. MS. Shelley adds. d. 7.*   PRINTED: *MWS, 1839/Hutch. 1904.*   DATE: *1839.* TEXT: *1904/1839/E. 4/d. 7.*
    1 and] and *above* or *uncancelled* E. 4   6 frail *edd.*] frail *below* [weak] *E. 4* or which *edd.*] or which *above* [is or] *followed by line beginning* [A Love] *E. 4*

'MY THOUGHTS ARISE . . .'.   AUTOGRAPH: *Bod. MS. Shelley adds. e. 16.*   PRINTED: *MWS, 1839/Hutch. 1904.*   DATE: *1839.*   TEXT: *1904/1839/e. 16.*
    Above the fragment [Why write I in my solitude / Why] *e. 16*   1–2 [The verse that would invest them is so frail] *e. 16*   3 in . . . day *edd.; changed from* [Clouds before the dawning day] *e. 16*   beam *e. 16*] heaven *edd.*   5 Freckling] Frekling *e. 16*   Flecking *edd.*

Fragment: A Hate-Song

1817

A HATER he came and sat by a ditch,
  And he took an old cracked lute;
And he sang a song which was more of a screech
  'Gainst a woman that was a brute.

Fragment: 'My head is wild with weeping . . .'

[2nd Version]

1817

MY head is wild with weeping for a grief
  Which is the shadow of a gentle mind.
I walk into the air yet no relief
  To seek, or haply if I sought to find—
It comes unsought . . . to wonder that a chief   5
  Among yon spirits should be cold and blind
And [

Ozymandias

1817

I MET a traveller from an antique land
Who said: 'Two vast and trunkless legs of stone
Stand in the desert . . . Near them, on the sand,
Half sunk, a shattered visage lies, whose frown,

A HATE-SONG. SOURCE: *Recollection of Hunt, related to Browning and by him to Rossetti. See n., p. 411.* PRINTED, DATE: *Ross. 1870/Hutch. 1904.* TEXT: *1904/1870.*

'MY HEAD IS WILD WITH WEEPING . . .', 2nd Version. AUTOGRAPH: *Bod. MSS. Shelley adds. e. 12, e. 19.* PRINTED: *Ross. 1870/Hutch. 1904.* TITLE, DATE: *See n., p. 411.* TEXT: *e. 12. Cf. nn., pp. 366 & 411.*
  2 mind. *1904, 1870*] mind *e. 12*   3 yet *e. 12*] but *1904, 1870*   5 comes *e. 12*] came *1904, 1870*   to *1904, 1870*] to *possibly* no *e. 12*   6 yon] men's *1904, 1870*   yon *apparently, followed by* mid *uncancelled e. 12*   7 And *possibly* As *e. 12 ; omitted in 1904, 1870*

OZYMANDIAS. AUTOGRAPH: *Bod. MS. Shelley E. 4.* PRINTED: *Hunt, in the* Examiner, *11 Jan. 1818, signed 'Glirastes' (see n.)/with Rosalind and Helen, PBS, 1819/Hutch. 1904.* DATE: *See n., p. 411.* TITLE: *1818/1819.* TEXT: *1904/1819/E. 4.*
  2 said: 'Two *Loc. 1911, Ross. 1870*] said: Two *other edd., E. 4*

And wrinkled lip, and sneer of cold command,   5
Tell that its sculptor well those passions read
Which yet survive, stamped on these lifeless things,
The hand that mocked them, and the heart that fed;
And on the pedestal these words appear:
"My name is Ozymandias, king of kings: 10
Look on my works, ye Mighty, and despair!"
Nothing beside remains. Round the decay
Of that colossal wreck, boundless and bare,
The lone and level sands stretch far away.'

[*Fragment of an earlier draft*]

THERE stands by Nile a single pedestal,
On which two trunkless legs of crumbling stone
Quiver through sultry mist; beneath the sand
Half sunk a shattered visage lies, whose frown
And wrinkled lips impatient of command   5
Betray some sculptor's art, who [

Fragment: 'Serene, in his unconquerable might . . .'

1817

SERENE, in his unconquerable might
Endured, the Almighty King, his steadfast throne
Encompassed unapproachably with power
And darkness and deep solitude and awe,

9 these words appear *edd.*] this legend clear *E. 4*   13 bare,] bare *edd. & E. 4*
14 away.' *Loc. 1911, Ross. 1870*] away. *other edd., E. 4*

OZYMANDIAS. Fr. of an earlier draft.   AUTOGRAPH: *Bod. MS. Shelley E. 4.*   PRINTED:
Loc. 1911.   TEXT: *1911/E. 4.*
    1–2 There . . . On *cancelled in E. 4*

'SERENE, IN HIS UNCONQUERABLE MIGHT . . . '.   AUTOGRAPH: *Bod. MS. Shelley E. 4.*
PRINTED: *Loc. 1903/Hutch. 1904/Loc. 1911.*   DATE: *See n., p. 412.*   TEXT: *1911/*
1904/1903/E. 4.
    1 Serene, *1911*] Serene *1904, 1903, E. 4*   2 Endured, *E. 4*] Endued, *1911,*
1903. See n., p. 412.

Stood like a black cloud on some aëry cliff 5
Embosoming its lightning. In his sight
Unnumbered glorious spirits trembling stood
Like slaves before their Lord; prostrate around
Heaven's multitudes hymned everlasting praise.

Fragment: 'Address to the Human Mind'

1817

Address to the human mind; representation of its being a perpetual flame.
Burning on the altars of Greece and Rome and Egypt. Gods its ministering
⟨? Powers⟩. Temples, Juggernaut, China ⟨? Sanctuary⟩. [*Shelley's synopsis.*]

THOU living light that in thy rainbow hues
Clothest this naked world; and over Sea
And Earth and Air, and all the shapes that be
    In peopled darkness of this wondrous world
The Spirit of thy glory dost diffuse 5
            truth   thou Vital Flame
Mysterious thought that in this mortal frame
Of things, with unextinguished lustre burnest
    Now pale and faint now high to Heaven upcurled
That eer as thou dost languish still returnest 10
    And ever

Before the   before the Pyramids

So soon as from the Earth formless and rude
One living step had chased drear Solitude
Thou wert, Thought; thy brightness ⟨? charmed the lids⟩ 15
Of the vast snake Eternity, who kept
The tree of good and evil.—

6 lightning. In] lightning—in *1911*   8 Lord;] Lord— *1911*
'ADDRESS TO THE HUMAN MIND'. AUTOGRAPH: *Bod. MS. Shelley E. 4.*   TITLE:
From Shelley's synopsis. See n., pp. 412–13.   PRINTED, DATE: *Loc. 1903/ Hutch. 1904.*
TEXT: *1904/1903/E. 4.*
    Shelley's synopsis. ⟨? Powers⟩/⟨? Sanctuary⟩ *cj. Loc. Two very doubtful words in E. 4;
the second possibly* something.   2 Clothest *edd.*] Clothest *above* Dost clothe *uncancelled
E. 4*   5 The . . . glory *underlined, possibly intending revision E. 4*   7 this *edd.*]
possibly the *E. 4*   9 *in the experience of Loc.* 'Shelley's most illegible line'
15 brightness *is not clear. It might be* light step *E. 4*   ⟨? charmed the lids⟩ *edd.;
replaces* [closed] [sealed] *in E. 4; 'might be* chained the lips' *Loc.*

Fragment: 'Soft pillows for the fiends . . .'

Probably 1817

soft pillows for the fiends
Of power to renovate their blighted pinions
For [

Fragment: 'Arise, sweet Mary . . .'

1817

ARISE, sweet Mary, rise
For the time is passing now,
My head is heavy, my limbs are weary
And it is no bliss that ⟨two or three illegible words⟩
And my way is [5

Fragment: 'Heigh-ho, wisdom and folly . . .'

1817

HEIGH-HO, wisdom and folly!
Heigh-ho, Edward and Molly!
He'll wear the willow and she'll wear the holly.
There's dear Mr. Mug going wild for our Dolly;
Let us follow him out to his ⟨? cave ? lake⟩ in the colly   5
And bother him out of his melancholy!

'SOFT PILLOWS FOR THE FIENDS . . .'.   AUTOGRAPH: *Bod. MS. Shelley E. 4.*   PRINTED: *Loc. 1903/I and P, 1927.*   DATE: *See n., p. 413.*   TEXT: *1927/E. 4.*
  1 pillows *very like* buttons *Loc.*   fiends *doubtful Loc.*

'ARISE, SWEET MARY . . .'.   AUTOGRAPH: *Bod. MS. Shelley E. 4.*   PRINTED: *1-2, Loc. 1903, 1911.*   UNPRINTED: *3-5.*   DATE: *See n., p. 413.*   TEXT: *1911/1903/ E. 4.*

'HEIGH-HO, WISDOM AND FOLLY . . .'.   AUTOGRAPH: *Bod. MS. Shelley E. 4.*   PRINTED: *Loc. 1911/I and P, 1927.*   DATE: *See n., p. 413.*   TEXT: *1927/1911/E. 4.*
  5 Let us *E. 4*] Let's *1927, 1911*   ⟨? cave ? lake⟩ *blank in 1927, 1911*

Translation: Epigram of Plato
cited in the Apologia of Apuleius

[*Anth. Pal.* vii. 669; *Ap. Apol.* x. 24.]

1st Version

1817

SWEET child, thou star of love and beauty bright,
Alone thou lookest on the midnight skies;
Oh! that my spirit were yon Heaven of light
To gaze upon thee with a thousand eyes.

EPIGRAM OF PLATO, 1st Version. AUTOGRAPH: *None traced.* TRANSCRIPTS: *a. MWS, SH II; b. MWS, Bod. MS. Shelley adds. d. 7.* DATE: *See n., p. 413.* PRINTED: *W. E. Peck,* Boston Herald, *21 Dec. 1927.* TITLE: *None in MSS.*/'Star of Love' *1927.* TEXT: *1927/SH II/d. 7.*

Fragments of 1817 which appear among the drafts for *Laon and Cythna* will be found among the Notes on that poem. See above, Contents, pp. viii–ix, and Introduction, pp. xvii–xviii.

NOTE BY MARY SHELLEY ON THE POEMS
OF 1817

THE very illness that oppressed, and the aspect of death which had approached so near Shelley, appears to have kindled to yet keener life the Spirit of Poetry in his heart. The restless thoughts kept awake by pain clothed themselves in verse. Much was composed during this year. The *Revolt of Islam*, written and printed, was a great effort—*Rosalind and Helen* was begun—and the fragments and poems I can trace to the same period, show how full of passion and reflection were his solitary hours.

In addition to such poems as have an intelligible aim and shape, many a stray idea and transitory emotion found imperfect and abrupt expression, and then again lost themselves in silence. As he never wandered without a book, and without implements of writing, I find many such in his manuscript books, that scarcely bear record; while some of them, broken and vague as they are, will appear valuable to those who love

Shelley's mind, and desire to trace its workings. Thus in the same book that addresses 'Constantia, Singing,' I find the lines:—

> My spirit like a charmed bark doth swim
> Upon the liquid waves of thy sweet singing . . .[1]

And the apostrophe to Music:

> No, Music, thou art not the God of Love,
> Unless Love feeds upon its own sweet self,
> Till it becomes all music murmurs of.[2]

In another fragment he calls it—

> The silver key of the fountain of tears . . .[3]

And then again this melancholy trace of the sad thronging thoughts, which were the well whence he drew the idea of Athanase, and express the restless, passion-fraught emotions of one whose sensibility, kindled to too intense a life, perpetually preyed upon itself:

> To thirst and find no fill—to wail and wander . . .[4]

In the next page I find a calmer sentiment, better fitted to sustain one whose whole being was love:

> Wealth and dominion fade into the mass
> Of the great sea of human right and wrong . . .[5]

In another book, which contains some passionate outbreaks with regard to the great injustice that he endured this year, the poet writes:

> My thoughts arise and fade in solitude,
> The verse that would invest them melts away . . .[6]

He had this year also projected a poem on the subject of Otho, inspired by the pages of Tacitus. I find one or two stanzas only, which were to open the subject: 'Thou wert not . . .' and 'I wrong thee not . . . '.[7]

I insert here also the fragment of a song, though I do not know the date when it was written,—but it was early:—

> TO——.
> Yet look on me—take not thine eyes away,
> Which feed upon the love within mine own . . .[8]

He projected also translating the Hymns of Homer; his version of several of the shorter ones remain, as well as that to Mercury, already published in the *Posthumous Poems*. His readings this year were chiefly Greek. Besides the Hymns of Homer and the *Iliad*, he read the Dramas of Æschylus and Sophocles, the *Symposium* of Plato, and Arrian's

---

[1] *Cf. above, p. 303.*   [2] *Cf. above, p. 304.*   [3] *Cf. above, p. 303.*
[4] *Cf. above, p. 317.*   [5] *Cf. above, p. 318.*   [6] *Cf. above, p. 318.*
[7] *Cf. above, p. 316.*   [8] *Cf. above, p. 6.*

Historia Indica. In Latin, Apuleius alone is named. In English, the Bible was his constant study; he read a great portion of it aloud in the evening. Among these evening readings, I find also mentioned the *Faerie Queene*, and other modern works, the production of his contemporaries, Coleridge, Wordsworth, Moore, and Byron.

His life was now spent more in thought than action—he had lost the eager spirit which believed it could achieve what it projected for the benefit of mankind. And yet in the converse of daily life Shelley was far from being a melancholy man. He was eloquent when philosophy, or politics, or taste, were the subjects of conversation. He was playful—and indulged in the wild spirit that mocked itself and others—not in bitterness, but in sport. The Author of *Nightmare Abbey* seized on some points of his character and some habits of his life when he painted Scythrop. He was not addicted to 'port or madeira,' but in youth he had read of 'Illuminati and Eleutherarchs,' and believed that he possessed the power of operating an immediate change in the minds of men and the state of society. These wild dreams had faded; sorrow and adversity had struck home; but he struggled with despondency as he did with physical pain. There are few who remember him sailing paper boats, and watching the navigation of his tiny craft with eagerness—or repeating with wild energy 'The Ancient Mariner' and Southey's 'Old Woman of Berkeley' —but those who do, will recollect that it was in such, and in the creations of his own fancy, when that was most daring and ideal, that he sheltered himself from the storms and disappointments, the pain and sorrow, that beset his life.

No words can express the anguish he felt when his elder children were torn from him. In his first resentment against the Chancellor, on the passing of the decree, he had written a curse, in which there breathes, besides haughty indignation, all the tenderness of a father's love, which could imagine and fondly dwell upon its loss and the consequences.[1]

At one time, while the question was still pending, the Chancellor had said some words that seemed to intimate that Shelley should not be permitted the care of any of his children, and for a moment he feared that our infant son would be torn from us. He did not hesitate to resolve, if such were menaced, to abandon country, fortune, everything, and to escape with his child; and I find some unfinished stanzas addressed to this son, whom afterwards we lost at Rome, written under the idea that we might suddenly be forced to cross the sea, so to preserve him. This poem, as well as the one previously quoted, were not written to exhibit the pangs of distress to the public; they were the spontaneous outbursts of a man who brooded over his wrongs and woes, and was impelled to shed the grace of his genius over the uncontrollable emotions of his heart. I ought

[1] *See above, p. 305, 'To the Lord Chancellor'.*

to observe that the fourth verse of this effusion is introduced in *Rosalind and Helen*.[1] When afterwards this child died at Rome, he wrote, *à propos* of the English burying-ground in that city: 'This spot is the repository of a sacred loss, of which the yearnings of a parent's heart are now prophetic; he is rendered immortal by love, as his memory is by death. My beloved child lies buried here. I envy death the body far less than the oppressors the minds of those whom they have torn from me. The one can only kill the body, the other crushes the affections.'

[1] *894–7.*

NOTES ON THE TEXT AND
CONTENT OF THE POEMS

SHORTER POEMS, 1814, 1815

p. 3, STANZA, WRITTEN AT BRACKNELL. 'I have written nothing but one stanza, which has no meaning, and that I have only written in thought . . . This is the vision of a delirious and distempered dream, which passes away at the cold clear light of morning. Its surpassing excellence and exquisite perfections have no more reality than the colour of an autumnal sunset. Adieu!' So Shelley wrote to Hogg on 16 March 1814 (Jones, *Letters*, i. 384). This was the time immediately preceding the rupture with Harriet. He was staying in the house of Mrs. Boinville, and the lines seem to be addressed either to her or to her daughter, Cornelia Turner.

p. 3, STANZAS.—APRIL, 1814. Forman and Hutchinson print this poem as six four-line stanzas. I have restored the three-stanza arrangement used by Shelley in the *Alastor* volume and followed by Mary Shelley. It was composed at Bracknell, and is supposed to be a self-exhortation at the moment of his departure from the Boinville household: cf. the preceding poem and note.

5: There seems some suggestion of a quarrel. Claire Clairmont asserted that Shelley had fallen in love with Cornelia Turner, Mrs. Boinville's daughter, that both ladies were indignant, and that relations were broken. Some have believed that trouble arose because the Boinville family were on Harriet's side.

8: *solitude*: Harriet was away from home in the latter part of April.

15: *or this world*: Both metre and sense would be complete without these words. Locock suggests that they were written in the margin of the manuscript as an alternative to 'thy soul', and wrongly put in by the printer.

22: In the letter to Hogg referred to in the note on the preceding poem Shelley wrote '. . . my heart sickens at the view of that necessity, which will quickly divide me from the delightful tranquillity of this happy home—for it has become my home.'

24: Locock quotes T. Constable's *Memoir of the Rev. C. A. Chastel de Boinville*, p. 365: '[Cornelia's] smile was as sunlight, and radiated the love of which it was the expression directly into the hearts of those who looked on her.' The libertarian connection is not uninteresting. Her father was an *émigré* and a friend of Lafayette; he died on the retreat from Moscow in 1812. Her assistance with Shelley's Italian studies had a considerable influence on his poetry. She lived till 1874, having moved much in Anglo-Italian circles and staunchly supported Risorgimento exiles.

p. 4, To Mary Wollstonecraft Godwin. *Date*: This is a considerable enigma. Mary Shelley assigned the poem to 1821, and headed it 'To——'. In *Relics of Shelley*, 1862, pp. 160–1, Garnett wrote thus: 'Much light has been recently thrown upon the feelings which actuated Shelley at this critical period [i.e. the period of his separation from Harriet] by an interesting and unexpected discovery made during the preparation of this volume. It appears that [this] poem, hitherto referred to the date of 1821, was, in fact, written in June 1814, and addressed to Mary . . .' I do not know the ground for Locock's statement that Mary believed the poem to concern Jane Williams. The proximity of the draft in e. 12 to drafts for *Epipsychidion* make a connection with Emilia Viviani more likely. Locock considers it curious that Mary should not recognize in 1824 a poem addressed to herself in 1814; I see no reason, however, to suppose that Shelley always showed her the vehicles of his feeling. One possibility is that the draft in e. 12 is a *redrafting*, from memory. When a situation produced the recurrence of an earlier feeling Shelley was liable to revert in this way to an earlier poem. The Emilia Viviani situation—cf. *Epipsychidion*, 267–8—had had several Platonic predecessors: I have discussed this in *Shelley at Work*, chs. 4 and 13, more specifically on pp. 230–2. With much hesitation I have decided to follow Forman, Locock, and Hutchinson in accepting Garnett's date of 1814. The legend that Garnett was somehow a 'coadjutor' of Lady Shelley's in falsifying documents and thrusting a 'Shelley legend' upon the world has been long ago exploded, and I cannot see why he should refer to a 'discovery' which did not exist. His reference may be to something since lost; possibly to something that may yet be rediscovered. Some slight support for my decision is afforded by the heading given to the poem in Mary Shelley's fair-copy book, d. 9, of which the mysterious cancellation has left the final letter, *y*, decipherable.

Text: The sources are a wild pencil draft, or redrafting, of Shelley's, and Mary Shelley's work in bringing out the latent meaning. Her work has four stages: transcript, *1824*, erratum slip, and *1839*. Since we do not have the poet's *ultima manus* the main witness to our text must be her editorial *ultima manus*, that is to say *1839*, though a re-examination of the draft will here and there reveal a point at which her work needs to be extended. The main problems, as so often with Shelley's drafts, are syntactical. What has happened is that, having written sentences with a 'thou . . .' construction, he has decided to prefer a 'you . . .' one; then, encountering obstacles from his rhyme-scheme, has left his adaptation incomplete. From *1824* to the erratum slip Mary aims to restore the workable 'thou . . .' in place of the unworkable 'you . . .' which Shelley had had to abandon. Not unnaturally she makes some slips, and these too call for her correction. Three lines (cf. Frontispiece) will illustrate the stages of textual progress: First, line 30:

a. As Shelley left it we have 'for you and me'.

b. Mary so transcribes the phrase in d. 9.

c. In *1824*, trying to complete Shelley's original thou-construction, started in line 2, she prints the ungrammatical 'for thou and me'.

d. In the erratum slip she prints 'for you and me', thereby correcting her own grammar but restoring Shelley's original confused construction which had appeared in *a* and *b*.

e. In *1839*[1] she forgets the erratum slip and reverts to 'for thou and me'.

f. In *1839*[2] she corrects both her own grammar and Shelley's confusion by printing 'for thee and me'.

Next, line 32:

a. As Shelley left it we have 'Nor can I'.

b. Mary correctly transcribes this in d. 9.

c. In *1824* she wrongly prints 'Nor I can'.

d. In the erratum slip she fails to pick up her error.

e. In *1839* she does so.

Then line 36:

a. As Shelley left it we have 'you feel'.

b. Mary transcribes this in d. 9.

c. In *1824* she tries to bring this into line with the original thou-construction and prints the ungrammatical 'thou feel'.

d. In the erratum slip she corrects her grammar but, unfortunately, emends the wrong word, thereby restoring Shelley's original, confused, construction which had appeared in *a* and *b*.

e. In *1839* she corrects both her mistake and Shelley's by printing 'thou feel'st'. It needs to be added here that, although I cannot see a trace of the 'st' in Shelley's rubbed pencil draft, a suggestion of this has been oddly brought out by the camera in my photostat copy.

Mary Shelley and the editors who succeeded her missed two further grammatical errors which I have now corrected: 'thou should', in line 14, and 'thou . . . requited', in line 16. A third solecism, 'thou appear', in line 32, cannot be corrected because it is tied up with the rhyme-scheme.

p. 6, To ——. *Date*: Mary Shelley printed this poem among her Notes on the Poems of 1817, but remarked: 'I do not know the date when it was written but it was early.' The Notebook in which Shelley's rough pencil-draft is found contains material mostly belonging to the second half of 1819, There can be no doubt that this draft was the source of Mary Shelley's text, the differences between *1839*[2] and *1911* being all due to problems of deciphering. Her comment, therefore, can only mean that she knew the draft to be a redrafting; such a re-drafting from memory as I have suggested in relation to the manuscript of the preceding poem. I follow Forman, Locock, and Hutchinson in interpreting 'early' as 1814. Some have suggested that it was addressed to Mary herself in June of that year; others connect it with Harriet. *Text*: Before *1911* the poem was printed without a break after line 9 and, since that line as customarily printed was a foot shorter, it was thought to be part of an incomplete sonnet. Forman's restoration of the alexandrine then showed that what we really have is a Spenserian stanza followed by the fragment of a second one.

12: *pityest*: For examples of grammatical solecisms which Mary Shelley failed to correct cf. nn. on the preceding poem. My correction was anticipated by Rossetti.

p. 7, MUTABILITY. *Date*: I follow editors in my dating, but am inclined to think that the mood fits 1814, being comparable to that of the 'Stanzas' printed by

Shelley as belonging to April of that year. The title is an echo of Spenser's Platonism. Shelley, no doubt, got it from his reading of *The Faerie Queene*, *VII*, *Two Cantos of Mutabilitie*: cf. Canto viii. 2:

> But stedfast rest of all things firmely stayd
> Upon the pillours of Eternity,
> That is contrayr to *Mutabilitie*:
> For, all that moueth, doth in *Change* delight . . .

Shelley is describing an experience in terms of the Heraclitean flux, which characterizes earthly and human experience generally, and contrasts with the permanence of the divine and ideal realm. In this poem he is concerned only with the lower realm; the contrast between the two was soon to be a common motif in his poetry. In the first line we have the Platonic image of life as a veil, which half reveals and half conceals the ideal world of permanence. This concept had appeared in *Queen Mab*, I. 181. See Rogers, *Shelley at Work*, ch. 8, 'The Veil, Mutability'. For the darkness–light imagery cf. also ibid., pp. 148–9.

p. 8, A SUMMER EVENING CHURCHYARD. Written during a ten-day boating expedition on which Shelley embarked about the end of August 1815 in company with Mary, Charles Clairmont, and Peacock. Cf. above, p. 17 n. 1.

p. 8, 'OH! THERE ARE SPIRITS OF THE AIR'. *Epigraph*: From Euripides, *Hippolytus*, 1144, 'With tears shall I endure an ill-starred fate'. *Date*: Notopoulos, *Platonism*, p. 194, considers that, since 'some plays of Euripides' are recorded in Shelley's reading for 1815, the poem should be ascribed to that year. *Title*: Editors have followed Shelley's 'To ——'. Mary says (see p. 17) that the poem was 'addressed in idea to Coleridge, whom he never knew'. A more likely view, generally accepted today, is that Shelley is addressing himself. This is consistent both with the epigraph and with the general idea of *Alastor*, which treats of the spirit of solitude as a spirit of evil. Such was Shelley's sense of loneliness and uncertainty at the time of his break with Harriet.

13–14: Cf. 'Stanzas.—April 1814', 23–4.

19–20: A Platonic realization of the inconstancy of the relative world. See, above, n. on 'Mutability'.

p. 10, TO WORDSWORTH. Shelley's attitude to Wordsworth was a mixed one. Medwin in his *Life* tells us that, in his early years, he considered Wordsworth's poetry 'too simple', and in 1814 he amused himself by enacting 'The Highland Boy' by sailing a washtub in a pool at the bottom of a garden; his amusement at the banality of some of Wordsworth's verse developed, in 1819, into the delightful parody 'Peter Bell the Third'. At the same time, as an admirer of Wordsworth's more inspired poetry, Shelley yielded to none. He had a natural affinity with Wordsworth's nature-poetry and with his Platonism, and the effects of this are noticeable not only in *Alastor*, with which this poem appeared, but in his poetry at large. During Shelley's stay in Switzerland, in 1816, the mountain scenery, as was not unnatural, set his mind and his verse moving along Wordsworthian lines which may be traced in the 'Hymn to Intellectual Beauty', 'Mont Blanc', and a good deal else that he wrote just then. They may be traced too in the Wordsworthian tone of many of the best passages in the third canto of *Childe Harold's Pilgrimage*, for, in Byron's phrase, Shelley had been heavily 'dosing' him with Wordsworth and had practically forced him to override his previous prejudices and to perceive Wordsworth's real greatness. It is not without significance that Shelley's draft of 'Mont Blanc' is written in his Swiss Notebook over a draft of the poem 'On Receiving a Celandine'; see p. 80 and n., p. 355. Wordsworth had recently published odes and sonnets glorifying the Battle of Waterloo and in the Celandine poem Shelley is sad that a deathless poet can stoop so low as to glorify bloodshed. The last few lines of this sonnet of 1814–15 are similar in feeling. Shelley's disgust at the way a former republican had sacrificed his independence out of venal motives is compared by Forman with Browning's treatment of his defection in 'The Lost Leader'.

p. 10, FEELINGS OF A REPUBLICAN, ETC. Shelley had lived through the era when the republican ideals of the eighteenth century had led to revolution, revolution to mob rule and anarchy, and then, from the chaos, to the power of a dictator whose tyranny invited comparison with that of the monarchical system against which eighteenth-century idealism had struggled. Welcomed widely by the victims of the older tyrannies as an apostle of French libertarian ideals, Napoleon had brought war, devastation, and a newer tyranny which had paralysed Europe for a generation and more. Perhaps the most significant thing about the poem is its title, which implies 'it is to *this* that republican ideals can lead'. Shelley was by no means the starry-eyed young revolutionary that he has been believed to be, both in his own time and later. It was because of his clear perception that the cycle of violence which begins with revolution must inevitably lead through anarchy to newer tyrannies that he preached moderation in *The Mask of Anarchy* and elsewhere. With his reactions in 1814 is to be compared Byron's 'Ode to Napoleon Bonaparte', written at the same time. A finer poem on the same subject is the neglected 'Lines written on the Death of Napoleon Bonaparte', of 1821. See Rogers, *Shelley at Work*, pp. 196–9, 280–1.

p. 11, TWO FRAGMENTS, ETC. These fragments, together with 'The Sunset', are the only known examples of Shelley's blank verse between *Queen Mab* and *Alastor*. I quote from White, *Shelley*, i. 702:

. . . The blank pages [in Claire Clairmont's journal, on which Shelley wrote out the lines] contain, in Shelley's handwriting, several scraps of Latin and Italian—chiefly the Latin Motto of *Alastor*, about half a dozen lines from the Paolo and Francesco episode in Dante's *Inferno*, and some half-obliterated lines in Latin . . . Since the lines centre on the subject of love and one is definitely connected with *Alastor* it might be possible to suppose that the idea of *Alastor* was germinating in Shelley's mind . . . in that case the notes and the English verses were probably written in the spring of 1815, before Claire's departure from the Shelley household.

TRANSLATIONS, 1814, 1815

p. 15, SONNET FROM DANTE. *Date*: usually ascribed to 1815. Probably among the fruits of Shelley's Italian studies with Cornelia Turner, daughter of Mrs. Boinville; see above, p. 327, nn. on 'Stanza, written at Bracknell' and 'Stanzas.— April, 1814'. The Italian original was quoted by Shelley in one of his letters to Emilia Viviani which preceded the writing of *Epipsychidion*: see Rogers, *Shelley at Work*, pp. 238–40 and 341–2.

5 *So*: preferred here, since the Italian is 'sì che'.

10: Since 'Bice' is but a shortened form of the name 'Beatrice', who was Dante's 'gentle love', the line makes no sense as it stands. The name is a mistake in the text used by Shelley: 'Lagia' is found in the better texts.

p. 16, SONNET FROM CAVALCANTI. *Date/Text*: see preceding n. As Forman remarks, it seems odd that Shelley should not have printed this sonnet in his *1816* volume as a companion piece to the preceding one. Garnett drew Forman's attention to the similarity between Cavalcanti's mood of disillusionment and the mood of Shelley's sonnet to Wordsworth: see above, p. 10. Forman explains that he gave a facsimile of the manuscript because it is 'curiously punctuated': he wanted to furnish a specimen of Shelley's finished 'copy' and to show, at the same time, how far it had been necessary to depart from the copy. Shelley's 'curious' punctuation is, in fact typical. It is limited to the following stops:

> line 1 quest,
> „ 5 lost.
> „ 6 men.
> „ 10 inspire.
> „ 11 wert.
> „ 12 wont.
> „ 13 words.
> „ 14 integrity.

p. 21, THE DAEMON OF THE WORLD

Text: The two copies of *Queen Mab* bearing the emendations with which Shelley condensed the poem and presented it in a new form as 'The Daemon of the World' are, of course, the equivalent of manuscripts. They are quite different in character. BM^b contains only the changes made in Cantos I and II. Pf. contains changes in Cantos I, II, IV, V, VI, VIII, and IX. The revisions in Pf. have, more or less, the character of a draft, being full of cancellations, interlineations, and renumbering of sections; the insertions in BM^b are neat, uncancelled, and obviously a fair copy made from some earlier draft. That it was not copied from Pf. is evident from a number of divergences; e.g. it contains passages, some of them quite long, which do not appear in Pf. I have been able to study the original of BM^b and to make an analysis of it by means of photostats. The results have been collated with the text and annotation of Pf. provided by Mr. Cameron in *Shelley and his Circle*, iv. 487–568, and I have made use too of the admirable collation of both BM^b and Pf. made by Forman, when he himself owned the latter (see Vol. I, p. xliii n., for its designation in that volume as 'Fn.') and the former was in the possession of Wise. Two copies of the *Alastor* volume are known to have borne annotations made by Shelley to the text of 'The Daemon'. One of these is unlocated, though the few changes, mentioned by Ingpen, were known to Forman, from whom they have been included in my collation. The second copy, now in the Pforzheimer Library, is not yet available for study. The text of 'The Daemon' as printed by Shelley with *Alastor* corresponds to that of BM^b. The only passage peculiar to Pf. printed by Shelley is one from *Queen Mab* VI (72–102), to which he gave the title 'Superstition'. In the last line:

> Converging, thou didst bend and called it God

the last five words are changed to

> give it name and form

and a final line has been added:

> Intelligence and unity and power.

Forman, first in a private printing, and later in his 1876 edition, published, as 'Part II' of 'The Daemon of the World', the revised passages from Pf. of which Shelley did not make use: that is to say the passages adapted from Cantos VIII and IX of *Queen Mab*—the changes made in Cantos IV and V being but slight ones, he relegated them to his textual footnotes. Mr. Cameron is anxious to show that this was an error, and that, instead of treating the passages from Cantos VIII and IX as a second part to the revised poem, we should regard them, together with the rest of the material in Pf., as a second version of *Queen Mab*, and give it the title which Shelley wrote on the front endpaper of the volume, 'The Queen of the Universe'. I must confess that I regard this as having a good deal less than academic interest. Furthermore, Mr. Cameron's own evidence is against him. Forman's 'contention', he says (*Shelley and his Circle*, iv. 501), 'is supported only by one fact: the revisions in Cantos I and II [in the Pf. copy] do not call the presiding spirit a *Daemon* in the passages in which it is so called in the British Museum copy, but a *Queen* . . . whereas in the revisions of Cantos VIII and IX the spirit is referred to as a *Daemon*'. To me, as to Forman, no other fact seems necessary—unless it is the two facts produced by Mr. Cameron himself, namely that ink, pen-pressure, etc., show that there is unlikely to have been any time-lapse between the penning of the early and later sections of the Pf. corrections, and that above the Canto-numbering 'VIII' Shelley has written 'Second Part'. All this would seem to show that, as he revised and composed in Pf., the concept of 'The Queen of the Universe' gave place in his mind to that of 'The Daemon of the World'—a differentiation (see below) most significant of the way in which the evolution of his mind from Godwinism towards Platonism, half-unconscious in *Queen Mab*, was deliberately emphasized in the new version in which he sought to repair his immaturities. Since what Shelley heads 'Second Part' follows logically upon the Daemon-part, as copied out in BM^b and subsequently printed by him, rather than upon the 'Queen of the Universe'-part of Pf., Forman's ascription must, surely, be sound. We do not need, I think, to ask why Shelley left so much work unprinted; it could be simply that, like any good literary artist, he wanted to relate the proportions of his poem to the proportions of his volume.

In Part I, since BM^b corresponds so closely to the text printed by Shelley with *Alastor* in 1816, it has the authority of a manuscript fair copy, and I have treated it as such. Pf., in Part I, must be treated as a draft: I have given its readings only where they differ from BM^b (see Introduction, pp. xvi–xvii). In Part II Pf. has the authority of a manuscript fair copy.

Of great textual interest are the illustrations afforded by Shelley's labours in the rehandling of *Queen Mab* of his confession to Stockdale in 1810 (Jones, *Letters*, i. 20, see Vol. I, Intr. § 1) that he was 'by no means a good hand at correction'. As printed in 1813, *Queen Mab*, VIII. 232–4 reads

> Whilst each unfettered o'er the earth extend
> Their all-subduing energies, and wield
> The sceptre of a vast dominion there;

—a triple syntactical solecism which escaped not only Shelley himself but Mary Shelley and the successive editors who have corrected other passages of the sort. When adapting the lines for *The Daemon of the World*, 465–7, Shelley substitutes 'mind' for 'each', and makes both 'extend' and 'wield' singular by adding the *s* which they ought to have had in the first place; he forgets, however, to change the 'Their' to 'Its'. Forman, who on occasions could piously accept a solecism or two, very properly makes the necessary change. Similarly with lines 497, 499 of 'The Daemon': in his adaptation from *Queen Mab*, IX. 126–9, Shelley forgot to complete his tense-changes and printed 'Pealed' and 'were'; then, in line 507 he prints 'its wall', not noticing that in his substitution of a plural subject for the singular one of *Queen Mab*, IX. 108 he ought to have changed 'its' to 'their'. (See Forman, 1876, iii. 374–5.) Another incomplete tense-changing appears in line 480, where in adapting *Queen Mab*, IX. 57–70 he has printed 'Has', instead of 'Had'. This, though missed by Forman and Hutchinson, was picked up by Locock: see *1911*, i. 548. In 422–3 Shelley takes the opportunity of getting rid of the unwanted rhymes 'late' . . . 'create' which had crept into *Queen Mab*, VIII. 190–1; however in 500–1 he allows a new rhyme 'more' . . . 'war' to intrude.

In lines 522–3 Shelley printed 'the past / Fades from our charmèd sight'. But, in accordance with the argument of the poem, the past was finished with in Part I, as Locock points out, and from lines 316–19 it is clear that Part II is concerned entirely with the future. In view of Shelley's other slips I feel justified in agreeing with Locock that 'past' is another unadapted word and ought to be adapted to 'future'.

Epigraph: In Lucan's context the meaning is 'Nor may the prophetess divulge as much as she knows; all time comes crowding upon her, and so many centuries weigh upon her unhappy breast.' Appius Claudius Pulcher consults the Delphic Oracle before deciding to take up arms on behalf of Pompey against Caesar; he gets the usual ambiguous reply and makes a decision which leads to his death. In the lines that follow, Lucan queries the divine purpose behind oracles. It may be that Shelley's quotation implies no more than an expression of agnosticism, such as underlies the epigraphs he chose for *Queen Mab*. But since *vates* can mean 'bard' as well as 'prophet/prophetess' he may be projecting the uncertainty and ambiguity of the Delphic Oracle on to himself, and implying, perhaps, that since he wrote *Queen Mab* he is just a little less cocksure than he then was of the validity of what he then believed and disbelieved.

Content: The 'Daemon' of the title is Love, conceived of by Plato as an intermediary spirit between gods and men; cf. *Symposium*, 203a, as translated by Shelley:

The divine nature cannot immediately communicate with what is human, but all that intercourse and converse which is conceded by the Gods to men, both whilst they sleep and when they wake, subsists through the intervention of Love; and he who is wise in the science of this intercourse is supremely happy, and participates in the daemoniacal nature; [ὁ μὲν περὶ τὰ τοιαῦτα σοφὸς δαιμόνιος ἀνήρ] whilst he who is wise in any other science or art, remains a mere ordinary slave.

It is usually agreed that Shelley's rehandling of *Queen Mab* does not constitute a particularly successful poem. But we should, I think, consider not so much his achievement as the significance of what he was trying to do. As Mary Shelley rightly observed, 'the alterations his opinions underwent ought to be recorded, for they form his history'. *Queen Mab* (see Vol. I, nn.) marks not a point but a phase in his development; a phase in which he passed from the cold, unrelieved gloom of the Godwinian doctrine of Necessity to the Platonic concept of Love as a power in the Universe. The concept of the 'Daemon of the World' is in sharp contrast to the feeling of '*Écrasez l'infâme*' in which he embarked upon *Queen Mab*; here, indeed, is a record of 'the alterations his opinions underwent'. And the poem needs to be considered too in relation to its place in the *1816* volume. Platonic daemons were many: some of them benevolent, among whom Love was the most powerful, but others were malignant, and it was sometimes difficult to know which kind was possessing you: sometimes what appeared to be a good δαίμων might prove to be one of the evil ones, κακοδαίμονες—such were 'the furies of an irresistible passion' which pursued the Poet in *Alastor*, and the furies of an unhappy mind which were pursuing Shelley at the time when he moved to Mary from Harriet. In a sense, therefore, the one poem is an offset to the other—Shelley is suffering the torments of passion in his own life, but recording still his faith in Love as a force in the Universe.

100: The Snake can be one of the most puzzling of Shelley's symbols, because of its Old Testament associations with the conception of Evil. Shelley's reference, however, is to the δράκων οὐρυβόρος, the tail-eating serpent whose figure signifies Eternity because it is without beginning or end.

Its origins are very early and it is prominent in the alchemical writings of Hermes Trismegistus, the Egyptian Thoth, from whom, it was believed, all Greek philosophy was derived: in Hermetic literature it became a symbol of the Platonic formula ἕν τὸ πᾶν which makes its appearance in *Adonais*—'The One remains, the many change and pass'; it was among the many Neoplatonic notions which were embodied in this literature. Shelley is thought to have met it in such works as Volney's *Les Ruines* and Lord Monboddo's *Of the Origin and Progress of Language*. 'The subject which he loved best to dwell on', says Mary Shelley apropos of *Prometheus Unbound*, 'was the image of One warring with the Evil Principle', and this subject indeed is fundamental in the poem: more than once the Snake appears as the representative of the One. As such it represents also the principle of the Good; this happens notably in the first canto of *Laon and Cythna* where Evil, correspondingly, is represented by its adversary the Eagle, both daemons of the Shelleyan mid-space.

For a detailed bibliography of the symbol see Notopoulos, *Platonism*, 186–8, from which this note is, in the main borrowed, though I cannot wholly agree with my late friend's identification of the Eagle in *Laon and Cythna* with the principle of Evil.

102: Means 'All of love that inspires thy voice . . .' A Latin genitive of the type of *Surgit amari aliquid*. Cf. *Alastor*, 72, 112, and there are instances in *Queen Mab*.

214: *dome*: cf. 224; this with 'mazy motion' (244) suggests 'Kubla Khan', though in 1812 Shelley could not have read it. For the dome-image see Rogers, *Shelley at Work*, ch. 7.

292: *reality*: realization. Locock comments that this part of the poem may be regarded as a first study for the climax of *Prometheus Unbound*, III.

350 ff.: Shelley has dropped into an eighteenth-century style, reminiscent of Pope.

p. 43, ALASTOR

Title: Shelley asked the advice of Peacock, who tells us in his *Memoirs of Shelley*:

I proposed that which he adopted: *Alastor; or, the Spirit of Solitude*. The Greek word Ἀλάστωρ is an evil genius, κακοδαίμων; though the sense of the two words is somewhat different as in the φανεὶς Ἀλάστωρ ἢ κακὸς δαίμων ποθέν of Aeschylus. The poem treated the spirit of solitude as a spirit of evil. I mention the true meaning of the word because many have supposed *Alastor* to be the name of the hero of the poem.

Text: As will be seen from my collation, the present text is the combined work of several hands. Shelley's *editio princeps*, in addition to some of the usual deficiencies in punctuation, contains one probable and one certain misprint. In line 219 I have followed Hutchinson in printing 'Conducts' in place of Shelley's 'Conduct' which had been favoured by all editors except Rossetti. There has been much talk of the 'Shelleyan subjunctive': analogous instances have been sought in *Laon and Cythna*, 2269 and 3025, and *Epipsychidion*, 100. My own view is that on such occasions Shelley has not intended any such linguistic anomaly but has simply allowed grammatical logic to be carried away by the sound of words. Where such awkwardness can be corrected it is, surely, pure pedantry to preserve it. Hutchinson makes two good points in favour of his correction: first that the final *s* is often, as he says, 'a vanishing quantity' in Shelley's manuscripts and, secondly, that the compositor's eye may have been misled by the 'Conduct' in line 212 above. Possibly some such mistake, either on the part of the compositor or in Shelley's own copying from his draft, may explain the word 'roots' in line 530: either this or the 'roots' in the following line *must* be wrong. Rossetti, at the suggestion of James Thomson, printed 'trunks'. Hutchinson suggested 'stumps' or 'stems', but did not emend the word. I have adopted his first suggestion. In *1824* errors crept into lines 62, 79, 115, 196, 207, 262, 274, 424, 432, 485, and 712. All but three was corrected by Mary Shelley in *1839*[1] or *1839*[2]. My impression is that she intelligently corrected what was obviously wrong but lacked a copy of *1816* from which she could have mechanically corrected the other errors: for instance her 'rippling' (485) is an intelligent conjecture to replace the obviously erroneous 'reaping' of *1824* but, had she possessed *1816*, she would have seen that Shelley's word was 'leaping'. This, together with her errors in 424 and 712, was corrected by Forman in *1876*. Unfortunately, in *1839*, new errors crept into lines 2, 60, 65 (*1839*[2]), 161 (*1839*[2]), 181, 327, and 556. It is a little difficult to see why, if she was without a copy of *1816*, she did not check with *1824*. It may be that, having discovered some of its previous errors, she began to distrust it and used her brains in an intelligent but unsuccessful conjecture: this would explain 'have' (2), which has a Shelleyan sound, 'Himself'(161), and the intelligent, but wrongly interpretative, comma in 'Silence too,' (65). The other four errors of *1839* could be seen as normal misprints which any author might fail to pick up. All these seven mistakes, fortunately, were picked up by Forman in *1876*, and I print Hutchinson's inheritance of his work. Locock, in *1911*, advanced, at several points, the punctuation both of Shelley and his editors: I have gladly adopted, as I am sure Shelley would have done, his adjustments in lines 446, 476, 490, 499, 564, 614, 641, 687. My own adjustments are noted in the commentary.

Content:

Introduction: We should compare Mary Shelley's comment (see her Note, p. 65) that 'none of Shelley's poems is more characteristic than this'. It does not, I think, exactly convey what she meant. What she probably did mean was that, by expressing 'the Poet's' quest for a loved one, the 'prototype of his conception', *Alastor* is itself the prototype of much poetry that was to follow. *Epipsychidion* is the culmination. Its 'Advertisement' presents Shelley's feelings, no less transparently than this Introduction, as those of a 'Writer [who] died at Florence'. For 'the furies of an irresistible passion' cf. above, pp. 334–5, where δαίμονες and κακοδαίμονες are discussed. The poem is a haunted one, and belongs to the time when Shelley was divided between Harriet and Mary. The fourth sentence is a reminder of the current influence upon Shelley of Wordsworth and Coleridge: it may be traced both in the poem itself and in the poems that accompanied it in the *1816* volume. The quotation is from Wordsworth, *The Excursion*, I. 500–2; I have corrected two small slips.

Epigraph: Shelley had used this quotation before, in his 'Advertisement' to the Mary poems written out in the Esdaile Notebook. The meaning is 'I was not yet in love and wanted to be in love: I was seeking something to love, liking [the idea of] loving'. It well sums up his quest for 'a prototype of his conception' and succinctly expresses the natural Platonism found in many people. See Vol. I, p. 369, n. on p. 139.

1–49: The invocation is Wordsworthian in feeling and diction; cf., more particularly, the borrowed phrases in lines 3 and 26.

18–23: Shelley makes use of Plato's favourite image of shadow versus original; see Rogers, *Shelley at Work*, pp. 148–9. For his development of this symbolism see below, pp. 344–5, nn. on the 'Hymn to Intellectual Beauty'; lines 23–9 anticipate lines 49–60 of that poem.

45–9: Locock compares ll. 83 ff. of the extract from *The Recluse* given in Wordsworth's 1814 edition of *The Excursion*. Cf. also 'Peter Bell the Third', V. VII–VIII.

67–75: The nature of infancy is conceived here in a Wordsworthian Neo-platonism; for Wordsworth, Plato, and Shelley see Notopoulos, *Platonism*, pp. 162–7. The education in the 'good and lovely' of divine philosophy is autobiographical: Shelley is endowing his Poet with the fruits of his own reading in Plato and other philosophers.

72: For this classicism cf. above, p. 336, n. on 'The Daemon of the World', 102.

109–17: Cf. Erasmus Darwin, *Temple of Nature*, III. 223, 231–4.

119: The Zodiac of the temple of Denderah, in Upper Egypt, is alluded to in Volney's *Les Ruines*, a book much studied by Shelley. Mythological figures are arranged, in Zodiac fashion, around the ceiling of its portico. The Zodiac was removed to Paris in 1822 and is now in the Bibliothèque nationale.

151: As an image for something dividing the seen from the unseen, the known from the unknown, the Veil suggests itself quite naturally to poets. For Shelley it is almost always a profoundly Platonic symbol; see Rogers, *Shelley at Work*, ch. 8, where this is discussed in detail. The natural Platonism of Shelley's own soul manifested itself in a continuous search in this earth for a physical counterpart of an ideal beauty. The sphere in which ideal beauty manifested itself for him is (1) nature, which is a veil of ideal beauty, a realm in which 'some spirit of great intelligence and power' invests the visible world with beauty and (2) woman, who is for the poet the prototype on earth of his own soul, a 'veilèd maid'. I quote Notopoulos, *Platonism*, p. 190:

> It is important to realize the significant and basic differences between Shelley's and Plato's natural Platonism. Shelley's natural Platonism is determined by his nature, temperament, and experiences. Whereas Plato seeks a completely intellectualized and unsensualized idea, Shelley seeks a 'veiled maid' who incarnates Ideal Beauty. The symbolic incarnation of ideal love and beauty in the form of beautiful women in contrast to Plato's completely intellectual otherworldliness is the identity-in-difference between Plato and Shelley. Our poet is not a dialectician, but a poet who, even though he searches for truth and 'the fountain of divine philosophy,' is always in love with earthly forms which he, to his sorrow, often confuses with the ideal; he follows the Platonic gleam in his own romantic and image-clinging way. Shelley's expression of Platonism is the poet's way, which Milton has described as

> > what surmounts the reach
> > Of human sense, I shall delineate so,
> > By lik'ning spiritual to corporal forms
> > As may express them best . . .
> > (*Paradise Lost*, V, 571-574)

The notion of a 'veilèd maid' is inherent in the epigraph from St. Augustine: see above. And cf. line 176.

154: *its music long*: I take 'long' as an adverb. Locock thinks that it might possibly be an adjective, sc. 'long drawn out'.

159: *divine*: For the poetical accentuation of the first syllable cf. *Epipsychidion*, 135, where both accents are used:

A divine presence, in a place divine.

210: Woodberry compares Aeschylus, *Agamemnon*, 420–6. One might also compare the line from Sophocles, *Oedipus Tyrannus*, 67, by which Shelley was so fascinated:

Πολλὰς δ'ὁδοὺς ἐλθόντα φροντίδος πλάνοις

('Having come by many ways in the wanderings of careful thought'). See Mary Shelley's Note on *Prometheus Unbound*, and Rogers, *Shelley at Work*, pp. 15–16.

211–13: Cf. Plato, *Apology*, 40 c–41 c. For Shelley the relation between death and sleep was full of Platonic significance and the Dream is a symbol, like the Veil, for something which lies between the world of mutability and the world of reality, and represents the problem of which is which. The most famous use of this symbol is in *Adonais*, XXXIX. The symbol is discussed in detail in Rogers, *Shelley at Work*, ch. 10.

227: Fights between a serpent and an eagle, or some other powerful bird, are not infrequent in Shelley's poetry; see line 325. Cf. also *Laon and Cythna*, 190 ff., *Prometheus Unbound*, III. i. 72, *Hellas*, 308. The serpent is usually symbolical of the good. See above, pp. 335–6 n. on 'The Daemon of the World', 100.

311: The idea of the underground voyage in a little boat is thought to derive from Southey, *Thalaba*, XI. 31 ff. In his own life Shelley delighted in boats. In his poetry he delights in spiritual vehicles—usually a small boat, but often a space-ship: the distinction is unimportant. They symbolize the freedom of the human soul to escape from the world of mutable things (including tyranny, ignorance, and all human miseries) towards the ideal realm of eternal values—truth, beauty, goodness, liberty. For boats cf. *Laon and Cythna*, 4729 ff., the conclusion of *Prometheus Unbound*, II, and *Adonais*, 487–95. For space-ships cf. *Queen Mab*, I. 187, 'To Constantia, Singing', III, where the poet himself becomes a kind of aircraft, and the Sonnet from Dante, translated by Shelley, of which he made use in his Platonic wooing of Emilia Viviani: see nn. on this, above, p. 15. The Boat symbol is discussed at length in Rogers, *Shelley at Work*, ch. 6.

337–9: Cf. 'A Summer Evening Churchyard', 3–5, p. 7, above.

374–5: Cf. Coleridge, 'Kubla Khan', so frequently echoed in Shelley's poetry, and Southey, *Thalaba*, VII. 6 ff.

382: *alternating*: sc. 'greater and lesser succeeding one another', *The Shelley Concordance*.

398: *expanded*: used, as Locock notices, proleptically; so too with 'far' in line 402.

420–5: Whether through his own miscopyings or for some other reason Shelley is not wholly in control of the syntactical flow. I follow Locock in adding a comma after 'rocks' in line 424, which seems to help a little. I find, however, difficulty in believing, as he does, that 'its' in the next line refers to the 'torrent', back in line 402. Surely it must refer either to the 'forest' in 421 or to the 'vale' in 423, either of which could be said, poetically, to 'moan'.

455: *Silence and Twilight here*: Locock places the comma after 'Twilight', on the ground that, otherwise, 'here' is tautological with 'Through the dell'. But 'Here, through the dell' is a perfectly normal expression, and all Shelley has done is to split it up and displace the first word—used, anyhow, not repetitively, but for emphasis.

502–14: I quote Notopoulos, *Platonism*, p. 194:

Grabo (*The Magic Plant* [Chapel Hill, N.C., 1930], pp. 176–8) sees in the boat (see ll. 299 ff.) and stream Neoplatonic symbols of the soul and its voyage through life. That Shelley was conscious of any Neoplatonic symbolism in these lines seems doubtful. W. B. Yeats in his study of Shelley's symbolism has pointed out that the symbol of the stream was inspired by Shelley's sailing on rivers and streams in an open boat. In his preface to *Laon and Cythna* Shelley lists among the things that helped to make him a poet sailing down mighty rivers and streams. Shelley was a natural Platonic symbolist, and one can even go so far as to read in these lines an analogous expression of the Neoplatonic relation of the microcosm and macrocosm. A simpler expression of the same thought appears in *Adonais*, line 370: 'He is made one with Nature,' where a portion of the Eternal goes back to its ultimate source, even as in Plotinus's philosophy of emanation. . . . For the boat and stream as a symbol, see W. B. Yeats, *Ideas of Good and Evil* (London, 1903), pages 115 ff.; A. T. Strong, *Three Studies in Shelley* (Oxford, 1921), pages 89–105; G. Wilson Knight, *The Starlit Dome* (London, 1941), pages 186–7, 228–30.

543–50: A much-disputed passage. Here again Shelley has allowed his syntax to get a little out of hand: we cannot know whether it was he or his printer who failed to interpret the intentions revealed, in so far as they were revealed, by his manuscript, because this has not survived. I think, however, that the general syntactical pattern is this: 'Rocks rose, which lifted etc., and, its precipice [i.e. the dell's precipice] obscuring the ravine [Latin and Greek absolute construction], disclosed, above, black gulfs etc.'

551: For the accent on the first syllable cf. n., above, on 159.

583–6: Shelley seems to echo this in *Laon and Cythna*, 2578 ff.

608: *Danger's grim playmates*: cf. Shelley's Preface to *Laon and Cythna*, § 6, sixth sentence.

610: *sightless*: sc. 'invisible'. Cf. 'valueless' (= priceless), *Prometheus Unbound*, IV. 281, and the similar use of 'sightless' in Wordsworth, *The Excursion*, IV. 797.

613: *devastating*: for the shortening of the penultimate syllable by Shelley, and by other poets, Locock compares

alternăting	vibrăted	alligătors
penetrăted	congregăted	contemplăting (common
radiăted	animăted	in Wordsworth)
satiăted	illustrăting	inculcăted
emulăting	unexpiăted	prostrăted.

650: *still as*: i.e. 'as still as': the 'still', caught up by the repeated 'still' in 653.

671: Locock quotes Stopford Brooke's paraphrase: 'the lute is still, the stream is dark and dry, the dream is unremembered.'

677: *one living man*: Ahasuerus, the Wandering Jew, a character who held a great attraction for Shelley. Cf. his juvenile poem, *The Wandering Jew*, Vol. I, pp. 183–228. Ahasuerus appears in *Queen Mab* and in *Hellas*.

680: The broken rhythm, as has been more than once noted, is in apt relationship to the broken life of the Wandering Jew.

682: *visioned*: sc. 'peopled with visions'. Cf. 'visioned bowers' in 'Hymn to Intellectual Beauty', 65. Shelley uses the word in two other senses: 'seen in visions' and 'inspired with visions'. Cf. also *Queen Mab*, I. 68.

713: '*deep for tears*': Shelley's quotation marks acknowledge yet another echo from Wordsworth: the last line of the 'Immortality Ode'.

MISCELLANEOUS SHORTER POEMS AND FRAGMENTS
1816

p. 69, THE SUNSET. *Date/Text*: Mary Shelley says in her Note (see p. 94) that the poem was written at Bishopsgate, in the spring of 1816. Those who have not penetrated into Shelley's habits might well be puzzled by the fact that the e. 12 manuscript, clearly a draft, and a much laboured one, occurs among drafts for *Epipsychidion*. But this is, no less clearly, an example of Shelley's tendency to redraft a poem from memory when some situation produced a recurrence of the feeling that had evoked it. The Platonic symbolism is closely akin to that in which he was thinking and writing about Emilia Viviani in 1821. The editors of the Julian edition printed the redrafting as a 'correction' of the printed version based on the original draft. Since both versions were known to Mary, as well, it would seem, as the circumstances of composition, I have no hesitation in preferring the first one; the points of difference are given in my collation. This is how he worked, trying to remember his old poem:

At the top of the first page of the e. 12 draft he has drafted the fragment 'Dear home . . .' (see p. 86). It ends with the half-line

I visit thee

A little further down the page 'The Sunset' begins:

There was [a *omitted*] youth on whom

This does not please Shelley, and he builds up, above it, three lines of corrections which overlap the half-line of the abandoned fragment giving this effect:

late was one
[I visit thee] there [was a youth]

But for a variation in penmanship, it would be easy to think that the two poems were one. To make things a little more complicated he has not only cancelled, specifically, the concluding half-line of the fragment, but cancelled the whole of it with oblique pen-strokes. Then, underneath the point where the two poems collide, he writes

I had a friend within whose subtle being

Subsequently he cancels the first four words. The point of collision now looks like this:

[I visit thee] there late was one
[I had a friend] within whose subtle being

Here, with the uncancelled words, Shelley has recaptured the first line of his earlier drafting. It is, of course, identical with the line, derived from that earlier drafting, that Mary Shelley printed. The Julian editors did not discover this, because they failed to notice the cancellation of 'I had a friend'.

The restoration of line 37, unaccountably dropped by Mary Shelley and by subsequent editors from Hunt's text, is to the credit of Hutchinson. In line 49 I have introduced one small change. My 'a', in place of 'or', is conjectural, but it is based on three points, (1) that 'drop' as a verb has an inferior sense, (2) that e. 12 shows that Shelley did not intend a verb, (3) that since, in Shelley's handwriting, as in that of many other people, 'or' and 'a' are frequently indistinguishable, he may well have written 'a', or what was intended for it, in the missing manuscript.

Content: The basic idea of the poem is inherent in the title. The antithesis between sunshine and sunset is the Platonic antithesis between light and darkness, symbolizing the two worlds of reality and mutability, real values and false values, and the death of the youth is a variant on the Dream of Life symbolism and the Veil: see nn. on *Alastor*, above. Cf. also Rogers, *Shelley at Work*, pp. 148–9. Forman was much concerned about line 22. He found this nonsensical and suggested reading 'sunrise' in place of 'sun'. But if the symbolism is understood, his difficulty, I think, disappears. The meaning is still clearer if we regard 'never' as having an emphatic rather than a literally temporal sense; as in the sentence 'I never locked the door', which implies 'how remiss of me not to have done so!' The point of the line is the awakening of the youth, through love, to reality, symbolized by light—his physical death has no reality; cf. much of the imagery of *Adonais*. The cancelled line drafted in e. 12 to succeed line 8 expresses the basic idea of *Epipsychidion*, and is evidence in itself of why Shelley redrafted his poem in 1821. The name 'Isabel', in line 21, is a link with 1816, when Isabel Baxter, one of Mary Shelley's closest friends, had been forbidden to communicate with her because of her association with Shelley, and she had been deeply grieved. It was in connection with this incident that Shelley wrote the 'eclogue' entitled *Rosalind and Helen*, in the manuscript of which, as here in e. 12, the name 'Rosalind' is a substitution for the original 'Isabel'.

p. 71, HYMN TO INTELLECTUAL BEAUTY. *Text*: The work, successively, of Shelley, his printers, and his editors. Verbally Hutchinson's text is satisfactory, apart from the inherited misprint 'birds', in line 58, which I have emended from the correction in SH II. Both e. 16 and SH II are useful not so much by reason of any new contributions they can now make to the text of the poem, but for the evidence they afford about Shelley's textual habits and the editorial treatment they demand. The manuscript is an intermediate copy of some sort, with cancellations and changes here and there. Stanza IV is missing from the Notebook, and Stanzas VI and VII are in reverse order. It would seem that, in his first draft, his inspiration, as often happened, worked so fast that certain details had to be omitted for the moment: the blank spaces which he left in his draft are blank in this copy, awaiting the time when he would fill them with the right word or phrase. Another curiosity is the way he has underlined certain words. To the uninitiated it might seem that he intended italics, but here, as in other manuscripts, this merely indicates his intention to make some subsequent change. The following are some of the points which emerge:

2: 'Walks', underlined in e. 16, is duly improved in print to 'Floats'.

Shelley has 'amongst' in e. 16, prints this in *1817*, does not change it in SH II, when correcting *1817*, but in *1819* gets rid of an unnecessary sibilant by printing 'among'.

3: An improvement made in e. 16 is further improved in print.

13: The ungrammatical 'doth' gets into print in *1817*, is not corrected in SH II, but is corrected in *1819*.

14: A syllable short in e. 16. Shelley has miscopied an earlier manuscript by omitting 'own' before 'hues'.

16: Similarly miscopied in e. 16: 'and' has been omitted before 'leave'.

18–19: Emended in e. 16 for euphony; further improved in print.

27: I have followed what Shelley twice printed, though it seems that in SH II, as in e. 16, he wished to record his aversion to what he considered 'Christian superstitions'.

43: *lovers'*: Singular or plural? A typical example of a place where neither manuscript nor editions give certainty, and an editor must make up his mind.

44: *art*: correct in *1817*; in *1819* became the ungrammatical 'are'. Put right in *1839*.

67: *envious*: underlined, in e. 16, but Shelley could not better it in print.

83: The *SPIRIT fair*, which Shelley printed, is more in keeping with the title of the poem than the 'awful power' of e. 16.

Though Hutchinson's text is verbally satisfactory it is ruined by its inheritance of Shelley's notorious all-purpose dashes. They derive from the *Examiner* text into which they had been allowed to creep from his manuscripts. In *1819* they were corrected, Forman thinks, by Peacock, who was one of the friends on whom Shelley relied for such help. Mary Shelley corrected them and so did Rossetti, but Forman with, one may suppose, a bibliophile's reverence for *1817* as a 'first edition', decided that its pointing should be preserved. Hutchinson uncritically followed him. My changes are as follows:

line		*for*	
4	flower;	flower,—	
8	evening,	evening,—	
9	spread,	spread,—	
10	fled,	fled,—	
19	river;	river,	
20	shown;	shown,	
26	given:	given—	
28	endeavour—	endeavour,	
29	spells,	spells—	

44 Thou	Thou—	
54 heard, not:—	heard—	not—
55 When,	When	
67 night:	night—	
70 slavery—	slavery,	
71 thou,	thou—	
74 past:	past—	
81 calm,—	calm—	

These changes are based on an independent study of the syntax. I have compared them with the punctuation of Locock in his 1911 edition and am gratified to find that we differ very little. On one or two small points of difference I have deferred to a stop of his which seemed superior to mine: on others I adhere to my own. I have compared my punctuation also with that of Mary Shelley and Rossetti. My view is that, although, as workers in the matter, they are both far superior to Shelley, they have allowed their reaction against this weakness of his to go a little too far. Stylistically both his early rhetoric and his more mature classical syntax do need to be sustained by an occasional application of the dash; his trouble is not that he uses this stop, but that he cannot ration his use of it. The result of misplacing it is that its effectiveness when properly placed is masked, and—as may be perceived by anybody who can intelligently read a poem aloud—a series of false syntactical parallelisms are suggested to the reader's eye, which hide the meaning from his understanding.

Title/Content: The poem is a manifesto of Shelley's Platonism. It is a natural Platonism which had haunted Shelley since childhood: see the fifth and sixth stanzas. The poem is not, like 'Prince Athanase', the result of a reading of Plato; it was written out of the emotions aroused in him by the scenic beauty of Switzerland. *The Prelude*, which Wordsworth had written but not yet published, describes a similar awareness of an immanent, transcendent beauty. 'As Shelley grew older and pursued this Beauty with "studious zeal", he found in Plato's pages a similar experience, and in shaping the articulation of his own native experience he gave it a Platonic title' (Notopoulos, *Platonism*, p. 201). The title derives from the Platonic tradition rather than from Plato himself, in whose Dialogues the phrase 'intellectual beauty' does not occur. It seems to have originated from Plotinus, *Enneads*, V. viii, which is entitled Περὶ τοῦ νοητοῦ κάλλους,—however, Plotinus and the other Neoplatonists do not appear in Shelley's reading. 'Plato's intellectual beauty' is referred to by Lord Monboddo in *Of the Origin and Progress of Language* (3 vols., 1773-6), a book which Shelley ordered from Clio Rickman in 1812; the passage (i. 105-6) shows that the phrase had become a commonplace Platonic formula. Again the phrase 'Beauté intellectuelle' occurs three times in Pernay's French translation of Wieland's *Agathon*, which Shelley had read in 1813 and 1814, and in contexts (see Notopoulos, p. 197) which must have been very attractive to him. Notopoulos suggests that Shelley's title may represent a grafting of the Platonic formula upon the title of Spenser's 'An Hymne of Heavenly Beautie'. It is not uninteresting that in 1818, when translating the *Symposium*, he rendered the phrase ἀλλ' ἐπὶ τὸ πολὺ πέλαγος τετραμμένος τοῦ καλοῦ (210 d) as 'would turn towards the wide sea of intellectual beauty'. The skilful interpolation of the word 'intellectual' is evidence of how closely Shelley's experience had become associated in his mind with Plato's. To understand Shelley's idea of Intellectual Beauty we need to compare it with Plato's, as expressed first in the *Phaedrus* and then in the *Symposium*. Between the Hymn and the *Phaedrus* there is much similarity. We find in both the natural philosophy of a mind which feels the immanent and tran- scendental relationship of the intellectual world with the relative world, and in both the feeling is expressed in terms of the imagery of light and shadow; again, Shelley's lover, like Plato's, after being moved, first of all, by the most intense excitement, to the pitch of which poetical language magnificently soars, is later refreshed, consoled, and calmed. But between the lover in the Hymn and the lover in the *Symposium* there is a basic difference: it is that whereas the former is constantly seeking on this earth for the shadow of an abstract, eternal Beauty, the latter 'starts with the shadow of earthly beauty and imme- diately transcends it in a dialectical pursuit of its shadows in morals and sciences.'[1] In the *Symposium* the conception is essentially an intellectual and objective one, each step in the upward progress of the soul being attained by reason alone, there being only in the preliminary stage a suggestion of the senses. In the Hymn, despite the 'Intellectual Beauty' to which it is dedicated, the con- ception is mystical and emotional, being biographical in origin: in Shelley, says Notopoulos, 'we have an imaginative leap with very little distinction between emotion and idea'. The basic distinction between the pure Platonic and the Shelleyan-Platonic could hardly have been better put. It is that 'imaginative leap' which gives him his greatest power as a poet, an interpreter, symbolically, of the universe. The Hymn is a manifesto, explaining and exemplifying that power. It was to such a power that he was laying claim when he wrote the highly significant letter to Godwin which Mary Shelley printed in her Note on *Laon and Cythna*; see above, pp. 272–3, and below, p. 394 n.

2–3: The concept of the two realms of shadow and original stems from Plato, *Republic*, 510 e ff., where the world of Becoming is related to that of Being as a shadow to its original. The imagery was taken over by Neoplatonism, whence it permeated European thought, becoming a favourite philosophical, religious, and poetical idiom. It became a favourite with Shelley: typical instances are *Epipsychidion*, 116, 137, 268; *Prometheus Unbound*, II. iii. 13. For other instances and analytical discussion see Rogers, *Shelley at Work*, *passim*. It is to be classed as a literary commonplace which he had picked up rather than as a direct borrowing from Plato.

13–15: These lines are a close parallel to Plato's conception of Beauty, even to the extent that Beauty consecrates the object it visits: cf. Notopoulos on φαντάσματα θεῖα in *Republic*, 532 c, *Classical Philology* xxxiii (1938), 99–100. Cf. too Shelley's use of 'illumed' in line 68, which is akin to the way, in the *Republic*, Plato speaks of the Good in terms of light: for this symbolism see Notopoulos, *Classical Philology*, xxxix (1944), 163–72 223–40. For the imagery of light and darkness in Shelley see Rogers, *Shelley at Work*, *passim*.

16–24: Shelley's lament for mutability is in sharp contrast with the Platonic belief in the *Phaedo* that it is not worth tears. Cf. above, pp. 329–30, n. on the poem 'Mutability'.

[1] See p. 348.

17: *vale of tears*: This well-known phrase probably originated from the Vulgate's *in valle lacrimarum* (Psalms 83: 7). It is found, in various forms, in other related scriptural passages and was given currency by hymnologists from the seventeenth century onwards. One famous reference to it is Keats's: in the journal letter written to George and Georgiana Keats between 14 Feb. and 3 May 1819 he objects to the 'little circumscribed notion' in the phrase and suggests, and develops, the alternative idea of a 'vale of soul-making' (Hyder E. Rollins, *Letters of John Keats*, 1958, ii. 101–2). Cf. also Mrs. Gamp, in *Martin Chuzzlewit*, ch. 25, 'this Piljian's Projiss of a mortal wale'.

27: *Demon*: Shelley is not here thinking of the Platonic daemon but of the Demons of Christian theology. Sometimes (see Rogers, *Shelley at Work*, ch. 5) he is not very concerned to distinguish between one category of spirits and another.

32–5: Shelley is in harmony with Plato in his belief that the ideal world is what gives 'grace and truth to life's unquiet dream'. Whatever of truth or beauty there is in the relative world is derivative from the ideal world; (see *Phaedo*, 100, *Symposium*, 212). The use of 'light' (32) is again Platonic. The Dream is a Platonic concept closely akin to the Veil: see Rogers, *Shelley at Work*, ch. 10. It stands for something which comes between the ideal and the relative world. In line 34 the 'still instrument' probably has reference to the 'Aeolian harp, or lyre', which consisted of a box containing strings of different lengths and which, when suspended in the wind, would produce chords of music. See Coleridge's poem on the subject. For Shelley, as for him, the sweeping of the wind across the strings symbolized the operation of the creative power upon poetic sensitivity (cf. *Shelley at Work*, pp. 195–6). See also 'Ode to the West Wind', 57: 'Make me thy lyre, even as the forest is'.

47–8: For the notion that the vanishing of Beauty takes with it the hope of immortality which makes man fearless of death cf. Plato, *Phaedo*, 107 c.

52: Cf. Thomson: *Seasons, Winter*, 432:
> Hold high converse with the departed dead

56–7: Cf. Wordsworth 'To the Same Flower' (i.e. 'the Small Celandine' subject of a preceding poem), 17–18:
> Soon as gentle breezes bring
> News of winter's vanishing

59–62: The 'ecstasy' of the poet on feeling the impact of Beauty is expressed in terms of the ecstasy of the lover in Plato's *Phaedrus* (245 b, 250–1) when he beholds the beloved one. The poetic ecstasy is similarly described by Coleridge in 'Kubla Khan':
> A damsel with a dulcimer
> In a vision once I saw:
> It was an Abyssinian maid,
> And on her dulcimer she played,
> Singing of Mount Abora.
> Could I revive within me
> Her symphony and song,
> To such a deep delight 'twould win me,
> That with music loud and long,

> I would build that dome in air,
> That sunny dome! those caves of ice!
> And all who heard should see them there,
> And all should cry, Beware! Beware!
> His flashing eyes, his floating hair!
> Weave a circle round him thrice,
> And close your eyes with holy dread,
> For he on honeydew hath fed,
> And drunk the milk of Paradise.

Not everybody has understood that 'Kubla Khan' is a poem about the act of poetic creation. Even the great Livingston Lowes considered that these lines are 'inconsequential' and thought the 'flashing eyes and floating hair' represented the sudden intrusion into the poem of some 'Tartar youth'. As Humphrey House remarks, this supposition is only possible on the part of somebody who has forgotten the *Phaedrus* and *A Midsummer Night's Dream*; he was thinking, of course, of Theseus' famous speech (v. i. 7 ff.) beginning 'The lunatic, the lover and the poet . . .' Shelley would certainly not have failed to connect these lines with the *Phaedrus* or to understand the real theme of the poem; cf. the language in which he described to Peacock, on 22 July 1816, how he beheld 'the aerial summits' of the Swiss Alps with 'a sentiment of extatic wonder, not unallied to madness' (Jones, *Letters*, i. 497). When published in the following year 'Mont Blanc' was dated 'July 23, 1816'. The 'hymn', Mary tells us, was written during Shelley's excursion on Lake Leman with Byron, between 23 and 29 June 1816. On 17 July (Jones, *Letters*, i. 490) he wrote to Peacock saying, 'Coleridge is in my thoughts'. Possibly this was due to the recent publication of the volume containing 'Kubla Khan' and 'Christabel'; if so the 'extatic wonder' of both poems may have a triple Shelley–Coleridge–Plato connection. The effect of 'Kubla Khan' on Shelley's scenic imagination was very great: see *Shelley at Work*, ch. 7, where I have described the extraordinary drawing, reproduced in my frontispiece, in which he portrayed the Boat, the Dome, the Isle, and the Eye of Creative Imagination; this drawing, as I have shown, connects directly with 'Kubla Khan', with scenic features in *Laon and Cythna*, written in 1817, and with similar scenic features in the 'Fragment of an Unfinished Drama', written five years later.

Commenting on lines 59–62, Notopoulos (*Platonism*, p. 206) points out that the conversion described in the 'Hymn' is aesthetic only, whereas in Plato it is the conversion of the entire soul: see *Republic*, 518, and *Apology*, 21 ff., for a conversion which had a profound effect on Socrates' life. His discussion of the Shelley–Plato relationship in Stanzas v and vi is a penetrating piece of critical insight which needs to be quoted in full:

> For a better understanding of the *Hymn* it is well to compare and contrast Shelley's conception of Intellectual Beauty with Plato's Ideal Beauty. The kinship of these two conceptions consists in identity-in-difference. Both reveal a fundamental kinship in that they are expressions of the natural Platonism of a mind which sees an immanent and transcendent relation between the intellectual and relative world. Both conceptions make use of the imagery of shadow and original to express this relationship. Shelley's conception of Beauty is more akin to that in the *Phaedrus* than that in the *Symposium*. The lovers in the *Hymn* and the *Phaedrus* have much in common. Shelley's lover is desolate in a vale of tears; he shrieks and clasps his hands in ecstasy when the shadow

of Beauty falls on him. Plato's lover is pierced, maddened, and pained in his soul; he is 'like a bird fluttering and looking upward and careless of the world below'; at the sight of beauty 'first a shudder runs through him, and again the old awe steals over him'; his 'soul is all in a state of ebullition and effervescence' and like Shelley's lover is refreshed after communion with Beauty, 'and has no more pangs and pains.' A comparison of Shelley's conception with that in the *Symposium* shows the one fundamental difference between Shelley's lover and Plato's lover: Shelley's lover is constantly seeking the shadow of Beauty on this earth; Plato's lover starts with the shadow of Beauty on the earth and immediately transcends it in a dialectical pursuit of its shadows in morals and sciences. Though it is titled *Intellectual Beauty*, Shelley's poem is emotional and mystic rather than intellectual and objective, as is Plato's conception. In Plato we have a progressive ascent from particular beauties to Beauty, each step attained by the use of reason alone, with only the suggestion of the senses in the preliminary stage; in Shelley we have an imaginative leap with little distinction between emotion and idea. Shelley's approach is purely aesthetic, whereas Plato's is ethical, logical, and metaphysical as well. Shelley's is biographical, and Plato's is objective and universal; the poet's joy and sorrows find intense romantic expression, whereas the philosopher's revelation has the calm soaring, bursting to white heat of ineffable emotion only when the ultimate 'ocean of Beauty' is reached. A realization of these differences will serve to clarify the difference between the Platonic experiences of the poet and the philosopher. Yet even here the difference verges on similarity, for Shelley's lover, after the visitation of Beauty in childhood, outwatches the envious night with studious zeal (ll. 65–7). Shelley's lines appear to be a compressed version of Milton's lines in *Il Penseroso*:

> Where I may oft out-watch the *Bear*,
> With thrice great *Hermes*, or unsphear
> The spirit of *Plato* to unfold
> What Worlds, or what vast Regions hold
> The immortal mind that hath forsook
> Her mansion in this fleshy nook.

Since Shelley had been reading Milton in 1815 and 1816, this may well be the case. If so, then Shelley's outwatching the night with studious zeal might well mean a pursuit of Intellectual Beauty through the study of Plato and other Platonic writers which he had been reading since his Oxford days; if we finally associate these lines with Shelley's intention in the preface to *Prometheus Unbound* to 'familiarize the highly refined imagination . . . with beautiful idealisms of moral excellence,' we can see that Shelley's pursuit of Intellectual Beauty possesses much in common even with Plato's conception in the *Symposium*.

p. 75, MONT BLANC. *Text*: Hutchinson's *textus receptus* derives from Shelley's 1817 printing, itself derived, in the first place, from e. 16—a wild draft in ink, written over an earlier pencil draft, with much cancellation and changing of words and phrases; the manuscript, as a whole, is cancelled by vertical pen-strokes, suggesting, it would seem, that Shelley marked it off as 'copied and finished with'. Its general appearance is a reminder (see n. on the preceding poem) of the 'extatic wonder, not unallied to madness' characterizing his Platonic reactions to the beauties of the Alps. There must have been intermediate copies. Somewhere, between draft and first printing, errors crept in which are traceable to his own misinterpreting of his confused scrawl: the omission, for instance, of two lines (27a and 28a) which threw a long passage out of its syntactical shape, and (79) the transcribing of a cancelled phrase instead of his emendation. Sometimes I am uncertain whether editorial change is improvement—e.g. Mary Shelley's 'tracks her there' of line 69. But the minor verbal changes in lines 103, 107, and 125 are to the good, and (80) the change of 'Ye' to 'Thou', which concentrates Shelley's apostrophe on the single mountain instead of a range of Alps, strengthens the whole poem. My text, therefore, must be based, verbally, on *1817*. In my collation I have shown only those changes which reveal significant points of evolution. The punctuation of *1817* and derived texts is, for the most part, unskilful, and the syntactical drift, which it hampers rather than assists, has required a new and independent consideration. I hope that the need for this will be shown by my giving, section by section, the text inherited from Shelley, accompanied by an account of what I have tried to do.

As printed by Hutchinson lines 1–11 appear thus:

I

The everlasting universe of things
Flows through the mind, and rolls its rapid waves,
Now dark—now glittering—now reflecting gloom—
Now lending splendour, where from secret springs
The source of human thought its tribute brings   5
Of waters,—with a sound but half its own,
Such as a feeble brook will oft assume
In the wild woods, among the mountains lone,
Where waterfalls around it leap for ever,
Where woods and winds contend, and a vast river   10
Over its rocks ceaselessly bursts and raves.

The four 'now' phrases quite clearly require to be linked by commas, not separated by Shelley's ubiquitous dashes; they also need to be divided off as a parenthesis. Then, in line 4, the adverbial phrase 'from secret springs' needs to be tied together between commas, the comma after 'splendour' then becomes redundant. The main construction should now be plain: 'The . . . universe . . . rolls . . . waves . . . where . . .'

And here, as inherited from Shelley, are lines 12–34:

II

Thus thou, Ravine of Arve—dark, deep Ravine—
Thou many-coloured, many-voicèd vale,
Over whose pines, and crags, and caverns sail
Fast cloud shadows and sunbeams: awful scene,   15
Where Power in likeness of the Arve comes down
From the ice-gulfs that gird his secret throne,
Bursting through these dark mountains like the flame
Of lightning through the tempest;—thou dost lie,
Thy giant brood of pines around thee clinging,   20
Children of elder time, in whose devotion
The chainless winds still come and ever came
To drink their odours, and their mighty swinging
To hear—an old and solemn harmony;
Thine earthly rainbows stretched across the sweep   25
Of the aethereal waterfall, whose veil
Robes some unsculptured image; the strange sleep
Which when the voices of the desert fail

Wraps all in its own deep eternity;—
Thy caverns echoing to the Arve's commotion,   30
A loud, lone sound no other sound can tame;
Thou art pervaded with that ceaseless motion,
Thou art the path of that unresting sound—
Dizzy Ravine!

When so printed, this long sentence is almost incomprehensible. One difficulty comes with lines 27–9, which, as noted by Rossetti and Locock, have no syntactical position. In the draft the word 'strange' does not appear, but above 'even the' is a cancelled word which, though I read it as 'shadowy', could, just conceivably, be mistaken for 'strange'. The word 'even' restores the syntax of these two and a half lines. It is not without great hesitation that I add to a text based on Shelley's own printing the lines I have numbered 27a and 28a, but they improve the symmetry of the whole passage, and there is at least one other instance (in the Silsbee–Harvard Notebook MS. of 'To Constantia, Singing') in support of my belief that he was capable of missing a line in copying from his draft. If we look for the construction of the passage as a whole, we find that the rhetoric hangs on the double 'thou', which introduces the descriptive apostrophe in lines 12 and 13, and is caught up by the 'thou' of line 19, which introduces the first main verb, 'dost lie'. Here description broadens out from apostrophe to statement—a highly involved descriptive statement which runs down to lines 32 and 33, where the opening pair of 'thou's is balanced by a final pair, introducing and co-ordinating a second main verb, 'art'. The main difficulties arise between lines 19 and 34. They are syntactical, and their principal cause is the failure of Shelley to mark off the parentheses in lines 21–4 and 27–9. I have placed brackets round both passages. Shelley has rightly placed a strong stop, semicolon-plus-dash, to mark the syntactical hinge in line 19, but another, corresponding, stop was required where I have placed it, in line 31. After 'Ravine' in line 34 a special, dramatic, pause seemed needed, and to differentiate this from the strong stops used above I have used dotted suspension points.

The symmetry of the structural features just noted is sustained by an arrangement of three participial phrases at five-line intervals—20, 25, 30—on the model of the Greek genitive, and the Latin ablative, absolute. Of the first participial phrase (20) the whole of the first parenthesis is an extension, it being in apposition to the word 'pines'. The second (25) is extended first by the adjectival clause 'whose . . . image', qualifying 'waterfall', and then by the second of the parentheses, which is in apposition to 'image'. The third, 'Thy caverns . . . commotion' (30), is correspondingly followed by 'A loud, lone sound . . .', in apposition to 'commotion'. In marking my parentheses I have preferred brackets to dashes; it was necessary to economize in these to avoid confusion with the function of the dashes used to mark the main structural pivots.

From Shelley to Hutchinson lines 34–48 have been punctuated as follows:

and when I gaze on thee
I seem as in a trance sublime and strange   35
To muse on my own separate fantasy,
My own, my human mind, which passively
Now renders and receives fast influencings,
Holding an unremitting interchange

With the clear universe of things around;   40
One legion of wild thoughts, whose wandering wings
Now float above thy darkness, and now rest
Where that or thou art no unbidden guest,
In the still cave of the witch Poesy,
Seeking among the shadows that pass by   45
Ghosts of all things that are, some shade of thee,
Some phantom, some faint image; till the breast
From which they fled recalls them, thou art there!

Here too are parentheses, two of them, which need to be marked. For the longer
one (40–4) I have used dashes, in order that it may stand clear of the two parallel
ones above. Since the shorter one (46) needs further differentiation, I have
used brackets. In line 48 'thou' is, of course, the Ravine, and the introduction
of the word in the last line of the stanza completes its syntactical unification.

Here is the Shelley-derived text of lines 49–83:

III

Some say that gleams of a remoter world
Visit the soul in sleep,—that death is slumber,
And that its shapes the busy thoughts outnumber   50
Of those who wake and live.—I look on high;
Has some unknown omnipotence unfurled
The veil of life and death? or do I lie
In dream, and does the mightier world of sleep   55
Spread far around and inaccessibly
Its circles? For the very spirit fails,
Driven like a homeless cloud from steep to steep
That vanishes among the viewless gales!
Far, far above, piercing the infinite sky,   60
Mont Blanc appears,—still, snowy, and serene—
Its subject mountains their unearthly forms
Pile around it, ice and rock; broad vales between
Of frozen floods, unfathomable deeps,
Blue as the overhanging heaven, that spread   65
And wind among the accumulated steeps;
A desert peopled by the storms alone,
Save when the eagle brings some hunter's bone,
And the wolf tracks her there—how hideously
Its shapes are heaped around! rude, bare, and high,   70
Ghastly, and scarred, and riven.—Is this the scene
Where the old Earthquake-daemon taught her young
Ruin? Were these their toys? or did a sea
Of fire envelop once this silent snow?
None can reply—all seems eternal now.   75
The wilderness has a mysterious tongue
Which teaches awful doubt, or faith so mild,
So solemn, so serene, that man may be,
But for such faith, with nature reconciled;
Thou hast a voice, great Mountain, to repeal   80
Large codes of fraud and woe; not understood
By all, but which the wise, and great, and good
Interpret, or make felt, or deeply feel.

In line 52 the full-stop-plus-dash seems to be an example of Shelley's antici-patory stopping: he had felt the need for a specially strong stop and put it, as he sometimes did, a little too soon. After 'live' a full stop is quite sufficient. It is at the end of the line that dramatic effect requires a strong stop: not a full stop, which would separate what precedes from what follows, but a colon to connect and explain. I have strengthened mine with a dash. In line 54 I have changed 'or' to 'Or: this is a small point but the change brings the sentence into line with the sentences that precede and follow. In line 61 the comma-plus-dash usefully marks a dramatic pause, but its effect is spoiled by the squandering of another dash at the end of the line, which to the reader's eye might convey a momentary impression of a parenthesis; a semicolon can be easily substituted. The semicolons in lines 63 and 66 are disastrous: as printed, both the passage from 'broad vales' (63) to 'steeps' (66) and the passage from 'A desert' (67) to 'there' (69) are anacolutha. If we substitute a comma in line 63 it then becomes plain that the 'ice and rock' (in apposition, of course, to 'unearthly forms') are 'between broad vales / Of frozen floods'; 'between' being an inverted preposition, and not an adverb, as it might have seemed. If we substitute a dash at the end of line 66, 'A desert' is seen to be in apposi-tion to 'steeps', and what follows, is syntactically reconnected with what pre-cedes. Then, in line 69, where the sentence we have restored to sense comes to its end at 'there', we need to replace the dash by a full stop, and to capitalize the next word. That 'How' (69) does, of course, demand an exclamation mark; however, it is wanted not in the middle of line 70, where it wrongly divides a row of fine epithets from what they qualify, but where the sentence ends, at 'riven' in line 71; a dash in line 70 will reunite what Shelley's stop had divorced. (With exclamatory sentences Shelley is always particularly prone to antici-patory stopping: see Vol. I, p. xl.) In line 79 I have corrected the nonsensical 'But for such faith', which is due to Shelley's miscopying, and substituted from the draft 'In such a faith'. The semicolon at the end of this line wrongly divides 'reconciled' from what follows and explains the reconciliation: my comma-plus-dash leads 'reconciled' towards what follows. The semicolon in line 81 is another disaster; it cuts off 'not understood' from the 'large codes' which it qualifies; no stop was wanted here. I have added an exclamation mark at the end of line 83 because it seemed to me necessary, in order to mark the climax of a highly rhetorical stanza.

The Shelley-derived punctuation of lines 84–95 runs thus:

IV

The fields, the lakes, the forests, and the streams,
Ocean, and all the living things that dwell   85
Within the daedal earth; lightning, and rain,
Earthquake, and fiery flood, and hurricane,
The torpor of the year when feeble dreams
Visit the hidden buds, or dreamless sleep
Holds every future leaf and flower;—the bound   90
With which from that detested trance they leap;
The works and ways of man, their death and birth,
And that of him and all that his may be;
All things that move and breathe with toil and sound
Are born and die; revolve, subside, and swell.   95

The syntactical construction is a loose one: a catalogue of natural phenomena joined by a series of semicolons. The arrangement is quite effective, though three adjustments have been necessary. First of all an additional semicolon was needed after 'hurricane' in line 87, in order to divide two different categories of phenomena. Next, we need to remove Shelley's anticipatory dash from line 90 to the place where it really belongs, at the end of line 93; placed here after the semicolon, it can usefully lead the catalogue to the summary ('All things . . .') which is its climax. The five verbs in line 95 are closely joined in meaning, and the parallelism is spoiled by the semicolon after 'die' which wrongly divides them: they need to be reconnected by the substitution of a comma.

From lines 95 to 126 the Shelley-derived punctuation is, for some reason, quite effective, and I have made no changes. In the final stanza, lines 127–44, I have made three minor ones:

V

Mont Blanc yet gleams on high:—the power is there,
The still and solemn power of many sights,
And many sounds, and much of life and death.
In the calm darkness of the moonless nights,   130
In the lone glare of day, the snows descend
Upon that Mountain; none beholds them there,
Nor when the flakes burn in the sinking sun,
Or the star-beams dart through them:—Winds contend
Silently there, and heap the snow with breath   135
Rapid and strong, but silently! Its home
The voiceless lightning in these solitudes
Keeps innocently, and like vapour broods
Over the snow. The secret Strength of things
Which governs thought, and to the infinite dome   140
Of Heaven is as a law, inhabits thee!
And what were thou, and earth, and stars, and sea,
If to the human mind's imaginings
Silence and solitude were vacancy?

The strong colon-plus-dash in line 127 is really excellent: it marks, linguistically, the association of power with the mountain, which is the philosophical point of the whole poem. It is slightly weakened by the squandered dash in line 134, where a full stop is quite adequate. It seemed to me that both this effect and the interrogative note that is the rhetorical climax of the whole poem is further weakened a little by the exclamation marks in lines 136 and 141, and that both would be helped by the reduction of these exclamatory sentences to quiet, contrasting statements.

Content: Like the 'Hymn to Intellectual Beauty' (see nn. above) 'Mont Blanc' is an illustration of the madness of the soul in the presence of Beauty. Notopoulos (*Platonism*, p. 207) well summarizes the general metaphysical conceptions:

Shelley's genius as a natural Platonic symbolist is evident in his use of a mountain and a stream which has its source in this mountain to symbolize the transcendent yet immanent character of Platonic Reality. Mont Blanc is symbolic of Power, 'the secret strength' which governs thought and is the law to the universe; the various streams that flow from the mountain forming one majestic river are symbolic of the temporal experiences that flow through the human mind. The use of a stream for a symbol is as old as Heraclitus (see fragments 41–42), who uses it as a symbol of change; it is a favorite natural metaphysical symbol, as may be seen from its use by Coleridge in *Kubla Khan* and by Robert Frost in *West Running Brook*. In equating Mont Blanc and the Arve with mind and experience, Shelley makes a slight but significant change; the ravine is a passive recipient of the Arve, whereas for Shelley the mind through which the stream flows is, like Plato's conception of the soul (*Phaedrus*, 245 e), an active agent. The mind is endowed with a power which it derives from 'secret springs'; though not developed, the 'springs' are, as will be shown later, symbolic of a power emanating from the mind's immortal and divine heritage. The fusion of the stream of the external universe with the stream of the soul may be interpreted as a Platonic conception of the mind in contrast to the Lockean conception; it marks a turning point from materialism to immaterialism. The fusion of the two streams may further be interpreted either as the Platonic macrocosm and microcosm or, in the light of the *Timaeus*, as the world which is created by the imposition of divine form and values on the relative world. Perhaps this is why Shelley describes the stream as 'with a sound but half its own.' The result, therefore, of the fusion is an animate cosmos, a manifestation of the world soul which figures prominently in Shelley's conception of the universe.

1–11: Stanza 1 compares three physical phenomena with three metaphysical conceptions: (1) The Ravine, corresponding to the universal mind, (2) The Arve, corresponding to the everlasting universe of things, (3) The feeble brook, corresponding to the *individual human mind*, which draws its strength from the everlasting universe. This idea is developed in Stanza II, and finely rounded off in the last two sentences of the poem.

12–34: The relation of the Ravine of Arve to the river Arve is that of image and original, which, for Shelley, is a 'Power' or the ideal world.

29: *period*: A cycle of time (περίοδος) as opposed to time itself, eternity.

34–40: The mind is thought of as something like the prisoners in the Cave in Plato, *Republic*, 514 ff.: a passive receiver of images. The 'interchange' between mind and universe is a touch of Wordsworthian Platonism which Shelley may have got from 'Tintern Abbey': Wordsworth develops it in *The Prelude*, XIV. 60 ff., which, of course, was not published in Shelley's lifetime. Cf. Rogers, *Shelley at Work*, pp. 148–9.

43: *that or thou*: I think that 'that' refers to the poet's 'own separate fantasy'; 'thou' must refer to the Ravine—both welcome guests in the Cave of Poetry because the one provides a fitting poetical subject and the other a capacity for responding to it.

45: *Seeking*: This should probably be taken with 'fantasy' or, by a *constructio ad sensum*, with 'me', understood. The problem of the prisoners in Plato's Cave is the problem of the Poet in Shelley's metaphysics: how to distinguish between substance and shadow, truth and illusion.

47–8: I quote Locock's excellent note:

So far the sense of the passage beginning at l. 32 may be summed up as follows:— 'The Ravine is the path of the Arve's unresting sound. The poet, gazing on the Ravine, thinks of his own feeble imagination inspired by the untamed thoughts of the everlasting Universe. These thoughts of Nature's Mind seem sometimes to float above the Ravine (the Universal Mind), beyond his reach, sometimes to dwell in the cave of Poesy, where the poet's imagination seeks, among the ghosts (ἰδέαι) passing by the cave, some faint reflected image to express his conception of the Ravine.' The next line and a half, difficult enough in themselves, are curiously obscured by the misprint 'fed' for 'fled' in Rossetti's edition. I take the 'breast' to be the mind of the Universe of Things (Nature), and 'there' to mean 'outside the cave of Poesy.' The sense then continues—'Till Nature recalls these phantoms which are her thoughts, the phantom or Idea of the Ravine is within sight of the Cave of Poesy, and therefore accessible to the poet and describable by him.' An interpretation which Rossetti has recently suggested to me may be simpler:— 'Until my breast recalls certain other shadows which lately fled from it, thou art there (in my breast or mind). Though the last line is rhymeless it makes a not ineffective conclusion.'

49: *remoter*: 'future', according to the *Shelley Concordance*. But the meaning is probably 'beyond our ken', 'beyond the veil': cf. lines 53–4 below. For death and sleep (50) see Rogers, *Shelley at Work*, ch. 10.

53: *unfurled*: means 'drawn aside'. Cf. Shelley's sonnet of 1819, 'Lift not the painted veil . . .'. And for the Veil as a major symbol cf. Rogers, *Shelley at Work*, ch. 8.

62: Locock notices this, together with 65, 108, 113, 133, as a rhymeless line. Shelley's ear allowed such irregularities with fine effect.

72: *Earthquake-daemon*: Cf. 'The Wandering Jew's Soliloquy', 21–2; see Vol. I, p. 174 and nn. on p. 373.

86: *daedal*: a favourite Greek coinage of Shelley's: from δαιδάλεος, meaning 'cunningly or skilfully wrought'; connected with the name of Daedalus, the Cretan artist and mechanic.

105: *distinct*: Latin *distinctus*, 'adorned'. Cf. *Laon and Cythna*, 615, *Prometheus Unbound*, III. iii. 162. The usage is found in Spenser and Milton.

p. 80, MONT BLANC: REJECTED LINES. *Text*: These lines have usually been described as 'cancelled'. Though an occasional word or phrase has been scored through, the draft is not cancelled as a whole. It is pencilled on a loose sheet which once belonged to e. 16. The text is unsatisfactory, but the writing has now become too rubbed to permit improvement, and a commentary would be impracticable.
Content: Possibly the 'voice' connects with the 'voices' in 'Mont Blanc', 28.

p. 80, VERSES WRITTEN ON RECEIVING A CELANDINE ETC. *Text*: The fact that Shelley drafted the poem in pencil and then drafted the poem 'To William Shelley' on top of it led very easily to Garnett's mistake in printing as rejected from the latter poem the lines which I have printed as rejected from this one. In her Notebook, d. 9, Mary Shelley copied out the first four under the title 'To William S[helley]' but realized her mistake and cancelled the heading.
Content: It was natural that the receipt of a celandine should remind Shelley of Wordsworth, who had written lines about the same flower. Shelley's attitude to Wordsworth in the summer of 1816 was a mixed one: see above, pp. 330–51, n. on the sonnet 'To Wordsworth'.

p. 83, THREE LAMENTS. *Text*: Shelley's habits of composition have here presented a very difficult problem in editorial arrangement. The first two poems

B b

need to be connected in print because in the manuscript Shelley has connected them as one lament. They are written together on one side of a sheet of paper. On the verso side Shelley has made a sketch of a grave. Above it are clouds and trees, and around it are funerary urns on one of which he has written: 'I drew this flower-pot in October 1816 and now it is 1817.' To the right of the grave, and just above it, so penned that the letters have become part of the foliage, he has written the words 'Break them whose'. Just below, faintly penned, is the word 'miserable'. A little further down he has written 'When said I so? It is not my fault—it is not to be attributed to me.' There is a heavy mark under 'my', which may be intended for emphasis. The penmanship of these words and phrases varies a good deal, suggesting that they were written at different times. What all this illustrates is Shelley's tendency to revert to an old poem at times when there was a recurrence of the emotional situation which had produced it: see above, pp. 328–9, nn. on 'To Mary Wollstonecraft Godwin' and 'To ——' ('Yet look on me . . .'). Mary Shelley first printed the first lament as 'On F.G.' 'F.G.' was Mary Shelley's half-sister. She was known as 'Fanny Godwin', though she was really the elder daughter of Mary Wollstone-craft by an American named Imlay. On 9 Oct. 1816 she ended her unhappy life by taking laudanum at Swansea. Shelley probably last saw her in London, on 24 Sept. In a letter to Mary she had referred to a disagreement concerning Mrs. Godwin, and to his paying little heed to what she might say. It seems pretty certain that Shelley wrote the first lament and did the drawing in October 1816, and made his additions in the following year. Then, coming across this sheet of paper in the summer of 1819, when the death of little William had reduced him to despair, he joined an old grief to a new one by adding, on the recto side, above the poem on Fanny, some new lines about William. In print-ing the first two laments under '1816' I have had to prefer their poetical con-nection to the fact that this involves chronologically misplacing the second. Further complications arise from the facts (1) that the first two laments connect in turn with laments for Harriet Shelley, (2) that the first of these, the one printed here, was composed in 1816 but misdated 'November—1815', (3) that a second version of this Harriet-lament was composed in 1817 and misdated 'Nov. 5, 1815', (4) that a different lament for Harriet was also composed in 1817. For the two Harriet-poems composed in 1817 see below, 'Two Laments', pp. 312–13, and nn.

As will be seen from my collation, all three poems have required considerable adjustment of punctuation. The dotted suspension point, like the dash, is a stop that Shelley was frequently apt to squander and with which an editor of his verse must be economical. In the second lament I have used it three times, to mark the broken sentences which are so eloquent of his grief. Shelley's manuscripts of the two first laments are extremely difficult drafts. From the penmanship I am inclined to think that the last two lines of the first were added to the page at the time when the second was written: if so this is yet another link between the poems. The autograph of the third lament is a beautifully penned fair copy.

Content: In line 6 of the second poem '*one*' would seem to be a tender reference to Mary Shelley. A curious point arises from Shelley's dating of the third lament. About 9 Sept. 1816 Harriet Shelley left her father's house, where she had been living since her separation from Shelley, and went to live in lodgings in Chelsea. On Saturday, 9 Nov. she left these lodgings at about four in the afternoon and was seen no more till her body was taken from the Serpentine River on 10 Dec. That Shelley should write 'November —' seems natural enough, the actual date of her death being unknown to everybody. What is curious is that when writing his second version of the poem he dated it (see above, p. 312) specifically 'Nov. 5', which would imply that she died five days before she disappeared. I am inclined, however, to think that the figure which has been taken for a 5 in the manuscript ought really to be read as a 9.

p. 86, FRAGMENT: 'DEAR HOME . . .'. *Date*: I have followed Garnett's dating, but not without some misgiving. The draft of the fragment (see above, pp. 341–2) is closely entwined with that of 'The Sunset', a poem which, Mary Shelley tells us, was written at Bishopsgate in 1816. Perhaps Garnett dated the first poem from the known date of the second. The fact that a second version of 'The Sunset' is drafted in e. 12 among material of 1821 can be explained by the likelihood that it is a *re*drafting. It seems to me less likely that this fragment also had been written earlier. But for want of a certain date I allow for the possibility that Garnett may have had access to some other evidence unknown to me. *Text*: I have printed the lines as they appear in the draft. It will be seen, however, that the last three and a half lines are really a redrafting of the first two. Both drafts are cancelled by oblique pen-strokes. This might mean, here as elsewhere, that Shelley had made a later, possibly improved, copy.

p. 87, FRAGMENT: GHOST STORY. *Date*: The fragment is drafted in e. 16 among much material dating from the Shelleys' stay in Switzerland in 1816. It seems possible that it derives from the conversations about the supernatural between the Shelleys, Byron, Polidori, and 'Monk' Lewis, one fruit of which was Mary Shelley's *Frankenstein* and another Polidori's *The Vampire*. *Text*: the draft is in a thin, straggling scribble, and very difficult to decipher. The loose connection between the lines makes it difficult to punctuate them coherently. As with the laments on Fanny Godwin and William Shelley I have resorted to dotted suspension points.

p. 87, FRAGMENT: STANZAS ADDRESSED TO LEIGH HUNT. *Text/Date*: The stanzas are roughly drafted in pencil in two loose sheets detached from the Notebook, Bod. MS. Shelley adds. e. 16, which Shelley used in Switzerland in 1816. On the verso of one sheet is a drawing of Geneva. The second and third stanzas are drafted on the same page and the third is headed '3'. Though the second has no heading it must clearly be the second stanza of some poem of which the first stanza has been lost. The pencilling has become rubbed, and deciphering is extremely difficult. In lines 11–12 I have been unable to do more than offer conjectures based on a few clear letters and on rhyme possibilities. What I give here as Stanza 1 is drafted on the second sheet. Why Garnett, who printed it first, ascribed it to 1817 I do not know. His date has puzzled commentators, because Hunt left the prison, to which he had been consigned for libelling the Prince Regent, in 1815. The 1816 date, fixed by the Notebook, explains all:

Shelley's concern with Hunt was inspired not by his release from prison but by the publication of *The Story of Rimini*—'A gentle story of two lovers young'. It is odd that editors, including Mary Shelley, should have missed the reference, through Paolo and Francesca, to Hunt. And why Mary Shelley ascribed the third of these stanzas to 1819 is another puzzle.

TRANSLATIONS, 1816

p. 91, FOUR FRAGMENTS OF GREEK PASTORAL. *Title/Origin*: Some editors have printed nos. 2 and 3 as 'Sonnets from Moschus': no. 2 is in sonnet form though no. 3 is not. Shelley prefixed no. 2 with a quotation of the first line of the original Τὰν ἄλα τὰν γλαυκὰν ὅταν ὤνεμος ἀτρέμα βάλλῃ. In designating nos. 2 and 3 'Moschus, V' and 'Moschus, VI' I follow the Oxford Classical Text. The older designation, found in the text of Valckenaer, which Shelley probably used, was 'Moschus, IV' and Moschus, V'. The ascription of no. 4 to Bion dates from the Renaissance, and is based mainly on a reference to the poem in 'Lament for Bion', of which no. 1 is a partial translation; today, however, this latter poem is ascribed by many not to Moschus but to some disciple of Bion's.

Text: These fragments afford an excellent example, in miniature, of the demands constantly made by Shelley's manuscripts upon editorial judgement, and the history of the text provides an illuminating example of the recurrent struggle in the editorial mind between a consciousness of the need to exercise judgement and that fear of doing so which derives from an over-reverential attitude to the manuscript. In 1. 13 where a modern Fundamentalist would almost certainly have left a blank, as Shelley did in the manuscript, Forman very intelligently inserts, under cover of editorial brackets and a footnote, the words 'sweetest singer', a rendering of καλὸς τέθνακε μελικτάς which Shelley himself would, surely, have applauded as a substitute for his blank space. The manuscript of no. 2 lacks punctuation, which he rightly supplies, acknowledging in a footnote that he has done so. Yet in 3. 7 he rejects Rossetti's intelligent placing of the dash, believing, on manuscript authority, that Shelley would have preferred nonsense ('lack of syntactical standing') to an inversion which, although a little odd, as Rossetti admits, is by no means un-Shelleyan and turns nonsense into sense. Odder, surely, than Rossetti's inversion is Forman's readiness, after perceiving the total inadequacy of Shelley's punctuation in one poem, to assume about a point of punctuation in another that the manuscript is, in itself, a sufficient authority for printing nonsense. Herein he is followed by Hutchinson. Another interesting point arises in 3. 9. That Rossetti had seen the BM manuscript seems fairly evident: it was probably shown to him by Garnett, who had it from the Shelleys. That Forman had seen it is clear: it was probably shown to him by Wise who had subsequently acquired it. Rossetti prints 'in as much' as three separate words, on the ground that 'it appears to mean more than "because" and has its full primary force, "to that same degree wherein"'. 'This', he adds, 'would be more salient if we had "in so much"—which may perhaps be the correct reading.' Forman accepts 'in as much' on the ground that there are, 'literally, three words in the manuscript'. His literal mind is, however, somewhat troubled by a doubt as to whether Shelley really meant to write three words, *n* and *s* being letters which he frequently left unconnected. Since the habits of

Shelley the scribe were anything but consistent it is always dangerous to base any such reasoning on an enumeration of instances, and Forman did well to put his doubts aside. It is notable, however, that he reasons only from the work of the scribe and seems uninterested in Rossetti's reasoning about the meaning of the poet. He further notes, about 'in so much', that 'Shelley began a false start for the line with just those words, and struck them out.' Neither Rossetti nor Forman mentions a second manuscript, and I am sure that the fair copy in e. 12 was unknown to them. This is one of the many places in Shelley's text where a modern editor must bring to bear upon a single word not merely the evidence of a manuscript but his knowledge of Shelley's manuscripts as a whole. In e. 12 Shelley has clearly written 'inasmuch', in one word. For a beginner the mere fact that the manuscript *is* a fair copy would seem to give it an authority over the draft: wider experience, as will be exemplified throughout this edition, shows that Shelley's changes can very frequently represent carelessness rather than intent. I have to confess that I should like to print 'in so much', both because it best brings out the 'primary force' required by Shelley's line and because it best translates ὅσσον—since, however, Shelley not only cancelled it in the draft but did not revert to it in the fair copy, the weight of the manuscript evidence would be against me. I think, however, that, cancelled though it is, it is a strong indication that the 'primary force' which the single word 'inasmuch' would not give was in Shelley's mind, and 'in as much' at the same time comes closer to the Greek. These things being so, and since an editor cannot avoid judgement, I print the latter form.

Of the continuous battle in Forman's mind between courage and reason on one hand and, on the other, timidity and a religious faith in manuscripts, not untinged by a collector's pride in ownership, this group of translations affords three more examples. In a note on his reading of 4. 4 he says: 'The words "and weave the crown / Of Death" are struck out and Shelley has begun another reading with the words "beat your breast"; but as this is incomplete I leave the original reading.' Herein he is ahead, in courage and reason, of some of the Fundamentalists of today. Again in 4. 30 he makes bold, in spite of the manuscript, to correct Shelley's careless 'Ay! ay!' to 'Ai! ai!', the proper English equivalent of the Greek interjection of woe. But '*Tantum religio . . .*': how far faith and unreason could take him in the opposite direction may be illustrated by his note on 4. 23–4: 'I am sorry to say that there is not the remotest doubt that the possessive pronoun on these lines is *her*—whereas I presume it equally beyond doubt that it should be *his*.' His sad preference for the words wrongly penned by Shelley the scribe rather than the words demanded both by the context in Shelley the poet and by the Greek that he is translating is mitigated by some editors who have been courageous enough to change the first 'her' to 'his', but nobody hitherto has dared to change the other three silly possessives. For the characteristics of Forman's editing see Vol. I, p. xxv. What these examples show is the insecurity of even the most conscientious editor when he embarks upon the piecemeal editing of portions of a poet's text before acquiring the wider knowledge of both scribe and poet which can only come from a close preconsideration of the text as a whole.

In 4. 14 I am unable to account for Hutchinson's 'upon', printed also by Dowden and Woodberry: the Greek word is ποτικάρδιον.

Date/Content: 'Works of Theocritus, Moschus &c' head Shelley's reading-list for 1816 (see Jones, *Mary Shelley's Journal* (1947), p. 73). In his list for 1815 (ibid., p. 49) 'Theocritus' is mentioned, so that Shelley may be presumed to have been reading Moschus in that year out of the same volume; this fits in with the inclusion of no. 2 in the *Alastor* volume, which appeared in March 1816. The manuscript of no. 1, once owned by Leigh Hunt, was written on the same paper as the concluding portion of the *Essay on Christianity*, published in 1818, and Forman accordingly assigned the translation to that year. Noto-poulos (*PMLA*, 1943, p. 482) shows that late 1816 is a more likely date. This fits both with the reading-list and with the point that the period between October and December of 1816 marked the beginning of Shelley's enthusiasm for Leigh Hunt's company. Hunt's somewhat limited taste for Greek literature included a predilection for the pastoral poets, which may well have influenced Shelley's choice of these pieces. No very certain date can be assigned to no. 3, but it seems a reasonable guess that it followed consequentially on no. 1, and since it is drafted on the reverse side of the sheet on which Shelley drafted no. 4, it must be presumed to have been composed about the same time. The fair copy of no. 3 is adjacent in e. 12 to fair copies of 'The cold earth slept below' (2nd version) and 'That time is dead forever, child' (see pp. 312–13, 407–8), and the penmanship strongly suggests that the copying was a continuous one. It would be unsafe, however, to read into what may well have been no more than a fortuitous proximity any indication of a biographical connection for the transla-tion. A suggestion that Pan, Echo, and the Satyr allegorize the Shelley–Harriet–Hogg relationship has been made, but this seems to me to strain too far the principle of biographical interpreting: nor can I believe that the words 'Justice doomed them' in line 8 were interpolated by Shelley as a reference to Lord Eldon's decree of 1817 which deprived him of the custody of Harriet's children. I think it far more likely that his interpolation of words not found in the Greek was intended simply to strengthen the force of lines 9–10. This would be con-sistent with other examples of his technique in translation: compare, for exam-ple, in his translation of the *Symposium*, that phrase (214e) 'the original, the supreme, the self-consistent' which he applies to 'the monoeidic beauty itself, and which, though not in the Greek, is not so much an interpolation as an en-lightening transference of a relevant idea from a passage in 211b; cf. also his frequent translation of ἀρετή as 'virtue and power'. (See Rogers, *Shelley at Work*, pp. 140–1, and ch. 4 *passim*; for an example in his translation from Spanish see ibid., pp. 84–5.)

No. 4, 42–7: Cf. *Adonais*, XXVI.

p. 99, LAON AND CYTHNA, ETC.

Title: I follow Forman in preferring Shelley's fine original title but, since the second title has become more generally familiar, I have added it for convenience, omitting, however, its make-weight sub-title 'A Poem in Twelve Cantos'. The 'golden city' of Shelley's imagination is Byzantium, symbolical for him, as for Yeats, of the world of ideal beauty behind the Veil, where 'The unpurged images of day recede'. The poem is the tale of the purgation of Laon and Cythna through love and suffering: unlike the Revolution which had been the hope of 'trampled France' (line 127) in the previous century, Shelley's 'Revolution' is a visionary, nineteenth-century return to an ideal realm. For the relation of the poem to Zoro-astrian mythology see Carlos Baker, *Shelley's Major Poetry* (1948), pp. 64–70. *Date*: Mary Shelley's journal records the finishing of the poem on 23 Sept. 1817 and, as Shelley says in his Preface that it took six months to write, it must have been begun about mid-March.

Epigraph: 'But as for all the bright things that we, the mortal race, attain he reaches the utmost limit of that voyage. Neither by ships nor by land can you find the wondrous road to the festival place of the Hyperboreans.' The Hyper-boreans, in Pindar, are a distant, northern race devoted to Apollo and living in a state of blessedness—a realm akin to the world symbolized by Byzantium, the 'golden city'. The passage follows, somewhat inconsequentially, a discourse on the subject of athletic glory and the limitations of mortal achievement; Shelley, however, would be less concerned with context than with sound and beauty. It fits into the Boat symbolism of Canto I: see n. below, p. 382.

Text: Apart from Forman, editors have printed the poem in its second form, that is to say as revised by Shelley under the title of *The Revolt of Islam*. With the text, as with the title, I have preferred what Shelley preferred and restored what he was forced to change. As will be seen from my collation this has involved no more than putting back the final paragraph of his Preface and making forty-three changes in the text of the poem itself. Apart from a few instances—cf., for example, n. on line 1680, p. 369, below—it is hard to see why Shelley, on the one hand, and his publisher on the other should have felt so strongly on these points. But Ollier had taken fright at the implications of incest deducible from the brother-and-sister relationship of the hero and heroine; he saw danger too in an agnostic note indistinguishable in the early nineteenth century from atheism. Shelley's changes are designed to protect his publisher and himself against a possible prosecution for blasphemy.

For the textual problems raised by Shelley's two printings and for their relationship to the manuscripts see Introduction, pp. xiv–xviii. No complete manuscript, either fair copy or draft, is extant, though a considerable portion of the poem is covered by the Bodleian manuscripts. The following is a list of what survives and what is missing:

a. *Fair Copy*
   Preface: D. 3, complete
   Dedication: D. 3, lacks 21–94
   Canto I: D. 3, lacks 127–71, 181–9, 210–326, 492–517, 653–66
   Canto IX: c. 4, 3492–517 only

b. *Draft*
   Preface: lacking
   Dedication: e. 14, complete
   Canto I: e. 19, lacks 346–648
        c 4., 129–47
   Canto II: e. 19, lacks 838–46, 995–1107
   Canto III: lacking
   Canto IV: lacking
   Canto V: e. 10, lacks 1720–881, 1927–31, 2011–56, 2202
   Canto VI: e. 10, lacks 2474–501, 2659–720

Canto VII: e. 10, lacks 2884–914, 3064–99
Canto VIII: e. 10, lacks 3225, 3460–8
Canto IX: e. 10, lacks 3599–606
Canto X: e. 10, lacks 3991–9, 4045–80, 4205–24
     e. 14, 4207–15 only
Canto XI: e. 10, complete
Canto XII: e. 10, lacks 4720–818

The miscellaneous fragments which are known to exist, or to have existed, cannot always be traced or identified with certainty. They are few in number and I think it unlikely that, if they could be collected, a new examination of them would add more than a few very minor textual points to the gleanings of owners and editors through whose hands they have passed. Three sheets, not at present available for study, are in the Pforzheimer Library; I am indebted to Mr. Donald H. Reiman for the information that one bears a fragment of Canto I (151–72) and the other two consecutive passages (3625–47, 3648–75) of Canto IX. Forman (i. 80) refers to fragments once owned by Leigh Hunt: he had been able to make use of two of these, one of which had been acquired by Rossetti and the other by Townsend Mayer. Rossetti, in 1870, printed a facsimile of his fragment, a beautiful fair copy of Canto IX, lines 3625–48, which perhaps may be identified with the Pforzheimer manuscript of the same passage. The British Museum has a fragment, once owned by T. J. Wise: a fair copy of Canto I, lines 181–9, possibly (see above) this is one of the sections missing from the Bodleian fair copy, D. 3.

No descriptive summary of these manuscripts could be more than an approximate one. It is not always possible to distinguish draft from fair copy. Some passages in the draft Notebooks are well penned and have the appearance of a recopying; most of the writing, however, is confused by cancellation and change and almost illegible. Words, phrases, and lines in the embryonic form in which they appear in the draft are sometimes impossible to identify exactly with parts of the printed text. Pencilled passages have frequently become badly rubbed. Sometimes pencilled lines have been inked over. Sometimes something new has been written in ink on top of the pencilled work. The stanzas are not always drafted in the order in which they were printed: a stanza missing in the expected place may be found many pages ahead, or it may already have been encountered many pages back. In the Notebook e. 19 are some fine stanzas which Shelley rejected and which were printed by Shelley-Rolls and Ingpen. Here and there amid the draft are other, shorter passages, previously unprinted, and memoranda and broken snatches of extraneous verse which may or may not be connected in thought with the main poem. Doodlings and sketches abound.

Such a quantity of material presents considerable problems of arrangement. In my text the rejected stanzas have been placed, in accordance with the practice of Hutchinson, at the end of the poem; where their intended position in the poem is discoverable I have indicated it in my textual commentary. Previously unprinted phrases and lines have been printed in the Commentary, but verse-fragments and memoranda too long to be placed there have been relegated to the Notes, always with an indication of the place in the text to which they appear to relate. Since most of the broken snatches of extraneous verse are well-nigh indecipherable and usually too incoherent for punctuation or other normal editorial treatment I have had to content myself with transcribing them; this I have tried to do as literally as might be convenient—that is to say that I have not striven to preserve such non-significant anomalies as ampersands, queer spelling, capitalization, and dashes which Shelley would hardly have wished to inflict on his readers.

My text is based on Shelley's own printings, with which have been incorporated the corrections of his anomalies made by the generations of his editors; to these I have added a number of corrections of my own, more particularly where sense had been lost through failure to punctuate the syntax. Shelley's erratum slip is reproduced by Forman, 1876, i. 302–3; I have made use of it in lines 753, 1675, 2305. The amount of manuscript material is embarrassingly large: to record all the many changes in the long draft would be impracticable; only significant changes have been noted. For the principles on which these are selected, for the arrangements made for printing non-significant material elsewhere, and for the significance of the *Laon and Cythna* material as a whole in the illustration of essential textual principles, see Introduction, pp. xiv–xix. D. 3 is cited only when it differs from *1818*.

pp. 106–11, 1–126: The Dedication is drafted in the Notebook e. 14. Inside the front cover appears a memorandum:

> The aloe and the China Rose
> Solomon's Song Cap. 4—v. 9
>   particularly 4. v. 2
>   or Cap. 5. v. 2

As a poetical emblem the aloe signifies both 'bitterness' and 'everspringing beauty'. It will be unnecessary to strain biographical speculation, but the emblem could well concern his transition from Harriet to Mary, with the sad feeling or recollection of early 1818 out of which came 'The colour from the flower is gone . . .', and with the feeling of *Symposium*, 196b. This passage was one of those specially noted by Shelley in his memoranda in e. 16 as following what he called 'The wonderful description of Love' on p. 214 of his Bipont edition of Plato; see Rogers, *Shelley at Work*, pp. 43 ff. His own translation is

. . . for the winged Love rests not in his flight on any form, or within any soul the flower of whose loveliness is faded, but there remains most willingly where is the colour and radiance of blossoms, yet unwithered.

The passages about 'my sister, my spouse', noticed by Shelley in the Song of Songs, are germane enough to the brother-and-sister relationship of Laon and Cythna. Such relationships, a common motif in contemporary European literature, stem from German Hellenism and owe much to Wieland's novel *Agathon*; they represent a transference to modern man–woman relationships of the brother–brother aspect of Plato's idealized relationship between males in the *Symposium*. In the Dedication the implication is that the husband–wife relationship between Shelley and Mary involves a delicate touch of brother–sister relationship. The amalgam of the Biblical and the Platonic is typical.

p. 107, 22: Shelley's semicolon in e. 14, followed by three dots, is just worth noticing as a good example of his weird, hesitant punctuation; for another example cf. line 72.

p. 108, 54: *clod*: With Hutchinson and Forman I follow Rossetti's emendation; however, my friend and former student, Dr. Claude C. Brew, has drawn my attention to Byron, *The Island*, II. 390–1:

> Dissolve this clog and clod of clay before
> Its hour, and merge our soul in the great shore.

which suggests that the distinction between the two words may not have been a very clear or consistent one in Shelley's day.

p. 109, 60: I have thought it unnecessary to preserve the asyntactical 'thou . . . walked'.

pp. 111–40, 127–994: For this part of the poem (Canto I and part of Canto II) there are drafts in the Notebook e. 19, and drafts of a few lines on loose sheets in the box c. 4. For Cantos III and IV, and a good deal of Canto V, there are no drafts. The drafts in the Notebook e. 10 begin at V. 1882. (For the deficiencies in both drafts see above, pp. 361–2.)

On p. 1 of e. 19 is copied the following extract in French:

. . . et qu'enfin cette autorite ne s'ecroule ou ne se raffermit que par l'operation secrete d'une infinité des [*sic*] causes presqu'imperceptibles qui amenent [les *omitted*] choses au point d'un bouleversement total, un parfaite [*sic*] retablissement, l'on conviendra que toutes les entreprises de cette espece ont entre elles un rapport si semblables, quelles [*sic*] semblent differer plutot par le plus ou le moins de jeus [? *for* jeux] ou de l'habite dans les acteurs que par ce qui reste.

I have not attempted a proper editing of Shelley's hasty, careless French, though I have made a few adjustments for the sake of the sense. I am not altogether happy about 'jeus': my reading seems to match what follows, but seems a little odd in the context of what precedes. I have been unable to identify the passage but, both on stylistic grounds and from what we know of Shelley's reading, I would tentatively ascribe it to Holbach. Bodley's Librarian, Dr. R. Shackleton, who has been kind enough to check my text, agrees with me about this likelihood, adding that it is clearly by somebody who was influenced by Montesquieu. Below the French quotation is a memorandum, 'See Clarke's Travels in the Peloponnesus, p. 614'. The six volumes of Edward Daniel Clarke's *Travels in Various Countries of Europe, Asia and Africa* appeared between 1810 and 1823. Mary Shelley records in her Journal that Shelley read them on 7 Jan. 1818. I have checked Shelley's reference but can discover nothing of significance.

p. 111, 127–30: On a page of e. 19 facing the page on which these lines are drafted, just below the drafting of 151–3, are the following snatches of verse:

> Who with the Devil doth rage and revel
> When he keeps his Sabbath of sin
>
> [And] He ceased—and [music] approbation like the sound
>   grove of
> Of wind among a [thousand] pines was heard
> [Through this vast tem]
> [From] [that] [assembly] as [when a gust has stirred]
> [Descending the vast]
> Their thousand   another rose
>
>   I fear that I am hardly human

p. 116, 261–70: Between an ink draft of Stanza xv and a redrafting in pencil (in e. 19) is a memorandum by Shelley:

The seven spirits—the mild messenger friend in a ravaged city smiling by a fireside. A dead woman near him.

Following lines drafted for Stanza xvi is a memorandum in Mary Shelley's hand:

Is this an imitation of Ld. Byron's poem? It is certainly written in the same metre. Are Coleridge and Wordsworth to be considered?

Underneath Shelley has written two words: the first possibly decipherable as 'else', the second 'never'. Below these is another memorandum by Shelley:

Araucanus [sic] Don Alonso d' [sic] Ercilla

Araucana was a poem in thirty-six cantos by Alonso de Ercilla (1533–94); its subject was the revolt of the province of Araucania against the Spaniards in 1554, which he was sent out to help suppress. Voltaire, in his *Essai sur la poésie épique*, groups him with Homer, Virgil, Camoëns, Tasso, and Milton; Cervantes thought him the equal of any of the epic poets of Italy.

p. 117, In e. 19, above Stanza xxi, is scribbled 'Demon Lover'. For the symbolism of Stanzas xxi–xxiii, and their connection with Coleridge, see Rogers, *Shelley at Work*, ch. 7.

p. 118, 331–3: To put a comma after 'embarked' would seem to imply, rather absurdly, that the embarkation was somehow responsible for the way the mountains were hanging. The dash in Shelley's fair copy is against this, and, if we do not prefer to substitute a colon, as Locock does, I think that we may, for once, accept this overworked stop of his. I take the 'starry deep' to mean 'the water in which the stars are reflected', and 'A vast expanse' as being in apposition to this: if we take 'below' as an adverb, meaning 'below the mountains', as I do, it then needs a comma to mark this: to omit the comma would be to make it a preposition, and thereby to give an inferior sense to the passage.

p. 118, 345: Shelley's memorandum which follows this line would seem to connect with lines 361 ff.:

> A vision of evil
>   spirit
>   witch
>   ⟨? Harpy⟩
>   ghost

Then, on the next page, come these broken lines of verse:

> Like a sunbeam on a tempest streaming
>
> And with thy sweet eyes awful glance
>   nature
> Would wake the world from its cold trance
> Hast thou
>
> Breathless withdrawn   Like the Heaven of night
> Over a lake star-paved   azure
> Whose columns are the snowbright ⟨mountains⟩ round

> When the light of the rising moon is in the east and
> the setting sun yet in the west

A page further on come these lines

> To Wilson
>
> My head is wild with weeping for a grief
> Which is the shadow of a gentle mind
> I walk into the air yet no relief
> I seek yet haply if I sought should find—
> It comes uncalled—the woes of humankind   5
> Their actual miseries their false belief
> Fair Spirit thou art cold as clean and blind
> As beautiful

To the right of the heading, 'To Wilson', are two capital letters, the first 'S', and the second, I think, 'F': these I have failed to interpret. 'Wilson' may possibly be John Wilson, 1785–1854 ('Christopher North'), whose *City of the Plague* (1816) was read by Shelley in 1817, and is probably reflected in Canto X of *Laon and Cythna*. A powerful reviewer, Wilson surprised Shelley by his defence of his poem in *Blackwood's Edinburgh Magazine*, in January 1819—a defence the more surprising since *Blackwood's* had vied with the *Quarterly* in its attacks on Keats.

That this fragment originated in 1817 is plain from this draft among the pages of the draft of *Laon and Cythna*. For a second version, derived from a manuscript in Bod. MS. Shelley adds. e. 12, see p. 319. This version was placed by Rossetti among the minor poems of 1818. See n. on this version, p. 411 below.

On the page facing that on which Shelley has drafted 'To Wilson'—a wild pencil scribble, hardly decipherable—appear eight lines which seem to be a stanza drafted for *Laon and Cythna*, but lacking its final alexandrine:

> He ceased. Another rose: one pale and ⟨? weak⟩
> As he had been subdued by sufferings
> Too deep and dread to leave upon his cheek
> Aught but those lines which high endurance brings
> And scorn of anguish—like the peak that flings   5
> The sunbeam ⟨? on⟩ its snowy rocks—and smiled
> Gently in innocent pride, while on its wings
> His golden locks the wind spread wide and wild.

I have been unable to determine for what part of the poem these lines were intended. In line 1 the last word has been lost through tearing of the page: my conjecture is based on rhyme, sense, and what might perhaps be an initial 'w'. In line 6 Shelley originally wrote, and cancelled, 'The lightning from its rocks he stood and smiled'; the last two words are left unreplaced. A similar intention to revise is indicated in line 7, where 'innocent pride' is scored through. There is no punctuation except for the usual all-purpose dashes in line 1, needing to be replaced by some such strong stops as I have inserted, and the dash in line 5, indicating the parenthesis which Shelley, characteristically, forgot to close in the following line.

p. 120, 397–402: Hutchinson and Locock have, in my opinion, done the right thing, though for the wrong reason. I cannot accept Locock's statement that

Shelley uses suspension points to 'indicate a longer pause than that of a full stop'. The truth is that he uses them, as he uses the dash, quite indiscriminately, and they almost always need to be replaced—as was done in his own printings— by some such strong stops as the syntax demands. If, in print, they are not strictly rationed, they lose their meaning and corrupt syntax everywhere. But if sparingly used they can, sometimes, suggest a longer, dramatic pause, and that is what the syntax of Stanza XXXI does seem to demand.

p. 129, 665: Following this line, under the number '4', is a snatch of verse, evidently the beginning of an abortive stanza of *Laon and Cythna*.

> And I remember wandering through the shadow
> Of the young myrtle woods.

The stanza-numbering in the draft usually denotes some interim arrangement made during the course of composition: it seldom relates to the final order of stanzas.

p. 129, 675: Mary Shelley's emendation is justified by the Italian version of the opening of 667–82 which Shelley made for Emilia Viviani (see Rogers, *Shelley at Work*, ch. 13): his rendering is 'del [*sic*] spirito'.

p. 131, 729: On a page in e. 19, following the drafting of Canto II, Stanza VII, come some broken lines of verse, drafted in pencil. The straggling, barely legible, handwriting seems to suggest that Shelley was sleepy, or was writing in a bad light. Lines and passages, as shown by my square brackets, are lightly scored through, though whether this indicates cancellation or, as so often, merely an intention to revise, is difficult to judge. The mood of these lines seems to have an affinity with other laments of Shelley's, and may well have a biographical significance.

> My   maiden
>   eyne
> Thy delightful anguish
> That their spirit over-laden
> Might repose on thine
> [The simoon to the tulip-tree]
> [Is that which I have been to thee]
> [Heavily oh heavily]
>   [weight not on me now]
> [Why is the same]
> [Which thou hast not forborne to show]
> [Alas] [I found the [*sic*] too [Into the griefs]
> Oh! that there had been no morrow
> To one sweet eve
> Doubles not divides our sorrow

On the next page of e. 19 are lines, similarly drafted, which appear to be a continuation. Two lines and three other words are in ink, and seem to have been added later.

> [Thou must have seen it was ⟨? ruined⟩] ⎫
> Thou must have known it not well]   ⎬ [*in pencil*]
>
> [Yet thou didst sit and sing and smile
> Lifting those sweet eyes the while]

almond
A simoon to the [ches[t]nut flower] blossom
[The lightning to the mountain pine]
Nay worse [*in ink*]
[A child that mocks the mothers bosom]
Which feeds it, have I been to thee
[When human hopes are ever guilt]
Death, and the everlasting [grave] [tomb]
[Is that] which I have been to thee

p. 137, 910–27: As hitherto printed, Stanzas XXVIII and XXIX are nearly incomprehensible. The syntax is ungainly, but just functional if assisted by punctuation. The draft in e. 19 is, as usual, of no assistance, and recourse must be had to grammatical analysis. In *1818* three stops of Shelley's disrupted the syntax: the exclamation mark at 'melody' (914), the semicolon at 'be' (916), and the full stop at the end of the first stanza (918). As often in a rhetorical passage, an exclamation mark is a mark of Shelley's excitement rather than a logical contribution to syntactical sense. Neither Mary Shelley nor later editors seem to have noticed that by divorcing 'melody' from the noun 'Hymns', which is in apposition to it, the one in line 914 makes an anacoluthon of the next four lines. I have reunited the words with a dash. The semicolon in line 916 was rightly removed by Mary Shelley in *1839* since she realized that 'be' must not be divorced from its complement, 'Triumphant strains'. She did not, however, remove the full stop at the end of Stanza XXVIII, with the result that, in the next stanza, the participial phrase 'Her white arms . . . hair' either becomes unattached or must be taken, ridiculously, as suggesting the reason why (920–1) Laon's purpose seemed so great. What really inspired and strengthened him was, quite clearly, the 'Triumphant strains'; the hair and the arms were but an attractive concomitant. My comma at 'sung' (918) attaches the participial phrase where it belongs, namely to what precedes, and my exclamation mark at 'hair' (920) divorces it from what follows, and to which it does not belong. Editors have strangely ignored Shelley's anomalous semicolon in line 916. Hutchinson's dash at the end of Stanza XXVIII was an improvement, but, in my opinion, still tended to make a wrongful division, so I have substituted a comma. Rossetti in *1870* rightly perceived that a strong stop was needed at 'Freedom' (915) and used a full stop—I thought this too strong and have preferred a comma-plus-dash.

p. 140, 994: Here the drafts in e. 19 terminate and there are no manuscripts till line 1882, where the drafts in e. 10 begin.

p. 143, 1104: Mary Shelley's emendation, which gives a more obvious sense, is preferred by Locock. But I venture to think that 'calm with passion', though less obvious, is both Shelleyan and psychologically sound.

p. 152, 1369: *As, lifting me, it fell*: means 'As it fell when he lifted me'. The misrelated participle is a good example of the kind of Shelleyan solecism that cannot be emended.

p. 152, 1370: *Were*: Though this solecism could be corrected without damage to metre I preserve the more euphonious *constructio ad sensum*.

p. 152, 1377: Here I am with Rossetti in seeing no reason for retaining Shelley's misused 'lain'.

p. 162, 1680: *brother's*: the stanza suffered when Shelley was forced to substitute 'lover's': here his indignation was certainly justified.

p. 165, 1765: *Thus while*, meaning, I think, 'while we thus'.

p. 169, 1882: From here, in Canto V, to 4719, in Canto XII, the draft continues in the Notebook e. 10: for the deficiencies in the two drafts see above, pp. 361–2. On the outer cover of the Notebook e. 10 Shelley has written two sayings of Antisthenes, recorded in Diogenes Laertius, VI. 12:

κρεῖττόν ἐστι μετ᾽ ὀλίγων ἀγαθῶν πρὸς ἅπαντας τοὺς κακοὺς ἢ μετὰ πολλῶν κακῶν πρὸς ὀλίγους ἀγαθοὺς μάχεσθαι.

It is better to be in the company of a few good men fighting against all bad men than to fight against a few good men in company with a number of bad men.

ἀνδρὸς καὶ γυναικὸς ἡ αὐτὴ ἀρετή

Virtue is the same in woman as in man.

p. 177, 2151: *beat*: I have not thought it necessary, as Mary Shelley did, to correct this particular piece of loose grammar. It is a *constructio ad sensum*, meaning 'the pulses of both hearts now beat together'.

p. 182, 2295: *flame*: This obvious conjecture, originally Rossetti's, is justified by e. 10, where Shelley cancelled 'light', substituted 'flame', and, as happened elsewhere, printed the cancelled word.

p. 185, 2397: I follow Hutchinson, Dowden, and Forman in substituting a comma for the full stop at the end of the line placed there in *1818* and followed in *1839*. The passage is obscure and the line unmetrical. Hutchinson ingeniously suggested 'lift' for 'light', but e. 10 is against this.

p. 188, 2480: With Mary Shelley I capitalize 'Pest', to match 'Want' and 'Moon-madness' with which it logically belongs; 'bane' should not be capitalized because it stands outside this group.

p. 192, 2604–14: Shelley printed a full stop at the end of Stanza xxx and a colon-plus-dash after 'speech' in the next stanza (2608). These stops were preserved by Mary. Rossetti rightly saw that in place of a syntactical break between the stanzas a stop was needed to lead from the first 'in silence' to the second; he printed a colon-plus-dash. He felt too that a full stop was needed in 2608. Forman would not accept Rossetti's changes. Hutchinson accepted the first but in place of the full stop printed a second colon-plus-dash. I have accepted Rossetti's full stop—wherein, for what draft punctuation is worth, he has the support of e. 10—but, to join the stanzas syntactically, I have preferred a comma-plus-dash in line 2604.

p. 195, 2690: The clause starting here ends in 2697 where, in Virgilian fashion, the 'as' of the simile is caught up by 'thus'. In 2694–5 the parallel main sentences having 'clasps' and 'clings' for their verbs should not be divided by so strong a stop as a semicolon: I have substituted a comma. I have removed the comma from 2695 in order that the 'when'-clause may come closer to the 'clings' which it qualifies, and balance the 'while'-clause, properly untrammelled by a comma, which qualifies 'clasps'.

p. 201, 2885–6: Though defended by Forman, the punctuation of *1818* is meaningless. With Hutchinson and others I follow the suggestions of Rossetti.

p. 201, 2887–8: With Rossetti and Locock I print the brackets suggested by A. C. Bradley, which make clear that the two clauses within them qualify 'whirlwinds'; I do not agree with Hutchinson that they are unnecessary. Hutchinson's comma-plus-dash usefully shows that the comparison refers back to Cythna.

p. 205, 3024–5: Editors who have accepted Shelley's 'when the red moon on high / Pause' have been at pains to explain the 'Pause' as a 'Shelleyan subjunctive' or as the subordination of syntax to euphony. On this occasion the draft—probably miscopied by Shelley himself—does supply us with his real syntactical intention.

p. 206, 3041: I follow Rossetti in removing Shelley's sense-obscuring colon. The sense, as explained by Rossetti to Locock, is 'The dream [that I had borne a child] vanished, and left unreturned the more than human love which I had bestowed upon the supposed infant.'

p. 207, 3076–8: The meaning, as yielded by Locock's pointing, is 'My spirit felt again like one of those spirits (such as thine) whose fate it is . . .'.

p. 208, 3105: *are*: in the Platonic sense of 'are real', as opposed to things that belong only to the world of Mutability. My colon was necessary to point to Shelley's list of the 'real' things.

p. 211, 3188/3191: These and some twenty other unnecessary capitals in Cantos VIII and IX, which I have silently removed, were unaccountably introduced by Hutchinson. The nouns in question are uncapitalized both in *1818* and e. 10 and only three have capitals in *1839*.

p. 214, 3271–5: With Locock's pointing, adopted here, 'thereon' means 'on Opinion'. See below, p. 390, for n. on the content of this interesting passage.

p. 214, 3289: Shelley wrote first

> O [human] love [*subsequently capitalized*] which to
>   the hearts of [erring] man
> [Is as]
> Art as

When he personalized Love and moved into the vocative his reason for leaving 'hearts' in the plural may have been to avoid the jingle of 'heart . . . Art'; then at some stage subsequent to the draft the sense required him to substitute 'men' for 'man'. I think that we should accept this Shelleyan half-rhyme.

p. 215, 3311: It does not seem to have occurred to Forman that Shelley might have changed the word in proof. He cites 4165–6 where Hate is masculine, being the mate of Fear who is feminine, but, surely, this is to credit Shelley with a totally unlikely degree of consistency.

p. 215, 3315: Here, for some reason, it does occur to Forman that Shelley might have added the comma to 'man' in proof; he considers that it prevents 'a shocking tautology'. To me, as to Locock, it seems rather to cause one.

p. 217, 3379 ff.: The construction of Stanza XXI is, as Locock observes, 'obscure and ungrammatical'. The general meaning would appear to be something like this: 'It is Hate whom self-contempt arms with a mortal sting, which becomes useless when enfolded in a human heart—i.e. a heart filled with love which, according to Shelley–Plato notions of *Prometheus Unbound*, etc., is its antidote.' Then Shelley awkwardly confuses the personification—Hate has been 'Whom' in line 3381, but becomes 'it' in 3383. But the meaning proceeds, I think, like this: 'When Hate revolts from such horrible food it attacks other hearts within its reach with ninefold rage: just as Amphisbaena, when it has entangled a bird in its coils, rears itself over the putrefying body and threatens to strike at everything within range.' For the content of this passage see below, p. 391.

p. 223, 3564–7: Thus *1904*, *1818*, *1839*. Syntax obscure. Rossetti makes a parenthesis of 'like . . . earth.' 'Hung [in the minds of men]' was Shelley's first thought in e. 10; 'have' is omitted in e. 10—'had' might be consistent with 'Hung', which is quite clearly written.

p. 223, 3573: *fame*: In e. 10 the line ends with three words, all uncancelled: 'fame', written above 'glory', which is written above 'grace'. To make a sense for the last the whole stanza would have needed redrafting and re-rhyming; however, 'grace' somehow got printed, nonsensically, without this. The conjecture of 'flame' is a very reasonable one, in view of other instances in the poem of repeated rhyme-words. The thought behind 'fame' is made plainer by the fact that 'glory' was in Shelley's mind as an alternative: likewise by the Homeric tag which he scribbled in e. 10 below the stanza (see note on line 3577 under 'Content' below, p. 391).

p. 226, 3642–3 Perhaps the draft is a little less obscure than the revised and printed version. The general meaning seems to be that, by her union with Laon, Cythna participates in his poetic capacity.

p. 229, 3743: After the page in e. 10 which bears the preceding lines comes a page bearing doodled profiles and a few figures. On the next page, pencilled barely legibly, partly above and partly below a drawing of a sailing boat on a lake, with mountains in the rear, come the following lines (cf. 'Dear Home . . .', p. 86):

> I visit thee but thou art sadly changed
> Thy former home is now made desolate
> It has become the path of homelessness
> The moon and stars and sun find a new
>
> From tired
> [For weary] beams where once this busy heart
> From many beatings and in many thoughts
> After ⟨? her⟩ wandering ⟨? found a few⟩ brief years
> And I am changed and many things are changed
> The earth the forests and the sky remain

From 'and many things' the pencilling is lighter, suggesting a later addition. In the centre of the next page, written with the first, darker, kind of pencilling, are two more lines (cf. 'Death', p. 134):

> These things remain
> And unforgiving memories linger there

In a different script and a different shade of pencilling, with the crowded words hardly separated, another line is just decipherable:

> Which leap forth anew

On the next page are fragments unrelated to what precedes them. First a line almost certainly related to 'The Ancient Mariner', 350–66 (cf. also *Laon and Cythna*, 2586):

> A music wild and soft that filled the moonnight air.

About halfway down:

> The pine is here
> The sky where ⟨*possibly* when⟩ the moon was
> The grass, the hawthorn
> blooming now

Next a comment, apparently referring to 'The Ancient Mariner', 200 ff.:

> The star scene too with ice there! Coleridge's etc. And each dreadful moment afterwards telling in

Five words at the top of the next page may be the completion of the comment on 'The Ancient Mariner':

> truer and more sorrowful truth.

A little lower on this page is another snatch of verse:

> Thou *above* [One] was [*sic*] a homeless cloud—the other rested
> Upon a pinnacle of mountain snow
> So pure and beautiful, that time who wasted
> [All] With his swift footstep mark [
> Past over it and left no ruin there
> But cold—too cold

On the page following this Shelley has drafted an advertisement indicative of his plans for leaving England for Italy:

> Wanted to purchase by exchange for an equivalent secured on a large [prosperous] property in England, a villa in the neighbourhood of Naples.

p. 230, 3775: *with stream*: Shelley probably omitted the definite article to avoid rhythmic distortion and an ugly clash of '-th th-'. His phrase may be coined on the analogy of 'down stream' which itself would neither fit his sentence nor a context in which his river is not a literal but a purely metaphorical one. No need, I think, to see in the 'flow' a reference to Heraclitus' doctrine of πάντα ῥεῖ.

p. 232, 3834: Another instance where the cancelled word somehow got copied and printed, in place of Shelley's correction.

p. 234, 3898: Explained by Locock as a condensed expression, probably modelled on some Greek passage, for 'faithless to the agreed-on duty of continuing the non-betrayal of fear'. This meaning seems supported by the words originally drafted: 'the fear they strove to hate'. Once again—cf. 3642–3— Shelley's revision has failed to clarify. But I agree with Locock's general summary of 3894–8: 'Peace in the silent streets, save when the cries of some [not all] of the victims caused friendly bystanders to dread that some victim of their own kindred, hitherto faithful and silent, should be induced by the cries of his fellow victims to the expression of fear,—a fear which he had not yet exhibited.' It has been suggested that 'fear' is a misreading of 'few'. In e. 10 the *ductus litterarum* might just conceivably be held to support the suggestion, but my judgement is against it.

p. 234, 3900: After Stanza XII, in e. 10, Shelley has scribbled six barely legible lines of verse and two memoranda:

> The wild bull in the mountain and the horse
> Perished, the fish were poisoned in the streams
> A cloud of ⟨? horrid⟩ exhalation ⟨?⟩
> From the earth ⟨? up⟩ and to Heaven steams
> The birds are killed which float among the ⟨? skies⟩
> And winds they have drank poison

> In the pestilence—its effects on man—destroying the memory of things—the imagination of ghosts—⟨? Daphnis⟩ Thebd—see Senecas

> The dogs become hydrophobic and the wolves—the horse—cold sweat—tear their [teeth] flesh with their teeth—the birds and beasts of prey become mild

These passages, clearly, connect with the description of the pestilence which begins in the following stanza. 'Daphnis'—what Shelley wrote looks more like 'Daphies'—is presumably the hero of Longus' pastoral romance, *Daphnis and Chloe*, which he praised in a letter to Peacock in 1820 (Jones, *Letters* ii. 213). He may have read it earlier. 'Thebd' is, presumably, the *Thebaid* of Statius. I cannot perceive any thought-connection that either of these works may have with *Laon and Cythna*, and I am unable to guess what work of Seneca's Shelley has failed to specify.

On the page that follows are three words, perhaps the start of an abortive line:

> The ships that

p. 248, 4321: *wreathed*: It is certainly arguable that Shelley intended to add 'writhed' to the archaisms which occasionally colour his poem. But meaning is not seriously affected and I assume that the 'wreathed' of *1818* is not a miscopying from the draft but a correction. Cf. n. on 4361.

p. 249, 4341–65: Above the page of e. 10 on which Shelley drafted Stanza XV and part of XVI is a memorandum:

> This somewhat resembles an incident in *The Corsair*. The catastrophe and tendency of this involuntary imitation of it is widely different and an allusion to it might justly be considered presumptuous.

p. 250, 4361: *the . . . the*: Another editorial dilemma—but, though Shelley's 'the' and 'tho' are frequently indistinguishable, the word is perfectly clear in e. 10, and since both sound and sense are, I think, slightly improved by it, I here opt for the draft rather than for the *editio princeps*. Cf. n. on 4321, above.

p. 255, 4450–76: At the bottom of the second of two pages in e. 10 bearing the draft of XII. I–III, Shelley has jotted down Μελάγχλαινοι Πρίηποι, 'black-garmented Priapi', from Moschus, III. 27, a poem of which he translated part (see above, p. 91), probably about the time when he was working on *Laon and Cythna*. The context of Moschus' lament is remote from Shelley's Canto; but here, as often, Shelley has simply been fascinated by a phrase. The comment is obviously a wry, private, unprintable one on the 'Priests' (4460) with their 'gloomy cowls' (4464); a smile at concealed sexuality which would have amused the young Rimbaud—cf. 'Les Châtiments de Tartuffe'.

p. 255, 4535–9: The received text of these lines is almost nonsense. The draft in e. 10 does afford one little piece of help: there is a carefully placed semicolon after 'loveliness' in 4535. Locock, who saw that a stronger stop than the traditional comma was necessary, printed a comma-plus-dash, which points the syntax quite as well as Shelley's semicolon, which I follow. For the rest the draft is unpunctuated, and an editor can only punctuate the sense. The inverted commas, indicative of what the Priest was thinking, are mine, and so are the full stops after 'ice' (4537) and 'self' (4539) with which I have strengthened the confusing dashes of Hutchinson. 'One' (4534), of course, is the Priest; 'he' (4537) means 'any man'.

p. 261, 4699: In e. 10 the word certainly might be read as 'then'. But Shelley first wrote 'they have lent / To you' for which 'there is lent / To you' is surely a more natural emendation than 'then', which would have a somewhat pointless emphasis.

p. 262, 4728: Here ends the draft in e. 10, with the end of Stanza XXXI. There follow some lines of which the wild pencil draft has become badly rubbed, so that I can decipher only occasional words:

> As *over* Like the wintry skies ⟨?⟩ mountains
> Which the tempests shake *above* ⟨?⟩ roaring elements
> Like the young moon beside ⟨?⟩ fountains
> Which floats on the sunsets golden ocean
> Above the piny dells of   mountains

At the bottom of the page is a memorandum in the hand of Mary Shelley:

> £5—March 19, 1817
> 5191

Possibly this may refer to one of Shelley's loans to Godwin. On 9 Mar. he had written to him saying 'I enclose a check to within a few pounds of my possessions' (Jones, *Letters*, i. 536).

Above the memorandum, written with the page reversed, are three broken lines of verse:

> How long has Poesy, the widowed Mother
> Been childless in our land   he died
> Blind old and lonely, when

On a neighbouring page, at the top of which Shelley has noted

> [We all act out a false part in the world]

are some more near-illegible, pencilled lines:

> Shapes about my steps assembling
> [Hopes of youth] Ghosts of hope which unreturning
>   has ceased
> And [? and *for* un] returned [like spirits] trembling
> In my heart for ever burning
> Like a firebrand slowly dying
> [Dead] And in its own ashes lying
> The winds are soft the skies are blue

On the next page is a memorandum:

⟨? Her aversion⟩ from a stranger's touch shrinks with the modesty of natural meetings

pp. 262-3, 4746-55: As punctuated by Shelley, Stanza XXXIV is one long anacoluthon, which Mary Shelley, Rossetti, and Forman failed to set right. Hutchinson's semicolon after 4750 is successful in giving sentence-shape to what follows, but not to what precedes. Locock's dash after 4747 is a help. But if we now replace the full stop after 4746 by a comma-plus-dash, the next line will stand in intelligible apposition to 'maze', 4748 will yield an absolute participial clause in explanation of 4747, and two clauses, one of time and one of place, will complete the sense down to Hutchinson's semicolon.

At this point may be conveniently grouped seven Platonic memoranda from MS. Shelley adds. e. 10. Shelley wrote them with the Notebook held in reverse, and working backwards. Nos. 1–5 were printed by J. A. Notopoulos in his important article 'New Texts of Shelley's Plato' (*Keats–Shelley Journal*, xv, 1966); nos. 6 and 7 have not, I think, been previously printed. The first four are on p. 219 rev., the fifth on p. 217 rev., and the last two on p. 172 rev. I give Shelley's references to his Bipont edition of Plato, together with the reference in the Oxford Classical Text edition. The memoranda are given in Shelley's order, but in place of his accentless Greek, with its other non-significant anomalies, I have given the Oxford text:

1. [*Apology*, Bipont, i. p. 67; OCT, 29 a 4–b 2]

τὸ γάρ τοι θάνατον δεδιέναι, ὦ ἄνδρες, οὐδὲν ἄλλο ἐστὶν ἢ δοκεῖν σοφὸν εἶναι μὴ ὄντα·
δοκεῖν γὰρ εἰδέναι ἐστὶν ἃ οὐκ οἶδεν. οἶδε μὲν γὰρ οὐδεὶς τὸν θάνατον οὐδ᾽ εἰ τυγχάνει
τῷ ἀνθρώπῳ πάντων μέγιστον ὂν τῶν ἀγαθῶν, δεδίασι δ᾽ ὡς εὖ εἰδότες ὅτι μέγιστον
τῶν κακῶν ἐστι. καίτοι πῶς οὐκ ἀμαθία ἐστὶν αὕτη ἡ ἐπονείδιστος, ἡ τοῦ οἴεσθαι εἰδέναι
ἃ οὐκ οἶδεν;

Professor Hugh Tredennick has kindly allowed me to quote from his translation in *The Last Days of Socrates* in the Penguin Classics Series:

> For . . . to be afraid of death is only another form of thinking that one is wise when one is not; it is to think that one knows what one does not know. No one knows with regard to death whether or not it is not really the greatest blessing that can happen to a man but people dread it as though they were certain that it is the greatest evil; and thus ignorance, which thinks that it knows what it does not, must surely be ignorance most culpable.

To his Bipont reference Shelley adds 'et amplius'. It is not difficult to see what fascinated him in the whole long passage. No subject was nearer to the centre of his thought than the mission on earth of poets and philosophers, and Socrates' assertion of his own mission as something divinely imposed on him includes, logically, he says, the refusal to fear death. If he did subscribe to popular assumptions about death, as about any other subject, he would be himself guilty of the very kind of intellectual dishonesty which he had spent his life in exposing among the sophists and others.

Across the Greek text is drafted the first line of 'To Constantia' (see above, p. 302):

[Mouths] Rose which drink [*sic*] the fountain dew

2. [Note on *Apology*, Bipont, i. pp. 74–6; OCT, 32 b 1–e 1]

Socrates *alone* in the Senate opposed the condemnation of the ten captains, and ran great risk of his life.

Political hysteria, and resistance to it, was always a subject of Shelley's: as an exemplar he jots down Plato's reference to Socrates' courage after the battle of Arginusae, when six Athenian generals, despite their victory over the Spartans, were condemned to death on account of a heavy casualty list.

3. [Note on *Apology*, Bipont, i. p. 77; OCT, 33 c 4–7]

Socrates says that his proceedings were assigned to him by dreams and by prophesies

By 'proceedings' Shelley means the practice, which Socrates regarded as his duty, of cross-examining pretenders to wisdom—designated in the text τοῖς οἰομένοις μὲν εἶναι σοφοῖς, οὖσι δ'οὔ. For the whole big question of the significance of dreams to Shelley see Rogers, *Shelley at Work*, ch. 10.

4. [*Apology*, Bipont, i. p. 85; OCT, 36 d 9–e 1]

ὁ μὲν γὰρ ὑμᾶς ποιεῖ εὐδαίμονας δοκεῖν εἶναι, ἐγὼ δὲ εἶναι.

Before we can translate Shelley's quotation, or see the point of his memorandum, we must first look at the context in Plato. Socrates has been found guilty on the charge of corrupting youth. The prosecution has demanded the penalty of death and it now falls to him to propose an alternative penalty. He says that so far from punishment for what he has done—namely to safeguard the moral welfare of those whose minds he has spent his life in examining—he deserves, as a public benefactor, to be maintained at the public expense. Such a person as he, says Socrates (I quote again from Professor Tredennick's translation, the last sentence of which renders Shelley's quotation), 'deserves it much more than any victor in the races at Olympia, whether he wins with a single horse or a pair or a team of four. These people give you the semblance of success, but I give you the reality.' The conflicting worlds of popular values and true values—the two worlds of semblance and reality—are found everywhere in Shelley's metaphysical thinking and imagery. The words ἐγὼ δὲ εἶναι are underlined. Can this, perhaps, denote a quiet, private identification of the principles of the Socratic mission with those of the Shelleyan one?

5. [Note on *Apology*, Bipont, i. pp. 93–4; OCT, 40 c 4 ff.]

The immortality of the soul magnificently questioned.

By itself this might suggest the conventional delight of the conventional atheist-figure at reading something which doubted that doctrine of immortality so essential in Christianity. But reference to the *Apology* shows that, in the context, Socrates is in fact arguing in favour of the doctrine, and doing so by his usual method of raising questions and working out the answers. By 'questioned' Shelley does not mean 'doubted' but 'examined'—he is probably thinking of the Greek verb ἐξετάζειν.

6. [Note on *Symposium*, Bipont, x. pp. 93–4; OCT, 173 d]

Motto for an anti-worldling

Apollodorus has been talking of his delight in philosophic discourse and his preference of this to the society of the wealthy money-bag friends (τῶν πλουσίων καὶ χρηματιστικῶν) of his companion. His companion rallies him for being crazy and thinking everybody miserable except Socrates. Very much in line with the manner of such a passage were the railleries between Shelley and Peacock, the friend from whom he had caught so much of his enthusiasm for Plato. Writing to Peacock in June 1819 (Jones, *Letters*, ii. 98), he says of the caricature of himself as Scythrop 'I suppose the moral is contained in what

Falstaff says *"For Gods sake talk like a man of this world"* . . .' He neatly pushes
Peacock into the position of Apollodorus' companion, and neatly scores a point
in identifying 'a man of this world' with Falstaff, eternal prototype of tavern
wiseacres.

Once again Shelley's mind is moving on the semblance–reality conflicts.
The context is germane to that of no. 4 above, where just before the passage
I have quoted from the *Apology*, Socrates had spoken of his own unworldliness
and contempt for money.

7. [*Symposium*, Bipont, x, p. 186, lines 5 ff.; OCT, 182 c]

οὐ γὰρ οἶμαι συμφέρει τοῖς ἄρχουσι φρονήματα μεγάλα ἐγγίγνεσθαι τῶν ἀρχομένων,
οὐδὲ φιλίας ἰσχυρὰς καὶ κοινωνίας, ὃ δὴ μάλιστα φιλεῖ τά τε ἄλλα πάντα καὶ ὁ ἔρως
ἐμποιεῖν. ἔργῳ δὲ τοῦτο ἔμαθον καὶ οἱ ἐνθάδε τύραννοι· ὁ γὰρ Ἀριστογείτονος ἔρως καὶ
ἡ Ἁρμοδίου φιλία βέβαιος γενομένη κατέλυσεν αὐτῶν τὴν ἀρχήν.

Pausanias has been talking of the educative power of love among young men.
The barbarians, he says (meaning the non-Greek world), condemn this kind
of love and he proceeds to say why. I quote Shelley's translation:

> For I imagine it would little conduce to the benefit of the governors, that the governed
> should be disciplined to lofty thoughts and to unity and communion of steadfast friend-
> ship, of which admirable effects the tyrants of our own country have also learned that
> Love is the author. For the love of Harmodius and Aristogiton, strengthened into
> a firm friendship, dissolved the tyranny.

Harmodius and Aristogiton were the lovers who killed Hipparchus, brother
of the Athenian tyrant Hippias, in 514 B.C. and tried to kill Hippias himself.
Shelley's mind is moving on a favourite subject—the extension of love between
individuals to love as a force in politics. He is discovering in his direct study of
Platonism an extension of the ideas inherent in his natural Platonic feelings:
for which see nn. on *Queen Mab* in Vol. I.

Content:

p. 99, *Preface.*

[2] *vice not the object of punishment, etc.*: The doctrine seems drawn from
Godwin. Locock compares 'The Daemon of the World', II. 577–80, and
Prometheus Unbound, I. 403. The 'Rulers of the World' are the 'seven blood-
hounds' of *The Mask of Anarchy*, 8: Austria, Bourbon France, Portugal,
Prussia, Russia, Spain, and Sweden—Metternich's 'Holy Alliance' which, after
the fall of Napoleon, opposed reforms throughout Europe.

[6]: *I have considered Poetry in its most comprehensive sense*: Cf. the passage
from Shelley's letter to Godwin, quoted by Mary Shelley in her Note on *Laon
and Cythna* (pp. 272–3), which is as significant a passage as Shelley ever wrote on
his conceptions of his poetic function: see Rogers, *Shelley at Work*, pp. 24 ff.
This new poem represented his first attempt since *Queen Mab* at poetry 'in
its most comprehensive' (i.e. 'cosmic') sense. Notopoulos (*Platonism*, p. 213)
points out the significance of the last few sentences of this paragraph for the
study of the Platonism of the poem, which is poorly assimilated, as he says,
with its revolutionary character. Godwin loomed large in Shelley's life in 1817,
and the poem was written with one eye on him. From Godwin himself, his

troubles, and his demands, Shelley was never to be freed, but, when in the next year he escaped to Italy, the emancipation from Godwinism that had begun as *Queen Mab* progressed (see Vol. I, nn.) was to find its fulfilment in his most 'comprehensive' poem, *Prometheus Unbound*. *Laon and Cythna* might be described as a half-way house—rather a tumbledown one—between *Queen Mab* and *Prometheus Unbound*, Godwinism and Platonism, the young Shelley and the mature Shelley. See nn. on Canto I.

[7]: In paragraph 6 of the Preface to *Prometheus Unbound* this section was to be given new and magnificent expression: cf. 'The cloud of mind is discharging its collected lightning . . .'

[8]: *an alexandrine in the middle of a stanza*: e.g. lines 1652, 3788. Line 1575, which ought to be the concluding alexandrine of a stanza, has a syllable short. Lines 2115, 2361, and 2451, which should be alexandrines, have been extended to a seventh foot. I have not attempted an exhaustive inquiry into this anomaly.

[9]: *some of our greatest poets* . . .: Shelley is thinking, in particular, of Coleridge and Southey, whom he regarded as political renegades.

p. 106, *Dedication*.

Epigraph: From *Byron's Conspiracy*, by George Chapman (*c.* 1559–*c.* 1634). The preceding lines, as Claude C. Brew points out, are interesting in a context in which, beset by the difficulties of a stormy life, Shelley is offering his most ambitious and longest poem to the world:

> Give me a spirit that on this life's rough sea,
> Loves t'have his sails filled with a lusty wind,
> Even till his sail-yards tremble; his masts crack
> And his rapt ship runs on her side so low
> That she drinks water, and her keel ploughs air.

Cf. lines 125–6, where the Dedication concludes with the image of Shelley and Mary weathering together the storms of 1817, guided by the twin stars of their loves, the one for the other. Shelley's editions were inscribed 'TO MARY —— ——'; for the reason see below, n. on lines 7–9.

1–3: One of Mary Shelley's names for Shelley was 'Elfin Knight'. In writing for the *Examiner* he sometimes used the initials 'E.K.' as a pseudonym. This image of Shelley as a Red Cross Knight, returning to his Una from a hazardous but successful quest, is the first of the Spenserian echoes in the Dedication, the whole of which is cast in a Spenserian-Platonic form. For a discussion of this see Claude C. Brew's critical study of the text and poetical evolution of the Dedication, *Shelley and Mary in 1817*, 1971. *Faëry* is, of course, 'fairyland', as in Spenser.

7–9: *natal gloom*: Shelley's dark misfortunes are contrasted with the Platonic radiance shed by Mary the 'Child of love and light'; the radiance comes partly from their love for each other and partly from her parentage, for she is the daughter of two philosophers, Godwin and Mary Wollstonecraft. As explained in his Preface, he considered *Laon and Cythna* a test of his effectiveness in communicating with his public, and it is because of his 'doubtful promise' that he refrains from overt references that would link other names to his own.

12–17: Cf. Mary Shelley's Note, p. 272, [4].

21–36: For this description of Shelley's semi-religious call, and self-dedication, to poetry cf. 'Hymn to Intellectual Beauty', 55–62, and *Laon and Cythna*, II. XIV–XV. Biographers now consider that the incident referred to took place not, as Mary believed, at Eton, but earlier, at Sion House Academy, Brentford. It is possible, however, that Shelley has fused the imaginary and symbolical with the autobiographical.

37–40: refer to Shelley's interest in unfashionable poets such as Wordsworth and Southey, in the political teaching of Godwin, in scientific experiment, etc.

44–5: The mood of the poet in *Alastor*.

46–63: From the *Alastor* mood Shelley has passed to the mood of fulfilment: in Mary he has found the Una, the ideal woman of his lifelong quest. Cf. the mood of fulfilment in *Epipsychidion*, 267–80. A version of lines 51–2, from e. 14, was given by Garnett to Forman:

> One whom I found was dear but false to me,
> The other's heart was like a heart of stone.

Forman comments: ' "One" refers to Shelley's first love, his cousin, Harriet Grove, "the other" to his first wife, Harriet Westbrook.' No doubt he did well to cancel, at the time, so explicit a reference.

52: *Hard hearts, and cold*: Cameron, *The Young Shelley*, p. 238, takes this as referring to Harriet Westbrook and her sister Eliza. This would mean, in the context of Shelley's quest for an ideal love, that he once entertained romantic notions about Eliza, which few could believe. What Forman suggested of the rejected lines (see preceding n.) is probably true here as well.

59: *Custom*: commonly mentioned in Shelley's poetry as one of the enslavers of mankind. Cf. Wordsworth, 'Immortality Ode', 126–8.

60: *clouds*: symbolic, Platonically, of the evil through which the 'Child of love and light' could shine, dispelling it.

61: *slave*: a common term in Shelley for those who lack the will to repel evil in society. *breathed*: exhaled.

64–7: Cf. above, nn. on 7–9, 46–63.

77: *two gentle babes*: William, born 24 Jan. 1816, and Clara, born 2 Sept. 1817. Within two years the Shelleys were to lose both to sickness in Italy.

80–1: The notion of works of art as 'children of the mind', engendered by Platonic intercourse between people who love each other in a manner over and above the physical element, which may or may not be present, was a favourite with Shelley: cf. *Prometheus Unbound*, III. iii. 49–56. It originates in *Symposium*, 209 c.

82–90: Cf. the mood of 7–8 and 119–20.

86: Cf. 58–9 and n.

90: Cf. 'The Sunset', 1–4, and the prose fragment, 'Una Favola' (Julian edition, vi. 279–86).

91: Cf. 'Passages connected with *Epipsychidion*', 4 [Hutch, 1904, p. 426]:

What you are, is a thing that I must veil.

94: *ample forehead*: This attribute, a mark of beauty in the Middle Ages, is probably a conscious echo of *The Faerie Queene*, II. iii. 24.

102: *One*: Mary Wollstonecraft, first wife of William Godwin, who died in giving birth to Mary Shelley.

108: *Sire*: William Godwin.

109: *spirit*: Cf. 'Rejected Passages', line 54 (p. 267), where Shelley has a footnote identifying the 'spirit' as the author of *Political Justice*. This footnote comes from e. 14, and appears, in an abbreviated form, in D. 3. Some have thought that the omission of this note in the published version of the poem indicates a change of feeling towards Godwin. But this is inconsistent with the respect which, despite all personal differences, Shelley always showed for Godwin's work. For a more likely explanation see above, n. on 7–9. In support of this, as Claude C. Brew points out, is the fact that the 'Mary, thou and I' of the passage rejected from Stanza XIV becomes 'thou and I / Sweet friend!' in its final form: see 121–2.

118: *pauses*: seems to have troubled commentators, but the meaning must surely be that Shelley's voice, having uttered truth in his poem, pauses to see what effect he is making; see above, n. on 7–9.

119: *cry*: the poem, *Laon and Cythna*.

119–26: Cf. the substance of Shelley's prose pamphlet of Mar. 1817, *A Proposal for Putting Reform to the Vote*: cf. Julian edition, vi. 63–4.

p. 111, *Canto 1*.

127–9: *trampled France ... visions of despair*: Like Wordsworth, when emerging to maturity out of the Godwinian twilight of French revolutionary idealism, Shelley had often come near to 'yielding up moral questions in despair'. The tensions of his personal life had helped to increase the confusion of his thinking, which, in turn, is reflected in the difficult symbolism of *Laon and Cythna*. Keats, who knew him while he was composing the poem, shrewdly perceived his need to 'curb his magnanimity'—i.e. the breadth of his metaphysical conceptions—and not to let the attempt at 'comprehensiveness' (see above, n. on Preface [6]) result in an unintelligible sprawl of meaning. The letter Shelley wrote to a publisher on 13 Oct. 1817 reads rather like an attempt to explain away weaknesses in the poem of which he himself was conscious. Of the first Canto he wrote that it was (Jones, *Letters*, i. 563)

indeed, in some measure a distinct poem, tho' very necessary to the wholeness of the work. I say this, because if it were all written in the manner of the first Canto, I could not expect that it should be interesting to any great number of people.

Perhaps both he and Keats were thinking of the somewhat confused symbolism, which is as puzzling in the Canto itself as it is unsuccessful in giving a unity to the poem as a whole. See n. on I. 193, below.

136: *So as I stood*: means 'As I stood thus', a common Spenserian inversion.

172, 178–80: Cf 'The Ancient Mariner' 18, 149–82.

158: *serene*: Latin *serenum*. *The Shelley Concordance* says 'calm, brightness'. Imitation of such Latinisms as this substantival use of a neuter adjective was common between 1750 and 1850. Cf. *Epipsychidion*, 506, and Keats, 'On First Looking into Chapman's Homer', 7.

181–5: *Even like a bark . . . Sails*: Locock says that this solecism is not found elsewhere in Shelley.

193 ff.: *An Eagle and a Serpent*: For the symbolism of the Serpent see above, pp. 335–6, n. on 'The Daemon of the World', 100. Here too it is important to get away from Old Testament associations. Once again it symbolizes not Evil but Eternity. Since Eternity, eternal values, etc., are commonly associated by Shelley with the world of Beauty, Liberty, etc., the Snake does come very close here to symbolizing Goodness. Since the natural adversary of Goodness is Evil it is usually assumed that the Eagle that is here warring with the Serpent is a symbol for the Principle of Evil. Of this I am less certain. If we examine the occurrence of the word Eagle in Shelley's poetry we find, to start with, that, like the Cave and other symbol-words, it is not always used symbolically. When, however, it is invested with a symbolical significance that significance is a fairly consistent one. An interesting example is the fragment 'Mighty eagle! thou that soarest . . .'; see p. 304. The draft found by Forman scribbled on a letter of Godwin's of 29 Apr. 1817 gives, I think, the date of conception. With his conclusion, and that of later editors, that the lines were addressed to Godwin I am unconvinced—as well might one reason, if a fragmentary pane-gyric by the late Dame Edith Sitwell were found drafted on a letter from the Commissioners for Inland Revenue, that it had been inspired by her local Inspector of Taxes. Nobody seems to have noticed the connection of these lines with the Platonic epigram (*Anth. Pal.* vii. 62). In the Bodleian Notebook MS. Shelley adds. e. 8, Shelley wrote them out only a few pages away from the page on which he drafted his translation of this epigram, and in it the question 'Eagle, why soarest thou . . .' is answered by the Eagle: 'I am the image of swift Plato's spirit . . .' Cf. also *Hellas*, 76–7, 'As an eagle fed with morning / Scorns the embattled tempest's warning'. Here the symbolism is clear enough: the eagle, spirit of Greece, is triumphant over evil and tyranny because 'fed with' the Platonic radiance which drives away evil. Cf. also 'The Triumph of Life', 128–31, and 'Ode to Liberty', 8 (also drafted in e. 8). It seems to me that the struggle in *Laon and Cythna* between the Serpent and the Eagle is intended to symbolize the contemporary conflict not so much between Good and Evil as between two forces of idealism: the Godwinian revolutionary, which had failed and was outdated, and the Shelleyan-Platonic, which, the poet hoped, might bring about the new revolution in human affairs, the 'Revolution of the Golden City', wherein Shelley and Mary would be the protagonists, building their Byzantium, a Platonic paradise, in England's green and pleasant land.

Though this explanation of the Snake–Eagle conflict may not illuminate all the attendant obscurities, it does illuminate many of them: e.g. the denouement in lines 622–30; see n. I do not disagree with Mr. Cameron's suggestion (*PMLA*, lvi, Mar. 1941) that Volney's *Les Ruines* was a likely source of *Laon and Cythna*:

Queen Mab had owed much to it and it would not be surprising if its indirect Platonism merged with the direct Platonic studies of 1817.

For Shelley's Platonic memoranda among manuscripts of the poem see nn. above, p. 375.

248: *lifeless*: inanimate, exhausted; cf. Jane Austen, *Persuasion*, vol. i, ch. 12, where Louisa, after a fall, though by no means dead, is 'taken up lifeless'.

262-70: For the Woman-figure in Shelley's Platonism see Rogers, *Shelley at Work*, ch. 4; for the Boat-symbolism see ibid., ch. 6. Over and above the metaphysical notion of escape from a present world of unreality and despair—anticipatory, for example, of *Prometheus Unbound*, II. v. 78 ff., and *Epipsychidion*, 407 ff.—Shelley's feelings may be moving towards his escape, with Mary and their children, to Italy: cf. 'To William Shelley, 1817', p. 309, especially the last stanza. Possibly the actual 'boat of rare device' (line 325) may symbolize their union and recent marriage—an embarkation on a life-trip. Mary it was whom Shelley saw as his inspiration in the business of reconciling the triumph of Platonism with the defeat of Godwinism—he always remained a loyal supporter and friend of the philosopher whom, philosophically, he had outgrown. Cythna is a Mary-figure.

315: *voyage*: practically a monosyllable in Shelley. Locock compares 'betrayer' ('Ginevra', 94) and 'rowers' ('A Vision of the Sea', 153).

406-14: Notopoulos (*Platonism*, p. 215) comments: 'Shelley's tribute to Greece here reflects also his tribute to Plato, whom he had been reading at the time of composition.' See above, n. on line 193.

484-92: Notopoulos draws attention to the Platonic imagery (darkness and light) tangent to the theme of appearance and reality. Cf. Rogers, *Shelley at Work*, pp. 148-9.

497: *speechless*: 'unutterable'; cf. II. 944. Shelley uses 'sightless', 'viewless' 'quenchless', 'tameless', etc. in a similar manner.

514: *that vast and peopled city*: Paris; possibly an allusion, Locock suggests, to Mary Wollstonecraft's residence there during the Revolution.

554: *glode*: Cf. *The Faerie Queene*, IV. iv. 23. Cf. below, 2176, 4760.

559-603: Cf. the Temple in Erasmus Darwin, *Temple of Nature*, I. 65-80, itself based on Pope, *Temple of Fame*, 61-2 and 138-9.

578: Forman quotes Chaucer, *Troylus and Cryseyde*, II. 772
> And shadwed wel with blosmy bowers grene

but Shelley probably had in mind the 'bloosming' of *The Faerie Queene*, VII. vii. 8.

600: *poesy*: Shelley, as Locock notices, had not forgotten the original meaning of ποίησις: 'creation'. Cf. his Tasso quotation in *A Defence of Poetry*: 'Only God and the Poet deserve the name of Creator.' Cf. Rogers, *Shelley at Work*, pp. 95-6.

604-6: The 'Senate of the Great' is analogous to Socrates' conception in *Apology*, 41. For Shelley's memoranda on the *Apology* among the manuscripts of *Laon and Cythna* see nn. above, pp. 375 ff.

615: *Distinct with*: 'adorned with' (cf. above, n. on 'Mont Blanc', 105). Locock compares 2077 and *Prometheus Unbound*, III. iii. 162.

622–30: To those unable to get away from Biblical notions the metamorphosis of the Serpent into the Morning Star will seem odd enough. But see nn., above, on I. 193 and 262–70. The new-born star unites in itself the two forces of idealism, the Godwinian revolutionary and the Shelleyan-Platonic, out of which the 'Revolution of the Golden City', the subject of the poem, must come about.

632: *a Form*: Locock suggests that this may be the masculine equivalent of Queen Mab, and compares with the description *Alastor*, 175–6, *Prometheus Unbound*, II. i. 71 ff., and *Epipsychidion*, 77 ff. He does not develop this interesting suggestion, which depends on the association, if not identification, of the 'Form' and what it symbolizes with *Queen Mab*, I. 180–6. In view of the now well-known consistency of Shelley's metaphysical ideas, I think Locock's suggestion a likely one. By thus showing *Laon and Cythna* as a pivotal point in the Platonism that progresses from *Queen Mab* to *Epipsychidion*, and indeed beyond, it explains much that has hitherto been obscure in the poem. It is the more interesting since it preceded by about half a century the analysis, based on Shelley's working Notebooks, that showed the Platonic consistency of Shelley's Veil-symbolism; see Rogers, *Shelley at Work*, ch. 8.

649–59: *one . . . One*: Laon . . . Cythna.

662: *lines*: 'rays of light' (Rossetti). Locock compares 'radiant lines of morning', *Prometheus Unbound*, II. v. 56.

p. 129, *Canto II.*

667: From here down to line 4286 Laon becomes the narrator. From there till 4572 Shelley continues the narrative, after which Laon continues it to the end. This arrangement was intended to give variety: see Shelley's letter to a publisher, 13 Oct. 1817 (Jones, *Letters*, i. 563).

667–98: In the Notebook D. 1, in which he drafted parts of *Epipsychidion*, Shelley translated these lines into a somewhat odd Italian. For this 'Platonic wooing' of Emilia see Rogers, *Shelley at Work*, ch. 13. Notopoulos (*Platonism*, p. 216) notes the Platonic force of the passage: the objects described constitute the first stage in the ascent from an earthly to an ideal love. See *Symposium*, 210–11, also *Republic*, 401.

690–2: Rossetti explains: 'Who, by offering flattery to a supposed Almighty Power, had given to the ministers of that Power (priests) a show of authority in the world beyond the grave.' See Rogers, *Shelley at Work*, ch. 13.

742, 745: The repetition of 'pale', in order to get a rhyme, was, no doubt, due to carelessness of a not uncommon kind.

783: *impious trust*: impious because the trust is in something false.

825: Locock suggests that the allusion may be to Hogg; retracted, however, it would seem, in line 1761.

828: *had bled*: would have bled.

835–7: *it . . . its*: refer to 'my sorrow' (829). Locock compares 'The Sunset' 36, 'wisdom-working grief', and *Prometheus Unbound*, I. 58, 'ere misery made me wise'.

838–42: *deathless minds*: Cf. Shelley's Preface, sections 6–9.

849: *When I might wander*: 'Whenever I wandered', an imitation of the Greek optative usage, not uncommon in Shelley's poetry.

865–73: The description of Cythna is in terms of the theory of Beauty and Love in the *Symposium*: the Ideal Woman is a light cast upon the dark stream of life. The language anticipates *Epipsychidion*.

938–9: Cf. 1667–74 and *Prometheus Unbound*, II. iv. 136.

946–9: *communion with this purest being*: In the 'ladder' of the *Symposium* communion with Beauty leads to Wisdom. Cythna was to Laon what Diotima was to Socrates.

986: *half of humankind*: women. In his *Discourse on the Manners of the Ancients Relative to the Subject of Love* Shelley ascribes the Greek homosexual *mores* to the fact that 'one half of the adult population' (i.e. the women) were in bondage.

995: The theme of the equality of women (see also 1594–5) is analogous to *Republic*, 540 c; Mary Wollstonecraft had been the great advocate of the doctrine in Shelley's England.

1006: *The Golden City*: Byzantium. See n. on title, above, p. 360.

1015: Locock comments on the harsh elision, extending his censure, not unjustly, to the technical deficiencies that may be found in Stanzas XXXII–XL generally.

p. 144, *Canto III.*

1145: Rossetti regarded the metre as defective and proposed changing 'Through' to 'Thorough'; alternatively, the transposition of 'Through' and 'over'. The manuscripts being defective here, one can only rely on one's knowledge of the way Shelley's ear operated. With Forman and Locock I believe this to be an example of the by no means uncommon 'telling irregularity' of his rhythmical excursions.

1287: *poison*: because the hope was more like despair. Locock cites the *1820* fragment 'Such hope as is the sick despair of good'.

1292: *uprest*: Hutchinson thinks this a mistake for 'uprist', possibly borrowed from Coleridge, who misuses it in 'The Ancient Mariner', II. 16. Shelley often uses 'uprise' as a noun.

1330: *the giddy air*: Locock compares Keats's use of the phrase in his rival poem (*Endymion*, IV. 355).

1348: *an old man*: The Hermit stands for Dr. Lind of Windsor, Shelley's early mentor who first introduced him to Plato. He is the Zonoras of 'Prince Athanase'.

1360: *He struck my chains*: It has been suggested to me that Shelley is referring to 'his emancipation from Godwinism'. I think, however, the meaning to be simply that Lind gave him that training in the Socratic method which freed him from the bonds of dogmatic teaching; in particular that habit of reasoning which demanded the examination of the *entirety* of any matter under discussion; see his remarks to Godwin quoted on p. 273. It should be remembered (see Notopoulos, *Platonism*, pp. 146–7) that Godwin's philosophy, from its own Platonic inheritance, was an early source of Shelley's Platonic ideas. From *Queen Mab* onwards (see vol. i, pp. 380–1) they were enlarged and absorbed, rather than displaced, from his wider Platonic study. In 1817 he enthusiastically acclaimed the poetic Platonism in *Mandeville*, where the relationship of the lovers is akin to that of Laon and Cythna.

1389: *the starry giant*: Orion; cf. 2328, and 'Prince Athanase', 197.

p. 154, *Canto IV*.

1445: For the comparison of mortal life with a many-coloured sleep cf. the sonnet 'Lift not the painted veil', of 1819, *Prometheus Unbound*, iii. iii. 113 ff., and iii. iv. 190 ff.; also the famous image in *Adonais*, lii. For the Platonic symbolism of the Veil, and its origin in the *Symposium* and the *Phaedrus*, see Rogers, *Shelley at Work*, ch. 8.

1468: *slowly*: Cf. 1510; this 'milder madness' lasted seven years.

1472–4: Cf. 1555 and *Prometheus Unbound*, iii. iii. 170.

1475–6: *thought . . . not*: a not untypical Shelleyan rhyme.

1477–81: Cf. 'Prince Athanase', 214–29, where Shelley tells us, more specifically, of his reading of the *Symposium* with Dr. Lind and of his own reaction to the great minds that, through literature, moulded his own. With 1480–1 Notopoulos (*Platonism*, p. 218) compares 'Prince Athanase', 139, Shelley's paraphrase from Thomas Paine; cf. n. below, pp. 401–2.

1485: *among mankind*: to be taken with 'he read'.

1492: *one in Argolis*: Laon.

1570: *a maiden fair*: Till the end of the Canto Laon does not suspect that this is Cythna. The Platonic and other Greek lore referred to in 1477–81 (see n., above) is extended from the hero to the Ideal Woman; incidentally, of course, this is Shelley, sharing with Mary the inspiration he had derived from Dr. Lind. 'Educating the Beloved' was an important feature in the doctrine of the *Symposium* and Mary was very zealous with her Greek studies.

1575: What should have been an alexandrine is too short by a foot.

1627–8: "*she paves / Her path with human hearts*": Only Locock, I think, tried to identify this quotation. I might not have identified it myself, had I not studied Shelley's Platonic memoranda in the Bodleian Notebooks. One of the most important clues to his poetry is contained in a memorandum in MS. Shelley adds. e. 16, which I transcribed in *Shelley at Work*, p. 44; a magnificent reproduction of the actual manuscript appeared in *Keats–Shelley Journal*, xv, Winter 1966, with Professor Notopoulos's article, 'New Texts of Shelley's Plato'. This memorandum amounts to little less than an anthology of the passages in the *Symposium* that underlie Shelley's poetic thought and feeling. Amongst them is the passage which he describes as 'the wonderful description of Love'. Here it is. I forgo the Greek, but quote Shelley's translation:

He is young, therefore, and being young is tender and soft. There were need of some poet like Homer to celebrate the delicacy and tenderness of Love. For Homer says, that the goddess Calamity is delicate, and that her feet are tender. 'Her feet are soft,' he says, 'for she treads not upon the ground, but makes her path upon the heads of men.' He gives as an evidence of her tenderness, that she walks not upon that which is hard, but that which is soft.

Plato compares the Goddess Calamity to Love, in respect of her sensitive feet, and her sensitive response to the men over whom she walks. Plato's 'Calamity' (so is her name rendered by Shelley) is the 'Havoc' of line 1613 above. Plato just borrows words about Ἄτη which happen to fit Ἔρως, whom he wishes to describe. Shelley uses the passage, and its terms, to show how the Havoc (Ἄτη) of the post-revolutionary period (line 1613) might be 'baffled' by the young maiden who incarnated Shelleyan-Platonic love. The quotation here takes us to the centre of Shelley's Platonic thought and feeling. See *Shelley at Work*, ch. 4 *passim*.

1650: Cf. 1807.

1673: *Their*: Rossetti printed 'Its'. Locock says, 'Probably Shelley regarded the flush in the cheek and the flush in the lips as two distinct subjects.' I suspect that he meant to write 'objects', which might make both the comment and its subject intelligible.

1690: The beams and the moon stand for Cythna in this stanza, the cloud and the stars for Laon. This astronomical intercourse anticipates *Prometheus Unbound*, Act IV.

p. 164, *Canto V*.

1726: *sublunar*: terrestrial; cf. 'The Sensitive Plant', II. 10.

1798 means 'For the sake of which alone thou wert of any worth'. The next two lines are addressed to the 'patriot hosts' and the next stanza to the enemy.

1823, 1825: For the repetition of 'shed' in order to get a rhyme cf. 742, 745.

1833: *assay*: a Spenserian word, meaning 'perilous attempt'.

1877: *one*: Laone.

1897: *The fallen Tyrant*: Othman.

1908: *speechless*: Cf. above, n. on line 497.

1925: Locock quotes the letter to Peacock of 9 Nov. 1818 (Jones, *Letters*, ii. 51): 'It is as if he could have dipped his pencil in the hues of some serenest and star-shining twilight.'

1934–5: Cf. 4661–2. This child is, in fact, the daughter of Laon and Cythna, and identical with the dream-child of 2983–91; cf. 4645. She was born in the winter, and, as the time is now late spring or early summer, must now be about six and a half years old.

1949: *its*: of the 'gorgeous grave'.

2023: *were*: the subjunctive mood.

2041: *his straight lips*: Rossetti's suggestion that this should be 'strait' seems supported by 3610 as well as by *Rosalind and Helen*, 426; Locock thinks it equally likely that this was a word which Shelley was liable to mis-spell, so that both instances could be mistakes for 'straight'. I am inclined to agree with Forman and Locock that the idea is 'the cruelty of a curveless mouth'. The draft in e. 10 is defective here.

2061: *doom*: 'consummation of happiness', says Locock.

2063: *signs*: standards, Latin *signa*. Shelley's sentence gets a little out of hand, so that 'it was a sight' (2057) is followed not only by 'To see' (2062) but also by 'To hear' (2064).

2068–70: I find the meaning obscure. Locock paraphrases 'Almost made dumb companionship with the joy felt by men'.

2092: *Two only bosoms*: Laone and the 'youth' of V. v; cf. 2123.

2108: The construction is 'exhalations woven by winds'; cf. 'The Witch of Atlas', 466.

2115: Shelley's alexandrine has extended itself to a seventh foot.

2156: *Three shapes*: the Giant (2157) represents Equality, the Woman (2161) Love, and the third Image (2165) Wisdom. In the lyric ode which follows Laone addresses Wisdom, Love, and Equality in turn. This ode is a precursor of Shelley's later, and greater odes, as well as of the choric passages in *Prometheus Unbound* and elsewhere.

2217: *last*: probably used like the Latin *ultimus* to mean 'remotest, most distant'.

2231: *lawless*: 'unshackled' (Forman).

2253: *forms*: a literal translation of the Platonic εἴδη. For this imagery and its origin cf. the analysis of *Prometheus Unbound*, II. ii. 40 ff. in Rogers, *Shelley at Work*, pp. 134 ff.

2308–16: Once again Shelley's sentence seems to have got out of hand, though Locock somehow sees in the first lines of the stanza 'a good instance of zeugma'. The draft in e. 10 casts no light.

p. 183, *Canto VI*.

2337: *that dear friend*: the 'youth'.

2361: Another over-long alexandrine.

2374: *to have repelled*: thinking to repel.

2383: *drive*: sc. 'me'.

2419–22: *The old man*: the Hermit of Cantos II and III.

2426: *The horseman*: probably a Latin usage, *eques*, with a singular verb.

2449: *each sixth*: another Latinism, *sextus quisque*.

2451: Yet another abnormal alexandrine.

2499: *Tartarian*: appertaining to Tartary, not to Tartarus, as is shown by 2558.

D d

2536–9: *as . . . wild*: parenthetical, the main construction being 'The waters might be heard and the tents might be seen'. I do not think the awkwardness would yield to repunctuation.

2541: *Thence marking*: observing from the hill.

2543–4: *the two . . . / Each . . . the other*: Some have explained the construc-ion as synecdoche, some as metonymy, but a glance at the examples in any good English or American dictionary will show that neither is applicable. Locock (i. 565) says 'another classical figure of speech, the σχῆμα καθ᾽ ὅλον καὶ μέρος'. This 'whole and part construction' is illustrated in any good book on comparative Latin and Greek syntax. Reference to Buckland Green or R. W. Moore will show that it cannot be the explanation here. What is probably the real explanation may be seen from a comparison with such an ordinary English sentence as 'They killed each other' (or 'one another'). Here the subject is divided into 'each' (or 'one'). In reciprocal actions the object is always part (or all) of the subject. What Shelley has done is to replace the plural subject *the two* by the simple partitive (or distributive) apposition *Each*. The meaning is clear, though the syntax is complicated by the number of the verbs; I hope that it may be slightly assisted by my removal of the unnecessary comma in line 2543.

Linguistically this is an interesting example of the way in which Shelley could catch the feeling of a classical construction and vary it to express a nuance of his own. The nuance depends partly on the use of the co-ordinating conjunction *or*. Normally the three verbs *heard . . . saw . . . felt* would have applied to each of *the two* and would have been emphasized by the use of the co-ordinating conjunction 'and', whereas Shelley has deliberately substituted the equally co-ordinating conjunction *or* which is distributive or alternative in effect, while 'and' is additive. With 'and' the three verbs are predicated of both persons; by substituting *or* Shelley leaves open the possibility, and perhaps even positively implies, that if A, B, and C are the verbs and X and Y the people, A may be said of one, B and C of the other, or A and B said of one and C of the other.

2594–5: Notopoulos thinks that the Ocean of universal life may be a Platonic or Neoplatonic image, and compares *Symposium*, 210 d.

2596: *To the pure all things are pure!* This comes directly from St. Paul's Epistle to Titus, 1: 15; it is also an Orphic doctrine found in *Phaedo*, 67 b, 69 c, and *Sophist*, 191 d.

2617: The Meteor is not a shooting star, but glowing gas from a near-by marsh. Cf. *Prom. Unb.* II. ii. 70–82.

2633–4: *one interval / Made still*: still made one intermittent rhythm.

2639–40: Shelley fuses two Platonic notions. The union of two disunited spirits into one is analogous to, or an echo of, Aristophanes' conception of love in *Symposium*, 191 d.

2655–8: A Shelleyan version of Platonic love, which combines the notion of transcendence (see *Phaedrus*, 26 a ff., and *Symposium*, 210–11) with Aristo-phanes' conception of love in *Symposium*, 191 d.

2659: The language is borrowed from the first stanza of the 'Hymn to Intellectual Beauty'.

2659–60: An epigrammatic expression of the Platonic conception of Intellectual Beauty, as described in the *Symposium*, 210–11 and in Shelley's 'Hymn to Intellectual Beauty', see nn. above, pp. 344 ff. It is, says Notopoulos (*Platonism*, p. 219), both natural and direct Platonism refracted through Shelley's romantic temperament. The lines are permeated with Platonic connotations, such as the shadow of the divine, which infrequently visits blind mortality; see *Republic*, 514 ff.

2690: *as in*: the clause begun here ends in line 2697.

2702: The comparison between knowledge and the Nile is the theme of Shelley's sonnet 'To the Nile', written early in 1818.

2710–11: As Locock observes, the sense of the stanza was confused by the use of 'ruin' in two different senses; Shelley's comma at 'well', which I have removed, made things worse. The sentence is clearly a stop-gap but I agree with Locock as to its general drift: 'Fortunately for us this marble ruin (2530) constituted an unnoticed watch-tower so that we were now in safety.' The draft, which might have given a clue, is defective here.

2728: *at intervals*: to be taken with 'gleamed'.

2791–2: *making a dearth / Among the dead*: because the woman had collected the bread supply of the whole village.

2800: *absent looks*: absent because the mind was distracted, thoughts being elsewhere.

p. 199, *Canto VII.*

2841: *Liberty's uprise*: as reported to him by the Hermit in Canto III.

2848–910: Laon, as narrator, tells what Cythna told him.

2850: *firm assurance*: 'Probably the object of "impart" ' (Locock). But quite possibly, I suggest, the subject, the object being 'faith'.

2882: The image of a spirit in fleshly chains derives, ultimately, from Plato, *Phaedo*, 67 d.

2910: Cythna's speech goes from here to 3782, covering nearly three cantos. After the 'she said' of stanza XII in this canto (2929) Laon intervenes as narrator only in Stanzas XVIII and XIX (2990–5).

2935: *hupaithric*: ὑπαίθριος, 'open to the sky'. The passage anticipates *Prometheus Unbound*, III. iv. 116 ff., and the word, and probably both passages, owe something to Peacock's *Rhododaphne*: cf. I. 2 'Round Thespian Love's hypaethrian fane'.

2938 ff.: Cythna's cave anticipates the cave-dwelling of 'The Witch of Atlas', 185 ff., and the pleasure-house of *Epipsychidion*, as well as Asia's cave in *Prometheus Unbound*, III. iii. 10–64. None of these passages can be understood except in relation to *Republic*, 514 a ff., the famous passage where Plato deals with the progress of the mind from the lowest state of unenlightenment to a knowledge of the Good; this he illustrates by the allegory in which the world of appearance, in contrast to the world of reality, is compared to an underground cave. See Rogers, *Shelley at Work*, ch. 9.

3061: *a Nautilus*: This is probably a playful addition by Shelley to the Caveimagery. The Nautilus was a name he used for himself. It seems to have been an extended pun on his surname: see letter to Claire Clairmont, 29 Apr. 1821 (Jones, *Letters*, ii. 288). Cf. 'The Conchoid', the nickname used by Hogg and Peacock; another pun on 'Shelley'. Cf. also the punning self-reference in Shelley's use of the pseudonym 'Glirastes', see below, p. 412, paragraph 2.

3088: *By intercourse of mutual imagery*: conversation in Platonic terms, leading to an ascent to the world of enlightenment.

3100: Cf. n., above, on 2938 ff. The benefits resulting from this Platonic improvement of the mind anticipate the benefits that accrue for humanity in general when Prometheus, representing mind, and Asia, representing beauty, are united in the Cave in *Prometheus Unbound*, III. iii.

3104: *One mind, the type of all*: The Platonic concept of the World Mind of which the human mind can become a microcosm: the most famous appearance of this concept in Shelley is in *Adonais*, 460 ff.: 'The One remains, the many change and pass . . .'

3113–14: Shelley is referring to Pythagoras.

p. 211, *Canto VIII*.

3232: *Ye*: emphatic.

3244–48: Possibly an elaboration of the Sophistic doctrine of Protagoras that man is the measure of all things. The preoccupation of sophists with shadows is a Platonic theme: see *Sophist*, 233 c, 254 a.

3271–5: *Opinion . . . cloud*: Shelley's language seems to be feeling its way towards the convictions that sustained him through the writing of *Prometheus Unbound* (Preface, paragraph 6):

. . . The great writers of our own age are, we have reason to suppose, the companions and forerunners of some unimagined change in our social condition or the opinions which cement it. The cloud of mind is discharging its collected lightning, and the equilibrium between institutions and opinions is now restoring, or is about to be restored.

Shelley conceives of Opinion in the same epistemological way as Plato: see *Republic*, 479 d–e.

3276: *One shape of many names*: from Aeschylus, *Prometheus Vinctus*, 210, πολλῶν ὀνομάτων μορφὴ μία, a quotation jotted down by Shelley at the end of the Bod. Notebook MS. Shelley adds. e. 11.

3293 ff.: As Locock notices, this stanza and the next sound like a first study for *Prometheus Unbound*: not this time in respect of the Platonic ideas (cf. above, nn. on 2938 ff., 3088, 3100, 3104) nor in respect of the language (cf. n. on 3271–2), but in the syntactical pattern—with these concatenated infinitive subjects cf. Act IV, 570–end.

3304: An anticipation of *Epipsychidion*, 551–2.

3372: The notion that mind is a man's fate is analogous to that in *Republic*, 617 e, where the soul chooses its own fate to which it is irrevocably bound.

3377–8: See n., above, on 1627–8.

3382–7: See n. on 3379 ff. under 'Text', above, pp. 370–1. The Amphisbaena was a fabulous snake capable of moving in either direction (ἀμφίς, βαίνειν), cf. *Prometheus Unbound*, III. iv. 119, and *Paradise Lost*, X. 524. The epithet 'putrid' seems to show that Shelley attributed to the Amphisbaena one of the properties of the Seps: cf. *Prometheus Unbound*, III. i. 40 f. Both creatures are described in Lucan, *Pharsalia*, ix.

p. 220, *Canto IX*.

3499: *such*: emphatic, continuing the simile.

3523–4: Again the Platonic use of the Veil image.

3526: *the shades approve*: Shelley not uncommonly imitates the classical usage whereby an independent sentence continues a simile.

3577: In e. 10 Shelley has pencilled here 'painted by Νεφεληγερέτα Ζεὺς, a partial artist'; i.e. because of his cloud-colouring the 'cloud-compeller' might add this to his Homeric titles—a thought arising out of Stanza xii.

3595–603: As printed in *Laon and Cythna*, Stanza xv has ten lines. In *The Revolt of Islam*, where remodelling was necessary in order to get rid of the dangerous word 'God', Shelley still failed to achieve an authentic Spenserian stanza.

3617: possibly refers to the visits of the Homeric gods to dine with the Ethiopians.

3635: *human love*: Shelleyan love of humanity.

3641–3: Somewhat obscure. Locock suggests that, Laon having hitherto allowed his intellectual gifts to conceal his true emotional nature, Cythna, by her union with him, will combine intellect with emotion, and so become the inspired prophetess of regeneration. This would fit in well with the position of Mary Shelley in 1817, when she was supplying so much that poor Harriet had pathetically failed to supply; it is likewise in line with the Prometheus–Asia union, for which so much of *Laon and Cythna* supplies an early pattern.

3706–10: Notopoulos (*Platonism*, p. 221) notes that this is the last appearance in Shelley's philosophy of the doctrine of Necessity: from now on it is supplanted by Platonic idealism. The transition had begun during the writing of *Queen Mab*; see, *passim*, the nn. on that poem in Vol. I.

3711: *divided never*: i.e. evil from evil and good from good. Cf. Aeschylus, *Agamemnon*, 759–60, which Shelley quoted in a letter to Mary on 8, 10 Aug. 1821 (Jones, *Letters*, ii. 325) and later expanded into *Hellas*, 729–32: also *Choephoroe*, 794. The notion seems to have haunted Shelley. Locock compares 4359, and 'Euganean Hills', 231–2.

3730–3: Platonic notions of immortality: cf. the *Phaedo*. Shelley did not believe in the Christian notion of a personal immortality, though there are signs, e.g. in his notes to *Hellas*, that, had he lived longer, he might have moved in that direction.

3752: *seems*: The verb agrees with the last of its subjects. Locock cites similar constructions in 'Hymn of Apollo', 34, and in the fourth sentence of the Preface to *Alastor*.

3788: One of Shelley's alexandrines in the middle of a Spenserian stanza, for which he apologized in his Preface to the poem. It is not altogether ineffective, as it seems to bring the reader up with a jerk, making him receptive to the translated epigram (Plato, in *Anth. Pal.* vii. 669) which is the climax of the canto:

$$\text{Ἀστέρας εἰσαθρεῖς Ἀστὴρ ἐμός· εἴθε γενοίμην}$$
$$\text{οὐρανός, ὡς πολλοῖς ὄμμασιν εἰς σὲ βλέπω.}$$

For an earlier translation of this epigram, made by Shelley in 1817, see p. 323 and n. on p. 413. It is important to understand how Shelley, in the wake of the German Hellenists, was concerned to modernize Platonic doctrine by adapting to contemporary man–woman love relationships the philosophical and poetical ideas in Plato about idealized love-relationships between males. This is one of a number of poems addressed by Plato to the boy Ἀστήρ, in whose name, meaning 'Star', there is an untranslatable paronomasia. In 1821, in translating another of these epigrams (Ἀστὴρ πρὶν μὲν ἔλαμπες . . . , *Anth. Pal.* vii. 670—'Thou wert the morning star among the living . . .') Shelley tried to circumvent the linguistic difficulty by adapting the Greek feeling under his title of 'To Stella'. The irrelevance of this to points of sexual ethics is shown by his use of the second epigram as an epigraph to *Adonais*, where the expansion of the Platonic star-imagery is all-important. Misunderstanding of this has led to a general misunderstanding of 'The Triumph of Life', 256, and a consequent misinterpretation of the role of Plato in that poem. See Rogers, *Shelley at Work*, ch. 16.

p. 231, *Canto X*.

3795–8: Shelley here approaches vaguely the Platonic conception of the One and the Many: cf. *Philebus*, 15 ff.

3835–8: Shelley is depicting a clash between warring nations. He is probably more concerned to give a general, epical effect by using proper names, in the Homeric–Virgilian manner, than to identify specific nations. 'The Arctic Anarch' has been thought to refer to the Tsar of Russia. 'Idumaea . . . lies' is, I think, simply a reference to an area of Biblical history, thought of as a source of the religious superstitions which can underlie wars.

3865: Shelley seems to have forgotten that in 2493–4 we were told that no rebels were left.

3874–82: Apparently only a few days have elapsed since the events narrated in 2497–505, and, apparently, the rebellion has now spread over the entire country.

3901: The time now appears to be late summer or early autumn, while the events of the first half of Canto V seem to have taken place in the late spring or early summer.

3964: *blue Plague*: As the *Shelley Concordance* will show, Shelley was prone to use the word 'blue' when describing something pestilential or ghastly. Locock compares *The Faerie Queene*, I. iv. 23, and the 'blue meagre hag' of Milton's *Comus*, 434.

3999 refers to Pygmalion and Galatea.

4003–8: An obscure passage, on which examination of the draft in e. 10 can cast no light. The general meaning seems to be that while Famine can sometimes be placated by those who are able to hoard food, Plague is as implacable for the haves as it is for the have-nots.

4063: *and Christ*: Shelley's substitution of 'Joshua' in *The Revolt of Islam* was obstinate and artful, the name being a synonym of 'Jesus'. 'Oromaze' is Ormuzd, the Principle of Good among the Zoroastrians. 'Zerdusht', in the next line, is Zoroaster.

4212: *she*: not, I think, Cythna, as Forman suggested; see next n. Probably the mother of the children, as Rossetti thought.

4215: Explained thus by F. H. Bradley: 'One infidel, A, is going to be burned. Another infidel, B, comes up and says "Stop; that is not A; I am A." The orthodox find it an excellent joke to burn them both.'

4216: The 'that' in 4222 shows that ' 'Tis said' must be understood.

p. 245, *Canto XI.*

4262–9: The language anticipates a good deal of the Platonic imagery which was to be evoked by the figure of Asia in *Prometheus Unbound*: cf., for instance, II. v. 48 ff.; cf. also *Epipsychidion, passim.*

4286: See above, n. on 667.

4322–3: I am indebted to Mr. Desmond King-Hele for the following note: 'At Byzantium Arcturus is within 30° of the zenith, i.e. approximately 'overhead', at some time every night from January to June each year, whereas Shelley earlier implies that the season is autumn [see n. on line 3901 above], when Arcturus passes over in the daytime. Thus the astronomy is mere colour and no guide to the season.'

4375–7: Notopoulos (*Platonism*, p. 221) notes 'Another example in Shelley of the Platonic dualism of transience, and the immortality of Platonic love.'

p. 253, *Canto XII.*

4468: *His . . . his*: Now that Laon has been identified (4449) the use of the third person here and in Stanza VII shows that Shelley himself is the narrator, probably as far as 4572. See above, n. on 667.

4585: With Locock I think that the 'Yet' is temporal, and that 'one brief relapse' is an equivalent of the Latin 'accusative of duration of time'.

4592: *The tyrant's child*: So Laon thought, though she was really his own.

4594: *And is this death?* It was. The scene is no longer on earth: see 4279. Laon and Cythna are now 'two mighty spirits'. They are near the Temple of the Spirit, beyond the 'ocean which girds the pole'; cf. 550–8 and the Epigraph and n. The child, also dead (of the plague), is now a 'plumèd Seraph'. Cythna still has 'human hues and living charms'. Such is this Shelleyan eternity, neither Christian nor Platonic.

4613: *incense-bearing forests*: Forman compares 'Kubla Khan', 9.

4638: *the sunken meteor*: must be the moon; see previous line.

4645: *mine own child*: described in 2983–90.

4719: *change*: in the sentiments of the crowd. This is the point at which the child dies of the plague.

4721 ff. See above, n. on 604–6.

4724: Probably derived from the conception of Love as a beneficent Daemon in the *Symposium*, 203 a; see Rogers, *Shelley at Work*, ch. 4. Notopoulos (*Platonism*, p. 222) compares also *Timaeus*, 41 ff., 90 a, *Statesman*, 271 e, Plotinus, *Enneads*, III. iv. The conception may be derived, more generally, from Plato's notion of good and evil in the universe: see *Laws*, 896 c ff.

4814: *one hollow sky*: Locock has well understood Shelley's pictorial imagination (see Rogers, *Shelley at Work*, ch. 7): '. . . the temple in the distance seemed like a sphere hung in one hollow sky, consisting of the heaven above and the heaven of water below.'

p. 265, LAON AND CYTHNA: REJECTED PASSAGES. *Text*: The manuscript in e. 14 has the character of a first draft. In e. 19 some of the stanzas are quite neatly penned, and there are efforts at punctuation, suggesting that Shelley was recopying what had been drafted elsewhere: other stanzas look like freshly drafted additions to them. These are among the places (see Intro., pp. xvii–xviii) where the difficulty of the draft has obliged me to resort to literal transcription. Though *1934* is marred by a number of misreadings, I occasionally found its punctuation helpful: the editors perceived, for instance, the need to ration Shelley's usual, all-purpose dashes.

Content:

p. 268, *Canto I*.

19–27: Cf. the Platonic concept in the 'Hymn to Intellectual Beauty' of a Power which visits the world and leaves its imprint or shadow.

p. 269, 37–45: A variant expression of Shelley's tribute to classical literature and its association with the immortal Spirit; cf. 838–46.

p. 269, 53: See Commentary, p. 269. Where Shelley leaves uncancelled alternatives his editor must choose between them, and can but spin a coin.

p. 270, NOTE BY MARY SHELLEY ON LAON AND CYTHNA. *Text*: [6] Shelley's letter to Godwin: With two minor amendments the text is Mary Shelley's, of 1839. It differs only in a very few minor details from the text in Jones, *Letters*, i. 577–8.

Content: [2] *another poet*: Byron.

[6] Nothing Shelley ever wrote tells us more than this letter of his personal poetical aims. Cf. nn. above on the Preface, paragraph 6, on lines 127–9, and 193 ff.; cf. also Rogers, *Shelley at Work*, ch. 3.

[6] "*the agony and bloody sweat*": quoted from the Litany in the Book of Common Prayer. Cf. Luke 22: 44 and *Prometheus Unbound*, I. 597 ff. Geth-

semane and the Crucifixion, as well as the suffering Titan, not unnaturally lend colour to the thought and language evoked by Shelley's own, frequent, agony, both personal and intellectual.

p. 277, PRINCE ATHANASE

Title: See below, under *Content*.

Date: Lines 1–124 are dated by Mary Shelley 'December 1817', the remaining lines published by her, 'Marlow 1817'. Hutchinson says 'probably rehandled in Italy during the following year'. I know no authority for this.

Text: As printed by Hutchinson, the text is divided into 'Part I' (1–124) and 'Part II' (125–end). 'Part II' is subdivided into six 'Fragments' (125–63, 164–229, 230–9, 240–60, 261–78, 279–302), followed by 'Another Fragment (A)' (303–11) and 'Another Fragment (B)' (312–17). Since these divisions, while reflecting the history of editorial change, are a disturbance to the continuity achieved by editorial effort, I have removed them.

The textual complications require close consideration of:

   i. the nature of the manuscripts;
   ii. the achievement of Mary Shelley;
   iii. the achievement of subsequent editors;
   iv. the work of the present edition.

   i. The poem is a half-realized idea; the manuscripts comprise a series of fragments, varying in size, uncoordinated by Shelley. The existing holograph, in E. 4, was left in varying stages of correction; lines 1–60, roughly speaking, have the appearance of an intermediate, partly corrected fair copy; the remainder is a draft, or rather a series of drafts. In *An Examination of the Shelley MSS. in the Bodleian Library*, 1903, Locock rightly deduced that Mary's first printing, of 1824, must have drawn on some other holograph, so that the numerous variations from her text which E. 4 presents would have no authority: his deductions are illustrated by my collation of lines 1–124. He seems not to have known of the Claris MS. which, according to Sotheby's catalogue for their sale of 22–5 July 1918, included those lines. It may well have included more but not, I think, very much, since the rest of Mary's text varies so little from E. 4 that it may be presumed to derive from it. For John Chalk Claris (Arthur Brooke, the Shelley enthusiast) see White, *Shelley*, ii. 302, 356, 392–3.

In Mary's transcript in d. 9, lines 1–124 are missing. From 125 onwards, except that it unaccountably omits lines 271–8, it corresponds to E. 4. It follows Shelley's condensed versions of lines 125–9 and 168–81, which follow lines 124 and 167, rather than an extended version of the passage which occurs, inconsecutively, in E. 4 after line 239. In d. 9 she transcribed this passage, but cancelled her transcription. Hutchinson relegated it to his notes. I have printed it here as 'Additional Lines', following the poem. Except that line 270, though transcribed, was not printed, Mary's omissions in *1824* correspond to those in d. 9, and are the same in *1839*¹. In *1839*² she added from E. 4 lines 312–17, which are not transcribed in d. 9.

Clearly, then, our witness for lines 1–124 must be Mary's printing, drawn from the Claris MS., and, for the rest of the fragment, E. 4; for the interpreting of its somewhat confused evidence we have: (1) d. 9, (2) *1824*, (3) *1839*, (4) the textual commentary of Locock in *An Examination*, pp. 50–60, including his transcripts of passages previously unprinted; his 1911 edition also contains textual notes on the poem but I do not find that they add very much. Hutchinson's text, based on a collation of nineteenth-century editions, derived from Mary's, with the notes and transcripts of Locock, calls for a careful re-examination. Locock noticed that, apart from a few differences, to which he draws attention, E. 4 agrees with Mary's collected editions rather than with *1824*. In other words, Mary's work, from her transcription in d. 9 onwards, was a constant revision and improvement.

ii. What we know of the Claris MS., preserved in Mary's printings, gives an interesting glimpse into the relation between an intermediate fair copy of Shelley's and a later one. Locock comments, for instance, on his way, in E. 4, of putting a pen-stroke through, or under, a word or a phrase, not to cancel or to italicize, but to remind himself later of some intended revision. He is not particularly methodical about this: e.g. in line 62 he underscores both 'Piercing' and 'rifts' but, evidently, in the Claris MS., changed only the second. In lines 12, 25, 26, 29, 33, 37, 43 are examples of changes not prescribed in E. 4. From this point Mary has to sort out his clues. Sometimes, as in 219, 271, 273, he cancels words or lines without writing in an alternative; in line 261 he cancels a whole line, writing above it the word 'Prince' as an indication that this was to come first in the revised version of that line. Sometimes, as in 141, 169, he gives alternatives and cancels both. Sometimes he gives alternatives without cancelling either: e.g. 188, 262, 280 so that Mary can rely only on her good sense in choosing what to print; sometimes the choice is easy (e.g. in 262 'eagle-baffling' is obviously more impressive than 'wintry'), but not always. In 202, for example, her exclamation mark after 'light' skilfully replaces the deadening dash of E. 4: similarly with her exclamation mark in 204 after 'nightingale'—unwisely rejected by Hutchinson in favour of the comma-dash of E. 4. Where an extra word is needed to make Shelley's line scan, Mary once or twice adds it: e.g. the 'gentle' of 160, and the 'whole' of 215. Here and there she discreetly prints a cancelled word: thus in 229 she achieves a fine complete line by printing Shelley's cancelled 'dark' and inserting the well-chosen 'forgetfulness'. Sometimes Mary makes slips: e.g. the 'one piny' (206) which crept into d. 9, but was corrected to 'yon piny' in *1824*; the mistranscription 'the' (175) crept from d. 9 into *1824*, but was corrected in *1839* to 'that'. One or two errors remained to be corrected in the present edition, but, in view of her difficulties, her care and skill must be accounted remarkable.

Of her skill in detecting Shelley's intention and realizing it in print line 289 affords an outstanding example. First, at the foot of a page, Shelley makes three attempts at the line, all ending in abortive phrases. At the top of the next page we find, in E. 4:

> Thee like a garment   robe   [fairy woven]
> [Loveliness] and Beauty, [like] some light [garment] [whose woof is wind] thou ever
> soarest

Here, as often in Shelley's drafts, the process of emendation is incomplete, so that the literal transcriber's principle of picking out the uncancelled words and reproducing them would produce incoherence. As far as *words* go, three only are certain, the last three—they are needed to supply a rhyme for 'forest' (291) and 'implorest' (293). But Mary Shelley looks beyond the words of the scribe to the mind of the poet. The *idea* of the passage becomes plain from line 287: the wings of love falling over the scenery like a robe, or garment, whichever word scans the better. Relying on sense, metre, and syntax she releases the fine poetic image that had been hidden amid the uncertain cancellings.

I have ignored, as Mary Shelley did, Shelley's apparent cancellation of lines 130–61. Each of the pages which cover this passage in E. 4 is criss-crossed by a large X: this may denote, like many of his underscorings, or scorings-through, of words, his intention to revise, or it may denote that he had transcribed the lines elsewhere. Mary's acceptance of them is justified by their place in the continuity of the poem.

iii. Collation casts an interesting light on the reasoning of subsequent editors. Rossetti, who had not seen the manuscript, rightly suspected that, in line 152, 'blighting' was a clumsy anticipation, which needed emending, of 'blight' in the next line. That Shelley thought so too is shown by his underscoring: unfortunately his intended emendation was never made. Rossetti's suggestion of the plural 'shadows' (287) was rejected by Forman on the ground that the grammar was 'characteristic'; since, however, examples are not wanting to show that Shelley himself corrected such 'characteristic' solecisms, even at the expense of sound, when he happened to notice them, I have followed Rossetti.

As penned in E. 4, line 307 was correctly deciphered by Locock in *An Examination*:

their
Of those who love [man] kind and therefore [die] [perish] perish

In his 1911 edition he prints '[die]', not noticing, presumably, that, with lines 303, 305, and 309, this gives a quadruple rhyme which was what Shelley, already in difficulties with these tercets, must have been trying to avoid when he hesitatingly changed to the 'perish' which, with Hutchinson, I have preferred. In his editing of this poem Locock's reasoning is, I find, a trifle less sound than his reasoning on the text of *Laon and Cythna*, where he had less manuscript evidence to work upon. Despite his principles of caution (see Introduction, pp. xv, xvii), he sometimes tends to rely too much on an 'authority' which a manuscript fails to afford. Having remarked, for instance, in *An Examination*, that where E. 4 differs from the Claris-derived manuscript it is *not* authoritative, he proceeds to make several minor changes on its account. Two of his punctual changes, in lines 69 and 103, I have in fact followed—not because they are 'authorized' by E. 4, but because, like a number of his changes in *Laon and Cythna*, they remove obstacles to the sense. A minor, but significant, example of his over-reliance on the manuscript is the italicizing in line 57: '*that* vernal spirit'. The word is certainly underscored in E. 4, but the underscoring is clearly one of those examples, noted elsewhere by Locock, of places where Shelley is reminding himself of the need to revise. Cf. commentary on line 62.

iv. No poem of Shelley's better illustrates what Mary Shelley and her successors have achieved. Merely to understand their achievement, involving, as it does, the complicated relationships between manuscripts and printings and the manifold deceptions of the surviving holograph, is in itself something of a nightmare for a new editor, but I have tried to follow the principles of my predecessors and to extend their work by new study.

My principal revision of Hutchinson's text is my printing of the lines numbered 271–278b. Since the manuscript affords no clear indication of Shelley's intentions, the lines have been printed between brackets. Though nothing can be made of the syntactical structure, the words, phrases, and lines have a beauty that demands such reproduction as can be contrived. In 229a, 229b, 229c, and 229d I have, I hope, rescued another nugget, besmeared by Shelley's confused cancellings. The end-stop of line 193 is crucial: the crux is the meaning of the word 'seem'. I have little doubt that here, as in 'The Sensitive Plant', 124, it means 'have semblance', and is used in Platonic contrast to the things of the world of reality. This meaning can best be helped out by three dots, marking an aposiopesis. This will be masked if we do not remove Shelley's three dots after 'storm', where they are clearly an example either of his occasional 'anticipatory stopping' (see Vol. I, Introduction, p. xl) or of the way he was wont to squander this stop in places where it needs to be replaced by a period.

222 is another crux. In E. 4 the draft reads thus:

how in those beams we walked

[As at this hour]—[How we together strayed] [lost] half resting on the sea

Despite Shelley's cancellation, I cannot believe that he intended to say, as implied in Hutchinson's text, that it was 'the pupil and his master' who were 'half resting on the sea'. If we invoke his cancelled 'As at this hour' we get, surely, what he did intend to say—that it was the moon which was 'half resting'; this, incidentally, removes the alexandrine that he could hardly have intended to place in the middle of a tercet—a very different thing from the alexandrine in line 124, a typical Shelleyan variation, carefully designed to round off the final tercet of this section of his poem: different too from the out-of-place alexandrines that sometimes mar the Spenserian stanzas of *Laon and Cythna* and which are there, as he admits in his Preface, not because he intended them but because he simply failed to remove them.

231 presents a curious appearance in E. 4:

a blight had   lighted
Leaves of his opening [manhood] [blight] de

In *An Examination* Locock does not discuss the puzzle, does not notice the uncancelled 'de', and transcribes thus:

Leaves of his opening   a blight had lighted

Hutchinson, cautiously confining himself to what is uncancelled, prints Locock's transcription. As a result the word 'manhood', required by sense, has been lost and the jingling 'blight . . . lighted', unrequired by the sound, preserved. But I think that Shelley's process can be reconstructed if we consider the problems of a rhymer struggling with his English tercets—I do not dissent from a remark, which I heard made by T. S. Eliot, that Shelley was more capable than any other Englishman of reproducing Dante's *terza rima*: however, as Locock notes, he was never to finish a poem in that measure, and in 1817 he was still finding it difficult. I suggest that he first wrote

Leaves of his opening manhood blight de

but before deciding on 'descended', which might have somewhat awkwardly dictated the outer rhymes of the next tercet, paused and proceeded with line 232, starting it with 'He said', making an abortive continuation with 'you know not what', cancelling the latter, and then getting sense, line, and rhyme all together:

He said—my friend one grief alone can wean

He must now return to line 231. Perhaps we may suppose—as any practitioner of verse-technique would allow—that the ear, controlling rhyme, could be slightly ahead of the brain controlling meaning. Thus the 'de' could easily become 'delighted', a point suggested in the manuscript by the fact that the last two syllables, straggling upward at a slant, have the appearance of a later addition. The 'delighted' does not fit in with the idea of 'young manhood blighted', so 'manhood' and 'blight' are cancelled. Shelley's new rhyme-word is not getting him anywhere. But those two last syllables have given him 'lighted', so he hastily writes in front of it the unmetrical jingle 'a blight had', then takes along 'delighted' to the next tercet. Yet another tercet, and the first line of another, and the fragment breaks down. He never gets back to line 231 to restore the 'manhood' which completes sense, to amend the 'a', which destroys metre, or to correct the ugly jingle of the sound. For lines 236–9 Shelley's intentions are clear enough, in so far as he indicated them, and I have tried to follow up his indications. Hutchinson, following Locock, has doubts about line 237, but to me it is quite clear in E. 4. The meaning is simply that Zonoras's understanding words had seemed to change his weight of introspective woe into a state of bliss. Of line 239 Locock and Hutchinson give only the first two words. In E. 4 the rest is scored through; this however, as so often, indicates not cancellation but the need for later revision.

Against the draft of lines 185–90, written in the margin is a memorandum:

Twin daughters of a dim Enchantress who Xtened [*for* christened] them

Praxitelean shapes whose marble smiles
Filled the mute air [

The lines of verse were adapted for *Prometheus Unbound*, III. iii. 165–6. I am unable to explain the memorandum, but suspect some connection with Peacock's *Rhododaphne*.

Content/Title: As Notopoulos observes (*Platonism*, p. 224), the poem is an example of Shelley's direct Platonism refracted through indirect Platonism. Even though it was written at a time when he was fresh from a study of the *Symposium*, his primary source of inspiration is the poetically attractive account of Earthly and Heavenly Love in Peacock's *Rhododaphne*: from this poem too came the plot, the idea of 'intellectual soul' and the incarnation of Platonic abstractions in the form of women. Shelley started it on 5 Dec. 1817, immediately after reading Peacock's poem, which he read aloud, got Mary to transcribe, and later reviewed with enthusiasm. Perhaps, in view of the close classical companionship between Shelley and Peacock at this time, it might be fairer to consider the relationship of their writings less as the influence of one man upon another than as a community of conceptions arising from an interpenetration of ideas. Peacock was exceedingly friendly with Thomas Taylor, the translator of Plato, who considered the Neoplatonists the true interpreters of Plato, and from whom much of the theological and mythological information in *Rhododaphne* was derived—and, in due course transfused into Shelley's mind. Mary's statement in her Note (see p. 291) that 'Prince Athanase was a good deal modelled on *Alastor*' needs, I think, a slight adjustment, the truth being that *Alastor* just happens to overlap with what I have called the 'community of conceptions' between the two young men.

As first sketched (see Mary Shelley's Note), the poem was to have been entitled 'Pandemos and Urania'. Based on *Symposium*, 180 c–181, it was to have related a typical Shelleyan quest, involving travel, for an ideal female embodiment of Heavenly Love and the discovery, in place of this 'Urania', of 'Pandemos', the everyday earthly love which has been masquerading as the ideal.

I think this poem important among Shelley's compositions—not by reason of its achievement but because of the stage it marks in his development. Two significant questions are 'Why did he change the title?' and 'Why did he abandon it?' The answers are, I think, related. Apart from the last fragmentary six lines there is nothing whatever, in the text which we have, to tell us that Shelley intended a poem about the two conflicting types of woman-love—without Mary's Note we might never have guessed that. Quite clearly the poem, as it progresses, moved gradually further from the origin of the first title, but I do not think that the origin of the revised one has been noticed. It must, surely, derive from that passage in *Symposium*, 208 where Diotima is talking of the effects of Love on human nature—a passage particularly noted by Shelley in his memorandum on the dialogue: it occurred on p. 239 of his Bipont edition of Plato (see Rogers, *Shelley at Work*, pp. 43 ff.). 'For the mortal nature', says she (as translated by Shelley), 'seeks, so far as it is able, to become deathless and eternal.' She proceeds to speak of 'That which is called meditation' (ὅ γὰρ καλεῖται μελετᾶν)—that is to say philosophical meditation, which is 'the science of the departure of knowledge' (ὡς ἐξιούσης ἐστὶ τῆς ἐπιστήμης)—and concludes (again as translated by Shelley): 'By this contrivance, O Socrates, does what is mortal, the body and all other things, partake of immortality.' In Plato her words are ταύτῃ τῇ μηχανῇ, ὦ Σώκρατες, ἔφη, θνητὸν ἀθανασίας μετέχει, καὶ σῶμα καὶ τἆλλα πάντα. The eighth of these Greek words, 'athanasias', yields us the name of Shelley's protagonist—a self-projection, of course. Notopoulos, whose pages (*Platonism*, 51–4 and 224–5) give the full background of this matter, guessed rightly: '[Shelley] wanted to make the philosopher the central character of the tale, and changed the title to suit his purpose.' In his footnote on line 124 Shelley tells us as much himself. It was, I think, not so much something that Shelley wanted as something that happened by itself. The effect made upon him by the *Symposium* in 1817 was so tremendous (see Notopoulos, *Platonism*, pp. 46–54, and Rogers, *Shelley at Work*, ch. 4) that it proved a turning-point in his life. One immediate effect was that, becoming more and more conscious of the direct Platonism in his own mind, he could not help projecting himself more and more into the personality of Athanase, and he felt that this was 'morbid'. The fragmented poem that we have, had become, when he abandoned it, a half-finished monument to the *Symposium*, and the feeling had become curiously diverted into a touching reminiscence of his own early teacher (see below). 'Pandemos and Urania' had become something like 'Athanase and Zonoras'. It may not be wrong to see in the collapse of the poem a change in Shelley's attitude to Platonism itself. In the Notes to *Queen Mab* (see Vol. I, p. 319, and n., p. 396) he contrasted 'the reveries of Plato' with 'the reasonings of Aristotle' and, even after his direct studies of Plato had begun to advance, he still tended, in eighteenth-century fashion, to regard him mainly as a poet and a beautiful dreamer. Like *Alastor*, 'Prince Athanase' is itself a poetical reverie in the midst of which it may well be that Shelley awoke to the realization of the full power of Platonic thought to which he testifies in the Preface to *Prometheus Unbound*.

15: *Philosophy's accepted guest*: Though differing in many ways from the Platonic philosopher, Athanase shares many of his characteristics: cf. 17, 31–2.

34: *their dark estate*: The unenlightened multitude are like the prisoners, bound in darkness, of the Cave in the *Republic*: see Rogers, *Shelley at Work*, pp. 148–9.

74: *wake*: probably transitive.

90–2: These lines refer to *Phaedrus*, 245 (see above, pp. 344 ff., nn. on 'Hymn to Intellectual Beauty') and to the central doctrine of the *Phaedo* (72 e–73 a) where memories of an antenatal life make the philosopher despise earthly imprisonment. Shelley seems to have got the word 'antenatal' from Godwin's *Political Justice*, which he had been reading a few days before beginning on his poem. Notopoulos (*Platonism*, p. 226) observes that, whereas Godwin denounces the doctrine, Shelley here endows others with this Platonic belief. Paradoxically Godwin, like other anti-Platonic thinkers, had absorbed a good deal of Platonism and is sometimes a source of the indirect Platonism in Shelley. *Mandeville* appeared while Shelley was writing this poem and he compared the love motif with the speech of Agathon in the *Symposium*.

95–6: Cf. *Symposium*, 204 b. Shelley translates: 'For Wisdom is one of the most beautiful of all things; Love is that which thirsts for the beautiful, so that Love is of Necessity a philosopher, philosophy being an intermediate state between ignorance and wisdom.' Not a bad description, it happens, of the stage of his development at which Shelley wrote 'Prince Athanase'.

100: *But*: sc. 'But which'.

115–16: A useful reminder that Shelley not only got ideas from Plato, but drew from the Platonic Socrates his method of analysis. (See H. Tredennick, *The Last Days of Socrates*, Penguin edition, pp. 9–10, for an admirably succinct summary.) This is viewed, in its relation to Shelley, in William J. McTaggart's article, 'Some Inquiries into Shelley's Platonism', *Keats–Shelley Memorial Bulletin*, xxi, 1970.

125–9: An idealized account of Dr. Lind, Shelley's mentor in his Eton days, with whom he read the *Symposium*. Cf. Dr. Lind's appearance as the Hermit in *Laon and Cythna*, III. 1360–1; see n., above, pp. 384–5.

139: An adaptation of a sentence in Thomas Paine's *The Rights of Man*: 'it is the faculty of the human mind to become what it contemplates, and to act in unity with its object'—another example of how Platonism, absorbed among eighteenth-century writers from the general European tradition of culture, reached Shelley indirectly and became fused with his natural and direct Platonism. For this Platonic doctrine, very common in his writings, cf. *Prometheus Unbound*, II. iv. 83, IV. 484, 'Marenghi', 135 [Hutch.]. Locock compares its appearance in Byron, *Childe Harold*, IV. CLVIII. 8–9.

143: *A bloodier power*: Napoleon.

168–81: The Zonoras/Lind–Athanase/Shelley relationship is made to reflect the relationship of Socrates with his pupils and, particularly, with Plato, who, as Shelley aspired to do, 'outran his teacher'.

193–8: I am indebted to Mr. Desmond King-Hele for the following note: 'Shelley is deliberately progressing through a whole year. It is summer in lines 173–185½, winter in lines 185½–193, spring in lines 194–198, and summer again in lines 199–223 ("'Tis just one year"—very exact). It is in spring (March) that Arcturus rises after sunset and Orion is in the south (or strictly a little west of south) at the same hour. I see no reason to suppose, as Locock does, that Shelley is projecting into his poem the chronology of 1817: Athanase is a timeless sort of character, so an exact date, determined by the moon, seems inappropriate. Shelley is merely telling us it is spring in two complementary ways (*a*) "the wintry clouds are all gone by" and (*b*) it is the month when "bright Arcturus" is rising through the trees just after sunset (i.e. March). This is all accurate and specific, and there is no inconsistency anywhere.'

218–29 d : More spiritual autobiography, sentimentalized but of the first importance in relation to Shelley's poetry. The lines refer to his reading of the *Symposium* with Dr. Lind at Eton, and of its emotional impact 'recollected in tranquillity" when he re-read it in 1817. Of the far-reaching effects of this second impact we can judge from the clues left in the memoranda which are followed up in Rogers, *Shelley at Work*, pp. 43 ff. Of its immediate effects in 1817 there is evidence in his letter to Godwin of 7 Dec. 1817 (Jones, *Letters*, i. 574) where he over-reacts a good deal to Godwin's use of the speech of Agathon in the *Symposium*. The clues left among his memoranda lead us, *inter alia*, to the self-revelatory passages about Shakespeare's sonnets, Diotima and Agathon, which he wrote, but did not print, for *Epipsychidion*.

227: *the story of the feast*: Plato's *Symposium*: cf., *passim*, these notes on this poem, and Shelley's translation of the dialogue.

251–3: An analogy to the mental state of 'conjecture' (εἰκασία) in *Republic*, 510 d.

303–5: The first three lines, slightly altered, appear cancelled in a manuscript of *Prometheus Unbound*; they were used, still more effectively in *The Cenci*, I. i. 109–13.

MISCELLANEOUS SHORTER POEMS AND FRAGMENTS, 1817

p. 295, MARIANNE'S DREAM. *Title*: From the name of Leigh Hunt's wife, who was the dreamer. *Text*: Shelley wrote the poem to please Mrs. Hunt and it seems likely that Mary made her transcript before the holograph was dispatched to her. Hunt printed it anonymously. If the text is better than that of other poems he printed for Shelley, the reason is probably that, compared with, say, the 'Hymn to Intellectual Beauty', the style is simpler and the syntax less complicated. I have added quotation marks where the sense required them: only in line 2 is a quotation mark supplied in the transcript. In line 56, where the verbless sentence yields no sense unless exclamatory, I have added an exclamation mark. In line 18 Mary Shelley's 'gold' is unaccountable. The transcript leaves no doubt of the correctness of Rossetti's conjecture in line 62: as penned by Mary Shelley the letter 'a' can easily be mistaken for 'or', and so too sometimes when Shelley writes it. In line 63 Rossetti conjectured 'their' for 'its', but here the transcript is against him. The meaning of Stanza x, which puzzled both Rossetti and Locock, is 'Columns and fanes and gates, bright with workmanship of no mortal kind, shot a lustre, magnificent from the shapes it (the workmanship) had created'. In line 106 James Thomson ('B.V.') conjectured 'flames', but 'flood' is the reading in the transcript. In line 109 the uncancelled alternatives in the transcript probably represent something left similarly unsettled in the holograph: for this habit of Shelley's cf. nn. on the text of the preceding poem.

Content: The 'Hymn to Intellectual Beauty', printed by Hunt in 1817, was a manifesto of Shelley's Platonism and his self-dedication to poetry: this poem, though playful in tone, is coloured throughout by his usual semblance–reality symbolism. See Rogers, *Shelley at Work*, p. 172 and, for the dream-symbolism in general, ch. 10, *passim*.

p. 300, To CONSTANTIA, SINGING. *Title*: I have preferred Mary Shelley's title to that printed in *1818*, both because it is neatly descriptive and because it has long served to distinguish this poem from the one that follows.

Date: Newman Ivey White thinks that the poem is to be dated from Claire's entry in her Journal for 19 Jan. 1817 where she mentions 'copying part of verses to Constantia' (*Shelley*, i. 731–2). About the association of the poem with Claire, White is almost over-cautious. But the draft occurs in a Notebook started in 1817, and Shelley and Claire were not together till March or April, she being at Bath and he in London: she busied about the birth of her daughter by Byron (12 Jan.) and he with the matter of the Lord Chancellor and his children by Harriet. Perhaps it was some other lines to Constantia that Claire copied, e.g. the fragment that follows. And since a piano is postulated ('snowy fingers', line 3), the Marlow period seems likelier. Shelley's note of hand for the Kirkman pianoforte which he obtained for Claire through Vincent Novello was signed by him and witnessed by Leigh Hunt on 27 Apr. 1817: in 1952 I acquired it from Novello's descendants on behalf of the Keats–Shelley Memorial. See Rogers, 'Music at Marlow', *Keats–Shelley Memorial Bulletin*, v, 1953. Two days later Mary records the arrival of the instrument. I incline to think that this gives a *terminus post quem*.

Text: E. 4, a confused draft, must be considered inferior, on the whole, and so must the texts that derive from it: d. 7, *1824*, *1839*, *1904*. Theoretically *1818* should command authority, as having been printed by Shelley. But *did* Shelley print it? It is odd that, having broken, since 1812, his connection with the *Oxford Herald*, in which he had reason for publishing pseudonymously as an undergraduate (see nn. in Vol. I on his translations of epigrams) he should suddenly revert to it in 1817 under a new pseudonym, when other forms of publication were open to him. It seems not inconceivable that it was Claire herself who sent the poem to the *Oxford Herald*. The Notebook SH II was her preciously guarded property, given to her by Shelley. Not till its acquisition by Captain Silsbee, who presented it to Harvard, does its existence seem to have been known; had Mary known of it when preparing her 1839 edition she could hardly have printed from a wild draft a poem extant in a neat fair copy. A curious point about the fair copy in SH II is its lack of the final line. The line, as I have printed it, following Peck, from E. 4, has a warmth of feeling which, just conceivably, Shelley might have wanted to keep private: he and Mary had good reason to be discreet about Claire, in view of the rumours of Shelley's promiscuousness, to which the presence of her unexplained daughter seemed to lend colour. It seems to me, however, equally possible that Shelley omitted the line out of pure carelessness, confused by the wildness of the draft he was transcribing: cf. the way he missed lines in transcribing 'Mont Blanc' from the draft in e. 16. The comparative inferiority of the last line as printed in *1818* would be, at least, consistent with the possibility that Claire supplied it when printing from her manuscript where it was missing. Shelley's 'it' (line 2) in SH II is another example of careless copying, corrected in *1818*, whether by him or by Claire. Perhaps, as suggested by Mrs. Chernaik, 'Pleyel' was taken from the rationalist hero of Charles Brockden Brown's novel *Wieland*, published in 1798. It might equally well be borrowed from the name of Ignaz Pleyel, the famous musician and piano-maker, friend and professional associate of Muzio Clementi, who married the sister of Mrs. Gisborne, an old friend of Godwin, Claire, and Mary and, later, a close friend of the Shelleys in Italy.

Neither *1818* nor the manuscripts make much attempt to supply the punctuation demanded by the syntactical and rhetorical movement. I have done my best. A full collation with E. 4 or with the transcript and printed texts which derive from it would be hardly practicable since, apart from other forms of confusion, the stanzas appear in the wrong order.

Content: 27–33: 'The sprouting of wings on the shoulders and the ascent to 'Nature's utmost sphere', where 'the world's shadowy walls are past and disappear', is a Platonic feeling absorbed from the *Phaedrus*, 249 d–251. Music gave Shelley the feeling of escape that he felt physically in boats and, in his poetry, the Boat becomes a symbol of his imaginative, intellectual excursion out of the world of semblances and mutability into the realm of reality and eternal beauty; then, with the notion of ascent the Boat very easily becomes a space-ship.

p. 302, FRAGMENT: To CONSTANTIA. *Text*: 1: The three dots in E. 4 denote an unfulfilled intention to revise. Cf. the underscorings and apparent cancellations, made with the same intent, in the holograph of 'Prince Athanase' and in other manuscripts.

Content: 7–11: For this Platonic notion, from *Symposium*, 196 b, cf. 'The colour from the flower is gone . . .', 1819, usually given as 1818. See Rogers, *Shelley at Work*, pp. 49–51.

p. 303, Fragment: To One Singing. *Content*: For the Platonic concept of the Boat see above, n. on 'To Constantia, Singing', and Rogers, *Shelley at Work*, ch. 6. Clearly the 'One Singing' is, once again, Claire Clairmont. See Rogers, 'Music at Marlow', *Keats–Shelley Memorial Bulletin*, v, 1953. The Notebook E. 4 accompanied Shelley to Italy, and this fragment was recast as the opening of Asia's song in *Prometheus Unbound*, II. v. 72 ff.

p. 303, Fragment: To Music (2). *Text/Content*: 1: To an eye familiar with Shelley's drafts the manuscript is quite clear, and it seems odd that Mary Shelley should have missed the obvious echo of *Twelfth Night*, I. i. 1.

p. 304, Fragment: 'Mighty Eagle . . .'. *Date/Content*: For the connections and significance of this fragment see above, p. 381, n. on *Laon and Cythna*, 193 ff.

p. 305, To the Lord Chancellor. *Title/Date*: In order to connect the piece with Shelley's reaction to the English political scene of 1819 the lines printed in *1839*[1] were placed by Mary Shelley among her Notes on the poems of that year, though she made plain that they are to be dated 1817. As usual with pieces placed in her Notes, she gives no title, but, despite the discretion of most of the manuscripts, she makes it quite plain whom Shelley is addressing. Forman, Rossetti, and Hutchinson all assign the date of composition to August or September of 1817, on the ground that Lord Eldon's decree, depriving Shelley of his children by Harriet, was pronounced in August. With the dating is bound up that of the lines 'To William Shelley', about which (see *Shelley at Work*, p. 47) I formerly inclined to agree with Forman, Rossetti, and Hutchinson. I now confess to having shared an error. The decree was originally pronounced on 17 or 27 March (between which two dates documents differ), and Mary's Note—attested by the fierce immediacy of the poem—tells us that it was written in Shelley's 'first resentment against the Chancellor'; therefore, as Locock points out in his 1911 edition, we should date it, at the latest, Apr. 1817.

Text: The multiplicity of manuscripts is remarkable. A puzzle is suggested by the fact that the draft in the Notebook e. 9, which has every appearance of a draft, occurs in a Notebook belonging otherwise to 1820–1; this, however, becomes explicable in the light of Shelley's habit of redrafting poems from memory—see *Date*, above. Hutchinson, who, I think, had personally seen few manuscripts, may be forgiven for describing SH 1 as 'a much-corrected draft'. It is, in fact, a much-corrected fair copy, derived from e. 9, the basis of Mary's printing. Its occurrence in SH I would be consistent with a supposition that the poems in this Notebook were originally collected for the purposes of the 1820 volume. Its rejection, for reasons of discretion, would be natural enough. The purpose of d. 9 was, apparently, to incorporate the corrections made by Shelley in SH I. How the untraced manuscripts relate to the textual evolution I have no means of guessing; possibly the Hunt transcript was intended for publication in the *Examiner*. The Leeds transcript was probably intended simply as a gift from Mary to the Cowden Clarkes, her friends and sympathizers. I have collated such readings of 'Fred' as are recorded in 1904. Between the 'I curse thee' of line 17 and its repetition in line 61, the syntactical pattern of concatenated

'By . .', 'By in', has hitherto been obscured by unrationed Shelleyan dashes in lines 29, 30, 32, 40, 44, 45 (2), 48, 52, 53, 54, 56 (2). I have marked off the various curses by semicolons in lines 32, 38, 40, 44, 48, 52, 53, 56 (2), and 58. The rhetoric has been sustained at line 36 by an additional dash, and led to its climax by the exclamation-plus-dash in line 60. In lines 29, 30, 45, 46, 47, and 49 commas only were needed.

Content: Of this poem and the next one Mary noted, in *1839*, that they 'were not written to exhibit the pangs of distress to the public; they were the spontaneous outbursts of a man who brooded over his wrongs and woes . . .'.

4: *a buried Form*: 'the Star Chamber', says Mary Shelley.

19: *prove*: experience, feel; French *éprouver*, cf. 'Lines to a Critic', 13. *OED* compares Wesley, 'They only shall his Mercy prove'.

43: *which must be their error*: from which they will form a wrongful opinion of their father.

51: Cf. *The Mask of Anarchy*, 16–17, and *Oedipus Tyrannus*, I. 334.

62–3: Locock notes the similarity of this, and a good deal of the preceding, to the Incantation in Byron's *Manfred*, I. i, which may well have been a source: the poem was begun in the summer of 1816, when Shelley and Byron were together in Switzerland.

p. 309, To WILLIAM SHELLEY. *Date*: See n. on the date of the preceding poem.

Text: My main improvements are the corrections 'time' (14), 'thee' (41), and the omission in lines 5, 8, and 33 of words apparently put in to help the metre, but which the metre, as managed by Shelley, does not require. The wild draft perhaps reflects Shelley's agony.

Content: See above for Mary Shelley's Note on the preceding poem.

9: *thy brother and sister dear*: Charles and Ianthe, Shelley's children by Harriet, the custody of whom had just been denied him by the decree of Lord Eldon, the Chancellor.

18: *Another*: Clara, Shelley's daughter by Mary, who was to be born on 2 Sept. 1817.

25–32: Cf. *Rosalind and Helen*, 894–7; see above, pp. 325–6.

37–40: *we know . . . the storm . . .*: sc. to be *less cruel*. An adaptation into English, I think, of the Greek participial construction which follows verbs of knowing.

46 ff. It is significant that in the Notebook e. 16 the draft of these lines to William Shelley is followed by the momentous memorandum on Plato's *Symposium* which signposts so much of the poet's maturer thought and language: see Rogers, *Shelley at Work*, ch. 5. Greece, in 1817, had become for Shelley the symbol of all that was free and good and beautiful: apart from his own records of this we have the testimony of Hunt, Hogg, Peacock, and Horace Smith (see Notopoulos, *Platonism*, pp. 47–8). It should be remembered that Shelley—like Goethe some forty years earlier—did not clearly distinguish 'serene and golden Italy' from 'Greece the Mother of the free'; we shall understand his period better if we remember how the Romantic imagination tended to fuse the Greek, the Graeco-Roman, and the Roman-as-viewed-by-tourists.

p. 311, To WILLIAM SHELLEY. ADDITIONAL LINES. *Text*: As with the rest of the poem, the draft is a wild one. Shelley's intentions are hardly discernible. No editing or collation being practicable, I could do no more than print a transcription of such broken pieces as make sense. I have tried to make this as literal as possible, but at the same time to avoid adding to the confusion of the sense by recording non-significant anomalies or the confused processes of cancelling. The wild draft is on three sheets, two of them in the Notebook e. 16 and one among the loose sheets in the box catalogued c. 4. The loose sheet is f. 63ʳ and by a coincidence the pages of the Notebook—from between which f. 63ʳ has been torn at some time—happen to be numbered 63 and 64. The lines have two separate starts, one on p. 63 of the Notebook and the other on the loose sheet; after the second start there follow the lines Shelley drafted as an alternative follow-up to line 2 and which I have numbered 16 ff. The passage beginning 'The world is now . . .', which follows it, was printed by Garnett and subsequent editors preceding the opening line, 'Mild thoughts . . .'. I have removed from the Additional Lines some broken lines which Garnett took from e. 16, p. 42; they belong to the Celandine poem (see p. 80), over a pencil draft of which this poem was scribbled.

p. 312, Two LAMENTS. *Date/Text*: In 1816 Shelley wrote a lament on Fanny Godwin and a lament on Harriet Shelley. These are nos. 1 and 3 of the poems grouped on pp. 83–6 as 'Three Laments'. A minor complication is that the manuscript of no. 3, whether by accident or design, is antedated as 'November—1815'. A second complication is that coming upon these laments in 1819, just after the death of his son William, Shelley added to the manuscript of no. 1 the lament on William Shelley which is emotionally joined to it and which needs to be printed, as I have printed it, as 'no. 2' of these 'Three Laments'. Meanwhile, in 1817, with his grief for the previous winter's sorrows revived by their first anniversary, he had rewritten the third of the *1816* laments and added to it a new one, also about Harriet. These are the poems grouped here as 'Two Laments'.

The beauty of the first lament depends largely on the relation of rhythmic pattern, within each stanza, to syntactical shape. Stanzas I, II, and IV each start with a couple of lines carrying two separate statements, followed by five lines, of varied length and beautifully rhyme-patterned, containing a flow of description. These pairs of opening statement need to be marked off by something like the semicolons I have given them. In the third stanza the shape is varied a little by the opening enjambment and by the postponing till line 2 of the need for an end-stop. Stanza II is rhythmically differentiated by the fact that the descriptive flow of its last five lines is broken up by the division of the last three into two descriptive statements; the division needed to be marked, I thought, by the semicolon I have placed after 'soil'.

The witness to the text of the first lament is, of course, e. 12. Since d. 7 derives from it and is incomplete, it has no significance and is not collated here. With the second lament likewise e. 12 is the primary textual witness, but d. 9, derived from it, does contain some points of significance, and these I have collated. It may be forgivable, perhaps, if, faced with the editorial nightmare of dating and arranging five poems, separate and yet related, Mary Shelley made a sad verbal slip: the odd 'ghast' in line 5 is an obvious piece of dittography, and from the rhyming Edmund Blunden long ago conjectured the 'wild' of e. 12. Shelley-Rolls and Ingpen, who set out to fault Mary Shelley in the last line, may now be seen to be doubly wrong themselves, for, in the first place, their 'Mary blest' is a misreading, and, in the second place, they have mistaken the nature of the pen-stroke made by Shelley through 'In the light of'. It is not, I am sure, a cancellation but another instance (cf., for example, above, nn. on the text of 'Prince Athanase') of his way of signifying an intended revision. That the words 'From blest', misread in *1934*, indicated his *idea* for a revision I am prepared to believe. That 'From blest life's brief morning' represents his completed *verbal* revision I do not believe. Prone though he is to sudden changes of metrical pattern, this would be a most un-Shelleyan one since, apart from the ugly 'blest . . . brief', it would end the metrical movement of the whole piece with an unpleasant thump. I choose as Mary chose.

p. 314, DEATH. *Text*: Mary Shelley's source is two drafts made by Shelley in e. 16: a first rough draft, which begins on p. 47 rev. and ends about a third of the way down p. 46 rev, and a redrafting, more legible though incomplete, which follows the first draft on p. 46 rev.

Date/Content: The Notebook e. 16 contains a good deal that was written in 1816, during the Shelleys' stay in Geneva; it was taken up and used again in 1817. This is consistent with Mary's dating of the fragment as well as with the likelihood that it represents a reversion by Shelley to the grief-stricken mood that followed the deaths of Fanny Godwin and Harriet, his first wife. The mood might well have been evoked by his loss of Harriet's children through the Lord Chancellor's decree in 1817, and his fear that Mary's children also might be taken from him.

p. 315, OTHO, STANZAS, ETC. *Date*: The occurrence of the draft in the Note-book e. 16 is consistent with Mary Shelley's dating.

Text: The manuscript is perhaps as difficult as any manuscript of Shelley's and neither Mary Shelley nor Garnett deserves reproach for what they missed. Mary Shelley printed two stanzas and Garnett a third, together with two lines of a fourth. To these he added the fragment 'Once more descend', which I have removed here, since it is drafted in a different Notebook and its association with 'Otho' is based on metrical grounds that seem very odd.

Arrangement is the first problem. The six stanzas given here appear on four consecutive pages. That the draft begins on the second page is plain from the occurrence there, written close under the title, 'Otho', of the stanza that I place first. Stanza II comes below it, and on the top half of the third page comes Stanza III. The penmanship is similar throughout these three stanzas. On the third page, below Stanza III, comes Stanza V and, on the fourth, Stanza VI. Stanzas V and VI have been written first in pencil, which has become rubbed, and subsequently inked over by Shelley in a hand bolder than that in which the preceding stanzas are written. Stanza IV comes on the first of the four pages, below some lines drafted for *Laon and Cythna*, VII 3149–53, or adapted there. The penmanship on this page is similar to that in Stanzas I, II, and III. My placing of the stanza as number IV is based on the fact that the word 'Such' requires an antecedent. As I print Stanzas I–IV, the shape of the poem is this:

Stanza I gives a picture of the chaotic condition of Rome in A.D. 69 (the 'year of the four emperors'—see 'Content', below; Stanzas II and III give the 'thoughts' referred to in Stanza IV—they are Shelley's thoughts, and I have marked this by quotation marks; then, following 'To say' come Stanzas V and VI, again marked by quotation marks, which tell us what message the relics of Rome, as yet seen by Shelley in imagination only, appeared to be giving him.

A formal collation would be impracticable. A literal transcription would yield no meaning. But once the arrangement of the stanzas has been discovered, it is not impossible to work out the meaning buried away in Shelley's scrawl, provided we pay due attention, in the course of the deciphering, to syntactical shape, to metre, and to rhyme, and do not take Shelley's cancellings too literally. But Shelley sometimes scored through his manuscripts as an indication that he had copied them, and he may have made a fair copy now lost. Since each page of this manuscript is scored through with vertical lines I suppose that, according to Fundamentalist principles, it ought not to be printed at all. I note a few points:

22: *doubtful*: misread by Mary Shelley as 'deathful'.

23: *that*: I correct the 'and' of Mary Shelley and edd.

26: Deciphering of this complicated page is not made easier by the fact that this, the second line of the stanza, is written, apparently as an afterthought, above the first and marked with a '2' and an 'x'; beside line 25 is a possible but hardly perceptible '1'.

28: *gate*: almost illegible but not inconsistent with the *ductus litterarum*. Metre requires a monosyllable and no other monosyllable yields both sense and a rhyme for 'desolate'.

31: *visage*: clearly emended from [fair ghost]: I accept it with regret.

45: Mary Shelley printed 'buy'. Rossetti, with a regard for rhyme, conjectures 'wring'. Garnett, with a regard both for rhyme and *ductus litterarum* or, possibly, having seen the manuscript, suggested 'bring'.

Content: Mary Shelley suggests that the poem derives from Shelley's reading of Tacitus in 1817. It probably owes much also to Suetonius, whom he had read in 1814. It may be that this confused and violent period in Roman history appealed to the Godwinian element still remaining in Shelley's thought as an illustration of how tyranny perishes of its own corruption—four emperors, in A.D. 68–9 dying violently in succession. Nero killed himself to avoid being murdered by Galba, Galba was murdered by the soldiers of Otho, Otho committed suicide after defeat by Vitellius, and Vitellius was murdered by the Praetorian Guard as Vespasian advanced into Rome. Shelley's choice of Otho as a hero seems an odd one since, in addition to being the murderer of Galba, he had been a close associate of Nero's in crime and debauchery; however, Shelley's picture is not inconsistent with the legend created by Otho's behaviour in his last hours, when he showed great consideration and forethought for his soldiers before stabbing himself, and observed that it was better that one man should die than that all should be involved in ruin for his obstinacy. The legend is crystallized in Martial's epigram:

> Sit Cato dum vivit, sane vel Caesare major;
> Dum moritur numquid major Othone fuit?

9–10: An echo of Virgil's famous line, *Aen.* i. 462:

Sunt lacrimae rerum, et mentem mortalia tangunt

The echo is an apt one since Shelley's thoughts (see n. above, under 'Text') are being evoked, like those of Aeneas, by the contemplation of history preserved in stone.

11: *sweet mother*: Rome.

34: *"Last of the Romans"*: cf. *Julius Caesar*, v. iii. 99, for which Shakespeare drew on Plutarch. Here, and in 37–8, Shelley's source is Tacitus, who tells (*Annals*, iv. 36) of the defiant behaviour of the historian, Cremutius Cordus, when brought to trial for insulting Tiberius by using this phrase about a tyrannicide.

36: *Rest*: misread by Mary as 'Rests', which upsets the concessive sequence.

46: Above the page bearing Stanza VI Shelley has a memorandum 'Vitellius visits the field of battle'. This probably refers to an incident in Suetonius, *De Vita Caesarum*, Vitellius, 10, describing Vitellius' cynicism about the unburied slain and about the dead Otho.

p. 316, FRAGMENT: 'O THAT A CHARIOT OF CLOUD . . .'. *Date*: The occurrence of the draft in the Notebook e.16 is consistent with Hutchinson's date of 1817, though 1816 is a possibility. *Text*: 2: *tempest weaves*: one of the many places in Shelley's text where the vital question raised by the manuscript is not 'what did Shelley write?' but 'what would Shelley have wished to print?' What he first wrote was

Of cloud which the wild winds weave in air

then he changed 'winds' to 'tempest', forgetting either to adjust the metre, by cancelling the unwanted syllable, 'wild', or to rectify the syntactical conjunction of a singular subject with a plural verb. Editors, rightly assuming that Shelley would not have wished them to print a pointless solecism, have corrected 'weave' to 'weaves', but have hitherto preserved the false measure which I now take the liberty of correcting. It is arguable, of course, that Shelley might have preferred to print 'tempests weave', but an editor must choose one way or the other, and I see no reason to quarrel with the choice of my predecessors.

p. 317, FRAGMENT: 'A GOLDEN-WINGÈD ANGEL STOOD . . .'. *Date*: There are verbal similarities between this fragment and some irreligious lines belonging to 1819, written by Shelley to *bouts-rimés* supplied by Mary. But Garnett and Rossetti may have had grounds which are unknown to me for dating these lines in 1817, and it quite conceivable that the 1819 lines represent one of Shelley's memory-echoes.

p. 317, FRAGMENT: 'TO THIRST AND FIND NO FILL . . .'. *Date*: Mary Shelley's dating is consistent with the occurrence of the draft in the Notebook E. 4, on the same page as a stanza of 'To Constantia, Singing'.

Title: Ornamental titles, printed by some editors and rejected here, are 'Unsatisfied Desires' and 'Igniculus Desiderii'.

Content: See Mary Shelley's Note, p. 324.

p. 318, FRAGMENT: 'WEALTH AND DOMINION . . .'. *Title*: Earlier, ornamental, titles rejected here, were 'Wealth and Love', 'Love Eternal', and 'Amor Aeternus'.

Date: Mary Shelley's dating is consistent with the occurrence of the draft in the Notebook E. 4, among material dating from 1817.

p. 318, FRAGMENT: 'MY THOUGHTS ARISE AND FADE . . .'. *Title*: Earlier titles rejected here: 'Thoughts', 'Elusive Thoughts', 'Thoughts come and go in Solitude'.

Date: see n. on dating of the preceding fragment.

p. 319, FRAGMENT: A HATE-SONG. *Source/Content*: Rossetti's note: 'It seems that Hunt and Shelley were talking one day (probably in or about 1817) concerning Love-songs; and Shelley said that he didn't see why Hate-songs should not also be written and that he could do them; and on the spot he improvised these lines of doggerel.'

p. 319, FRAGMENT: 'MY HEAD IS WILD . . .' [2nd Version]. *Title*: Locock's 'The Lost Leader', based on this version, seems, in the light of the first version, to be a doubtful interpretation of the fragment. For Version I see above, p. 366. The association with Wilson revealed by Shelley's earlier draft makes plain that his 'grief' is occasioned by Wilson's attack on Keats, so that it may now be seen as an interesting anticipation of the mood of *Adonais*. The 'chief/ Among yon spirits' must, surely, be not Wordsworth, chief among poets, but Wilson, chief among critics.

Text/Date: This, the version of the poem printed by editors from Rossetti onwards, derives from a draft in the Notebook e. 12; its contents were composed over a wide period of time, so that the proximity of a poem to other work very seldom affords a safe clue to its date. I have little doubt that the version in this Notebook represents one of Shelley's redraftings from memory, and as the earlier version, in e. 19, seems, from its occurrence among the drafts for *Laon and Cythna*, to belong to 1817, I have placed both versions in the year of their origin. Rossetti does not state why he placed the e. 12 version in 1818. This dating would be consistent with a reference by Shelley to the attacks on *Endymion*. But, equally well, he might have been moved by the attacks on Hunt in 1817, in which Keats was included. The famous castigation of 'The Cockney School of Poetry' did not appear till October, but Keats may well have been aware much earlier of the hostility of the *Edinburgh Magazine*. His *Poems* appeared in March 1817, and during the ensuing period, when Shelley was composing *Laon and Cythna*, the two men met quite frequently.

p. 319, OZYMANDIAS. *Date/Content*: In a letter to his brothers, dated 14 Feb. 1818, Keats mentions how, on 4 Feb., he, Shelley, and Hunt had competed in writing sonnets on the Nile. From this, Middleton, Shelley's early biographer, was confused into believing that 'Ozymandias' was Shelley's contribution to the competition; Forman corrected this by printing the sonnet headed 'To the Nile' from a holograph owned by Hunt. The statement of the Julian editors that the poem was the result of a competition with Horace Smith is probably a further confusion of the truth, arising from the fact that Shelley's sonnet, published on 11 Jan. 1818, was followed up by a letter to the Editor in which Smith praised it and enclosed a sonnet of his own on the same subject. Smith's sonnet was published in the *Examiner* on 1 Feb. 1818. The title under which it was republished in 1821, 'On a Stupendous Leg of Granite Found in the Desert', brings it close to Shelley's earlier draft (written on the verso of the same page, 88, in E. 4). The two men had been reading Diodorus Siculus together, and the probability is that Shelley's imagination, primed by contemporary enthusiasm for ruins and for engravings of them, was finally fired off by his description of a funerary temple of Ozymandias, and, more particularly, by the sonorous phrases of the epitaph (I. 47), with their overtones of ironical understatement: Βασιλεὺς βασιλέων ᾽Οσυμανδύας εἰμί· εἰ δέ τις εἰδέναι βούλεται πηλίκος εἰμὶ καὶ ποῦ κεῖμαι, νικάτω τι τῶν ἐμῶν ἔργων.

In *Keats–Shelley Journal*, vii, 1958, Professor Pottle suggested that the word 'Glirastes' is probably a fusion of the Latin word for 'dormouse', *glis, gliris*, with the Greek suffix '-*astes*', as in 'Ecclesiastes'; Shelley was fond of such word-coinages. Professor Pottle then illuminated a small biographical corner by deducing that the 'dormouse' of Mary's letters is as likely to be a pet-name for Shelley himself as it is for her. Hogg is a witness to his frequent drowsiness at Oxford.

p. 320, FRAGMENT: 'SERENE, IN HIS UNCONQUERABLE MIGHT. . . '. *Date*: Hutchinson places this in 1820. Locock assigns it to 1817 for the good reason that, with the exception of the lines to Mary about crossing the Apennines, all the smaller pieces in the Notebook E. 4 belong to that year.

Text: 2: I think that the word is 'Endured', but admit a little doubt. That the 'Almighty King' should be 'serene' because the 'spirits' have to endure his 'might' makes good Shelleyan sense.

Content: Locock suggests that these lines may be an anticipation of the tragedy on the Book of Job which, early in 1818 Shelley was meditating on writing; see Mary Shelley's Note on *Prometheus Unbound*, para. 5.

p. 321, FRAGMENT: 'ADDRESS TO THE HUMAN MIND'. *Text*: Again I follow Locock, and wish that I could do better.

Content: The basic idea revealed by Shelley's synopsis is clearer than some of the words as he penned them. He did not believe in immortality as Christians do; as a substitute he believed in the immortality of the human mind as represented by its creations, works of art—in the words of his translation of the *Symposium* 'lovelier and more lasting progeny' than the children born of the body. For the Platonic background of this conception of his see *Symposium*, 206–11. In his memorandum of 1817 (see Rogers, *Shelley at Work*, chs. 5 and 8) these passages are specially marked for study. In 1817 the conception is in line with his self-projection, in the role of Platonic student, into the character of Prince Athanase, 'the deathless one'; see nn. above, p. 400. It was to become a seminal one in all his major poetry—*Prometheus Unbound, Adonais, Hellas*, to look no further. What seems to emerge, between the synopsis and the few broken lines Shelley here achieved, is the design for a poem that would develop his Platonic convictions of the immortality of human thought in a manner coloured with notions of the Eastern gods borrowed, perhaps, from Southey's

The Curse of Kehama. With lines 6–10 of the fragment compare the lines from Southey's poem (X. x. 6–10) which Shelley quoted to Miss Hitchener in a letter of 26 Nov. 1811:

> Earthly these passions of the Earth
> They perish where they have their birth;
> But Love is indestructible.
> Its holy flame for ever burneth,
> From Heaven it came, to Heaven returneth . . .

It is the essence of Shelley's belief in the immortality of the mind's 'lovelier and more lasting progeny' that they result from the Platonic love which brings about an intercourse of beautiful minds. For Southey's Platonism and its influence on Shelley see Notopoulos, *Platonism*, pp. 152–5.

p. 322, FRAGMENT: 'SOFT PILLOWS FOR THE FIENDS . . .'. *Text/Content/Date*: I print Locock's deciphering; I share his doubts about it, but I can do no better. The fragment occurs on the same page as the preceding one but need not, he observes, be connected with it. I think, however, that we may give it the same date. See n. on 'Serene, in his unconquerable might . . .', p. 412 above.

p. 322, FRAGMENT: 'ARISE, SWEET MARY . . .'. *Date*: 1817 seems safe enough, since these lines were drafted on the same page as 'To Constantia' and in the midst of material for 'Prince Athanase'.

p. 322, FRAGMENT: 'HEIGH-HO, WISDOM AND FOLLY . . .'. *Date*: See n., above, on 'Serene, in his unconquerable might . . .'. *Content*: A piece of fooling, referring perhaps to some characters at Marlow who amused the Shelley household.
   5: *colly*: an archaic word meaning 'soot, grime'.

p. 323, TRANSLATION: EPIGRAM OF PLATO. *Date*: On the page of SH II which bears Mary's transcript is a note in the handwriting of Captain Silsbee, who acquired the Notebook from Claire Clairmont in her old age and presented it to Harvard:

Shelley came in from his study and showed them this. They were delighted. C[laire] remembers it.

Clearly this a remembrance by Claire Clairmont about the composition of the translation. Since a version appeared in *Laon and Cythna* late in 1817, Shelley and Claire could hardly have hailed this as something new if composed later than that year.

   Content: See above, p. 392, n. on *Laon and Cythna*, IX. 3788 ff., which is Version II.

CORRIGENDA

page

viii penultimate line: *for* mid'night *read* moonnight

xxv mid: *omit* Stanza, Written at Bracknell

3 Commentary, lines 1–3: *read*
STANZA, WRITTEN AT BRACKNELL. MSS.: *Untraced.* TITLE, DATE: *letter to Hogg, 16 Mar. 1814.* PRINTED: *Hogg, 1858/Hutch. 1904.* TEXT: *1904/1858.*
5 control] control, *edd.*

5 Commentary on line 28: *for* Or pride *read* [Or pride]

16 Transfer italicized note 1 to page 17

17 paragraph 1, line 13: *read* July²
Change number of existing note to ²

21 Commentary, 3rd line from foot: *for* 9–21 *read* 9–20

32 Commentary, line 2: for *from*] ever read *from* ever

36 Commentary on line 507: omit *Pf.*

56 Commentary: *add* 455 See n., p. 340.

69 Commentary, line 6: read *1823/collated with e. 12.*

71 Commentary, 6th line from foot: for *pp. 341–2 ff.* read *pp. 343 ff.*

75 Commentary, lines 6–7: *for* 1–2 *read* 1
insert space between of *and* things
omit /Now move

136 Commentary, line 1: *for* 874 *read* 875

142 Commentary: *for* fire. *1839 read* fire, *1839*

155 Commentary on line 1452: *for* sadness, *edd.* read sadness; *edd.*

159 line 1567: *for* flow, *read* flow
Commentary on line 1567: *for* flow, *read* flow
Commentary on line 1568; *for* rise *1904 read* rise, *1904*

161 line 1649: *for* day *read* day,
Commentary, line 3: *after* 1649 *insert* day, *1818*] day *1904, 1839*

165 Commentary on line 1749: *for* hopes *edd.* read hopes, *edd.*

167 Commentary on line 1817 (2nd n.): *read* is, to be *1904, 1818*] is to be, *1839*

173 Commentary on line 2014: *read* earth, *1904, 1839*] earth *1818*

190 Commentary, line 1: *for* 2537–9 *read* 2536–9

210 Commentary on line 3167: *read* cataract, *1818*

217 Commentary, line 1: for *pp. 370–1* read *p. 371*

218 Commentary on line 3397: *for* reply *1839 read* reply, *1839*

CORRIGENDA

241 line 4094: *for* sacrifice, *read* sacrifice

260 shoulder head: *read* [CANTO XII
Commentary on line 4673: *for* beloved;—" *read* beloved;"—

277 Commentary, line 5: for *1903 all* read *1903/all*

305 Commentary, 3rd line from foot: for *from in SH I* read *in SH I from*

312 Commentary, line 3: for *I, II, III* read *stanzas 1–3*
Commentary on line 6 and on line 9: for *edd.* read *1934*

331 line 8: *for* Waterloo *read* Waterloo,

337 line 4: *for* was *read* were

340 note on line 551: *read* 551: *abrupt*: For

348–9 For last line page 348–first line page 349 ('Sometimes . . . But') *read*
One must assume (69) that 'tracks her', saved by Mary from a misprint,
was preferred by Shelley to his 'watches her' in e. 16. The

356 paragraph 1, penultimate line: *omit* below,

373 note on lines 4450–76: *for* p. 255 *read* p. 253

379 note on line 59: *for* 126–8 *read* 126–32

397 15 lines from foot: *for* pp. xv, xvii *read* Vol. I, p. xxvii

406 line 1: *for* 'By in' *read* 'By . . . '

409 line 2: *read* emperors')—

410 penultimate note, penultimate line: *read* it is quite

INDEX OF TITLES

'A golden-wingèd Angel stood . . .', Fragment   317
A Hate-Song, Fragment   319
A Summer Evening Churchyard   7
'Address to the Human Mind', Fragment   321
Alastor, 1815   43
April, 1814, Stanzas   3
'Arise, sweet Mary . . .', Fragment   322

Bion, I. 1–45, Translation: 'I mourn Adonis dead . . .'   93
Bonaparte, Feelings of a Republican on the Fall of   10
Bracknell, written at, Stanza   3

Cavalcanti, Sonnet from the Italian of: 'Returning from its daily quest . . .'   16
Celandine, Verses Written on Receiving a, in a Letter from England   80
Celandine, Verses Written on Receiving . . . , Rejected Lines   83
Churchyard, A Summer Evening   7
Clairmont, Claire, Two Fragments from the Journal of   11
Constantia, Singing, To   300
Constantia, To, Fragment   302

Daemon of the World, The, Part I   21
Daemon of the World, The, Part II   30
Dante, Sonnet from the Italian of: 'Guido, I would that . . .'   15
'Dear home . . .', Fragment   86
Death: 'They die—the dead return not . . .'   314

Epigram of Plato, cited in the *Apologia* of Apuleius: 'Sweet child, thou star of love
  and beauty bright . . .'   323

Feelings of a Republican on the Fall of Bonaparte   10
Fragment: 'A golden-wingèd Angel stood . . .'   317
Fragment: A Hate-Song   319
Fragment: 'Address to the Human Mind'   321
Fragment: 'Arise, sweet Mary . . .'   322
Fragment: 'Dear home . . .'   86
Fragment: Ghost Story   87
Fragment: 'Heigh-ho, wisdom and folly . . .   322
Fragment: 'Mighty Eagle . . .'   304
Fragment: 'My head is wild with weeping . . .'   319
Fragment: 'My thoughts arise and fade . . .'   318
Fragment: 'O that a chariot of cloud were mine . . .'   316
Fragment: Prince Athanase   277
Fragment: 'Serene, in his unconquerable might . . .'   320
Fragment: 'Soft pillows for the fiends . . .'   322
Fragment: Stanzas Addressed to Leigh Hunt: 'A gentle story of two lovers
  young . . .'   88

Fragment: Stanzas Addressed to Leigh Hunt: 'For me, my friend, if not that
    tears did tremble . . .'   87
Fragment: Stanzas Addressed to Leigh Hunt: 'Friend, this I hope . . .'   88
Fragment: To Constantia   302
Fragment: To Music 1, To Mary   303
Fragment: To Music 2   304
Fragment: To One Singing   303
Fragment: 'To thirst and find no fill . . .'   317
Fragment: 'Wealth and dominion . . .'   318
Fragments, Extraneous, found amid the draft for *Laon and Cythna*
    'A music wild and soft that filled the moonnight air . . .'   372
    'A simoon to the almond blossom . . .'   368
    'And I remember wandering through the shadow . . .'   367
    'And with thy sweet eyes awful glance .. .'   365
    'As the wintry skies . . .'   374
    'He ceased—and approbation like the sound . . .'   364
    'He ceased. Another rose: one pale and ⟨? weak⟩ . . .'   366
    'How long has Poesy, the widowed Mother . . .'   374
    'I visit thee but thou art sadly changed . . .'   371
    'Like a sunbeam on a tempest streaming . . .'   365
    'My head is wild with weeping for a grief . . .'   366
    'My   maiden . . .'   367
    'Shapes about my steps assembling . . .'   374
    'The pine is here . . .'   372
    'The wild bull in the mountain and the horse . . .   373
    'These things remain . . .'   371
    'Thou must have seen it was ⟨? ruined⟩ . . .'   367
    'Thou was a homeless cloud . . .'   372
    'We all act out a false part . . .'   374
    'Who with the Devil doth rage and revel . . .'   364
Fragments from the Journal of Claire Clairmont, Two   11

Ghost Story, Fragment   87
Godwin, Fanny, Lament On: 'Her voice did quiver . . .'   83
Godwin, Mary Wollstonecraft, To   4

'Heigh-ho, wisdom and folly . . .', Fragment   322
Hunt, Leigh, Stanzas Addressed to, Fragment: 'A gentle story of two lovers
    young . . .'   88
Hunt, Leigh, Stanzas Addressed to, Fragment: 'For me my friend, if not that
    tears did tremble . . .'   87
Hunt, Leigh, Stanzas Addressed to, Fragment: 'Friend, this I hope . . .'   88
Hymn to Intellectual Beauty   71

Lament, On Fanny Godwin: 'Her voice did quiver . . .'   83
Lament, On Harriet Shelley, Nov. [5], 1816, 1st version:
    'The cold earth slept below . . .'   85
Lament, On Harriet Shelley, Nov. 5, 1816, 2nd version:
    'The cold Earth slept below . . .'   312
Lament, On [Harriet Shelley], Nov. 5, 1817:
    'That time is dead for ever, child . . .'   313
Lament, On William Shelley: 'Thy little footsteps . . .'   84
Laon and Cythna (usually known as *The Revolt of Islam*)   99
Laon and Cythna, Rejected Passages   265
Lord Chancellor, To the   305

Lord Chancellor, To the, Additional Lines 308

Marianne's Dream 295
'Mighty Eagle . . .', Fragment 304
Mont Blanc 75
Mont Blanc, Rejected Lines 80
Moschus III, 1–7, Translation: 'Ye Dorian woods . . .' 91
Moschus V, Translation: 'When winds that move not . . .' 91
Moschus VI, Translation: 'Pan loved his neighbour Echo . . .' 92
Music 1, To, Fragment, To Mary 303
Music 2, To, Fragment 304
Mutability: 'We are as clouds that veil the midnight moon; . . .' 7
'My head is wild with weeping . . .', Fragment 319
'My thoughts arise and fade . . .', Fragment 318

'O that a chariot of cloud were mine . . .', Fragment 316
'Oh! there are spirits of the air . . .' 8
On Harriet Shelley, Nov. [5], 1816, 1st version:
    'The cold earth slept below . . .' 85
On Harriet Shelley, Nov. 5, 1816, 2nd version:
    'The cold Earth slept below . . .' 312
On [Harriet Shelley], Nov. 5, 1817:
    'That time is dead for ever, child . . .' 313
On William Shelley: 'Thy little footsteps . . .' 84
Otho: Stanzas from the Fragment of a Draft 315
Ozymandias 319
Ozymandias: Fragment of an earlier draft 320

Plato, Epigram of, cited in the *Apologia* of Apuleius: 'Sweet child, thou star of
    love and beauty bright . . .', Translation 323
Prince Athanase, A Fragment 277
Prince Athanase, Additional Lines 290

Reality: 'The pale, the cold, and the moony smile . . .'   See *Introduction, p. xix*
Revolt of Islam, The, see *Laon and Cythna* 99

'Serene, in his unconquerable might . . .', Fragment 320
Shelley, Harriet, Lament On, Nov. [5], 1816, 1st version:
    'The cold earth slept below . . .' 85
Shelley, Harriet, Lament On, Nov. 5, 1816, 2nd version:
    'The cold Earth slept below . . .' 312
[Shelley, Harriet,] Lament On, Nov. 5, 1817:
    'That time is dead for ever, child . . .' 313
Shelley, William, Lament On: 'Thy little footsteps . . .' 84
Shelley, William, To, 1817, Additional Lines 311
Shelley, William, To, 1817: 'The billows on the beach . . .' 309
'Soft pillows for the fiends . . .', Fragment 322
Sonnet, from the Italian of Cavalcanti: 'Returning from its daily quest . . .' 16
Sonnet, from the Italian of Dante: 'Guido, I would that . . .' 15
Stanza, written at Bracknell 3
Stanzas,—April, 1814 3
Summer Evening Churchyard, A 7
Sunset, The 69

The Daemon of the World, Part I 21
The Daemon of the World, Part II 30

'The pale, the cold, and the moony smile . . .'   See *Introduction, p. xix*

The Revolt of Islam, see Laon and Cythna   99

The Sunset   69

To ——: 'Yet look on me . . .'   6

To Constantia, Fragment   302

To Constantia, Singing   300

To Mary Wollstonecraft Godwin   4

To Music 1, Fragment, To Mary   303

To Music 2, Fragment   304

To One Singing, Fragment   303

To the Lord Chancellor   305

To the Lord Chancellor, Additional Lines   308

'To thirst and find no fill . . .', Fragment   317

To William Shelley, 1817, Additional Lines   311

To William Shelley, 1817, 'The billows on the beach . . .'   309

To Wordsworth   10

Translations, See:
  Bion
  Cavalcanti
  Dante
  Moschus
  Plato

Two Fragments from the Journal of Claire Clairmont   11

Verses Written on Receiving a Celandine in a Letter from England   80

Verses Written on Receiving a Celandine in a Letter from England, Rejected Lines   83

'Wealth and dominion . . .', Fragment   318

Wordsworth, To   10

Written at Bracknell, Stanza   3

'Yet look on me . . .', To ——   6

INDEX OF FIRST LINES

A gentle-story of two lovers young 88
A golden wingèd Angel stood 317
A hater he came and sat by a ditch 319
A music wild and soft that filled the moonnight air 372
A pale Dream came to a Lady fair 295
A shovel of his ashes took 87
A simoon to the almond blossom 368
'And I remember wandering through the shadow . . .' 367
And with thy sweet eyes awful glance 365
Arise, sweet Mary, rise 322
As the wintry skies [?] mountains 374
Away! the moor is dark beneath the moon 3

Beside the dimness of the glimmering sea 183
By all the terrors of thy fabled Hell 308

Dear home, thou scene of joys which now are cold 86

Earth, ocean, air, belovèd brotherhood! 44
Ere thou wert thus companionless 83

For me, my friend, if not that tears did tremble 87
Frail clouds arrayed in sunlight lose the glory 268
Friend, this I hope ⟨if it be⟩ thou hast ⟨cloven⟩ 88

Guido, I would that Lapo, thou, and I 15

He ceased—and approbation like the sound 364
He ceased. Another rose: one pale and ⟨? weak⟩ 366
Heigh-ho, wisdom and folly! 322
Her voice did quiver as we parted 83
How beautiful it sails 11
How long has Poesy, the widowed Mother 374
How wonderful is Death 21

I hated thee, fallen tyrant! I did groan 10
I met a traveller from an antique land 319
I mourn Adonis dead—loveliest Adonis— 93
'I sate beside the steersman then, and gazing 211
I thought of thee, fair Celandine 80
I visit thee but thou art sadly changed 371

Like a sunbeam on a tempest streaming 365

Mighty eagle! thou that soarest 304
Mild thoughts of man's ungentle race 311
Mine eyes were dim with tears unshed 4

My head is wild with weeping for a grief   319
My head is wild with weeping for a grief   366
My   maiden   367
My spirit like a charmèd bark doth swim   303
My thoughts arise and fade in solitude   318

No more beside the river's sunny foam   265

O Happy Earth! reality of Heaven!   30
O that a chariot of cloud were mine—   316
Oh, Music, thou art not the 'food of Love'   304
Oh! there are spirits of the air   8
Over the utmost hill at length I sped   164

Pan loved his neighbour Echo—but that child   92
Poet of Nature, thou hast wept to know   10
Prince Athanase had one belovèd friend   290

Returning from its daily quest, my Spirit   16

Serene, in his unconquerable might   320
Shapes about my steps assembling   374
She saw me not—she heard me not—alone   245
Silver key of the fountain of tears   303
So now my summer task is ended, Mary   106
So we sate joyous as the morning ray   199
Soft pillows for the fiends   322
Sweet child, thou star of love and beauty bright   323

'That night we anchored in a woody bay   220
That time is dead for ever, child   313
The awful shadow of some unseen Power   71
The billows on the beach are leaping around it   309
The cold earth slept below   85
The cold Earth slept below   312
The everlasting universe of things   75
The mistress and the monitress of earth   315
The old man took the oars, and soon the bark   154
The pale, the cold, and the moony smile . . .   See Introduction, p. xix
The pine is here   372
The rose that drinks the fountain dew   302
The starlight smile of children, the sweet looks   129
The thoughts of my past life   11
The transport of a fierce and monstrous gladness   253
The wild bull in the mountain and the horse   373
The wind has swept from the wide atmosphere   7
There is a voice, not understood by all   80
There late was One within whose subtle being   69
There stands by Nile a single pedestal   320
There was a youth, who, as with toil and travel   277
These things remain   371
They die—the dead return not. Misery   314
Thou living light that in thy rainbow hues   321